Image of the Region in Eurasian Studies

Image of the Region in Eurasian Studies

Edited by
Suchandana Chatterjee

Maulana Abul Kalam Azad Institute of Asian Studies
Kolkata

in association with

KNOWLEDGE WORLD

KW Publishers Pvt Ltd
New Delhi

2011 FPBA BEST PUBLISHERS AWARD (ENGLISH)

The **Maulana Abul Kalam Azad Institute of Asian Studies** (MAKAIAS) is an autonomous body under the Ministry of Culture, Government of India. It was set up at the joint initiative of the Government of India, Department of Culture, Ministry of Human Resource Development and the Government of West Bengal. Based in Kolkata, it was registered as a Society under the West Bengal Registration of Societies' Act of 1961 on the 4th of January 1993, with Prof. Nurul Hasan, the then Governor of West Bengal, as the President of the Society. It is funded by the Department of Culture, Government of India. Presently, His Excellency, Governor of West Bengal, is the President of the Society.

MAKAIAS is a centre for research and learning with a focus on social cultural, economic and political / administrative developments in Asia from the middle of the 19th Century onwards, with special emphasis on their links with India, and also on the life and works of Maulana Abul Kalam Azad. It operates out of Azad Bhavan in Salt Lake as well as the Maulana Azad Museum located at 5 Ashraf Mistry Lane, Kolkata.

ISBN 978-93-83649-23-5

KNOWLEDGE WORLD

Published in India by

Kalpana Shukla
KW Publishers Pvt Ltd
4676/21, First Floor, Ansari Road, Daryaganj, New Delhi 110002
Phone: +91.11.23263498/43528107
Email: knowledgeworld@vsnl.net • www.kwpub.com

Printed and Bound in India

Contents

REFLECTIONS

ANNEXURE

Introduction

The revived interest in the study of Eurasia's regions is not a sudden occurrence. In global terms, a multidisciplinary approach became the norm for most of the area studies programmes and the scope and span of Eurasian studies widened, combining European Russia and Asiatic Russia. The history of different disciplines of Central Eurasian studies became a research field in itself.[1] Hokkaido University's discourse on "regionology" entailed the study of "meso-areas" of Slavic Eurasia whereby attention shifted from the omnipotent centre to *krais* and *oblasts* of the post-Soviet space. An Asiatic gaze connecting the Islamic world also became popular in the Islamic Area Studies project of Tokyo University that focused on Islam as a religion and civilisation that spread beyond the Middle East to Central and Southeast Asia in the east and the Balkans and Africa in the west. The idea that gained ground within the revised format is not only how Eurasia's regions positioned themselves in the context of post-Soviet political transition but also how these regions reinvented themselves through a re-envisioning of spatial categories like Slavic Eurasia, Central Eurasia, Central Asia, Inner Asia, etc. with centuries-old and millennia-old time scales.

As new research directions opened up, there were fresh insights about historical time frames. The significance of historical interludes was emphasised and there was an urge to study Eurasia's Slavic, Turkic, Persian and Mongolian historical legacies. Some of these ideas echoed in India too but the ways in which the study of Eurasia developed were rather uneven. Prior to 1991, more particularly in the 1960s, 1970s and the 1980s, the study of Eurasia developed as a Soviet studies programme, with emphasis on the understanding of Soviet projects on education, planned economy, linguistics and nationality. There seems to have been an overall inclination towards the study of the Soviet bloc whereby East European studies were "combined" with Russian studies.

The result of this mixed study was a tendency to move towards European studies rather than pursuing a discreet Slavic studies programme. In the post-1991 period, Eurasian studies in India followed a completely different course. After the disintegration of the Soviet Union, the general assumption was the collapse of the Russia-centric Slavic superstructure. Hence, there was an urgency to disconnect from the Slavic component and concentrate more and more on the non-Slavic regions of the Soviet Union. From this emerged an interest in alternative insights, say a South Asian gaze of Central Asia, for instance looking northwest and exploring connected histories as Bactria and Sogdiana in ancient times, Balkh, Khorezm, Badakhshan, Mawarannahr and Mughalistan in medieval times and as Transoxiana during Tsarist and Soviet times.[2] The zeal to study interactive moments in early modern Eurasia (e.g., the Great Mongol moment) was also noticed. Sanjay Subrahmanyam has worked on a vast space of Asia—from Safavid Iran, Ottoman Empire and South East Asia to the Mughal dispensation in Bengal via Transoxiana to establish his argument about the significance of the model of integrative history and what he himself prefers to call "connected histories." Over the years, he has reworked the history of South Asia into a larger Eurasian space of conjunctural movements.[3]

Such ideas are a pointer to the "sprawl" in Eurasian studies, reflecting a deepening interest in theories about "spatial scales" which essentially means alternative spaces cutting across national and cultural boundaries.[4] This has led to a re-imagining of margins of Asia and beyond. The framework of research about a spatial surrounding has been modified substantially with scholars trying to argue about a variety of human settings that qualify this spatial surrounding. In the 2000s, Ansi Passi spoke about "constituents of the life-world" as integral to the study of regions.[5] More recently Prasenjit Duara has argued against the hypothesis of "spatial production" and identifies a region such as Southeast Asia as an area of interdependence and interaction.[6] The gaze has also shifted to cultural tropes and narratives of the Himalayan region that has an Asian individuality and was pitted against the imperial power of the Chinese, the British and the Russian. Reappraisals about the Himalayan borderlands offer fresh insights about alternative geographies—reflected in research about "*zomia* and beyond."[7] The spatial category "*zomia*"—sometimes called a trans-area, was rendered peripheral in conventional area studies categories of East Asia, South and Central Asia. Comparing the case of the eastern Himalayas with other cases as Burma, ocean spaces of the Mediterranean, Atlantic or the trans-Saharan desert spaces, van Schendel and James Scott and others have pointed out that area studies have conventionally been studied through the lens of power. The discourse about the "*zomia*" tends to open up blind spots and limits, and there has been a commitment to study both distant and near places and the connections between them.[8] The India connection has gained prominence in "decentred area studies" that take into consideration a series of glocal tropes, one of which is categorised as "trading powers and colonial endeavours: passages to India: golden triangles, silk roads."[9] A major component of this Himalayan link are the journeys across this Buddhist space with tangled histories and cultures.

What are interesting are the ways in which attention has shifted from discipline-centric investigations to critical interpretations of regions whereby pertinent questions are raised not only linked to geographical knowledge (e.g., cartography and geographical mapping) and geographical imagination of a particular region (reflected in the description of explorers, military adventurers, strategists, missionaries and men-on-spot) but also through cultural representations, for example, ways of living, art and architecture, symbols and sites of faith and worship. In the Eurasian context, images of the region varied from time to time as the regional perspective extended from geographies of spaces to geographies of weather, climate, people, terrain and culture of a vast continental space that is termed Eurasia or Central Eurasia or Slavic Eurasia. An entire gamut of ideas cutting across disciplines like historical geography, political economy, cultural anthropology and sociology tend to project alternative images of Eurasia. Most of these alternative images portrayed ruptures in the post-Soviet socialist countries, though not losing sight of continuities and survivals of tradition. What assumed centrality is simply not binary relationships but also community relationships, institutional arrangements reflective of interactive behaviour—all that have imparted dynamism to the region. A wide variety of regional matrices idealising (a) Turkic confederation, (b) Mongol commonwealth, (c) Altai Home, (d) Silk Road connectivity has gathered attention.

It is because of these images that discussions have shifted to the trans-regional and transnational phenomena stretching beyond Eurasia and including its eastern and western environs. In historiographical enquiries about the region, there is an unending appeal for perspectives, whether pre-Tsarist (Mongol, Turkic, Qing), Tsarist or Soviet that shaped those trajectories. Archival research indicates a strong ideological tenor in Soviet projects in Central Asia and the Caucasus, and in socialist projects of Eastern and Central Europe. One is also aware of the competing ideologies that cropped up within the Soviet bloc during the inter-war period. A multitude of images about a Eurasian ecumene has produced a great deal of interest in comparable situations about history-writing, group identity, political transition and economic transformation in South Asia and East Asia. In this context one is reminded about the look-north perspective of Barun De, a Calcutta historian, who mentored his young group of Calcutta scholars encouraging them to study Eurasia and Central Asia not merely as a geopolitical battlefield of Cold War giants. His suggestion was to look beyond the Cold War prism and analyse the internal dynamics of Asiatic Russia that was otherwise subsumed by the grand narrative of a Slavic Russia. As Founder Director of Maulana Azad Institute in Kolkata, De's premise about "bridges and buffers between Central Asia and South Asia"[10] has found a new meaning because it distances itself from the geopolitical tropes and tries to situate the discourse in the trans-regional historical and cultural framework, inspiring an entirely new generation of researchers in Kolkata to be engaged more and more in "critical Asian studies."

In appreciation of these variables and multiple settings of Eurasia i.e. the Slavic, the Asiatic, the Mongol, the Turkic, the Altai, the nomadic and the sedentary, the cosmopolitan and the transnational, the Maulana Abul Kalam Azad Institute of Asian Studies hosted the Fourth East Asian Regional Conference on Eurasian Studies on the theme *Image of the Region in Eurasian Studies* on September 4-5, 2012 in Kolkata in response to the

East Asian Slavic Associations' proposal to make it an all-Asian Eurasian Studies programme. The idea of hosting this regional conference in Kolkata was also to extend the associational base of International Council of Central and East European Studies (ICCEES). For India's Eurasianists affiliated to area studies centres and foreign policy institutes of universities in Kolkata, Delhi, Kashmir and Mumbai and to multidisciplinary research institutions (e.g., Indian Council of World Affairs in Delhi and School of Liberal Studies, Pandit Deendayal Petroleum University in Gandhinagar, Gujarat), this was an unusual opportunity of bridging minds on a bigger platform.[11] Also, this was an occasion to compare multiple experiences of the Soviet bloc (not limiting attention to Russia or Central Asia but extending it to the Baltics and Central and Eastern Europe from where popular front movements took birth). A meeting of Eurasianists of this scale (with 40 presentations accompanied by enriching discussions) was supported by the Ministry of External Affairs, Government of India.

The volume here comprises writings that reflect an array of opinions about spaces in Eurasian history, Eurasia's nomad-sedentary dynamics, Central and North-West Asian geopolitics, evolving nature of *konfliktologiia* in regional studies of the CIS, paradoxes of Eurasia's transition, sets and subsets of Eurasian integration, literary genres in Soviet and post-Soviet periods and representations of culture. An interesting feature in this collection is the Indian perspective—focusing on the intricacies of an Indian connection—reflected through two articles on Indian research about Comintern archives and the Central Asia-South Asia tangled relationships that is mired in the web of North-West Asian geopolitical competition. Because of their variety, the writings have been categorised as essays and reflections.

Essays

One set of writings in this collection indicate multiple dimensions of space as a category of research. Svetlana Kovalskaya's article deals with the dual representation of the steppe region—as the northernmost boundary of the Muslim world and as the southernmost border of the Eurasian landmass. Sergei Lyubichankovsky's essay deals with the annals of Tsarist military geography, showing intensive training and preparedness of the military elite in the art of war. The focus of attention is on the Imperial Military Academy of St. Petersburg. In both these compositions, the space in Eurasian history becomes a source of lively debate.

Research on Oriental studies or *vostokovedeniya* in the Soviet Union that included research on India was structured and institutionalised by the Academies of Sciences. Hari Vasudevan's essay projects Soviet professionalism and ideological rigour in the Comintern projects on oriental studies—a subject that was worked upon by Vasudevan and two senior researchers of Kolkata, Purabi Roy and Sobhanlal Datta Gupta. The Calcutta project was not just a collection of primary source material, but an acknowledgement of a trend in academic debate of the revolutionary period, i.e., 1917-1947. The idea, as Vasudevan explains, was "to locate the power and influence of a body of thought—in this case the Soviet construction of the Orient." In Datta Gupta's essay, we get a picture of the ways in which the nationalism issue and the colonial question were handled during the Comintern years. The Soviet Comintern, argues Roy, was the breeding ground of about 200 Indian revolutionaries who were negatively branded as anti-Soviet agents in the aftermath of India's independence. Nationalists like Netaji Subhas Bose and Rahula Sankrityayana became the icons of alternative ideologies and movements in Asia—an aspect that was underplayed in the diplomatic environment of Indo-Soviet friendly relations during the Nehru era.

The Russia-Central Asia trajectory (in Kothari's article) is a common feature in most Eurasia-centric studies. But it is not a very decisive factor in Eurasia's eastern fringe that is featured by Mongolia's nomad-sedentary dynamics that is based on multilateral options involving Northeast Asia. This Northeast Asian dynamic has hardly got the attention in Eurasian studies so far (argued by Sharad Soni).

Some essays are distinctively period-specific and country-specific—as in the case of Anwesha Ghosh's paper on India-Afghanistan relations, perceived as a byproduct of India's current priorities in Central Asia. The author feels that security considerations that converge on Central Asia rather than historical linkages have set the tone for India's Afghan policy. In Lopamudra Bandyopadhyay's case study of Turkmenistan, the rhetoric of national revival has had greater relevance since the Niyazov period.

Mohamad Reyaz surveys the reportage on 2011 elections in Central Asian newspapers. He argues that globalisation has had a positive effect on Kyrgyzstan where the civil society norms are comparatively more flexible than in the rest of Central Asia.

In comparative studies of political transition in the post-Soviet bloc, the emphasis is on regime transfer and elections that impacted on vertical power structures and power relations. External intervention and arbitration by the European Union (EU) in conflict-resolution have also been observed more closely by analysts—as in the case of Transnistria pointed out by Keiji Sato in this volume (and more recently in January-February 2014 during the Ukrainian conflict that saw an upsurge of mass demonstrations followed by the ouster of the Yanyukovich government). In Macedonia, since 1989, there were expectations about erasing century-old memories of Slavicisation and Balkanisation. Macedonia is a region where schisms were too deep set and therefore the euphoria was about democracy in Macedonia but more about appeasing the separatist-minded Albanians. In Russia, the localities' responses really did not matter in order to have any direct effect on post-1991 electoral processes. Dmitry Seltser makes a comparative analysis of elections in Russia and Macedonia and points to the implications of elections in small and big states like Russia and Macedonia. Keiji Sato analyses the grassroots initiatives for resolving the conflict in Transnistria.

Another paper on European affairs (by Minori Takahashi) is about "outside areas"—for example, EU norms pertaining to the whaling process which have brought Greenland and Denmark on a competition level. What stands out is the *essence* of EU norms—extending over a mosaic of issues including a complex range of environmental issues as well as health norms.

A section of the essays have tried to follow patterns of post-Soviet integration, sometimes being overly enthusiastic about an inward-looking integrationist paradigm like the Customs Union (Gidadhubli) as well as about a multi-starrer promotional campaign like the Silk Road project, with more and more involvement of Central Asian and non-Central Asian actors (argued by Sreemati Ganguli).

Various aspects of literature and culture have been addressed by scholars in their assessment of the literary environment in Tsarist Russia. What is interesting is the presence of Asiatic themes in Russian literature. The creation of a literary environment in nineteenth century Russia and the aspect of literary criticism as reflected in the works of Anton Chekov are the subject matter of Joyshree Roy's paper. Ranjana Saxena attempts to locate a Caucasian theme in nineteenth-century Russian literature, emphasising the strong presence of a Caucasian image. This is an interesting dimension given the contemporary challenges encountered by the Russian state due to separatist tendencies that have emerged in the region. The ideological content is very strong in Soviet and post-Soviet representations of culture. Akiko Honda's insightful essay is about the role of Soviet mass media in creating an environment of "socialist realism." Her case study of the All Union Agricultural Exhibition (VSKhV) reflects creation of an idealised space which becomes the goal of socialist realist architecture. Rashmi Doraiswamy portrays the ideological template in post-Soviet Kazakh films like *The Sky of My Childhood* (2011). Despite Soviet ideological control, cultural revival in post-Soviet Tajikistan has immense appeal, says Nandini Bhattacharya.

Reflections

A completely different set of writings (by Munira Shahidi and Umedjon Majidi) tends to bring out two different strands of association with Eurasian art/culture. On the one hand, the Soviet instructional norms were the guiding principles of the courses conducted by Academies of Sciences throughout Central Asia and in the rest of the Soviet Union. What is also significant are the ways in which Tajik-Persian literature flourished beyond this given structure. Ziyodullo Shahidi Foundation is popular in the Persian world for taking the initiative of popularising Persian drama, theatre and music. Majidi is ecstatic about Iranian-Tajik-Indian cultural linkages which are popularised by the *Zaboni Modari* Foundation.

The purpose of this volume is to integrate a variety of opinions about region as a pivotal subject in Eurasian studies but not limit its attention to the concept of region as a spatial category.

Notes

1. Foreword by Stephane A. Dudoignon and Hisao Komatsu, *Research Trends in Modern Central Eurasian Studies (18th-20th Centuries): A Selective and Critical Bibliography of works published between 1985 and 2000*, Part I, Tokyo: The Toyo Bunko, 2003, p. ix.
2. Barun De, the Founder Director of Maulana Abul Kalam Azad Institute of Asian Studies spoke of a southern perspective and South Asia's northern gaze in the inaugural session of the Institute's international seminar *Eurasia Twenty Years After: 1991 in Retrospect,* Kolkata, February 15-17, 2011.
3. Sanjay Subrahmanyam, "Connected Histories: Notes towards a Configuration of Early Modern Eurasia," *Asian Studies,* vol. 31, no. 3, 1997.
4. South Asian scholars like Arjun Appadurai have pointed to the theory of "scapes" as an alternative to the study of the core, whereby periphery mappings matter. Concepts of "worldliness" have moved from the West to the global South. Ananya Roy, "The 21st Century Metropolis: the New Geographies of Theory," *Regional Studies,* vol. 43, no. 6, July 2009.
5. Anssi Paasi, *Reconstructing Regions and Regional Identity*, Nethur Lecture, November 7, 2000, Nijmegen, The Netherlands. http://gpm.ruhosting.nl/avh/Paasi1.pdf
6. Prasenjit Duara, "Asia Redux: Conceptualising a Region of Our Times," *The Journal of Asian Studies*, vol. 69, no. 4, November 2010.
7. The concept of *zomia* was originally coined by the Dutch social scientist Willem van Schendel in 2002 when he proposed to reconsider the Asian highlands from the western Himalayan range through the Tibetan Plateau to the lower end of the peninsular Southeast Asian highlands. There has been a westward and eastward extension of the concept of *zomia*, including portions of Xinjiang and Qinghai in China, a fair portion of Central Asia encompassing the highlands. Jean Michaud, "*Zomia* and beyond" [Editorial], *Journal of Global History,* 5 (2010); C. Patterson Giersch, "Across *Zomia* with Merchants, Monks, and Musk: Process Geographies, Trade Networks, and the Inner-East–Southeast Asian Borderlands," *Journal of Global History,* vol. 5, issue 2, 2010.
8. Willen van Schendel, "Geographies of Knowing, Geographies of Ignorance: Jumping Scale in Southeast Asia," *Environment and Planning D: Society and Space,* 20, 6, 2002; C. Pattersen Giersch, *Asian Borderlands: the Transformation of Qing China's Yunnan frontier,* Cambridge, MA: Harvard University Press, 2006; James C. Scott, *The Art of Not Being Governed: An Anarchist History of Upland Southeast Asia,* CT: Yale University Press, 2009.
9. Mentioned in James D. Sidaway, "Geography, Globalization and the Problematic of Area Studies," *Annals of the Association of American Geographers* (2012), DO

I:10.1080/00045608.2012.660397. https://ap4.fas.nus.edu.sg/fass/geojds/intro/AreaStudies.pdf.

10. Barun De, "Central and North-west Asian Geopolitics in post-USSR International Relations," *Azad Institute Paper 2,* Kolkata, 1995.
11. Senior scholars like Hari Vasudevan, R. G. Gidadhubli, Mahavir Singh and Ajay Patnaik were appreciative of the global reach of the Azad Institute and its significant role as a nodal centre connecting India's research groups that focused on areas and diverse issues in Eurasian Studies.

1. The Kazakh Steppe of the 19th-Early 20th century: The Northernmost End of the Muslim World or the Southern Limit of the Eurasian Space?

Svetlana Kovalskaya

The concept of a "region" and the ideas, myths and images it is associated with evolve continuously from time to time. Human geography offers useful and valuable study material of these transformations. Kazakh history was traditionally treated within the framework of spatial and geographical categories. Perhaps it is this very factor that accounts for the so-called "drifting identity" of the region's population.

The external sociocultural and civilisational characteristics of the Kazakh steppe were substantially transformed during the period in question during the establishment and consolidation of Russian administration, alongside which continued to exist traditional Kazakh socio-political institutions. As a result concurrently in one territory, heterogeneous ethno-social, ethno-religious and ethnocultural structures coexisted and developed to a varying extent.

The problem of regionalism lie in the territorial expanse of Kazakhstan, in the history of state development, the diverse cultures that have historically composed the modern country's population and differences in these cultures' socio-economic and cultural development. Each region is distinct but fits uniquely into the country's unified cultural and social space.

Theoretically, the country's regionalism is defined by cultural distinctive features that have been analysed by many scholars. The work of F. Boas focuses on the geographic distribution of cultures and the geographical "binding" of certain cultural elements.[1] This idea was developed further in the writings of the American ethnologists K. Whistler and A. Kroeber.[2] Lev Gumilev argued about a relationship between the *ethnos* and the *Landschaft* (meaning the physical geography of a place).[3] Other Russian ethnologists also pointed to historical-ethnographic zones in their work. The most well-known works are those of M. Levin and N. Cheboksarov, who developed the idea of different economic cultural prototypes.[4]

The study of social and political processes in Kazakhstan requires attention at the regional level. Unfortunately, at the theoretical level, a sociocultural regional profile of Kazakhstan is yet to emerge. The Kazakh literature is based on the distinction between the five economic regions (North, East, West, Central, and South). But one has to note that there are other parameters of comparison.

Figure 1. **Yuri Bregel, *An Historical Atlas of Central Asia*, Leiden: Brill, 2003.**
http://elbilge.ucoz.com/_ld/0/39_geographyCA.jpg

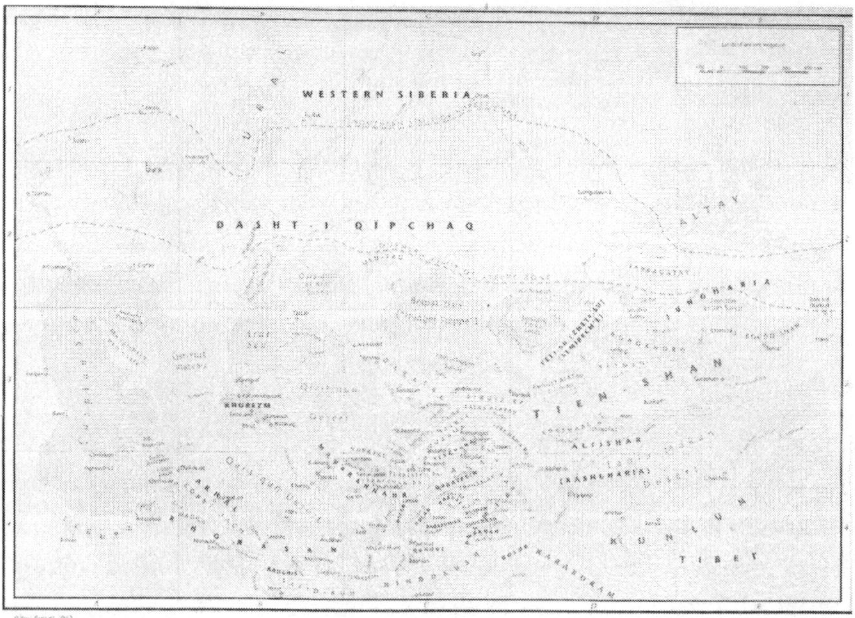

THE PRINCIPAL GEOGRAPHICAL FEATURES AND PROVINCES

This situation could be reconstructed with the help of historical references, such as: (1) narrative sources, (2) geographic descriptions, travel notes, and (3) personal sources—diaries, reminiscences, epistolary heritage, (4) official documents, including the official Party's documentation and (5) sources related to the cultural, social and psychological interactions between Russians and Kazakhs, Kazakhs and Cossacks.

The Turan-Iran controversy dates back to ancient sources that have, to an extent, survived to this day. The name *Turan* appeared in the Aryan period in the Persian sources as distinct from the Aryan country (Iran). In this case, there is no clear-cut physical boundary between them. In physical geography, the Turan-Iran distinction is defined by the area of the Aral Sea—i.e., the Turan lowland. Later the term became entrenched in Iranian mythology and *Shah-Nameh* of Ferdowsi. After a millennium, it became the basis of the new concept of *Turkistan* (land of the Turks) and in the wider context, became equivalent to the definition of Central Asia (the area from Russia to China).[5]

The distinction between the oases and the steppes of the Central Asian region can be traced back to the pre-Saka period. The ethnic boundary between the Eurasian steppe and the settled regions of Central Asia, seems to follow a pattern—i.e., Mangyshlak-Aral Sea—Syr Darya—Tashkent—Ketmen-Tyubinkskaya gorge—Torugart Pass.[6] The Syr Darya and the Tian Shan mountains were a natural geographical boundary dividing the steppes of Eurasia from the agricultural and oases regions of the south for several centuries, creating a substantial obstacle to the formation of new political associations.

As we trace the history of development and spread of the population and evolution of statehood in Kazakhstan, the following scenario emerges: the steppe area extending from the *Dasht-i-Qipchak* area (Qipchak steppe, Polovtsian steppe), as depicted in Russian, Persian and Islamic literature beginning from the ninth century, were designated as belonging to the great steppe—from Qinghai to the Danube. This space included the Kazakh and southern Russian steppe, which were populated by Kipchak-Coman tribal groups in the early Middle Ages. For over millennia, migration was from east to west, and only from the fifteenth century onwards did a small section of people move from the west to the east. Cossack migration, followed by industrial, agricultural, and political migration, began to gain momentum. This movement began to weaken in the Soviet period, especially in the 1970s, leading to the onset of a negative migration balance that reached its peak in the mid-1990s. The only factor that limited this influx was the scarcity of water resources, a problem that is increasing every year.

In the ancient period, the Kazakh regions were populated by nomadic tribes belonging to various dynasties—i.e., the Sakas, the Huns, the Usuns, and Qinghai. Then the great migration of peoples from across the steppe took place—the Huns, Avars, and sometime later, of the Turks, Arabs, Mongols, Dzhungars, Cossacks, Slavic and European people and the Chinese. From the second half of the first millennium AD, part of modern eastern and southeastern Kazakhstan belonged to the Western Turkic Khaganate, while the western part was included in the state of the Khazars. From the ninth century onwards the territory of Dasht-i-Qipchak was populated by tribes and state entities of Kaimaks, Turgesh, Karakitai, Qarluq, Khitan, Qipchaks, and the Oghuz Turks. Moreover, the localisation of these state entities can be seen quite clearly. In the steppe zone lived the Qipchaks, Kaimaks, Naimans, Kerei, while in the Semirech'e and the southeastern part, there were Turgesh, Khitan, and Qarakhitai. In the pre-Aral and pre-Syr Darian regions, the Oghuz Turks lived.

From the thirteenth century onwards, the north and west of the Kazakh steppe were incorporated into the Golden Horde (formerly the Juchi ulus, the Ulug ulus). Prior to this period, the western Dasht-i-Qipchak was already bounded—between the Ural (Yaik) and Dneistr Rivers—and the eastern Dasht-i-Qipchak, between the Irtysh and Ural (Yaik) Rivers, bordered on the south by the middle reaches of the Syr Darya River, and on the north by the Tobol River.

Southeastern Kazakhstan in that same period became included in the Chaghatai ulus, together with the territory of Eastern Turkestan and part of Transoxiana. Only a small portion of the northeastern Semirech'e became part of the Ogedei ulus; the northern Kazakh territory was part of the Siberian Kaganate, and the western part belonged to the Nogai Horde. The central region was part of the Ak-Orda. A group of nomadic Uzbeks (of the khanate of Abul Khair led by Janibek and Kerei), came to the state territory of the ruler Esen Buga and with his permission, founded the Kazakh Khanate between the rivers Chu and Talas.

In later history, the three Kazakh *zhuz* were politically isolated from each other after the death of Tauke Khan, but the ongoing conflict with the Dzhungars influenced their eventual geopolitical choice in favour of the Russian Empire (and facilitated their gradual entry into it). This is also unique in the sense of the formation of distinct historical and cultural regions. We must not forget that in the second half of the eighteenth to the first half of the nineteenth century, one part of the Elder Zhuz territory was divided between Qing China and the Russian Empire. Another part submitted to the Kokand Khanate. From the Younger Zhuz in 1802 in the area between the Urals and the Volga, the Bukey Horde became isolated, a condition which lasted till 1845. The khanates were restricted at the time of Russian administration—the territory of the Kazakh zhuzes was divided into three administrative entities or the governor generalates: Orenburg (Ural and Turgay area), West Siberia (with Akmola and Semipalatinsk regions), and Turkestan (Semirechenskaia and Syrdarya regions).

In 1882, the West Siberian governor-generalate was abolished, and the newly created steppe governor generalate (called the Steppe region) included Aqmola and Semipalatinsk, as well as the Semirechenskaia area (till 1898). The Turkestan governor generalate was retained in the same form. In this kind of territorial restructuring we see a return to the "usual" territorial division of Kazakhstan into the oasis and steppe regions. On the one hand, the Steppe governor-generalship largely corresponded with Russian civilising influence.[7] On the other hand, Turkestan was sufficiently influenced by the Central Asian khanates while in one or another form we also observe the Chinese presence. Some might object to the view that Russian state formation led to the Islamisation of the Kazakhs. Of course, we cannot disagree with this. However, the degree of Islamisation, its forms and methods, and its resultant nature were directed towards completely different goals than the Central Asian Islamic "exposure" of the Kazakh population and the region as a whole. Another important point must be emphasised here—the efforts of the Russian Empire to proselytise the Kazakh population. This policy was intended to maximise the goal of political assimilation through the merger and conversion of the people inhabiting the Russianised space, the imperial policy of religious tolerance, as well as in the future to serve geopolitical goals. It is sufficient to say that these efforts were too late and did not bring the expected results.

Thus, we see that attitudes and tendencies towards a particular cultural and historical space had their own set of rules and the characteristics were different in different regions of Kazakhstan. The state had a huge role and involvement in this process.

Those who came to the region in different times and to different territories, like the Turks (6th-12th centuries), Arabs (8th century), and Mongols (13th-15th centuries), as well as the Dzhungars (16th-18th centuries) and Russian and European peoples (18th and 19th centuries) influenced the Kazakh people's perception of themselves and of the settler population. The problem of "us and others" is increased when ethnicity and other identities (religious, ethnic, economic) identities become less relevant compared to self-reflection which leads to an active search for one's own self in a rapidly changing world and the need to develop a sense of self-preservation and self-defence.

Being part of the Great Turkic Khaganate meant a new style of life—it became prestigious to be known as a Turk. We know of several examples of people who were not of Turkic origin and were beginning to consider themselves as such for various reasons. This point can be explained by the fact that with the arrival of Turks on the scene of history, ended the period of mythological history of the legendary predecessors. Turks left behind a lot of texts in runic script, in which they indicated that their appearance is coincident with that of the blue heavens overhead and the brown earth underfoot. They knew that the texts that they were leaving after them were for the name of Turk to go down to posterity, to remain for centuries to come. Such self-presentation definitely points to their belief in themselves, in their fame lasting for millennia. Therefore, everything associated with the Turks in the early Middle Ages, their ambitions and victories convinced others of their special status and hence prestige of being a Turk. It explains why a number of nations ranked themselves as part of the Turkic world, allowing them to feel their own equality with the Turks and superiority over non-Turks. Figure 2. Map of Muslim World by M. Kashgari. *Divan Lugat at-Turk*

Almaty: Daik-Press, 2005 should be noted that many aspects of the Turkic nations' ethnogenesis are still the subject of much controversy in science. For example, there was a vigorous ongoing debate regarding the ethnogenesis of the Yakuts, Karaims, and others.

Figure 2. **Map of Muslim World by M. Kashgari. Divan Lugat at-Turk 7 Almaty: Daik-Press, 2005**

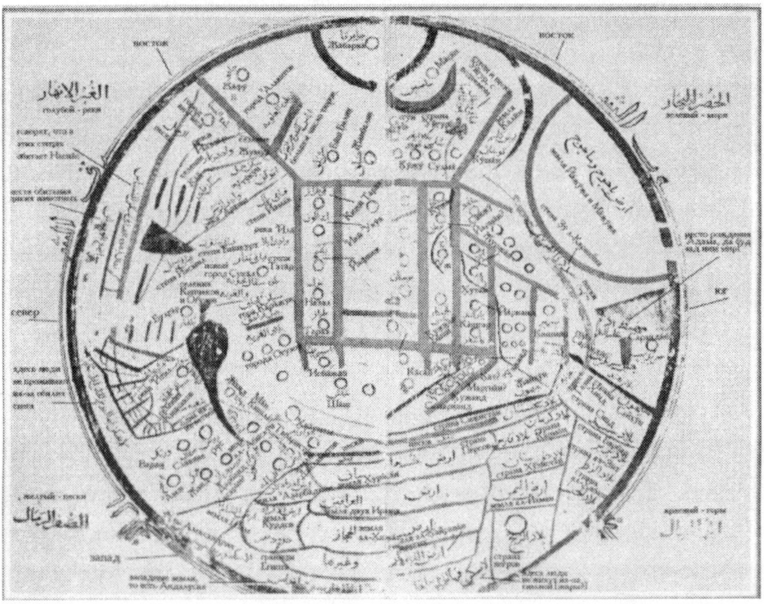

The convergence of three different civilisations—Turkish, Chinese, and Arabic—in the Kazakh region in the early Middle Ages led to the need to protect well-established traditions, languages, and cultural practices in the area. Most noteworthy is the work of Mahmud of Kashgar, *Divan Lugat at-Turk* in the eleventh century whose primary goal was the presentation of the Turkic world to the Islamic world.[8] His map of the Muslim world is represented as a closed circle, at the centre of which he placed Turkish cities—Barskhan, Shash, Farab, Ispidzhab, and others, clearly showing his readers the coordinates of the extent of Turkic space. Commenting on the map of M. Kashgari, it should be noted that most of the towns of the Turkic period owe their emergence to the development of trade and the Great Silk Road. According to written sources, these towns are Ispijab, Otrar, Taraz, Arsubaniket, Kulan and others. Ispijab was one of the main and big towns and trade centres in the south of Kazakhstan and Zhetisu was believed to be within its territory. The sources described its covered markets, cloth market and the cathedral Mosque. Another big town was Otrar (or Farab, Tarban, Turar). It was founded in early 5th-6th centuries and was developing as a typical early medieval town with its own mint. Taraz was first mentioned in the seventh century sources as the centre of a densely populated area. Around it, along the banks of the rivers Talas and Assa, lay many townships and settlements—e.g., Barskhan, Hamuket, Jikil, Adahet, Dah-Nadzhikent and others. For that time, the towns had a high level of development. The houses had sewage and heating systems. Aqueducts were commonplace in the life of major towns. Underground vaulted tunnels were built, in which ceramic pipes were laid. Every town had a public bathhouse. A medieval town consisted of several parts. The centre had a citadel or a castle, which was the seat of the government. The citadel was circled by shahristan—an area populated by urban nobility, wealthy merchants and land owners, clergy and the military. Around Shakhristan there were trade-artisan districts, the *rhabads*, where the main population of the town lived. Besides the town itself, there were small communities in the precinct area. The emergence of Islamic monumental buildings such as mausoleums of Aisha-Bibi, Karahan, Babaji Khatun, Syryltam and others point to the development of towns in the time in question. That explains why M. Kashghari knowingly paid so much attention to Turkic towns, placing them in the centre of the map and showing everyone that the Turks have become an integral part of the Islamic world. The Turks for him were part of the territory of Dar-ul of Islam, and not just a part of the outside world. This inclusion of the Turkic space with the connotation *Dar-ul Islam,* contributed to the strengthening of ideas about the unity of the region and the Islamic world in the minds of inhabitants of Kazakhstan and other Muslims.

In the formation of perceptions, the contemplation of visual information—in this case, the map—is very important. This information was quite effective, as it allows us to see not only the visual image of the Turkic world that was conceptualised, but also to understand the intent inherent in the map data leading to parallel interpretation of visual information. Thus, we see how the map becomes an important instrument in the formation and definition of ideas and images of the region. In this case, Mahmud of Kashgar was important because he showed that the Turkic and Muslim worlds were equivalent. This was an important fact because it showed that Islamisation among the Turks had intensified and it was Islam to which all positive, progressive, and modern thinking were attributed; in the Turkic world, many stood to lose their positions, which only till yesterday seemed to be strongly rooted and rock solid. This work was created under the auspices of the Abbasid Caliphate and was a Turkic-Arabic dictionary. The text was underlined on the last consonant of the root, according to poetic order and written in rhymed prose, just like the Quran. The equality of cultures was presented to the reader through the equality of the languages. The Turkish and Arabic languages were, "the two horses at the races," wrote Mahmud of Kashgar. It is said that the author was able to "raise the steppe, without degrading the mountain."

With the work of Mahmud of Kashgar and Yusuf Balasagun began a special period in Turkish literature, which can be described as Turkic-Muslim. Works were written either in Arabic or in Arabic script, began and ended with words of thanks for The Allah, and in the context of these texts, you can find many examples of behavioural imperatives characteristic of a true Muslim, etc. Included in the list of works of this kind are *Divan-i-Hiqmat* by Ahmad Yasavi, *Gift Truths* by Yugnaki and many others. More unique, in our view, is a product of the end of the seventeenth to the beginning of the eighteenth centuries, known under the code name *Treatise on the Holy Madinat al-Baida and Ispidzhab*, translated from the Chaghatai language into Russian by Professor Z. M. Tulibaeva. The uniqueness lies in the indication of a shift of the centre of the Muslim world directly to Sairam (Urungkent, Madinat al-Bayda, Ispidzhab).[9] The author emphasises that the city emerged straight from heaven, that it bestowed on him the light of God, that he was raised to heaven and blessed by Allah, that people living in this city would live a beautiful life, with God's blessing. Unfortunately, this work has not yet received sufficient attention from historians and religious scholars or educationists, and is not actively used in scholarship today. The text speaks for itself and shows us attempts about a priori approval of the Islamic self-identification of a section of the population of Kazakhstan and perceptions of the region not only as exclusively Muslim, but also with a claim to uniqueness and superiority. Lastly, there was substantial activity of the Sufi communities in Kazakhstan up to the eighteenth century, but much of these *tariqas* gradually disappeared with the consolidation of official Islam.

In general, the role of the elite, especially its spiritual component, on the formation of perceptions of the region and its correlation with a particular cultural and historical space should be noted. This segment of the population has usually referred to the previously-mentioned Sufis, as well as other Muslim representatives—the *ulema*, the *ishans*, and also the *Qadimis* and the *Jadids*. Each of them has contributed to the creation and modification of such terms as *milla*. Importantly, the term *milla*, originally referring to the Muslim community, was gradually transformed into the concept of a nation. It must also be emphasised that the Russian state's religious policy, even if not always coherent, had an important role in and influence on the process of identity formation of its Muslim subjects.

Figure 3. *Uchebnik Rodinovedeniya dlya shkol Zapadno-Sibirskogo uchebnogo okruga. Akmolinskaya oblast,* Omsk, 1916.

As pointed out, there has been a notable transformation in perceptions of the region and its designation in various public policy documents began with the gradual entry of Kazakhstan into the Russian Empire, from the first half of the eighteenth century till 1885 which marked the culmination of Russian Central Asia. Perceptions of Russian society in Kazakhstan, which had become part of the new space of "extended empire" also changed. In the northern part of the Kazakh steppe, which included a large part of the Middle Horde, the Russian state is traditionally addressed as the Siberian region. Evidence supporting this includes such documents as the *Charter of the Siberian Kirghiz* in 1822, which was developed by the Governor General of Western Siberia, M. M. Speranskii.

Figure 4. A. N. Sidelnikov, *Uchebnik Rodinovedeniya dlya shkol Zapadno-Sibirsk-ogo uchebnogo okruga.*

Here we need to turn our attention to the *Textbook of Native-origin Schools of the Western Siberian School District*, written and published in 1916 by an Omsk seminary teacher A. N. Sidelnikov. It is dedicated to the Akmola region, and covers features such as geography and the sociocultural plane.[10] Interestingly, the article points to the zonal divisions of Russia: A part of Russia between the Ural Mountains and the Great Ocean called Siberia; the Central possessions stretching between the Caspian Sea, River Irtysh and the Siberian Railway. The western part is called Turkestan and the eastern part is called the Steppe or Kyrgyz region. The Akmola region is part of the Steppes, and together with the Semipalatinsk region forms the Steppe General-Governorship.[11] The book has a map which has zones such as forest areas, grass steppe, sagebrush steppe, desert and sand.[12] In this passage, the naming of zones is fairly clear—i.e., Turkestan and the steppe (the latter denoting Kazakh territory). In other words—both nomadic and sedentary agricultural spaces are clearly defined in the map.

There is a whole range of ideas about the region in the nineteenth century. The ideas not only point to the Kazakhs and their perceptions of their native land, but also to the perceptions of the Russian government and the perceptions of the Russian population, perceptions of the foreign powers and their nationals about the Kazakhs, and in modern terms, about Kazakhstan as a whole. These perceptions were substantially influenced by the Islamic factor, which penetrated deep into Kazakh society and gradually became a signature of the Kazakhs' ethnic identity. Of course, the consolidation of the Islamic sentiments influenced understanding of the region and its relevance to a particular civilisation, with this or that state, and with a particular way of life.

Gradually, it became very popular among Kazakhs too to speak about their Arab origins. The reason for this mood was the growing influence of movements of pan-Turkism and pan-Islamism in the region. The Mongolian roots became less relevant and the revivalist discourse about Arabic origins became more popular and offered several opportunities. It was only a persuasive and knowledgeable scholar like Abai Kunanbaev who solely focused on the Mongol origins of the Kazakhs—but his work on the ethnogenesis of the Kazakhs has not survived to this day.

The intellectual and practical activities of the *Jadids* in educational reform, the influential role of the Muslim poet-scribes, the considerably active participation of Kazakhs in the affairs of the Muslim faction of the State Duma, the activities among Islamic political parties, and the subscription of Muslim journals were fairly widespread. The region became increasingly Muslim, although not in the manner as some people had wanted it to be. Nonetheless, the tendency toward an Islamised development became more and more attractive to the population of Kazakhstan. The party programmes and other documents of the Alash reveal divided opinions about Kazakh national autonomy and the voting rights on the question of organisation of Kazakh territorial limits. The delegates from southern Kazakhstan and the Central Asian regions abstained from voting and they had their own programme regarding the creation of an autonomous status for Turkestan which failed to materalise. Turkestan's autonomy came into being on November 27-28, 1917. The activities and views on autonomy of the Muslim parties (*Shura Islamia, Shura I ulama*) that were the most active in this region indicated a strong voice for Islam.

Figure 5. http://en.wikipedia.org/wiki/National_ delimitation_in_the_Soviet_Union

The leadership of Alash Orda outlined Kazakh national autonomy within the former governor-generalship of the Steppe, i.e., the four areas of Ural, Turgay, Akmola and Semipalatinsk, with the centre at Semipalatinsk. The draft programme called for the separation of church and state. The outbreak of civil war did not make it possible to bring this process to its logical end. With the approval of the Bolsheviks, voices about Turkestan autonomy were eliminated. What came in its place was the Turkestan ASSR, founded in 1918 encompassing the lands of the Elder Zhuz.

In August 1920, on the territory of the Elder and Younger Zhuz (called the steppe part), the Kyrgyz ASSR of the RSFSR was established, with its capital in Orenburg. In 1925, the national-territorial division of the republic resulted in the renaming of the region as Kazakh ASSR, including part of the lands of the Elder Zhuz, which was until then a part of the Turkestan ASSR. The capital was moved to Ak-Mechet, renamed Kyzyl-Orda, and then to Alma-Ata. On December 5, 1936, the Kazakh ASSR was transformed into a federal republic and parts of the south-Siberian districts were included into it. At the same time, the northwestern and northeastern borders of the Kazakh republic were reconfigured. In July 1930 the Karakalpak Autonomous Oblast was transferred to the RSFSR, and in 1936 it became part of Uzbekistan.

Thus, we see that the process of nation-building in the early twentieth century once again witnessed a traditional regrouping of steppe and nomad territories and the settled-agricultural-oasis parts remained in the same format. In this case, perceptions of the region differed. On the one hand, the levels of perception which resulted in the creation of certain images actually related to the region as a whole and there were some stereotypical images that influenced one another. The heterogeneity of Kazakh society, its socio-economic and sociocultural differentiation, active politicisation at the beginning of the twentieth century—all this influenced mixed sentiments about the region and new survival strategies by the Kazakhs. The Russian society too had diverse sentiments and with distinct political and socio-economic difficulties that it encountered, also perceived this region as heterogeneous.

There are many-sided opinions about the transformation of the Kazakh space. On the one hand, the Kazakh steppe became part of a single unit of the Russian empire and was geopolitically bound to the region while the efforts of the rest of the country were directed towards strengthening the base of the country. On the other hand, what part of it belonged to the Russian space remains an open question. Russia prevented the growth of pan-Islamic sentiment in the region and restricted the process of Islamic political revival. The reason for this is that among the Muslim population, Islam is not merely an ethnic identity but also as a form of struggle for national freedom, equality, and independence.

This duality of space composition—i.e., the nomad steppe as the geographic opposite to the sedentary areas makes Kazakhstan a unique case study. An example of this dual characteristic is the Kazakh steppe and its coexistence with Turkestan, a Kazakh region which is a settled agricultural cultivation area. By the nineteenth century, this duality had taken a geopolitical turn—the Kazakh space was at the same time the northernmost boundary of the Muslim world and the southernmost border of the Eurasian land space.

Notes

1. Franz Boas, *Race, Language and Culture* (New York: The Macmillan Company, 1940); Franz Boas, *Anthropology and Modern Life* (New York: Norton, 1928).
2. Clark Wissler, *Man and Culture* (New York: Thomas Y. Crowell Company, 1923); Alfred L. Kroeber, *Anthropology. Race, Language, Culture, Psychology, Prehistory* (New York: Harcourt, Brace and Company, 1923, Second Edition 1948); Kroeber, *Ethnographic Interpretation* (Berkeley: University of California Press, 1957).
3. L. N. Gumilev and K. P. Ivanov, "Etnicheskie protzessy: dva podhoda k izucheniu," in L. N. Gumilev (ed.) *Ritmy Evrazii: epokhi i tzivilizatzii* (Moscow: Ecopress, 1993).
4. M. G. Levin and N. N. Cheboksarov, "Khozyaistvenno-kulturnue tipy i istoriko-etnographicheskie oblasti (K postanovke problemy)" (In Russian). *Sovetskaya etnographiya*, 1955, no. 4, pp. 3-17.
5. Z. A. Djandosova, *Geographiya Tzentral'noy Azii*, SPb: Izd-vo SPb Universiteta, 2005, p. 7.
6. G. Sitnyanskiy, Problemy reintegratzii buvshego SSSR s tochki zreniya istoricheskogo naslediya narodov Evrazii', *Vestnik Evrazii,* 1996, no. 2:160-171, p. 162.

7. N. E. Masanov, *Kochevaya tzivilizatziya kazahov: osnovu zhiznedeyatelnosti nomadnogo obtzchestva* (Almaty-Moscow: Sotzinvest-Gorizont, 1995), p. 224.
8. *Divan Lugat at-Turk* (Almaty: Daik Press, 2005).
9. *Traktat o Sairame* (Astana: Izdatelstvo NTZAII, 2007).
10. A. N. Sidelnikov, *Uchebnik Rodinovedeniya dlya shkol Zapadno-Sibirskogo uchebnogo okruga. Akmolinskaya oblast,* Omsk, 1916.
11. A. N. Sidelnikov, *Uchebnik Rodinovedeniya dlya shkol Zapadno-Sibirskogo uchebnogo okruga. Akmolinskaya oblast,* Omsk, 1916, p. 2.
12. A. N. Sidelnikov, *Uchebnik Rodinovedeniya dlya shkol Zapadno-Sibirskogo uchebnogo okruga. Akmolinskaya oblast,* Omsk, 1916, p. 75.

2. The Practice of Regional Description in the Military Science of the Russian Empire "Military and Statistical Analysis" and Its Practical Uses Late in the 19th–Early in the 20th Centuries)*

Sergey Lyubichankovskiy

In Russian social and political thought of the second half of the nineteenth century the concept of "space" became the subject of enquiry by the establishment and military elite. It connoted the landscape in question along with its natural and geographical features. Russian military scholars wanted to find out the impact of space, applying this meaning on combat operations, their tactics and strategies.

By the early thirties of the nineteenth century the Russian Empire was badly in need of a military theory due to the lack of qualified experts in this field. The lack of able military scholars continued despite the establishment of the Imperial Military Academy in St. Petersburg. In 1832 General Headquarters, on the occasion of the inauguration of the Academy, announced the admission of officers eager to teach military subjects. The Academy's document read as follows: "On the admission of the teaching staff to the Military Academy."[1] It was especially difficult to find a Professor of Military Geography who studied the effects the space had on combat operations and strategies. As the Academy's Director Sukhozanet later wrote in his report to the War Minister: "Before the Military Academy was established, military geography was very little known in Russia; even foreign works on this subject were rather incomplete and not enough for teaching ... For this reason it was very hard to find a Professor of Military Geography and attempts were even made to invite one from abroad."[2] The specialist professor chosen for the post was affiliated to the Institute of Railways where this subject was taught by P. A. Iazykov. Academician I. O. Sukhozanet gave an explanation for the dismissal of P. A. Iazykov from the Academy: "Colonel Iazykov was the only one who could get rid of this inconvenient arrangement—as an aide to Adjutante General Zhomini[3] he translated the General's works and thus gained so much knowledge in military sciences that he was the right man for the position of the Chair of Military Geography in the Academy."[4] In fact in 1827 on His Majesty's orders P. A. Iazykov was entrusted with translating into Russian a book by Baron Zhomini titled *A Short Essay on the Art of War or New Analytical Revision of the Primary Military Strategies and Policies*. He was awarded 500 roubles by the Emperor for the translation of the work. Zhomini's book was a praiseworthy contribution as it brought the world's attention to the translator who worked on the importance of space in the art of war.

Professor Iazykov taught military geography at the Department of Theory (i.e., at the first course) in the Academy. He published *The History of the Theory in Military Geography* and was honoured with the Demidov award by the Academy of Sciences, translated in German and published in Berlin in 1840. This was his first work almost entirely devoted to the effects geography and space had on military strategy.

While in service Iazykov took an active part in the edition of the *Journal of Railways* that published some of his important works—*The Definition of the Theory of Arts in General, The Gains Brought by Theory in Practical Matters* (1838), *On the Use of Fortresses* (1837), *On the History and Development of the Theory of Strategy* (1839), *The Description of St. Gotthard Crossing, On the Advantage of Fortified Camps in Strategic Matters, News of a New Fortress in Tyrol* (1840), *On the Roads as Strategic Lines* (1841).The titles of these articles testify to Iazykov's main interest of study: in practical matters and the military and strategic significance of various factors. Of special significance is his book *The History of Theory in Military Geography*. It is a fundamental study devoted to the analysis of the effects of space on combat operations and military strategies in general. It is important to point out that Iazykov supported his thesis with historical evidence and vivid descriptions that are plentifully found in his book.

Iazykov highlighted the following factors that affected the strategic position of the country:

- Geographic position of the whole state in comparison to others. Thus the advantageous position of one state with respect to the other gives it a strategic edge and so directly has an effect on its own military strategy.
- The physical geography of the country. The author theorised that the elongated territory and extended boundaries force the state to disperse its armed forces which could be very negative in case of a conflict with its neighbour.
- Physical features of the state as a separate theatre of operations. Here Iazykov pointed out that this factor could have different effects in different countries. Depending on the peculiarities of geography combat operations can vary.

P. A. Iazykov further reiterated the argument of his European predecessors Archduke Karl and Zhomini about strategic routes and strong points that have an enormous effect on combat operations. "Strategic lines are those that exist in nature and become important in matters of strategy."[5] These can include roads, mountain chains, rivers, artificial waterways, etc. Strategic strong points according to P. A. Iazykov were those whose seizure could be very significant in war. Examples of geographical strong points include the state capitals where the main financial and state resources and bureaucratic personnel are concentrated. Other cities can be regarded as geographic and military strong points as well if they are situated on major crossroads, on long rivers, etc.

In accordance with their strategic significance the geographic locations were subdivided by Iazykov into the principal and subordinate ones.

- The principal geographic locations are those which are more important in strategic matters, namely: political boundaries, mountain chains, seas or their smaller parts, long rivers, artificial waterways, main roads, cities, ports and fortresses."[6] Thus, political boundaries should be evaluated from the viewpoint of their contours, length and distance from the capital, etc;

- Subordinate geographic locations are "those which are seldom regarded in strategic matters or have little effect in matters of strategy … and include high plains, large forests and swamps, great lakes, large and small islands, narrow isthmuses and capes."[7] In this regard, Colonel P. A. Iazykov often referred to the work of General C. Klauzevits[8] and also developed his ideas.

Summing up his study of geographic locations in strategic matters P. A. Iazykov noted that such a study could be well theorised as a specialised theory on military geography or the theory of strategy. He wrote about the advantages of the study of military geography for the future: (1) The theory of strategy is useful for those military men who have an important responsibility of carrying out the will and thought of their commander-in-chief. (2) The military officials should study the theory well in advance when they are still young for it takes some experience to put it into practice. (3) A true theory does not make one self-confident, on the contrary it teaches that theory is not enough in practical matters. (4) Theory combined with experience makes one confident of oneself."[9]

The Colonel pointed out that the theory of military geography could be widely used in practice: (1) it should be taken as a guide to plan strategic lines prior to warfare. (2) Geographic and topographic features of the region in question are important in warfare planning and techniques as well as combat operations and usually such information is revised on the spot. Military geography helps the officers during reconnaissance missions to note down the geographical features of special importance in strategic matters. (3) In peace situations military geography can be as well used to design roads, bridges and canals of great strategic importance. (4) Besides, P. A. Iazykov noted down specifically that one should be guided by the theory of military geography in order to select geographical locations for fortresses. They should be built at strategic geographic locations after a thorough investigation of all geographic factors using the provisions of military geography. But however fundamental his study was the author failed to put forward a theory of military geography which was based on some universal principles as he wanted to create a rigid science irrespective of any historical period. This attitude had considerable limitations on the development of the military geography. In fact, his study contained a detailed description of the facts supported by examples from history which showed the effects of space on combat operations while military geography needed the description of a certain sequence of measures for analysing the state's strategy, i.e., the descriptive military geography should have become an analytical and practical science.

Such was also the approach by the outstanding Russian military statesman Dmitrii Alekseevich Miliutin. In 1845 Miliutin was appointed Professor of the Chair of Military Geography at the Imperial Military Academy after the retirement of P. A. Iazykov. Miliutin subsequently was convinced about the necessity to establish a new scientific discipline—that of military statistics. Evidently he saw the limitations of military geography and thought it necessary to create a new modern science. On his request, in 1847, a course in military geography was replaced with a course in military statistics. His works include "A Critical Study of Military Geography and Statistics" (1846), "First Experiments with Military Statistics" (Vol. 1—Introduction and the Basis of Political and Military System of the German Union, 1847; vol. 2—Military Statistics of the Prussian Kingdom, 1848); was honoured with the Demidov award for *Warfare of 1939 in North Dagestan* (1850) and in 1852–1853 he wrote a study about the Italian expedition of Suvorov. After this, D. A. Miliutin was admitted to the Russian Academy of Sciences and his work was translated into French and German. In 1848 he presented the Emperor with his book *First Experiments with Military Statistics* and was awarded with 400 silver roubles. The book is recorded in his service list that is kept at RGVIA.[10]

Some scholars name D. A. Miliutin among the founders of Russian geopolitics as he was the first to establish it as a separate branch of science (it was only he who called it "military statistics"). For instance, the modern scholar of military geography and geopolitics E. F. Morozov wrote: "Dmitrii Miliutin founded the Russian school of military geography and as it were, the Russian military school of geopolitics."[11] It is quite true if we compare a popular definition of geopolitics by the modern geographer D. N. Zamiatin who said that "in geopolitical studies in general, the effects of geographical factors and geographical position on foreign policy of states and their political development and on the behaviour of any state or political formation in space (as proposed by Fridrikh Rattsel'[12])" [13] and the military statistics proposed by D. A. Miliutin, there is a lot in common.

His first serious work about the effects of space on military strategy was *A Critical Study of Military Geography and Statistics*. He wrote in his memoirs:

> It was supposed to put forward the idea that everything written about military geography, however varied in its contents, have little meaning scientifically and, on the contrary, military statistics aimed at all-round study of armed forces and their means must be one of the special branches of general statistics ... This brochure was noticed among the military and academic community as well as among the scientific community at large.[14]

From this it follows that D. A. Miliutin had studied other scholars' works devoted to military geography and found them unsatisfactory as P. A. Iazykov once did. He arrived at the conclusion that most of his predecessors' works were not scientific enough and thought it necessary to chart out a scientific theory of military geography. He supplemented his pioneering work *A Critical Study* with a more significant work *First Experiments with Military Statistics*. It is interesting to note D. A. Miliutin's review of the work of his predecessor P. A. Iazykov, i.e., *History of the Theory in Military Geography* (1838). Miliutin criticised Iazykov for his wish to turn military geography into "an abstract science" based entirely on theory. It has already been mentioned that according to P. A. Iazykov it is not enough to study the strategic conditions of the theatre of operations at a given period of time because this would signify that every historical period would have its own military geography. Instead P. A.

Iazykov offered that military geography had some theoretical provisions which were true irrespective of the period of time. In his lectures on military geography and statistics D. A. Miliutin wrote:

> So, General Iazykov's book aimed at becoming part of the theory of strategy. But the study of the conditions in which geographic factors were interpreted at different times should rather belong to the sphere of Military History.[15]

As to D. A. Miliutin, the realm of geography relates to the description of the earth and the geographic data should be timed in history. Therefore he thought it impossible to make a theoretical science only out of military geography. He noted that it was possible to overcome the problems connected with the changes in the landscape and space, provided that the strategic analysis included both geographical and other conditions. Therefore he avoided geographical determinism, though admitting the inseparable connection between space and other factors which influenced combat operations and military strategy.

Miliutin made it a point that the study of the theatre of combat operations should incorporate a greater number of factors, including all that affect the means of warfare as well as its results:

> … we should aim at the critical analysis of the theatres of war or whole countries from the strategic point of view rather than the collection of mere facts taking into consideration more factors besides landscape features which in every state in general affect the choice of means and ways of warfare. On account of this the study should embrace the entire state.[16]

Thus, D. A. Miliutin showed that only a study of military geography which basically denoted a study of geographical factors rather than strategy was insufficient. This was a new point in the field of military sciences at that time. In his opinion the study should be expanded to military statistics of a state. He specified the importance of "the study of military forces of states at a given period of time.[17] By coining the term "military force," Miliutin meant all the ways and means at the behest of the state to embark on war. The author's emphasis was on military statistics that combined with geographical factors that are bound to have an effect on combat operations and military strategies. He further added that the aim of the military statistical study was "to get some advantages in case of war with regard to the landscape on which the war was carried out and also other means of warfare."[18] So, this approach made it possible to solve a problem whether the country could take advantage of the resources well enough to undertake offensive or defensive operations successfully against any state, whether she needed to make allies or think of other options. The basic point is that a thorough military statistical study has some practical use—that is, to improve the military force of the country not only with regard to a specific conflict but also in general, that is with regard to the general condition of the armed forces. The idea of military statistical study for a qualitative evaluation of the armed forces of the country and the expectation of the results of that study on the character of warfare in a given territory was a completely unique theory that had enormous potential when put into practice. Moreover, it was to Miliutin's credit that he worked out the methodology of military statistical study and offered a detailed plan of this particular study:

- In the introduction there should be a general analysis of the state's character from the military point of view, i.e., consideration of its main potential and its effect on the armed forces.
- The study of the land and naval forces, their condition, supply and preparedness for warfare.
- A separate study of the strategic position of the country with respect to different theatres of war taking into account possible objectives and circumstances.

At the first stage the study should provide a general review of the political history of the country, its development and the modern position in the general political system of states; the evaluation of correspondence between the data which determine the means and ways of warfare to the political position of the country in question. These data according to D. A. Miliutin included the following:

- The country or its territory (i.e., the land surface occupied by the state). It should be regarded in accordance with its geographic position and general topographic features: "the contour of borders with respect to the most of domains and neighbouring states is very important in military matters in general: some state is elongated in length or dispersed, another is rounded and solid; one of them is entirely continental, the other is mostly maritime; some have to maintain comparatively more armed forces for their defence than others; one has to develop its land forces, the other—its navy."[19] Fertility of soil, climate and other natural conditions affect the army supply and determine its deployment in peacetime and so on. Of great importance are the land and sea ways of communication which affect the army supply, movement, deployment, communication, etc. D. A. Miliutin pointed out that the general features of various ways of communication and their direction should be considered from this viewpoint exclusively.

As one may notice the geographic position of the state, its land and other features of space have priority in military statistical analysis. It becomes evident, firstly, because of the significance of geography for the military statistical analysis and, secondly, the durability of the factor in question.

- Population, its numbers, concentration, well-being—all these factors do not only determine the strength of the army but its qualities too and show how much the government can rely on popular support. Here D. A. Miliutin noted down especially that it was very important to study the national character for it determined the political situation as well as the form of government and the political forces of the country in general. In doing so it was also necessary to consider the effect that the national character had on the army morale and therefore its loyalty. It is interesting to note that considering the military system of the German Union, D. A. Miliutin pointed to the lack of unity among the military forces of the union which he explained by the fact that the member countries missed coordination, where every man (hence every soldier) identified himself with his own land rather than the union as a whole. He wrote that "the armed forces of the union would not be united unless the people of the German union combined all together morally."[20]

- State system, budget, government's attitude to the people, foreign ties produce an enormous effect on the military system, warfare, military and administrative measures both in peace and wartime. In his lectures on military geography and statistics D. A. Miliutin wrote: "The fate of the Empire founded by Osman[21] after it attained the peak of its strength and power under Suleiman II[22] and then quickly declined may be cited as the best example of how much the government of the nation can affect its military power and explains why it is necessary to study this element in the military statistical review of the state."[23]

Therefore, the first part of the study combines the analysis of all statistical data from the military point of view.

At the second stage of the study one should analyse the military system of the state, its material, physical and moral conditions, strong and weak points including the auxiliary economic facilities required to maintain the army and make war. It is important to consider the strength and the type of the forces required against this country; advantages and limitations of the hostile armies are compared and the theory of warfare in the hostile country is analysed.

The third stage of the study comprises an enquiry into the strategic potential of those areas in the state where combat operations are very likely. Each of them should be analysed separately by taking into account the geographical position of the neighbouring countries and relations with them. It is very important to proceed from the most plausible assumptions based on the actual relationships between the states. According to D. A. Miliutin it is not unlikely that sometimes the study of a particular part of the country may be of greater significance from the strategic point of view. For instance, he considered Poland to be such a strategic belt with regard to Russia. Here, one should recollect his work titled, *Western border area of Russia*, in which he presented his military statistical analysis for the evaluation of the western border region of Russia: "Since 1815 (according to Vienna accords) the Polish kingdom was considered to be an inseparable whole along with the Russian Empire but strategically its geographic position is of special importance and therefore, should be regarded as a separate part of the western theatre of war."[24]

So, geographical and spatial factors belonged to one group of data that are evaluated at the first stage of the military statistical study. It is important to note that D. A. Miliutin did not give a detailed description of each factor separately evidently because it had been already clarified in the book by P. A. Iazykov.

D. A. Miliutin had quite succeeded in laying the theoretical foundation of a new military science. He suggested the methods of study and a detailed description of the stages in the military statistical analysis specifying the necessary data to carry it out. However he did not limit himself to his theoretical arguments only. His other notable work, *General Comparative Review of the Military Systems in England, Sweden, Prussia, Austria and France*, is an analysis of the condition of armed forces in the countries mentioned above. The second part of his *First Experiments with Military Statistics* showcased the military statistical study carried out by D. A. Miliutin as an example of his respect to the German Union. The character of this study becomes evident from the chapters of the book:

- A general military review of Germany—its principal forces. The plan of this chapter includes the following: the land (territory), topographic features, land and water ways of communication, railways, fertility and cultivation of soil, local features of the land, population and its well-being.
- The political system of the German Union: its components, distribution of the member countries according to the population, the basis of the political system in Germany before the Vienna Congress (1815) and at the present moment, the degree of political unity and autonomy of each member country, the political significance of Germany in strategic matters.
- The general military system of the German Union:[25] fundamentals, contingents, the general organisation of its army, readiness for action

in peace time, supplies and reserves, the military industrial system and supply in wartime, the military administration in the union army, its combat capabilities, the level of general control over it and the fortresses in the Union.

- The condition of the armed forces in German states: fundamentals of various military systems available in German states (conscription, terms of service, leave rules), full strength and its actual number, economic and combat conditions of the army.
- General conclusions about the strategic position of Germany: the extent of military efficiency acquired by Germany, the strategic importance of her different regions, the division into two theatres of war.

D. A. Miliutin suggested that the analysis of a separate theatre of war should be conducted in the following manner:

- First, after evaluation of the respective position of the hostile parties, their geographic and political characteristics as well as the possibilities of allied or neutral relations with other countries, it is necessary to make a clear demarcation between the general theatre of war and its separate spheres;
- Second, the space in question should be analysed from the military and geographic point of view, i.e., without going into particulars to describe the general features of the territory which facilitate the movement, supply, action of the army and so on. In doing so one should be very particular about the main features of the land, the rivers, the mountain systems, fortifications, etc;
- Third, the strategic study. Here D. A. Miliutin pointed out that the strategic study was focused at the analysis of the advantages and disadvantages of separate geographic locations and territorial features in general for one of the hostile states. The strategic study of a definite theatre of war shows the specific party in war the most advantageous routes, defence lines, etc., and therefore determines the general advantages and disadvantages of the given theatre of war which helps to work out a respective strategy.

The relative value of different geographic locations was brilliantly described by D. A. Miliutin in his guidebook—*The Manual to Seizure, Defence and Attack of Forests, Villages, Ravines and Other Local Objectives* (1843). The book provides various examples in the strategic analysis of different theatres of war with some recommendations for the advancing and defending sides. And it becomes clear how different appears to be the value of one and the same geographic location for either side, how differently it might be taken into consideration in matters of strategy.

D. A. Miliutin had done much to develop the idea of P. A. Iazykov—i.e., the significance of military science was growing in peacetime when strategic routes like new roads, canals, major plants, etc., were being constructed. Also, it is an important component in foreign policy, when concluding pacts and treaties, establishing border lines and so on.

There has been a reappraisal of Miliutin's works. E. Morozov writes that the Miliutin's thesis reflected the advancement in the field of Russian geopolitics: "firstly, his methodology was unique and never existed in the theories of foreign geopolitical schools. Secondly, these methods had been well put into practice by the Tsarist authorities while the German and Anglo-Saxon schools were only at the early stage."[26] One of Miliutin's major achievements was his integrationist approach to the military statistical review of states. His suggestion was that this study should take into account both the effect of the geographical factors (as his predecessors did) and other features of the state. Thus, he managed to broaden the strategic analysis considerably, and added to it the analysis of political, financial, social, historical and other factors which affected directly the state in general as well as its military strategies in particular.

Miliutin created a new science with its well-defined aim (of a general analysis of military forces and means used by the state including various factors which have an effect on the military forces and also to study separate theatres of war), theoretical foundations and specific methods of study. With some reservations one can say that D. A. Miliutin paved the way for the military dimension of Russian geopolitics in many ways.

Early in the twentieth century D. A. Miliutin's studies were continued in the works of A. E. Snesarev[27] who used the strategic analysis offered by D. A. Miliutin to study India as a likely theatre of war in his book, *North India theatre: A Military and Geographical Description*. A. E. Snesarev presented a detailed description of mountain passes, roads and villages of the Hindu-Kush and Kashmir—the data necessary for the troops to advance in the Indus-Ganges plain. His books, *Brief Essay of the Pamirs, The Pamirs: A Military and Geographical Description, East Bukhara: a Military and Geographic Essay,* gave a military and geographic description of the Pamirs and Eastern Bukhara. As E. F. Morozov notes down, "it was Snesarev who had formed the Imperial policy in the South ever since, and his recommendations were highly valued by the War Ministry and General Headquarters."[28]

In 1924 he wrote a book, *Introduction into the Military Geography*, which was in many respects a continuation of Miliutin's *First Experiments with Military Statistics*. The first one begins with a description of the enormous significance geography has in military matters in general and matters of strategy in particular: "If ... we raised to the level of great commanders, the Commander-in-Chief in fact, it would not be very hard to see how closely and attentively they study geographical factors, how very much dependent becomes every move, operational idea and even a fleeting tactical whim of theirs on the powerful means of geography that sets it in and rounds up in the end."[29] In this book Snesarev followed his predecessors Iazykov and Miliutin in studying the problems of military geography and military statistics. Especially interesting for him was Miliutin's *The First Experiments with Military Statistics* which he thought had done a lot for further development of this scientific study: "The concept and the contents of military geography, as conceptualised by D. A. Miliutin, are so exhaustive that they continue to influence the domain of modern science."[30] He wrote that historic changes, new times and, especially, the war in 1914-1918 had somewhat modified the programme and contents of the science created by D. A. Miliutin. For a full-scale analysis of the adversary's military forces, according to A. E. Snesarev, military geography had to be acknowledged more deeply and he suggested a wider range of factors that had to be considered during the course of military statistical studies. For example, he considered the importance of the level of trade, agriculture, politics as well as class distinctions as regards the country under study. However, A. E. Snesarev failed to continue his work because he was arrested in 1930 and died in 1937.

Thus, in the nineteenth century the Russian military was anxious to study the significance of space for successful combat action. The approach we have taken here is to show an exclusively practical comprehension of space which is limited by geographical characteristics. The followers of such an approach succeeded in a detailed analysis of the effect various geographic factors had on tactics and strategies of the state and described how this or that geographical location should be taken into consideration in strategic matters. They were convinced that evaluation of the landscape and its effect on combat operations and strategies should be of paramount importance during the military strategic studies. Moreover the Russian military science of the nineteenth century offered the algorithm of a thorough military strategic analysis for the state as a whole or its separate territory. At the same time the Russian scholars who followed this approach were far from geographical idealism and thought it necessary to consider not only the spatial factors, admitting a close relation between geographical and other characteristics of the state. The ideas suggested within this approach (for example, the political system of the state and its land may affect the military power and adequate military strategy) would appear later in the studies of Western scholars and lay the foundations of the role of the military in Western geopolitics. Another advantage of such understanding of space and its role reveals itself by its practical character, i.e., the ideas and concepts worked out within this approach aimed at the practical realisation and definite recommendations rather than theory.

Notes

1. *Rossijskij Gosudarstvennyj Voenno-Istoricheskij Arhiv (RGVIA)*, fond 544, opis 1, delo 13, list 8.
2. *RGVIA*, fond 544, opis 1, delo 252, list 3.
3. Zhomini (Antoine-Henri Jomini—in French; 1779-1869) was a Napoleonic and subsequently the Russian general. He was associated with the project of creating the Russian Academy of the General Staff. He also became the instructor of military strategy for the successor of the Russian Crown (since 1837).

4. RGVIA, fond 544, opis 1, delo 252, list 4.
5. Petr Iazykov, *Opyt teorii voennoi geografii* (Experience of the theory of Military Geography). (Saint-Petersburg: Pravo, 1870), p. 110.
6. Petr Iazykov, *Opyt teorii voennoi geografii* (Experience of the theory of Military Geography). (Saint-Petersburg: Pravo, 1870), pp. 66-67.
7. Petr Iazykov, *Opyt teorii voennoi geografii* (Experience of the theory of Military Geography). (Saint-Petersburg: Pravo, 1870), pp. 174-75.
8. Klauzevits (Carl Philipp Gottlieb von Clausewitz—in German; 1780-1831) was the Prussian general and the military theorist and the Director of the Prussian Military Academy. His main work is *About War* (1832).
9. Ibid., pp. 252-53.
10. RGVIA, fond 409, opis 1, delo 89128, list 4.
11. Evgenii Morozov, *Snesarev—velichaishii russkii geopolitik (Snesarev—the greatest Russian geopolitician).* (Moscow: Stella A, 2012), p. 12.
12. Rattsel' (Friedrich Ratzel—in German; 1844-1904) was German geographer, ethnologist and sociologist and a founder of the geopolitical school. He was also Professor of Leipzig University (since 1886).
13. Dmitrii Zamiatin, *Gumanitarnaia geografiia. Prostranstvo i iazyk geograficheskikh obrazov* (Humanitarian geography. Space and language of geographical images). (Saint-Petersburg: Universitet, 2003), p. 194.
14. Dmitrii Miliutin, Vospominaniia. *1843-1856 (Memoirs. 1843-1856).* (Moscow: Nauka, 2000), p. 120.
15. *Otdel rukopisei Rossiiskoi gosudarstvennoi biblioteki (OR RGB),* fond 169, opis 80, delo 10, list 27.
16. *Otdel rukopisei Rossiiskoi gosudarstvennoi biblioteki (OR RGB),* fond 169, opis 80, delo 10, list 28.
17. Dmitrii Miliutin, *Pervye opyty voennoi statistiki* (First experiences of military statistics). (Saint-Petersburg: Akademia, 1847), pp. 53-54.
18. Dmitrii Miliutin, *Pervye opyty voennoi statistiki* (First experiences of military statistics). (Saint-Petersburg: Akademia, 1847), p. 57.
19. Dmitrii Miliutin, *Pervye opyty voennoi statistiki* (First experiences of military statistics). (Saint-Petersburg: Akademia, 1847), p. 59.
20. Dmitrii Miliutin, *Pervye opyty voennoi statistiki* (First experiences of military statistics). (Saint-Petersburg: Akademia, 1847), p. 110.
21. Osman (Gazi Osman Paşa—in Turkish, 1258-1326) was the founder and first Sultan of the Ottoman Empire.
22. Suleiman II (İkinci Süleyman—in Turkish, 1642-1691), Sultan of the Ottoman Empire during 1687-1691. He encountered the Austrian army and seized Belgrade.
23. OR RGB, fond 169, opis 80, delo 10, list 152.
24. OR RGB, fond 169, opis 82, delo 3, list 2.

25. The German Union (Deutscher Bund—in German) was a union of German states (1815-1866). It included the Austrian empire, the kingdoms of Prussia, Saxony, Bavaria, Hanover, Wurtemberg, the duchies and principalities, and also four city-republics of Frankfurt, Hamburg, Bremen and Luebeck. The main power of the Union was in the hands of Austria and Prussia.
26. Evgenii Morozov, *Snesarev—velichaishii russkii geopolitik (Snesarev—the greatest Russian geopolitician).* (Moscow: Stella A, 2012), p. 43.
27. Andrey Snesarev (Andrej Evgen'evich Snesarev–in Russian, 1865-1937) was the Russian and Soviet military leader, military theorist, military geographer and orientalist. The Chief of Academy of the General Staff of Red Army in 1919-1921, the founder and the Rector of Institute of Oriental Studies during 1921-1930.
28. Andrey Snesarev (Andrej Evgen'evich Snesarev–in Russian, 1865-1937) was the Russian and Soviet military leader, military theorist, military geographer and orientalist. The Chief of Academy of the General Staff of Red Army in 1919-1921, the founder and the Rector of Institute of Oriental Studies during 1921-1930., p. 44.
29. Andrei Snesarev, *Vvedenie v voennuiu geografiiu* (Introduction to Military Geography). (Moscow: Politizdat, 1924), p. 1.
30. Andrei Snesarev, *Vvedenie v voennuiu geografiiu* (Introduction to Military Geography). (Moscow: Politizdat, 1924), p. 318.

3. The Soviet Study of India 1917-1947: A Report on the Soviet Archives Project, Calcutta

Hari Vasudevan

The Calcutta Soviet Archives' Project[1] was an initiative taken in India to locate important material relating to Indo-Soviet relations of the inter-war period in the (then newly-opened) Soviet archives, to obtain copies of some of this documentation and to draw attention to it in India. Among the various subjects the Project attempted to address,. the formation of Soviet knowledge of India was important, but has attracted least attention in the publications that came of the project. To compensate, a résumé of the implications of the project for the subject was included in the introduction to Volume 2 of the *Selected Documents* (2000) and in the general inventory of archival fonds (published in 2012). But this in itself could not provide a comprehensive sense of the implications of the documentation that has been brought to India and that still lies in Russian archives. This brief paper attempts to take the matter further—though some of the material that is provided will involve a repetition of what has already been stated in the publications mentioned above.

At issue is the structuring of research on Oriental Studies (*vostokovedenie*), which included research on India in the USSR, during 1917-47, when many of the new cadres in this field were trained and Soviet institutionalisation of the study took shape. It is worth noting for the record that this subject touches on a number of major themes in Soviet history and world history. These include the international authority of the USSR at a time when its material and military prowess was only beginning to develop in a manner that might rival that of Britain, France and Germany, the USA being a hardly reachable target; it was when the country's global political and ideological influence could not be discounted or confined to the territorial limits of its state-predecessor, the Russian Empire. Soviet self-awareness, research and self-direction, all reflected in the country's Oriental Studies, provided indications of such influence and range: yet *Vostokovedenie's* profile and resources in contributing to the political history of growing Soviet authority is hardly touched by traditional histories of Soviet foreign policy or the Comintern, the International that grew out of the Bolshevik Revolution. Regrettably, this broad subject could only attract passing attention in the Calcutta Project, given limitations of time and funds.

The subject of Soviet *Vostokovedenie* also touches on the "orientalist" content in Soviet Oriental Studies—an important theoretical and practical problem as far as the subject of Oriental Studies in the former Soviet Union is concerned and a matter of importance in international scholarship since the debates on Edward Said's arguments in his *Orientalism*. The subject—like others that touch on the specific character of Soviet *Vostokovedenie* (such as the character of professionalisation in a Communist environment)—certainly figured when the Calcutta Project agenda was established—but more as acknowledgement of a trend in academic debate than as a crucial factor in shaping the collection of material.

These issues are not, therefore, touched substantially in this paper, which attempts to show how the Project reworked the scope of the prevailing narrative in a slightly more mundane and piecemeal manner. This limited reworking, however, has broad implications for the subjects mentioned above. For it touches on the power and influence of a body of thought—in this case the Soviet construction of the Orient—matching it implicitly against other bodies of thought—for instance, the "imperial" and "national" constructions of the colonial world to mention two of the most significant.

The paper does not restrict itself to a description of the documentation, but points to directions that the Project indicated as far as fresh ground in the study of the subject may take. These directions point to a tentative argument in this paper that it originates on a standard refrain in the literature on Soviet Oriental Studies (*vostokovedenie*). The Soviet "project" while preserving the old points of focus in Oriental Studies in research bodies (including the study of India) on language and culture, moved such study from its normal ambit in the Tsarist past (the study of classical texts, comparative linguistics, etc.), to contemporary affairs.

I develop this argument to point out that archival material suggests the necessity to examine other issues more closely—especially discussions among Soviet Oriental Studies aficionados of diverse material, and the consideration among such "specialists" of the way Marxist categories concerning India should evolve. Such study was closely allied to political purposes and educational and research institutions that were geared to such purposes. The institutions pitched their discursive ambit more broadly than the Tsarist state, to include international scholarship and commentary on a scale seldom seen. The range of some of these organisations has been indicated in Oded Eran's study of policy studies in the USSR.[2]

The outcomes of such activity in the USSR may be adjudged to have been the equivalent of extended political reportage or material more akin to the policy briefs or project reports that are produced currently for international agencies, multinational corporates and well-funded government departments. This is certainly an implication of Eran's work. However, this is not quite adequate, since the studies fitted into a broader Comintern project—shared by Soviet institutions of higher learning and government bodies—to build socialism, and to understand society in terms of progress towards such a goal using categories of scholarship and debate. In fact, a failure to apply such a yardstick was said to be the reason for the rise and fall of some of the organisations that developed in this field at this time.

A deep involvement with Soviet and Comintern strategy and politics may have channelled this study and limited its scope in intellectual terms. But that did not diminish the fact that such study attempted to look beyond the specific and (in the Indian case) deal with local categories of caste and religion as well as apply Marxist categories of analysis in ways that were appropriate.

In the Soviet study of India, the upshot was that an interest in classical Sanskrit and its linguistic affiliations, together with an interest in Buddhism in India and Buddhist iconography and literature—the staple of Tsarist era scholars such as I. P. Minaev, S. F. Oldenburg and the Buddhologist Scherbatskoi—came to share the academic centre spot in the USSR with subjects of contemporary relevance. These included the state of the crisis of the British Empire through the world, specific national economic development, and, in the Indian case, the Indian economy under British rule, with a focus on landholding and industry, and aspects of the National Movement.

Significantly, the study of contemporary subjects involved local networks and research apparatus in the countries concerned and not just the involvement of Soviet experts. It was this aspect to it, I consider, that *ultimately* gave such study substantial intellectual force beyond the Soviet state—especially in countries (such as India) where the tradition of scholarship in the social sciences and economic and social history lacked the edge that had developed in Europe by the time of the October Revolution. That intellectual force began to make a showing in the inter-war period covered by the project. In the meanwhile, of course, such an edge was developed, within the framework of British debates and references easily available in these years in the growing number of universities in the subcontinent—or it stretched to include research and debate of US and European provenance. The coming of a Soviet Russian corpus of work, though, made its mark in a certain circle, creating a local presence in the case of South Asia for the Soviet lexicon—ultimately to develop in the post Independence era. The introductory work of R. Vaidyanath, which touches on the emergence of this literature, and the growth of this phenomenon, unfortunately has not developed, although it was pioneering in nature and provides important examples of the spread of Soviet profiles and ideas through the local languages of the sub-continent.[3]

This short report, however, while working with such considerations, will limit itself to a basic anatomy of the range of the Soviet study of the "Orient" and India specifically. Such an anatomy, it should be emphasised, is not exhaustive. It seeks to draw connections to research in bodies that are not considered mainstream centres of Oriental Studies, thereby casting light on the links and connections that were responsible for a greater diversity of research.

A. Traditional Centres of Oriental Studies in Russia and their Fate after 1917

The Calcutta Project took its cue from a base where the work of Kulagina and Kuznetsova,[4] on Soviet Oriental Studies, including the study of India, pointed to its concentration previous to the October Revolution in departments in various faculties at different universities as well as specific research-oriented institutions. The latter included the Asiatic Museum, St. Petersburg, with some limited presence for research in a language school that existed in Moscow and in the work of the Imperial Society for Archaeology. By 1917, the more material artefacts associated with Asian collections, and traditionally located in the Asiatic Museum, had long ago been transferred to the Institute of Ethnography of the Academy of Sciences, and the Asiatic Museum was primarily a repository of manuscript material that encouraged and stimulated research. As such it continued to be part of the Academy of Sciences as it survived into the period of Communist rule.

With time, however, the Museum came to form a part of the Academy's new Institute of Oriental Studies of the Academy of Sciences—formed from the Asiatic Museum, the Collegium of Orientalists of the Academy, and the Turkological Cabinet or Research Group. This developed its Moscow wing—a relatively small unit when compared with the elaborate institution that existed in Petrograd (later Leningrad). Both bodies were required to work with an agenda that involved an interest in contemporary spoken language and with subjects of contemporary history, and they developed a young scholarly tradition accordingly.

Unfortunately, in the case of the work of Kulagina and Kuznetsova, apart from the occasional details that come from the references to the lives of individual scholars, accounts of the training of the new scholarly community, except in the case of the Petrograd institutions, are not detailed. Again, Kulagina and Kuznetsova do mention the various associations that existed in parts of the USSR that devoted themselves to this branch of research, but the more substantial story of such bodies finds little place, obviously partly because of constraints of time but also as a result of the different status of the institutions concerned, oriented, as they are thought to be, to more mundane unifying and coordinating rather than research goals.

A major limitation of this approach was that centres that were seriously encouraged by the Russian state at this time failed to find a place in the narrative. Moreover, the profile of the forms of adaptation of the scholarly community to the agenda provided by the Soviet state was limited in the case of the institutions of the Academy of Sciences.

This deficit was substantially made up by Oded Eran, whose painstaking account ranged more broadly, albeit establishing a caesura at the beginning of the 1930s and being more concerned with the state of affairs of the post Second World War period.

The Calcutta Project attempted to develop in greater depth the fundamental accounts provided by Eran, Kulagina and Kuznetsova.

B. New Centres of Research on Oriental Studies and Indian Studies in the 1920s

In general, the Calcutta Project did not examine the areas brought into focus by Kuznetsova and Kulagina through an investigation of the scattered archival *fonds* that dealt with them. Some additional notes on new entrants in Petrograd, and some initial spadework on the life and work of the Director of the Moscow Centre, Snesarev, was undertaken. But the archives of the Academy of Sciences did not provide a ready source of material, divided as such material was into individual institutional holdings, and this aspect of the picture was left as it was.

Rather, the Calcutta Project dealt with two of the major areas of research and advanced teaching on Oriental Studies touched on by Eran, focusing on the Indian Studies component in these institutions. The institutions that were the focus of Project study were the All Russian Scientific Association for Oriental Studies and the Communist University for the Workers of the East. It may be mentioned that other institutions worthy of attention, besides the Academy of Sciences, were noted, such as the International Agricultural Institute, but these were not examined in depth at the time—substantially owing to the character of the archive, which was limited.

In what follows, I would like to draw attention to details that make up a new picture of Soviet *Vostokovedenie* generally and Indian Studies in the USSR specifically, that came to be formed from the archives. In the case of the Communist University, there is an aside on some of the groups that it affected, to provide a sense of the more general implications of the research for the Indian (and ultimately Pakistani) milieu. At a time when ideas cannot be seen wholly independently of their range and influence, this must be considered an important aspect of what transpired.

1. All Russian Scientific Association for Oriental Studies (VNAV)[5]

The Calcutta Project confirmed that, against the background of the emerging system of support for traditional Oriental Studies in Petrograd, as suggested by Oded Eran, VNAV emerged in 1922 in Moscow under the directorship of M. Pavlovich Veltman—a revolutionary of standing who had been associated with the Moscow branch of the Institute of Oriental Studies.[6]

The Association drew in the standard Orientalists into its debates, as is testified by its papers. It also organised the journal *Novyi Vostok*, with reviews, articles and information of importance to the profession of Oriental Studies. Most important, the Association encouraged the large-scale purchase of books (including a range of government reports and statistical compilations) from a variety of sources, to develop the weak information base in Soviet Russia concerning the contemporary state of the countries studied. The Association developed networks for the supply of material in a number of countries in Europe and Asia and also drew in visitors to Moscow.

Archival material enables those interested to trace Veltman through a career in the 1920s that was a little at variance with his associations with the Academy of Sciences immediately after the October Revolution. He took on the role of an academic impresario. Only too well aware of the range of those involved in post-war revolutionary politics globally and a gathering National Movement in India (where Congress activities had taken on a new shape after the Civil Disobedience Movement that followed the end of the war), Veltman was also aware of the network of Indian revolutionaries and migrant workers that operated outside the British Indian Empire. This was the product of his serious study of the work of the Profintern and the Krestintern as well as the Comintern, where he had many connections. While the members of the Academy of

Sciences in Petrograd were limited by their erstwhile concerns to more academic fare, Veltman was able to draw together informants and sources to lend vitality and excitement to contemporary questions concerning class struggle. The archives breathe a fervent energy—repeated travel, meetings and exhortations to pitch for new limits of academic enquiry, with a large storehouse of review and information that was hitherto seldom drawn into the academic milieu. The meetings of revolutionary organisations found regular mention in *Novyi Vostok*, just as Veltman engaged with them and their members—often fresh from the colonial world. The projection of Oriental Studies and Asia politics through the journal and the emphasis and energy that went into the journal—already conspicuous from its papers and the accounts of VNAV in it—acquire fresh strength from the archive. Clearly the venture gave the academic study of Asia a new standing and range that the content of the journal cannot elaborate beyond a point and that the archive brings out in sharp relief.

Significantly, also, it is apparent that Veltman's activities and his close links with the powers that be gave his activities a different status from that of the institutes of the Academy of Sciences. VNAV's agenda for enquiry, as stated by *Novyi Vostok,* challenged the significance and influence of Petrograd institutions, even if they were now on the move and attempted to revise their orientation. Unlike these academic institutions, moreover, VNAV reached out to a non-Russian revolutionary clientele that it included in its activities and references.

To say this does not imply that *Novyi Vostok* was a best-seller, that the perspectives of its writers now moulded both Soviet statesmen and foreign activists and that VNAV became a nerve centre of sorts for inputs into Soviet and Comintern policy towards the colonial world and guiding points for response in turn towards this policy. Such a status was foreclosed, not the least by language. The reference to the scope of journal and institution, though, does imply that they made a dent in this readership and such a constituency, at least by presence if not by grip, through the instrumentality of the cosmopolitan ambience of Moscow and the world of the Hotel Lux. What has to be recorded moreover is that in terms of international literature, it had no serious rivals.

2. The *Kommunisticheskii Universitet Trudiashchikhsia Vostoka* (KUTV) or Communist University for the Workers of the East[7]

Beyond such a picture of VNAV, the Calcutta Project established that the Association was ably supported by a major university project and research initiative that predated its formation—the Communist University of the Workers of the East and the Communist University for the Workers of China. Of these, the Project was able to look closely at the Communist University of the Workers of the East (KUTV). Here, it was able to use an excellent introduction by N. N. Timofeeva.

In the years immediately following the October Revolution and Civil War, as a gesture to the development of the capacity of local *ethnoi* in the former Russian Empire, a number of institutions were either upgraded into universities or new universities were founded in relatively far-flung areas of the RSFSR. Among bodies that already existed that were given new strength were those in Siberia (the Tomsk State University, founded in 1878), Bashkir country (the Bashkir State University, founded 1904) and the Russian Far East (the Far East National University founded 1899). Special attention was also given to teacher training establishments (Tomsk, Gori, etc.). New universities were formed in Omsk (the Omsk State Agrarian University, founded in 1918), Irkutsk (Irkutsk State University founded in 1918) and the various universities of the Caucasus (founded in Tblisi, Baku and Erevan in 1918-19). In early 1918, a People's University was formed in Tashkent, with the assistance of a number of research-oriented institutions of the town.

More in keeping with international goals that were part of the Revolution's aspirations, though, and yet concerned with the same goals as the above institutions was the Communist University of the Workers of the East.

(i) Character and Range of the Work of the Communist University of the Workers of the East or Kommunisticheskii Universitet Trudiashchikhsia Vostoka (KUTV)

The Communist University for the Workers of the East was founded in April 1921. It functioned under the Russian Komissariat for Nationalities until 1924, under the Central Committee of the CPSU during 1924-

29, and, during 1929-36, under the Scientific Association for National and Colonial Problems, (*Nauchno-Issledovatel'skaia Assosiatsiia Natsional'nykh i Kolonial'nykh Problem*, or NIANKP), a registered social body which had close connections with the Comintern, and the Komissariat for Foreign Affairs (Narkomindel). KUTV passed over to the Central Committee of the CPSU after 1936 and it was closed in 1939.

The prime preoccupations of the University were the training of "eastern" peoples of the Russian Soviet Socialist Federation/Soviet Union and foreign Communist parties. In 1936, though, it is likely that the training of foreign Communists passed out of the hands of the University and to the Scientific Institute for National and Colonial Problems (*Nauchno-Issledovatel'skii Institut Natsional'nykh i Kolonial'nykh Problem* or NIINKP). The University had departments in Tashkent, Baku and Irkutsk.

KUTV was run by a Council and a Rector. The first Rector was G. I. Broido (d. 1956), a Red Army activist on the Siberian and Central Asian front, a member of Bolshevik committees on Central Asia and vice-Commissar of Nationalities (1921-23). Broido held the latter position simultaneously with his tenure of the Rectorship of KUTV until 1923, when he ceased to be vice-Commissar. He relinquished his Rectorship in 1926, going on thereafter to be a major figure in the Communist Party of Tajikistan and in the RSFSR's Ministry for Education. He was succeeded by B. Z. Shumiatskii, an old Bolshevik, Ambassador in Persia during 1923-25, and head of the Far Eastern Secretariat of the Comintern.[8]

At its inception, students from the "Soviet east" were normally put through a 3-year course after a preparatory year equivalent to that provided in a "workers' faculty" or *rabfak* for those who came from underprivileged backgrounds. From 1922, foreign students were placed in a well-defined *Inostrannaia Gruppa* (Foreign group), and their course carried on for about 2 years. This group was also designated as "Section A" or as "specialist group" at various times. In 1927, the course of study was reorganised, and a 4-year course established for Soviet students. Here stress fell on lectures on (i) Marxism-Leninism and the history and tactics of the Communist Party, (ii) Economics, (iii) History, (iv) the East outside the USSR, (v) Historical Materialism. Special courses were set up in the Natural Sciences, Linguistics, and Military studies. The 2-year course for foreign students appears to have been based on the general subjects, with some additions regarding the evolution of Imperialism/ Capitalism and the Liberation Movement in their own countries.

Teaching followed a pattern specific to KUTV. Lectures were given in foreign languages or translated into the relevant language of the student group. Russian was the language of lectures only in senior classes. From the stronger students, special groups were formed to lead seminars or to undertake translations. Once trained, these monitors were given supplementary material and organised tutorials. By the mid-20s, KUTV gave out assistants to other Universities to help them cope with unusual problems of language or culture. It also drew on the assistance of other institutions (such as the Institute of Oriental Studies, Moscow). Among well-known teachers were V. Ya Vasileva (who handled foreign students), who prepared reports on Liberation Movements for the Comintern's Executive (ECCI) and who later went on to the South-East Asia Sector of the Institute of Oriental Studies, Moscow. Members of the Eastern Secretariat of ECCI, including L. I. Madiar, Mazut, B. Friar, and M. Pevsner, taught at the University, as did distinguished Oriental specialists A. A. Guber, G. N. Voytinskii, the Indianist D'iakov and members of the Institute of Red Professors. The Head of the Military Unit was V. E. Gorev, a former Soviet military advisor in China and the author of books on the Chinese army. The University organised special courses for the preparation of teachers, and the students of this unit went on to pedagogical work in various state universities.

As is clear, research at the University began on a low key in the work (1922-23) of a research group on social sciences (*kabinet obshchestvennykh nauk*) which was linked directly to the All Russian Scientific Association for Oriental Studies (*Vserossiiskaia Nauchnaia Assosiatsiia Vostokovedeniia*) and its journal, *Novyi Vostok*. In 1924, a research group on Oriental Studies and Colonial Politics (*Kabinet Vostokovedeniia i Kolonial'noi Politiki*) was established and formed a library, gathered documents and liased with various specialists on Oriental Studies. This developed into a Science-History Group (*Nauchno-*

istoricheskaia gruppa) in January 1925, which was the forerunner of the Scientific Research Association (*Nauchno-Issledovatel'skaia Assosiatsiia*) or NIA of the University, which was created in 1927.

The formation of the NIA (which acquired the name *Nauchno-Issledovatel'skaia Assosiatsiia Po Izucheniiu Natsional'nykh i Kolonial'nykh Problem* [NIANKP] or Scientific Research Association for the Study of National and Colonial Problems) in 1929 marked a crucial point in the history of teaching at the University and in research in Oriental Studies in the Soviet Union. The Association undertook work on the Soviet east and on Oriental countries outside the Soviet Union. The cadre of professional researchers who grew out of its activities published in the journal *Revoliutsionnyi Vostok* (The Revolutionary East), and taught subjects associated with the liberation movements of different countries. The NIANKP was eventually responsible for the reorganisation of KUTV, separating the teaching sections and the research sections. It also separated the foreign students from the Soviet students. The final result of such activity was the division of KUTV in 1937, and the concentration of its research and its training activities for foreign students in a newly formed Scientific Research Institute for National and Colonial Problems (*Nauchno-Issledovatel'skii Institut Natsional'nykh i Kolonial'nykh Problem* or NIINKP).

(ii) The Calcutta Project and Indian Studies at KUTV

The Calcutta Project confirmed the narrative established by Timofeeva and extended it in certain cases. The division of KUTV, for instance, in the 1930s, was poorly documented by Timofeeva, but its story figures in the archives. The Project was able to make the following clear with regard to the study of India.

Teachers and Researchers

At the height of its activities (1934), well-known teachers and research workers dealing with India at KUTV and NIANKP were included:

- I. I. Kozlov (b. 1902)—graduate of the Leningrad University's Institute of Oriental Studies, a political worker in 1918, a volunteer of the Red Army during 1919-22, and teacher in Barnaul and Saratov at a *rabfak* in 1922-25 before he returned to the Leningrad Institute for higher studies (1926-33) and received appointment at KUTV in 1934.

- S. M. Mel'man (b. 1903)—a medical student, who rose to senior rank in the Red Army during 1919-20 in the cultural section and at Groznyi, where he undertook political-educational work. He taught at the Tolmachev Military-Political Academy (1922-26) before being demobbed and attached to KUTV.
- K. A. Mikhailov (b. 1904)—who was an active Komsomol worker (1921-23), before attachment to Komsomol local agencies in Kazakhastan, and working with youth papers in Orenburg and Moscow (1925-26), finishing his education at the Institute of Oriental Studies (Moscow) (1926-31) and receiving attachment to KUTV in 1929.
- F. D. Stalina (b. 1904)—a Komsomol worker who began in Poltava and worked in Novgorod in party propaganda (both in factory and at an instructor level) before joining KUTV in 1929.

Mel'man, Stalina and Mikhailov were senior scientific workers at this time, along with A. A. Pronin and D. M. Gol'dman and one Kibenev, who were junior scientific workers. The head of the "Kabinet" (Research Group) on Indian affairs was Par'ian.

Research papers of the period and the memoirs of students also mention that V. V. Balabushevich (1900-1970) and A. M. Diakov (1896-1974), who later became the foremost specialists on India in the mid-twentieth century, were important figures in the India programme. The former came from a rural clergy background (Korbinsk region, Brest), and was trained at the Institute of Oriental Studies (Moscow) from 1921, when A. N. Snesarev was the Head of the Indology group. He completed his diploma from the Indo-Afghan Unit of the Economy and Foreign Affairs Department of the Middle Eastern Faculty, and thereafter worked for the Profintern as a research expert (*referent*). He was associated with the KUTV, clearly, while he held this position, until 1937, when the Profintern was abolished, when he transferred initially to a research agency of the Soviet Trade Unions' organisation and later to the Institute of World Economy and World Politics (1939). He came to head a section of the Institute of Oriental Studies (Moscow) after 1953.

A. M. Diakov came from a revolutionary family of Tver' province (which closely intermarried with the family of Mikhail Bakunin), and graduated as a doctor from Moscow State University in 1921. He then moved to Central Asia, where he served as a military doctor, and later (1924-26) as Kommissar for Health in Tajikistan. He was recruited from here for specialisation on India at the Institute of Red Professors (1932), where he finished his courses in 1936, and became a member of the staff of the KUTV. Diakov was a popular teacher, with a flair for languages. His ability to crack jokes in Punjabi has been well remembered by Indian students of KUTV. Like Balabushevich, he joined the Institute for World Economy and World Politics in 1939, and shifted to the Institute of Oriental Studies (Moscow) in 1950. His writings on India were already well known at this time, and he proceeded to become one of the USSR's major specialists on modern South Asian affairs.

Research Apparatus

The Calcutta Project was not only able to provide this basic story; it was able to deal with how research evolved. The character of research and the material that was the focus of interest were available in the archives of KUTV. As indicated in the Inventory, a range of official reports were integrated into specific surveys of strikes, the agrarian situation in Bengal, the United Provinces and other parts of India and the financial policies of the British government of India. Short résumés were made and presentations delivered. In addition, "obzory" were made of the Indian press—with translations that the staff prepared. Further translations of the press were provided to the researchers from the Soviet representative in Afghanistan.[9]

The archive also indicates a large range of coordination with students in India and a special concern with the translation of regional material from India. Reports of Indian newspapers highlighted the work of students trained in KUTV. Steps were taken to keep in touch with students and obtain on hand information from them.

(iii) Indian Students at the University and at the NIINKP

Information about Indian students at the University is limited for the 1920s. Hence, the archive was not helpful for information on the formative stage of the Communist Party of India and the operations of the Workers and Peasants' Parties during the 1920s.

The archive does indicate student numbers in the 1930s, associated with the arrival of a number of activists of the Gadr Party. The Calcutta Project was able to establish lists, working names and some histories of students concerned.

The Gadr Movement and The Soviet Union

A number of documents refer to Gadr Party activists who were trained in the Soviet Union and of whom some joined the Kirti Kisan Party and some joined the Communist Party in the Punjab. The interaction between Soviet authorities and such activists began in 1920-21, when Gadr leaders in the United States called for training of Gadr members in the USA. Initial interaction began with the visit of Santokh Singh and Rattan Singh to Moscow in 1923. Thereafter, five activists were sent with the assistance of the Communist Party of the USA, for training in Russia in 1926 (Pritam Singh, Karam Singh Dhoot, Harjap Singh, Santa Singh and one other). They were joined in the same year by Prem Singh Gill, who also came by way of the USA. All were admitted to the Communist University for the Workers of the East (KUTV). Thereafter, from centres of the Gadr Party in Rosario (Argentina) and Panama, further activists were recruited, and, between 1926 and 1935, a number of batches were sent to the Soviet Union for training at the Communist University. Five groups went during this period from Rosario. Four batches went from the USA (including Achhar Singh Chhima, Jaswant Singh Kairon, Nidhan Singh Mahesari and Sodhi Harminder Singh). One group went from Canada, and groups of four went from Panama and Nairobi. Teja Singh Swatantar went to the University alone. Altogether, some 76 activists are known to have received training in Moscow during this period, and the bulk of them returned to India. In the odd case, activists were returned to the Punjab: for instance, Hazara Singh Hamdam was rejected, possibly on the grounds that his family owned sufficient land (30 acres) in the Punjab for him to be considered "kulak."

In most cases, activists joined the Communist University and received a period of training. Some of these students were hardly literate in Punjabi, let alone any other Indian or non-Indian language. They seem, nevertheless, to have found adequate response from teachers in Moscow, according to a number who were interviewed by the veteran CPI leader, Sohan Singh Josh. Of the students, Rattan Singh Gholia Kalan and Sardara Singh attended the Seventh Congress of the Comintern (1935). Most of the students were gradually fed back into India by diverse routes (Paris, Pondicherry and Colombo being the most common). They returned, in some cases, to quick imprisonment (as in the case of Bachan Singh Gholia Khurd and Harbans Singh Bundala). They also had to deal with a confused situation in the Punjab, where the Communist Party, the Kirti Kisan Party and the Naujawan Bharat Sabha were at odds with each other. It was in such circumstances that the Moscow students came to constitute one more faction in the conflicts in the Punjab, as described in the documents here.

Instructed, apparently in Moscow, to unite different communist groups into one single Communist Party (Rattan Singh), if the CPI's presence was restricted, the Moscow students came to run a parallel party called the Kirti Communist Group by 1935, which took the title of the Communist Party of India. Teja Singh Swatantar was the acknowledged leader of the Party, which refused to acknowledge the existing Communist Party of India as a valid Left force, and which also refused to work with the Congress. With the assistance of Bhagat Singh Bilga and Chanan Singh, Teja Singh Swatantar attempted to make an all-India organisation of the Kirti Communist Group, sending representatives to Jamshedpur and Kharagpur. Although Swatantar's arrest in January 1936 impaired the working of the organisation, it continued as an independent group until a degree of unity with the CPI was achieved during the internment of both Kirti and CPI activists at Deoli (1939-42). Teja Singh's independent leanings, however, were to find expression after 1947 in his manoeuvres to establish a Communist Party of Pakistan.

The Calcutta Project established some of this narrative—allowing an extension of much that was known. The Project also detailed the problems of a Communist education, the approach of teachers and the lives of students. This fixed the doubts expressed by the teachers and the reluctant acceptance by students of what was taught. From the picture, a degree of clarity may be established that this was not indoctrination straight and simple, but a disputed process of education, where the links between the USSR and the students was maintained not always through the university or by commitment but by a process of networking that followed. The profile established by research, therefore, did not form the basis of a thorough and profound making of a Comintern man (there were no women). Rather, there was a two-way process of research accumulation where the ultimate research product and its significance was the product of interaction, chance and Comintern policy (both doctrinal and political).

3. Endnote: Profile of *Vostokovedenie* in the mirror of the Calcutta Project

As is clear from the above cameos, there were new dimensions that came to play in the development of *Vostokovedenie* in the 1920s and 1930s that made of it a far different social and cultural phenomenon from that which had existed under the Imperial Russian state. The archive indicates that not only did *Vostokovedenie* extend the range of its concerns, but that it was associated with those who had "feet on the ground," often coming from experience in Asia and dealing with those who were colonial subjects. This had seldom been the case of the Imperial Russian state, except in the case of native informants on Russia's borders who worked with the army, or a few members of the elite of the Empire's periphery.

The integration and training of informants into a regime of education and information was more akin to that which existed in "metropolitan" institutions of Empire in the west in the inter-war era (the School of Oriental and African Studies for instance), than standard foreign students' education programme that was to be found in Europe.

This aspect of *Vostokovedenie*, together with the political goals which Soviet institutions were expected to follow, could not but affect the intellectual character of the disciplinary area and the nature of its evolution. Figures such as I. I. Kozlov, S. F. Oldenburg and A. M. Diakov, representing different approaches to the study of Asia, all became specialists in Oriental Studies of equal weight.

The main success of the Project, it may be argued, however, did not only lie in this advance in the picture of the subject. The Calcutta Project took selections of the work done by the institutions mentioned above and established a small collection from which the subject could be examined in both intellectual and social terms. In this respect, the importance of the Project was not simply that it drew attention to what has been mentioned above. Rather, its significance lay in the fact that it allowed scholars to assess the degree to which various facets of this phenomenon developed, as well as to draw attention to its complexity. True, bringing together the way in which different aspects of what was considered an academic pursuit came to run into one another, it pointed to the anatomy of the discipline under Soviet rule. But beyond this, through the complexity of the documentation it provided in India, it also allowed those concerned to delineate different strands of what transpired, permitting them to establish a more open-ended processual profile than that which a straightforward anatomical profile might suggest.

Notes

1. For the range covered by the Soviet Archives Project see Purabi Roy, Sobhanlal Datta Gupta and Hari Vasudevan (eds.), *Indo-Russian Relations 1917-1947. Select Archives of the former Soviet Union. An Inventory*. (New Delhi: Shipra, 2012). Hereafter *Inventory*.
2. Oded Eran, *Mezhdunarodniki* (Tel Aviv: Turtledove Publishing, 1977).
3. R. Vaidyanath, *Soviet Studies in India* in Canadian Slavonic Papers, 1969, vol. 11, no. 2. I am grateful to Arup Banerji for drawing my attention to this little known but extremely rich article.
4. N. A. Kuznetsova and L. M. Kulagina, *Iz istorii sovetskogo vostokovedeniia 1917-1967* (Moscow: Nauka, 1970).
5. The various papers that establish the nature of VNAV's activities are to be found in the State Archive of the Russian Federation and are described, file by file in *Inventory* pp. 114 ff.
6. Pavlovich's complex background is not developed in the available archives, but is worth the mention here. Volonaire Mikhail Pavlovich was the pseudonym of Mikhail Lazerevich Veltman (b. Odessa 1871, d. Moscow 1927). He was a revolutionary who came from the family of a clerk. Veltman joined the RSDRP in Odessa and was arrested and exiled. He worked with Iskra in Paris from 1901 and joined the Mensheviks. He was present in St. Petersburg during the 1905 Revolution, working

with the RSDRP, and went into emigration, which he spent mainly in France (1907-17) and where he took an interest in the study of Asia. After 1917, he worked with the Kommissariat for External Affairs, joined the Bolsheviks, worked with the Main Committee of Armaments and was sent to the southern front and participated in the organisation of the Baku Conference for the Peoples of the East. During 1921-23, he was with the Kommissariat for Nationalities, during which time he formed the VNAV. See *Bolshaia Sovetskaia Entsiklopediia*, "Pavlovich."

7. The primary source of the institutional history of KUTV are the excellent articles by N. N. Timofeeva, "Kommunisticheskii Universitet Trudiashchikhsia Vostoka {KUTV} 1921-25" in *Narody Afriki I Azii* No. 2, 1976 and "Kommunisticheskii Universitet Trudiashchikhsia Vostoka {KUTV} 1926-1938" in *Narody Afriki I Azii* No. 5, 1979. This contains information on the various research institutes, but the bulk of the material in this article is also drawn from the archives of the State Archive of the Russian Federation and the Russian State Archive for Social and Political History. For the range of papers that make up some of this description see *Inventory,* pp. 113-14 and p. 88ff.

8. The Comintern's *Vostochnyi Sekretariat* or Eastern Secretariat provided many who were associated with Soviet Oriental Studies and also drew from the products of the institutions that were concerned with the area. Within the Comintern, the bulk of work regarding South West Asia and South Asia fell under the charge of the Eastern Department (*Vostochnyi Otdel*) and Eastern Secretariat (*Vostochnyi Sekretariat*) of the Third International. The former was established after a decision of ECCI of December 11, 1919. It became responsible for some activities of the CC of the RKP (b), took charge of the work of the Council for Propaganda and Action, and absorbed the Near East Section (*Otdel Blizhnego Vostoka*), as well as its sub-department, the Near Eastern Buro of ECCI (or Turkestan Buro). The Eastern Department was reorganised into the Eastern Sektor of ECCI by the autumn of 1922. From this time it was required to oversee not only the departments mentioned above, but also to supervise the work of the Department for the Near and Middle East and Northern Africa, which had been established by an ECCI decision of August 1921. Further reorganisations followed after the IVth Congress of the Comintern (1923) and in March 1926. Indian affairs on this last occasion went to the Secretariat for England, Holland, Australia and South Africa, where there was a "sub-group" for British India, under M. N. Roy. And this dispensation prevailed under the ECCI decision of July 8, 1927, by which an "Eastern Landsekretariat" continued to oversee the affairs of the Near and Far East as defined earlier, while the affairs of India came under the British-American Landersekretariat. It was only by the ECCI decision of September 1928 that India returned to the "eastern" group of countries which worked within the Comintern—i.e., to the "Eastern Landsekretariat," which was divided into three sections. The latter were: the Far Eastern Section (China, Japan, Korea, Mongolia,

Philippines), the Middle Eastern Section (India, Indo-China and Indonesia); and the Near Eastern Section (Turkey, Palestine, Syria, Persia, Francophone colonies). This position continued unchanged until 1935. A number of other important international organisations were a reference point for the work of South West Asian and South Asian revolutionaries in the 1917-28 period. The Trade Union International [*Profintern*], and its main affiliate to handle Indian affairs, the Pacific Labour Union, requires mention; equally the Peasant International [*Krestintern*] was a regular reference point for the Gadr Party.

9. Inventory, p. 92, ff.

4. The Soviet Union, Nationalism and the Colonial Question: Revisiting the Comintern Era

Sobhanlal Datta Gupta

I

The end of the Soviet era has led to revision of many of our earlier perceptions of history. This, however, does not suggest that all that was said or written in the Soviet period was necessarily wrong or distorted. It is true that non-accessibility of the archives did not provide the complete picture of what happened in history; but what was revealed later did not in all cases necessarily turn the truth upside down. One such issue was the Soviet Union's understanding of the colonial question in the wake of the October Revolution. The claim that was often made by the Soviet authorities that it was post-revolutionary Russia which, for the first time in human history, frontally opposed colonial domination and championed the cause of the anti-colonial struggle was quite correct. Indeed, the architect of this understanding was Lenin, and its antecedents can be traced to his critique of the Second International (1889-1914) for its failure to appreciate the cause of the oppressed people in the colonies. The implication of Lenin's critique was, methodologically, quite far-reaching, the reason being, first, that it was essentially a denunciation of Eurocentrism, which predominantly constituted the mindset of the European Left. Second, he made a distinction between bourgeois nationalism of the oppressor and that of the oppressed. While in the West bourgeois nationalism made way for imperialism, annexation and domination; nationalism in the colonies, despite its class limitations, was directed against colonial oppression. Third, Lenin highlighted the revolutionary potential of the peasant masses in the colonial countries, while at the same time pointing to the importance of organising the nascent proletariat in these countries. This position of Lenin was unique in the sense that it was a critique of the Narodniks who believed in a peasant utopia as well as of the Mensheviks and the Socialist Revolutionaries who were deeply sceptical of the revolutionary potential of the latter. Initially the Soviet position on the colonial issue was primarily guided by Lenin's understanding. It is the clearest manifestation of the colonial question being worked out by the Communist International (Comintern) [1919-1943], the dream child of Lenin, although major shifts took place thereafter, as the Stalin era commenced. Broadly speaking, three such phases can be identified in this context.

Phase One: This was primarily the Leninist phase of the Comintern, a phase which witnessed at one level the Soviet critique of the Eurocentric orientation of the West European Communist Parties, a position that was echoed by a large number of revolutionary parties in the colonies. This mainly refers to the marginalised status of the colonial question in the discourse of the Communist Parties of the West. In an article entitled "The Communist International and the Colonies" in *Pravda*, dated March 6, 1919, Bukharin significantly highlighted not only the importance of revolutionary movements in the colonies for the metropolitan countries but also warned against the false consciousness of the metropolitan proletariat vis-à-vis the colonies. Bukharin wrote:

> Up to now the so-called civilised world has been based on the merciless plunder of the colonial peoples. It is there, in the colonies, that all the filth and dirt, all the barbarism and contempt of capitalist relations finds its fullest expression. There you find the most repulsive decay and the most active agent generating it: capitalism. …
>
> Furthermore, it was not only the American, European, and Japanese bourgeoisies, but even to some extent the proletariat of these countries who benefited from this, for crumbs fell to them from the master's table. The proletariat looked down on the "barbarian people" and thought them worthy only of being fertiliser for European civilisation. …
>
> But though imperialist rule saps the strength of the enslaved peoples, the colonial countries are beginning to stir. For decades, for whole centuries, they have groaned under the yoke of these "civilised"

> bandits. Now that the proletariat has seen that its enemies are at home, it *welcomes* the uprisings of the colonial peoples. The rebellion of the colonies *hastens the collapse of imperialism*. The movement in the colonies, therefore, although it may not be socialist at all, has joined the broad stream of the great liberation struggle that is shaking up the entire immense structure of world capitalism.[1] [emphasis, original]

Karl Radek, a leading member of the Russian Communist Party and Secretary of the Comintern, strongly criticised the attitude of the West European Communist Parties in a speech in the Comintern's Second Congress:

> It is impossible for the British proletariat to free itself from the yoke imposed on it by capitalism unless it steps into the breach for the revolutionary colonial movement. .... In this situation the fate of the British revolution will in large part depend on whether the peasants and workers of Ireland, India, Egypt and so forth will see the British workers as their defenders, or whether they will have grown accustomed to seeing the British working class as the accomplice of British imperialism.[2]

In response, William McLaine, one of the British representatives in the Congress, admitted that it was their duty "to fight in the revolutionary struggle at home and to assist all real colonial revolutionary movements," since "revolutionary national movements that are fighting for real separation from the British Empire are helping advance the world revolution because they are striking at the fountainhead of imperialist reaction, namely, Great Britain."[3] Notwithstanding the British admission of the importance of the colonial question, Lenin in his "Report of the Central Committee RKP(b) to the Ninth All-Russian Conference of the Communist Party" dated September 20, 1920, made the following remark:

> When an English workers' delegation visited me and I told them that every decent English worker should desire the defeat of the English government, they understood nothing. They made faces that I think

> even the best photograph could not capture. They simply could not get into their heads the truth that in the interests of the world revolution, workers must wish the defeat of their government.[4]

In fact, from the archival sources it is now evident that the idea of providing arms and finances to the colonial countries was on the agenda of Lenin immediately after the Russian Revolution, since the colonial question engaged the attention of the young Soviet state from the very beginning. At the time of the founding of the Comintern, the vision of an outbreak of revolution in the East, with direct military help from Soviet Russia, figured in Lenin's initial perception of the colonial question, following the victory of the October Revolution, which is evident from a letter of Lenin dated October 16, 1919, addressed to Sh. Z. Eliava, an old Georgian Bolshevik:

> We will not spare money, and will send sufficient gold and foreign gold coins if you will arrange to buy military equipment (from English soldiers and officers, from merchants via Persia, and so on) and also establish ties through Persia, India, and so on, with Europe and America. To this end you must immediately begin looking for dedicated people capable of getting through to the right coastal locations and from there finding connections with steamships from neutral countries, with merchants, sailors, smugglers, and so on. Of course, the matter must be conducted in an extremely conspiratorial manner (as we knew how to work under the tsar). Weapons, connections with America and Europe, and aid to the peoples of the East in the struggle against imperialism.[5]

That the countries of the East occupied a key position in this strategy is now confirmed by the late D. Volkogonov, who, having the sole privilege of accessing the entire mass of archival holdings of the Comintern and the Soviet Communist Party, informs us that, on Lenin's initiative, Lev Karakhan had drawn up a proposal whereby the Central Committee was to allocate large sums for Bolshevik agitators sent to the Eastern countries. Thus, a trip to China or Korea amounted to ten thousand gold roubles, while Persia, India and other Asian countries had their own rates of pay.[6]

Notwithstanding this all-out support to the struggle of the colonial people, there were two issues which distinguished the position of the colonies from that of the Soviet Union. One: while the Soviet policy was to consider the cause of the colonial people as inseparably linked with the struggle of the proletariat in the West, persons like M. N. Roy considered the colonial question as an independent issue. Second, they quite sharply differed on the contentious question of nationalism. Lenin's idea of an anti-imperialist united front, which in the colonial countries envisaged the idea of alliance with bourgeois nationalism, was contested by representatives of a number of Communist Parties of the East. It is now evident that this idea figured in Lenin's mind following the defeat and retreat of the Left all over Europe and collapse of the dream of world revolution in the aftermath of the October Revolution. The most vociferous opponent of Lenin's position was M. N. Roy, who in his Supplementary Theses on the colonial question, which was adopted (with amendments) in the Second Congress of Comintern in 1920 along with Lenin's Colonial Theses, rejected the idea of going for an alliance with the nationalist bourgeoisie in colonies like India.[7]

II

Phase Two: This refers to the period between Comintern's Fifth (1924) and Seventh Congress (1935). It is generally believed that the Soviet policy in regard to the colonial question witnessed a major shift after 1927, following the collapse of the first United Front in China between the CPC and the Guomindang. Furthermore, it is also a standard argument that the Sixth Congress of Comintern (1928), which introduced an ultra-left turn in regard to the colonial question, and which was accelerated by the Chinese debacle, was another pointer to the shift away from a united front strategy in the Soviet position. But what remains somewhat underplayed in these explanations is the theoretical position of Stalin on the colonial question, which was not only different from Lenin's understanding but which set the tone for this ultra left turn even before the China episode and the Sixth Congress. What is especially noteworthy in this connection is, first, that Stalin's understanding of the colonial question was at variance with the Comintern's official position. Second,

Stalin's position closely resembled M. N. Roy's outlook, and one may argue that it is this understanding which was eventually reflected in the Comintern's new position in the Sixth Congress in 1928. Ironically, however, by 1928 there was a distinct shift in Roy's position, as he was moving away from his original ultra leftism to a distinctly moderate position.

Thus, in the Fifth Congress (1924) of Comintern, which was held after the death of Lenin, the Draft Resolution on the Colonial and Eastern Question could not be finalised, as there emerged sharp differences between the views of D. Manuilsky, representing the Soviet as well as the official Comintern position, and those of M. N. Roy, a central figure in the Comintern who worked out the colonial question. Two crucial differences between Roy and Manuilsky led to the impasse. One: while Manuilsky defended the idea of united front, calling for a direct link between bourgeois nationalism in the colonies and the Comintern notwithstanding the limitations of nationalism in these countries, Roy dismissed this idea, since in his opinion bourgeois nationalism in the colonial countries was a spent force. Two: for Manuilsky the colonial question had to be viewed as a homogeneous notion, cutting across boundaries; for Roy this undifferentiated understanding was unacceptable, since colonies differed in terms of their socio-economic development. According to the late Soviet historian, A. B. Reznikov's archival findings, the aforementioned Draft Resolution was submitted to Stalin. On July 31, 1924, he sent the following remarks to Manuilsky:

> You mention differences with Roy who underscores the social aspect of the struggle in the colonies. I don't know how these differences concretely express themselves. But I should say that there are certain places in the resolution of the congress which I do not agree with precisely from the standpoint of the social aspect. … I believe that the time has come to raise the question of the hegemony of the proletariat in the liberation struggle in the colonies such as India, whose bourgeoisie is conciliatory (with British imperialism), and the victory over whom (i.e., over the conciliatory bourgeoisie) is the main condition for liberation from imperialism. A whole number of points in the resolution speak

> of criticising the national bourgeoisie, exposing its half-heartedness and so forth. That is not what is needed. It is necessary to smash the conciliatory national bourgeoisie, i.e., to wrest the worker and peasant masses from its influence in order to achieve genuine liberation from imperialism. Without fulfilling this preliminary task it is impossible to achieve victory over British imperialism. The basic feature of the new situation in colonies such as India, is that the national bourgeoisie (i.e., the most influential and wealthy bourgeoisie) is afraid of a revolution and prefers a compromise with foreign imperialism to the complete liberation of their country from foreign imperialism. In order to smash this bloc it is necessary to concentrate all blows at the conciliatory national bourgeoisie and advance the slogan of the hegemony of the proletariat for leadership of the liberation movement in colonies such as India, and to push the conciliatory national bourgeoisie out of this honourable post. The greatest shortcoming of the congress resolution on the eastern and colonial question is that it does not take this new decisive aspect in the situation into account and lumps all the colonies together.[8]

That this note of Stalin was clearly a critique of the official position of Comintern and strongly inclined towards the position of Roy, introduced a new twist, leaving the fate of the colonial question undecided in the Fifth Congress, as the Congress ultimately did not endorse the Draft Resolution and it was decided to put off the decision till the commencement of the next Congress. It is now known that Manuilsky, the leader of the Eastern Commission in Comintern, later told the Executive Committee of Comintern (ECCI) that there was now a tendency in the Comintern to review some of the basic positions on the policies in the colonies, and to touch up Lenin. This meant the revival of old tendencies, i.e., the role of the bourgeoisie was exhausted in the colonial countries, since they constituted a class of reactionaries. Significantly, Manuilsky thereafter was removed from the leadership of the Eastern Commission.[9]

To understand the significance of Stalin's intervention it is, however, necessary to keep in mind that, despite Roy's criticism of the Comintern's position on the East at the Fifth Congress, the ECCI continued to reiterate its position, especially in regard to India, in the period that followed. Since the Fifth Congress could not take any decision on the colonial question, the ECCI's "Resolution on India" dated April 6, 1925, in its Fifth Enlarged Plenum, was crucial, as "it is necessary for the Communists in India to continue their work inside the National Congress and in the left wing of the Swaraj Party as well as in the nationalist organisations and unions with the objective of building up a national-revolutionary mass party and an all India anti-imperialist bloc."[10]

To appreciate the full meaning of Stalin's difference with the ECCI position, one has to consider the following documents, namely, his report to the Fourteenth Conference of the Soviet Communist Party on May 9 and his speech to the students in the Communist University of the Toilers of the East (KUTV) on May 18 in 1925. In the third section of the first document, which focused on the tasks of the Communists in the colonial and dependent countries, Stalin made it unambiguously clear that it was no longer possible to consider the East as a "homogeneous whole," since colonies were divided into "capitalistically developed," "developing" and "backward and lagging colonies" with the following consequence:

> Until now the national-liberation movement has been regarded as an unbroken front of all the national forces in the colonial and dependent countries, from the most reactionary bourgeois to the most revolutionary proletarians. Now, after the national bourgeoisie has split into a revolutionary and an anti-revolutionary wing, the picture of the national movement is assuming a somewhat different aspect. Parallel with the revolutionary elements of the national movement, compromising and reactionary elements which prefer a deal with imperialism to the liberation of their countries are emerging from the bourgeoisie.[11]

The second document further explicated the spirit of the first document. In his speech to the students of KUTV on May 18, 1925, Stalin reiterated that the colonies and dependent countries could be no longer considered "an all-embracing colonial East," Morocco being "quite undeveloped" having "little or no proletariat," China and Egypt being listed as "underdeveloped industrially," "having a relatively small proletariat," and India being categorised as "capitalistically more or less developed," having "a more or less numerous national proletariat." Accordingly, he emphasised the need to pursue three different lines for the Communists in respect of the three categories of countries. For the first category, the prescription was that of a united national front against imperialism, which would include the national bourgeoisie as a homogeneous category. For the second category the understanding was that the bourgeoisie had already split into two wings, revolutionary and compromising, but where the latter had not yet joined the imperialist camp. Consequently, here it was possible to think of a bloc of two forces in the form of a single party, a workers' and peasants' party, which would actually represent "a bloc of two forces—the Communist Party and the party of the revolutionary petty bourgeoisie," keeping in mind that such a dual party would not hinder the freedom of the Communist Party to conduct agitation and propaganda and bind the latter hand and foot.[12] Coming to the third category, which specifically referred to India, Stalin stated, distinguishing it from China:

> The fundamental and new feature of the conditions of life of colonies like India is not only that the national bourgeoisie has split up into a revolutionary party and a compromising party, but primarily that the compromising section of this bourgeoisie has already managed, in the main, to strike a deal with imperialism. Fearing revolution more than it fears imperialism, and concerned more about its money-bags than about the interests of its own country, this section of the bourgeoisie, the richest and the most influential section, is going over entirely to the camp of the irreconcilable enemies of the revolution, it is forming a bloc with imperialism against workers and peasants of its own country. The victory of the revolution cannot be achieved unless this bloc is smashed. But in order to smash this bloc, fire must be concentrated on the compromising national bourgeoisie, its treachery exposed, the toiling masses freed from its influence, and the conditions necessary for the hegemony of the proletariat systematically prepared. In other words, in colonies like India it is a matter of preparing the proletariat

> for the role of the leader of the liberation movement, step by step dislodging the bourgeoisie and its mouthpiece from this honourable post. This task is to create a revolutionary anti-imperialist bloc and to ensure the hegemony of the proletariat in this bloc. This bloc can assume, although it need not necessarily do so, the form of a single workers' and peasants' party, formally bound by a single platform. In such countries, the independence of the Communist Party must be the chief slogan of the advanced communist elements, for the hegemony of the proletariat can be prepared and brought about only by the Communist Party.[13]

The above documents thus confirm the impression that, while Stalin's position was not in agreement with the official Comintern position, as reflected in the ECCI Resolution of April 6, 1925, it virtually echoed and thereby vindicated the position of M. N. Roy.[14] Thus, on one level like Roy, Stalin too rejected the notion of a homogeneous concept of colonialism and embraced the idea of differentiation of colonies. On another level, however, although Stalin's position on the role of the nationalist bourgeoisie apparently seemed identical with Roy's position and stood in contrast to the position of the ECCI, a closer analysis would suggest that Stalin's outlook was somewhat different from that of Roy, notwithstanding their quite striking similarities. For Roy, bourgeois nationalism in countries like India was already a spent force. But in Stalin's understanding the nationalist bourgeoisie had split into a revolutionary and a compromising wing, demanding concentration of fire on the compromising wing and its isolation;[15] however, on the question of leadership in the liberation struggle in countries like India, Stalin's position was very close to Roy's understanding, as it underscored the necessity of securing the hegemony of the proletariat by building up the Communist Party. Evidently, that Stalin was becoming closely inclined to Roy's understanding of the colonial question, the root of which is to be traced to Roy's Supplementary Theses adopted by the Second Congress, was made unambiguously clear by him in 1927:

> Why were the Supplementary Theses needed? In order to single out from the backward colonial countries which have no industrial proletariat such countries as China and India, of which it cannot be said that they have "practically no industrial proletariat." Read the Supplementary Theses, and you will realise they refer chiefly to China and India .... How could it happen that Roy's special theses were needed to "supplement" Lenin's theses? The fact is that Lenin's theses had been written and published long before the representatives from the colonial countries had arrived, and prior to the discussion in the special commission of the Second Congress. And since the discussion in the Congress Commission revealed the necessity for singling out from the backward colonies of the East such countries as China and India, the necessity for the "Supplementary" theses arose.[16]

The Chinese debacle of 1927 acted as a catalyst to Stalin's understanding, which set the new direction of the Soviet position on the colonial question. This constituted a major break with the stand of Lenin which was reflected shortly in the Comintern's Sixth Congress (1928) when it adopted the new Colonial Theses. By 1929 Stalin's position underwent a further shift to the Left. It was now concluded that the bourgeoisie in the colonies had become a completely counter-revolutionary force, and that since this was sought to be concealed by the so-called "Left" elements within the parties that represented the bourgeoisie (Wang Cheng-Wei of Guomindang, Jawaharlal Nehru and Subhas Chandra Bose of Indian National Congress), the main attack would have to be concentrated on them, exposing their allegedly subversive and hypocritical character. As stated earlier, till the time of the Sixth Congress, he maintained a distinction between the revolutionary, petty bourgeois wing and the reactionary section within the camp of the national bourgeoisie. Now it was argued that the entire camp had become an accomplice of imperialism. Ironically, this was the spirit of Roy's Supplementary Theses, although by the time Stalin adopted this position, Roy had shifted to a moderate position on the colonial question, while increasingly turning out to be a trenchant critic of Comintern's ultra leftism. This was evident in Stalin's following characterisation of the Indian bourgeoisie in 1930:

> As regards India, Indo-China, Indonesia, Africa, etc., the growth of the revolutionary movement in those countries, which at times assumes the form of a national war for liberation, leaves no room for doubt. Messieurs the bourgeois count on flooding those countries with blood and on relying on police bayonets, calling people like Gandhi to their assistance. There can be no doubt that police bayonets make a poor prop. Tsarism, in its day, also tried to rely on police bayonets, but everybody knows what kind of a prop they turned out to be. As regards assistants of the Gandhi type, Tsarism had a whole herd of them in the shape of liberal compromisers of every kind, but nothing came of this except discomfiture.[17]

III

Phase Three: This was the period between Comintern's Seventh Congress (1935) and its dissolution in 1943. By 1934 it was evident that the Soviet policy on, and its understanding of, the colonial question had completely gone wrong. The original position of Lenin that, while the Soviet Union would, by providing material support to the anti-colonial struggles, prepare the ground for an effective linkage between the USSR and the oppressed people in the colonies, was now completely belied. As the Comintern increasingly became the instrument of Soviet foreign policy, as Stalin's understanding of the colonial question became the guideline for the Communist Parties in the colonies, it led to rapid isolation of the parties from the national mainstream. By 1934 it was evident that the strategy of the Sixth Congress had failed to reap dividends. In Indonesia, the Philippines, Turkey, Korea, Palestine, Tunisia and Egypt the Communist Parties had been reduced to small groups, as they were driven deep underground. In Iran, the Communists were victims of cruel terror. In China, the Communist Party had suffered serious erosion of its base under the impact of the disastrous Li Li-san line after the Sixth Congress; in India, the CPI was in wilderness, especially after the Meerut arrests.

All these now called for a change and the architect of this change was Georgi Dimitrov, the Secretary of Comintern since 1935. With the publication of Dimitrov's Diary[18] and the Stalin-Dimitrov correspondence, it is now evident that it was because of Dimitrov's persuasion that Stalin ultimately agreed to switch over to the "popular front" strategy in view of the growing menace of fascism and the looming shadow of the War. In the case of Europe it meant alliance between the Communists and the Social Democrats, while in the colonial countries it called for an alliance between the Communists and the nationalist forces. The Seventh Congress of Comintern gave it the final seal of approval. One may, therefore, be tempted to suggest that it was Comintern's return to the original Leninist line, which had been discarded after Stalin came to power. But this was not at all the case, since nowhere in the documents of the Seventh Congress was it admitted that the position of the Sixth Congress, its strategy of "class versus class" had been wrong. This was glaringly evident in the speech of Harry Pollitt of the Communist Party of Great Britain (CPGB) in the Seventh Congress when he said:

> There are people who believe that the slogan of "class against class" raised in the Sixth Congress has been incorrect. This slogan was correct and helped in strengthening the Communist Parties in warding off right opportunist as well as left sectarian deviations. Today's united front policy is only the resultant continuation of the slogan of "class against class"...[19]

Moreover, the rather lackadaisical attitude of the Seventh Congress towards the colonial question deepened this confusion. Thus, in a letter dated November 4, 1935, on India from one "Mac" to Comintern, it was stated:

> From a perusal of the literature sent by you we did not find any detailed discussion of the Seventh Congress on the Colonial question excepting Wang Min's speech. Was there no report or discussion on the question of the colonies and dependencies? Does it mean that the theses of the Sixth Congress hold good? Please let us know.[20]

This lack of clarity on this crucial question at the Seventh Congress was a major hurdle in materialising the idea of an anti-imperialist united front, particularly with the Congress Socialist Party (CSP) in India.

But this ambivalence was no longer there after June 22, 1941, when the Soviet Union was invaded by Hitler's Germany, when the "imperialist war" had become "people's war" as by this time the Comintern had become virtually an instrument of Soviet foreign policy. As defence of the Soviet Union became the sacred duty of all Communist Parties, the Communist Parties in the colonies too had to fall in line. India was a classic illustration in this regard. As the nationalist forces were now out to wage the "Quit India" movement in August 1942, the CPGB tried to persuade the Congress leadership to abandon its line of opposition to the British Raj and accept the position that it was high time to forge a united front of communists and the nationalists in defence of the USSR and its allies, namely, Britain. Thus in a statement dated August 30, 1941 the CPGB said:

> In the new world situation the Colonial and semi-Colonial people are conscious of the great role that they can play in winning the battle of freedom. They will understand the need for the immediate building of a great united front for the defeat of Hitler. This takes precedence over every other issue of the present moment.
>
> In India the release of Nehru and all political prisoners would assist in preparing the way for direct negotiations between the British Government and the National Congress in order to find a basis of collaboration in the present crisis.[21]

Harry Pollitt, General Secretary of CPGB, wrote to Nehru (addressing him as "Comrade Nehru" and marked "personal") on July 29, 1942, in view of the impending adoption of the August Resolution:

> I would not presume to write to you at this particular moment unless I felt it to be vitally necessary to the common interests of both of our countries, and in particular to what you and I stand for in regard to our socialist principles …
>
> I write to you now because never in the history of the world struggle for freedom have we had to face such a critical situation as now, one in which the future of world progress is being decided upon the battlefields of the Soviet Union …

> It is from this basis that I think your own policy ought to be formulated. You would make the politics of Congress a thousand times stronger if, while fighting for the complete independence of India and without in any way lowering your fundamental demands, at the same time in the present urgent situation you put to one side the suggestion of non-cooperation. It appears to me that the last two paragraphs of the recent resolution of the Working Committee will, if operated, lead to a weakening of the active struggle against fascism, bringing serious danger to the entire people of India and making more remote the prospect of India gaining its independence.
>
> ...
>
> This is why I ask you to reconsider the present draft policy of Congress. I ask you to see how, in the fundamental interests of your own country, a policy of non-cooperation with the British Government is not strengthening your cause but weakening it; for it would amount at best to a policy of neutrality, of standing aside from the present desperate conflict which will decide the fate of Indian independence ...[22]

While the Congress leadership refused to yield to the CPGB's persuasion, the CPI toed the Comintern line, despite serious internal differences within the Party.[23] But just as the adoption of the Sixth Congress line had led to the CPI's isolation from the national mainstream, adoption of this new line of Comintern on "People's War" led to its second isolation. The case of the CPI was a classic illustration of how a blind adherence to the Soviet understanding of the colonial question, mediated through the Comintern at two different historical moments, severely damaged its credibility, future possibilities and prospects.

Notes

1. Nikolai Bukharin, "The Communist International and the Colonies," in John Riddell (ed.), *Founding the Communist International: Proceedings and Documents of the First Congress, March 1919* (New York: Anchor Foundation, 1987), pp. 307-08.
2. John Riddell (ed.), *The Communist International in Lenin's Time*, vol. I (New York: Pathfinder Press, 1991), p. 231.

3. Ibid., pp. 262-63.
4. Document 59, "Political Report of the Central Committee RKP(b) to the Ninth All-Russian Conference of the Communist Party," in Richard Pipes (ed.), *The Unknown Lenin: From the Secret Archive* (With a new Afterword) (New Haven and London: Yale University Press, 1998) p. 99.
5. Document 40, "Lenin's letter to Sh. Z. Eliava dated October 16, 1919." Ibid., p. 74.
6. Dmitri Volgokonov, *Autopsy for an Empire: The Seven Leaders Who Built the Soviet Regime* (New York: The Free Press, 1998), p. 54.
7. For details of amendment of M. N. Roy's original Draft Theses on the colonial question, see Gangadhar Adhikari (ed.), *Documents of the History of the Communist Party of India*, vol. I: 1917-1922 (New Delhi: People's Publishing House, 1971), pp. 173-77, and Sibnarayan Ray (ed.), *Selected Works of M. N. Roy*, vol. I: 1917-1922 (Delhi: Oxford University Press, 1987), pp. 20-21.
8. Cited in A. B. Reznikov, "The Strategy and Tactics of the Communist International in the National and Colonial Question," in R. A. Ulyanovsky (ed.), *The Comintern and the East: The Struggle for the Leninist Strategy and Tactics in National Liberation Movements* (Moscow: Progress Publishers, 1979), pp. 169-70.
9. P. M. Shastitko, *Obrechenniedogmy: Bolshevizminatsionalnyivopros* (Moscow: Izdatelskaya Firma "Vostochnaialiteratura," RAN, 2002), p. 106.
10. Document 86, "ECCI's Resolution on India dated 6.4.25," in Purabi Roy, et al. (eds.), *Indo-Russian Relations: 1917-1947. Select Documents from the Archives of the Russian Federation, Part I: 1917-1928* (Calcutta: The Asiatic Society, 1999), p. 210.
11. J. V. Stalin, "The Results of the Work of the Fourteenth Conference of the RCP(B). Report delivered at a meeting of the Active of the Moscow Organisation of the RCP(B), May 9, 1925," in *Works*, vol. 7 (Moscow: Foreign Languages Publishing House, 1954), p. 108.
12. J. V. Stalin, "The Political Tasks of the University of the Peoples of the East. Speech delivered at a meeting of Students of the Communist University of the Toilers of the East, May 18, 1925." Ibid., pp. 148-50.
13. Ibid., pp. 150-51.
14. This, for instance, has been the interpretation voiced by K. Damodaran, "The Past," *Seminar*, 178, June 1974, p. 14 and, more recently, by Sibnarayan Ray, *In Freedom's Quest: A Study of the Life and Works of M. N. Roy*, vol. II: The Comintern Years (1922-27) (Kolkata: Minerva Associates, 2002), pp. 145-46.
15. This difference between Roy, Stalin and the ECCI was first pointed out by Adhikari but not very satisfactorily, as in his analysis he mainly focused on Stalin's Report of May 9 and not on his speech of May 18, 1925. See G. Adhikari (ed.), *Documents of the History of the Communist Party of India*, vol. II: 1923-1925 (New Delhi: People's Publishing House, 1974), pp. 547-57. Compared with the Report of

May 9, Stalin's speech of May 18 was far more negative in his assessment of the compromising wing, as the latter was considered to be the key enemy to be attacked and it cannot be denied that Stalin's position, despite his methodological difference with Roy, was certainly very close to Roy's position in spirit.

16. J. V. Stalin, "Concerning questions of the Chinese Revolution. Reply to Comrade Marchulin," in *Works*, vol. 9 (Moscow: Foreign Languages Publishing House, 1954), p. 238.
17. J. V. Stalin, "Political Report of the Central Committee to the Sixteenth Congress of the C.P.S.U.(B). June 27, 1930," in *Works,* vol. 12 (Moscow: Foreign Languages Publishing House, 1954), p. 259.
18. See *The Diary of Georgi Dimitrov: 1933-1949.* Introduced and edited by Ivo Banac (New Haven and London: Yale University Press, 2003) and Alexander Dallin and F. I. Firsov (eds.), *Dimitrov and Stalin 1934-1943: Letters from the Soviet Archives* (New Haven and London: Yale University Press, 2000).
19. *Rundscahuueber Politik, Wirtschaft und Arbeiterbewegung*, 4(36), August 8, 1935, p. 1728. According to Vile¢m Kahan, in the absence of publication of the stenographic records of the Seventh Congress, the most complete version of the proceedings of the Congress is to be found in the relevant issues of *Rundschau*, published in 1935.
20. Document 82, "Letter from 'Mac' to Comintern dated 4.11.35. Re: Confusion in the CPI Concerning the Idea of United Front, After the Seventh Congress," in Purabi Roy et al. (eds.), *Indo-Russian Relations: 1917-1947. Select Documents from the Archives of the Russian Federation.* Part II: 1929-1947 (Calcutta: The Asiatic Society, 2000), p. 235.
21. Labour History Archives and Study Centre, Manchester (LHASC). CPGB archives. CP/CENT/STAT/1/3. "The War and the Colonial Peoples." Statement issued by CPGB, *World News and Views,* August 30, 1941.
22. LHASC. CPGB archives. CP/IND/POLL/3/11. "Pollitt's signed letter to Jawaharlal Nehru dated 29 July, 1942" (marked "Personal" in pencil at the top).
23. I have explored this question in detail by a study of inner-party and archival documents in Sobhanlal Datta Gupta, *Comintern, India and the Destiny of Communism in India: 1919-1943. Dialectics of Real and a Possible History.* Second revised and enlarged edition (Kolkata: Seribaan, 2011), Chapter 4.

5. Russia's Policy Towards Central Asia in the Post-Soviet Period

Raj Kumar Kothari

In the post-Soviet period, the bilateral relations between Russia and Central Asia received more attention than in the past. In the Soviet period, Central Asia hardly played any role in the framing of Russia's foreign policy. With the dissolution of the Soviet Union, major attention was diverted towards the Caspian belt mainly for its energy resources and from this time onwards all major powers in the region and beyond, including the USA, China and Russia became involved in competition for Caspian shelf's energy resources. US international oil companies and others took keen interest in the region. The Caspian Basin became an arena of energy rivalry between the US and Russia. Central Asia by default drew attention of the major powers for strategic and economic reasons.

In the post-Soviet years Central Asia also emerged as a zone of conflict as clashes erupted between ethnic groups in the Ferghana Valley. The civil war in Tajikistan that took place from 1992 to 1997 had a spill-over effect on Afghanistan. The situation became conducive for the germination of radical groups, the infiltration of radical forces and the influence of organisations like the Islamic Movement of Uzbekistan (IMU). After the 9/11 incident, the linkage between terrorist groups operating in Afghanistan and Central Asia became a well-publicised issue and a matter of serious concern for Russia. Besides the security issue, Russia's involvement in Central Asian energy, arms sale and trade became the cornerstone of Moscow's foreign policy. It is in this backdrop that the present article tries to make a very humble attempt to focus on Russia's policy towards Central Asia in the post-Soviet years.

In India, scholars have analysed the problem from a historical perspective.[1] The Central Asian economy—even before the 1917 October

Revolution—was largely dominated and controlled by the Russians. The Tsarist administration paid great attention to cotton cultivation. Russian control over Central Asia with Russian as the *lingua franca* changed its ethnic and linguistic character. Russian settlements and Russian language in Central Asia became the thrust of Russia's Asiatic policy. Gradually, civil and military officials, intellectuals, scholars, scientists, teachers, artisans and workers from Russia settled down in Central Asia. People of European origin, including Russians, Ukrainians and Germans had also settled in Central Asia which changed its ethnic structure and composition. In the process Central Asia became more responsive to a Soviet order. It is therefore only natural that Russian influence in Central Asia, even in the post-Soviet period, remains deep-rooted.

The Central Asian states cannot be studied as a single entity. Today, each and every Central Asian state has distinct political cultures and has different levels of socio-economic development. All the countries have different foreign policy goals. However, they share common concerns about terrorism, illegal trafficking and other social evils—all that have led to a breakdown of social security. In fact, these states have many things in common: a volatile security environment, caused by weak civic and state institutions in all states of the region; socio-economic crises; and ethnic, religious and political tensions.[2] Russia, because of its traditional links with Central Asia, viewed the region as her responsibility and opposed the involvement of other external powers. However, since the collapse of the Soviet Union, other foreign countries—the US, China, Japan—also developed bilateral relationships with Central Asian countries. In 1993, Russia adopted a new foreign policy doctrine which declared Central Asia as part of Russia's "near abroad." Due to a number of factors, Russia's involvement in the region declined in the 1990s and then gained momentum with Vladimir Putin becoming the next President of Russia after Boris Yeltsin. From 2005 onwards, Russian presence was more strongly felt in Central Asia.[3]

Central Asia has the image of being the heartland of Asia. In the last two decades, there has been economic, political and military involvement of Northeast Asian countries like China, Japan and Korea in Central Asia. China has given utmost priority on promoting relations with Central

Asia in order to foster development and stabilisation of its vast western province, Xinjiang. Beijing also sees the region as a potential market, a source of energy and other natural resources, and as a communications bridge to Iran and the Middle East. In recent years, Japan has become the largest donor country to Central Asia and sees the region as a potential market, source of raw materials, and bridge to the Middle East. It is expected that China will have a greater influence in terms of prospects of trade and connectivity in the region.

The US intervention in Afghanistan and its tackling of the Taliban menace in the aftermath of 9/11 substantially altered the security equation in Central Asia. The United States established a military base in Kyrgyzstan. Russia and the Central Asian states welcomed US action in Afghanistan. Russia thus demonstrated its solidarity with the United States in the fight against international terrorism and strengthening Russia realised the importance of its support as a way to stabilise its border with Afghanistan, to better control the tense Ferghana Valley, including radical elements and to diminish differences in Tajikistan. As far as the US is concerned, till date it has no major energy projects in Central Asia. US interests focus mainly on military assets, crucial for the war effort in Afghanistan. In view of the tense situation in the Af-Pak border, the US and NATO have asked Russian support for opening a Central Asian route for the allied forces on the ground. This also reinforces the argument that Russia plays a more active/assertive role in the region.[4]

Out of the 25 million ethnic Russians who lived outside Russia, 9.5 million lived in Central Asia. Russian interest in Central Asia is strengthened by the presence of large numbers of Russians and Russian-speaking people in the region. The collapse of the Soviet Union brought into the limelight the brewing hostility between the ethnic Russians and the Central Asian population. Today Central Asia is witnessing a reverse migration of its Russian population. Thousands of Russians have left Central Asia since Soviet disintegration, which has changed the ethnic composition of the region.[5] The security of this population has been crucial from Moscow's point of view.

Russia has military bases in Kyrgyzstan, Uzbekistan, and Tajikistan and has signed a bilateral defence treaty with Kazakhstan. Russia has been playing a proactive role in Central Asia in recent years because of the rise of terrorist activities. Afghanistan has emerged as a key player, with border security and management becoming a priority. In fact, the Afghan situation might be a basis for enhanced cooperation with the US. Russia has been pressing for an increased regional involvement in the Afghan problems in collaboration with Central Asian republics and other regional states, such as Pakistan and the Shanghai Cooperation Organisation (SCO) which provides a solid basis for Moscow's involvement, strengthen its position and counterbalance Washington's presence. Actually, Russia is eager to regain its leadership status in Central Asia; China seeks markets and energy resources; and the Central Asian states need the SCO as their guarantee for political survival. China has also developed close ties with the Central Asian states bordering the province of Xinjiang, namely Kazakhstan, Tajikistan and Kyrgyzstan, based essentially on economic diplomacy within the SCO framework. It is important to note that China has made considerable investment in the region in transport infrastructure.[6] Therefore, complementarities of interest have been the basis of cooperation between Russia, China and the Central Asian states.

Russia's most important interest in the region is in Central Asian energy development, with a new focus on gas, as markets expand in Europe and Asia. Together, Russia, Iran, and the Central Asian states hold more than half of world gas reserves. Gas is not as mobile as oil and is destined for regional rather than world markets. Therefore, retaining a major role in Central Asian gas production and export is a key issue for Russia's energy industry. Energy experts doubt that Russia can both meet its domestic demand and its growing ambitions for gas exports in the coming decades without having access to and influence over the flow of Central Asian gas.

Energy development is seen as the key to Central Asia's economic future, and Kazakhstan, Turkmenistan, and Uzbekistan all have considerable oil and gas reserves. However, the location of Central Asian states is such that they do not have direct access to the European and Asian markets. Lack of pipeline infrastructure has constrained the states' efforts to become independent producers and exporters. In the 1990s, a series of ambitious international projects to transport Central Asian gas to world markets—from Kazakhstan to China, from Turkmenistan across the Caspian to Azerbaijan and Turkey and again from Turkmenistan across Afghanistan to Pakistan and India—failed to make any breakthrough. In 2002, Russia promoted Eurasian Gas Alliance to coordinate gas production and guaranteed long-term purchase of Central Asian gas for Russia's domestic market. Russia's energy industry plays the dominant role in Central Asian gas and Russia's participation is therefore unavoidable in any project.

Russia is also keen to restore trade and communications and to transform Central Asia into a route for trade between Europe, Afghanistan and South Asia. Given Moscow's present interest in reviving the North-South freight transportation corridor, Russia can play a particularly important rôle in developing infrastructure and bringing the landlocked Central Asian countries into the global marketplace. In this regard, the United States could also play a role by encouraging and assisting Russia in the development of this route to complement the East-West transportation routes from Central Asia across the Caspian, to the Caucasus and the Black Sea. While the East-West route became a focus of early competition between America and Russia, the development of a North-South route that binds Central Asia to Europe and Asia could become a basis for cooperation.

In fact, Moscow's objective has been to restore the Soviet-era communications and trade infrastructure between Russia and Central Asia. Accordingly, Russia has initiated a major project to revive and revitalise the former North-South transportation corridor from Russian Baltic ports down the Volga River, across the Caspian to Central Asia and Iran, and from there extended to Pakistan and India. During the Soviet period, this served as a major freight route and an alternative to the transportation of goods from Europe to Asia through the Mediterranean and Suez Canal. Thus Russia's main focus in the region has been to further economic interests along with military and strategic factors, and hence Central Asia's stability and development are its primary objective. To realise this goal Russia has framed a two-pronged strategy: (a) to integrate the Central Asian states in the CIS sphere and make them into close allies; and (b) to control external powers' strategic access to Central Asia. Both the CIS and Shanghai Forum are important mechanisms that are related to security related matters like drug trafficking, regional conflicts and extremism, and ensure Russia's position in the region, as well as restrain the Central Asian states from getting closer to the US and NATO.

The Central Asian states on their part are keen to strengthen their ties with western powers, especially through the NATO Partnership for Peace. Thus by the late 1990s, Russia's previously influential role as the regional security provider had mostly eroded. Its partners like Uzbekistan had estranged itself from collective security arrangements managed by Russia. At the same time NATO started expanding its operation in the region. In view of this altered strategic configuration in the region, the foreign policy of the Russian Federation of June 2000 signified a major departure in Moscow's strategy towards Central Asia. The concept entailed a more active involvement of Russia in the region than in the previous decades. Putin prioritised this by making Central Asia the most important destination of his foreign visits as President. In the process, the CIS fabric weakened and the Central Asian states sought to step up bilateral relations with other powers. Russia in turn focused on alternative mechanisms to step up bilateral relations with CIS member states. However, the two formal structures—the Collective Security Treaty and Eurasian Economic Community—emerged within the framework of the CIS that involved the Central Asian states in multilateral engagements with Russia.

The Treaty on Collective Security was signed by Russia, Kazakhstan, Uzbekistan, Tajikistan, Kyrgyzstan and Armenia (later joined by Azerbaijan, Belarus and Georgia) in Tashkent on May 15, 1992. In April 1999, Uzbekistan, Georgia and Azerbaijan withdrew from the CST on the grounds that the organisation was not doing enough to promote the interests of the concerned parties. Nevertheless, since the growth of radicalism in the Ferghana Valley in 1999, Russia, Tajikistan, Kyrgyzstan and Uzbekistan took part in the joint military command-and-staff exercise. In April 2000, Russia, Kazakhstan, Kyrgyzstan and Tajikistan agreed to create a CIS anti-terrorism centre, supported by the Russian Federal Security Service. In May 2001, the creation of a Collective Rapid Reaction Force was decided within the framework of the CST as a response to regional crises and a means to secure porous border areas against terrorist attacks and incursions. In May 2002, the Collective Security Council decided at its Moscow session to transform the CST into the Collective Security Treaty Organisation with the aim of deepening military and military-technical cooperation among its member states.

In May 2001, Russia, Belarus, Kazakhstan, Kyrgyzstan and Tajikistan created the Eurasian Economic Community (EEC) in Minsk with the aim of harmonising their customs, tax, trade and labour policies. The regional organisation was later joined by Moldova and the Ukraine as observers. An important objective of the EEC is to create conditions for future cooperation with the European Union. However, the multi-level participation of Central Asian states in different institutional arrangements put them in a difficult situation especially when they had to deal with management of policies. It also prevented these organisations from becoming effective forums for cooperation.

During Yeltsin's presidency, Russia's Central Asia policy was pursued with vigour within the CIS framework, which was reviewed and revised later on during the presidency of Putin. By the end of 2003, the security arrangements within Central Asia with a strong Russian presence were well in place. Putin, during his first term as President, introduced a new military doctrine. Russian foreign policy focused on three arenas of engagement: the CIS as arena of strategic importance, Western Europe and the United States and finally the Asia Pacific region. Power projections rested on domestic stability and economic growth, mainly sustained by increasing oil and gas revenues. These revenues conferred more independence and self-confidence about Russia's presence in international affairs. Constructive cooperation programmes initiated by Moscow included the following: substantial political-military cooperation, joint plans with border guards to respond to criminalisation and joint cooperation mechanisms that entailed the involvement of special services of the Central Asian countries in the struggle against terrorism, drug trafficking, organised crime and illegal migration.

Medvedev, the next President after Putin, however, adopted a soft approach towards Central Asia which was reflected in the new foreign policy document of 2008. Russia under Medvedev extensively focused on development programmes like (a) infrastructure building and participation in the reconstruction of pipelines; and (b) inter-regional cultural activities. In fact, cultural, ethnic, and linguistic links with the Central Asian states gave Russia considerable advantage when compared with other external powers, particularly the US, and EU.[7] According to Sergei Lavrov, "Russian foreign policy today is such that for the first time in its history, Russia is beginning to protect its national interest by using its competitive advantages."[8]

Russia thus tries to perpetuate its influence in Central Asia through signing agreements on realisation of big investment projects, writing off debts of the regional countries, deepening cooperation with them in the military-security field, extending the terms of military bases and attracting them to the membership of the integration organisations led by Russia. Russia in association with the Central Asian states is keen to form Customs Union (CU) and Single Economic Space (SES) as the first step towards establishing long-term Russian supremacy in Central Asia. It may also be added that Kazakhstan has already joined the Customs Union led by Russia. Kyrgyzstan and Tajikistan are officially considering membership of CU. It is only Uzbekistan that has had a turbulent relationship with Russia.

Vladimir Paramonov and Aleksey Strokov have made a pertinent point about Russian policy towards Central Asia in the aftermath of the Cold War. The analysts have pointed to the policy change—from one of isolated tactic in the early 1990s to direct involvement through institution-building especially by setting its own terms in the oil and gas sectors. The overall impression is that Russia has failed to frame a coherent strategy towards Central Asia, where the role of the region in the scheme of Russia's national interests is clearly defined.[9] The policy is reflected in the trade figures provided by analysts:

Trade between Russia and Central Asia, Year	Volume of trade (millions of US dollars)	Russian exports to Central Asia (millions of US dollars)	Russian imports from Central Asia (millions of US dollars)	Russian trade balance (millions of US dollars)
1991	59,226	33,785	25,441	8,344
1992	6,360	5,767	593	5,174
1993	6,750	4,703	2,047	2,656
1994	6,143	3,771	2,372	1,399
1995	7,679	4,230	3,449	781
1996	7,244	3,920	3,324	596
1997	6,833	3,402	3,431	-29
1998	5,411	3,165	2,246	919
1999	3,695	1,903	1,792	111
2000	6,469	2,730	3,739	-1,009
2001	5,924	3,517	2,407	1,110
2002	5,464	3,492	1,972	1,520
2003	7,088	4,520	2,568	1,952
2004	10,463	6,103	4,360	1,743
2005	13,227	7,525	5,702	1,823
2006	14,869	7,982	6,887	1,095
2007	21,787	13,489	8,298	5,191

(Source: Paramonov and Strokov, pp. 3-15)[10]

Russia's Role Reversal

It is clear from the above that Russia's policy towards Central Asia has been country-specific. Its security policy essentially framed by counterterrorism focuses on Tajikistan and Kyrgyzstan and its economic policy, dominated by energy considerations, revolves round Kazakhstan and Turkmenistan. In the process, Russia has successfully established its supremacy in the region. The Central Asian states also support Russia as their main regional partner. However, each individual country has its own preferences in relation to Moscow. Kazakhstan prefers direct engagement with Moscow, Tajikistan is Moscow-dependent, Uzbekistan prefers to maintain a balanced partnership and Turkmenistan is completely aloof to a Russian initiative. What is more interesting is that the authoritarian regimes of Central Asia are cautious about making a complete departure from their erstwhile domestic and foreign policies. The reason for this is pragmatic in nature. Till date, Russia remains the major arms supplier to the region. The Central Asian states welcomed military and financial contributions from Russia. In May 2002, an agreement between Russia, Kazakhstan, Kyrgyzstan, Tajikistan, Belarus and Armenia was reached that led to the establishment of a joint military command in Moscow, a rapid reaction force for Central Asia, a common air defence system and coordinated action in foreign, security and defence policy.[11]

Russia has set up its bases and stationed its forces in Kyrgyzstan, Tajikistan and Uzbekistan, ostensibly to defend these regimes against terrorist threats. Russia has also sought cooperation between CSTO (Collective Security Treaty Organisation) and the Shanghai Cooperation Organisation (SCO). CSTO has also gained observer status for SCO military exercises. That apart, there is also the Central Asian Cooperation Organisation (CACO), founded in 1994, of which Russia is a party (since May 2004) along with Kazakhstan, Kyrgyzstan, Tajikistan and Uzbekistan; and the Eurasian Economic Community—EurAsEC—set up in 2001, where Russia is joined by Belarus, Kazakhstan, Kyrgyzstan, and Tajikistan. In 2005, EurAsEC and CACO were merged. In this complex web of organisations, Russia's hegemony in Central Asia was reasserted.

Russia's relations with China within the Shanghai Cooperation Organisation (SCO) have been of immense significance. It serves a double purpose: restricting US influence in the region and restraining China's expansionist designs. Russia's assertions have been combined with soft-power approaches, particularly in relation to Central Asia, resulting in a more balanced and efficient approach. These include the negotiation of economic agreements, energy projects, and deepening cultural and educational activities.

Today, Russia's paramount concern is Central Asian security. Russia's own territory has been threatened by the spill-over of the internal strife in Afghanistan through Central Asia bringing in the ill effects of militancy, terrorism, and drug trafficking. Russia actively supported the Northern Alliance in its struggle with the Taliban in Afghanistan. In December 2000, Moscow joined Washington in supporting United Nations sanctions against the Taliban, and demanded additional sanctions against Pakistan for aiding the Taliban.

Central Asia today faces many important challenges from different directions. Russian interests in the stability of Central Asia are challenged by the domestic tensions within these states. The transition from the Soviet command economy and the authoritarian political model has been much more complex and difficult than anticipated. The Central Asian states were dependent on Soviet subsidies and had to begin development initiatives in a completely new way. In the post-Soviet years, the Central Asian states lost crucial subsidies for budgets, enterprises and households, inputs for regional industries, markets for their products, transportation routes and communications with the outside world. The World Bank estimated that as a result of these losses, during 1990-1996 the Central Asian states saw their economies decline by 20%-60% of GDP. Landlocked, resource-poor Tajikistan and Kyrgyzstan have fared particularly badly. A staggering 70%-80% of their populations have now fallen below the poverty line, which puts them among the poorest of the developing countries. Besides, Soviet-era attainments in health, education, infrastructure, and industrial development have gradually eroded. As a result of these failures, there has been a massive exodus of ethnic Russians and highly-skilled members of indigenous ethnic groups from Central Asia. The Central Asian states have by and large failed to develop effective institutions for governance in the post-Soviet period. In many respects, the Central Asian governments lack legitimacy. Regimes resorted to authoritarian measures—repressing the opposition groups, clamping down on dissenting voices, checks and balances on radical religious groups and denial of human rights. Under such uncertain circumstances, Russia needs to be proactive in regaining confidence of the Central Asian governments.

Conclusion

Russia's policy in Central Asia in the post-Cold War years has been unsystematic. In the early 1990s the Yeltsin administration's foreign policy was guided by strategic calculations that Russia had about integration into the Euro-Atlantic community. Central Asia was largely irrelevant to this Russian ambition. Towards the latter part of the 1990s, there was some rethinking among policy analysts and Moscow began to pay more attention to its eastern flank, including Central Asia.

The evolution of relations between Russia and Central Asia largely depends on the extent that Kremlin finds Central Asia's regional policies acceptable. At the same time, one must not forget the fact that Russia cannot ignore the resource options that Central Asian states have and can gamble with. Russia needs to look for stability on the Central Asian borderlands. For this, a rational Central Asian policy cannot be ruled out.

Notes

1. Bijaya K. Das, "Russian Minorities in Central Asia and Russia-Central Asia Relationship," *Jadavpur Journal of International Relations*, vol. 11-12, no. 2006-2008, pp. 64-88.
2. Maria Raquel Freire, "Russian Policy in Central Asia: Supporting, Balancing, Coercing, or Imposing?" *Asian Perspective*, vol. 33, no. 2, 2009, p. 126.
3. Andrey A. Kazantsev, "Russian Policy in Central Asia in 1991-2010: A Disappearing Power?" *EUI Working Papers* (RSCAS 2010/59), Robert Schuman Centre for Advanced Studies, European University Institute, Italy, July 2010. Available at www.eui.eu/RSCAS/Publications/ accessed on January 20, 2013.
4. Maria Raquel Freire, pp. 136-37.
5. Jed C. Snyder (ed.), *After the Empire: The New Geopolitics of Central Asia and Emerging New World Order*, Washington DC, 1996, pp. 28-29.
6. Subodh Atal, "The New Great Game," *The National Interest*, no. 81, September 2005.
7. Joseph Ferguson, "Russian Strategic Thinking toward Central, South and South East Asia" in Gilbert Rozman, Kazuhiko Togo and Joseph Ferguson (eds.), *Russian Strategic Thought toward Asia* (New York: Palgrave Macmillan, 2006).
8. Quoted in Margot Light, "In Search of an Identity: Russian Foreign Policy and the End of Ideology," *Communist Studies and Transition Politics*, vol. 19, no. 4, 2003, p. 48.
9. Vladimir Paramonov and Alexey Strokov, *The Evolution of Russia's Central Asia Policy*, Advanced Research & Assessment Group, Defence Academy of the United Kingdom, June 2008, p. 1. http://www.defac.ac.uk/colleges/arag accessed on May 20, 2013.
10. From the above table it is clear that in 1992-1993 the volume of trade between Russia and the countries of the region fell to about a tenth of what it had been in 1991 (from about 60 billion dollars to about 6.3-6.7 billion dollars), and in 1994-

1995 it remained at the same low level. In the second half of the 1990s, the volume of trade between Russia and the Central Asian countries reduced further even below the level it was in the first half of 1990s. In the period 1996-1999 the trade turnover virtually fell from 7.2 to 3.7 billion dollars. There was acute shortage of hard currency in Russia and Central Asia and analysts have indicated that in many cases trade between them was carried out on the basis of barter. Then there has only been a significant increase in trade since 2003. In the period 2003-2007 the mean annual level of trade went up to 10.7 billion dollars, 83% higher than the mean annual level in 1996-1999 and 57% higher than in 1992-1995. Thus during 2003-2007 the trade between Russia and Central Asia virtually tripled, from 7 to 21 billion dollars. However, the region's share of Russian foreign trade decreased, falling from 3.96 to 3.76%. Paramonov and Strokov, *The Evolution of Russia's Central Asia Policy ...*

11. Roy Allison, "Strategic Reassertion in Russia's Central Asia Policy," *International Affairs,* vol. 80, no. 2, 2004, p. 469.

6. Debating Nomadism versus Modernism: Some Reflections on Mongolian Identity Issues

Sharad K. Soni

In today's world we find that all human societies have become increasingly interlinked through global markets and the spread of global consumer culture. In that sense, the twenty-first century, which has been described as the century of globalisation, offers immense opportunities to Mongolia as well. New progress through democratisation and market economy in the internal and external environment of this small and tiny populated country provides much better opportunity to overcome the disadvantages of its landlocked location and develop itself by relying on the intellectual capability of the Mongolian people.[1] However, there have been serious concerns within the country that modernisation in the era of globalisation has been eroding traditional culture and values, especially the Mongolian nomadic civilisation based on Buddhist culture.[2] Majority opinions point to the fact that while, internally, nomadism continues to be a powerful symbol of a collective Mongolian identity that evokes a lot of sentiment and is often linked to the "glorious past," externally Western influences have threatened the very existence of a nomadic lifestyle. Herein lay the origins of the debate, both within and outside the country, about nomadism versus modernism—a debate that has been reflected in the pertinent issues about Mongolian identity or, more precisely, the notion of being a Mongol in contemporary Mongolia.

It is in this context that this paper seeks to map the Mongolian situation of identity formation that gave way to the debates on nomadism versus modernism. While not ignoring the continuing importance of nomadism as an aspect of identity, it seeks to emphasise the Mongolians' own quest about finding their place in the fast-track modernisation of the global community. The argument in this paper is also about whether the Mongolians should find a proper combination of modernism and traditionalism based on the nomadic culture, taking into account the current realities in the contemporary world.

Debates on Mongolian Identity Formation

A sizeable number of Mongolia's 2.9 million population still give due importance to the aspect of nomadism and practise the ancient tradition of nomadic herding. Most families have retained the tradition of keeping herds that include five types of animals—goats, sheep, cattle, camels and horses. These animals are useful because they provide meat and dairy products for consumption, can be used for transportation and are indispensable in Mongolian climatic conditions for their wool. The Mongolians are among those communities that have preserved horse-based cultures. Outside the capital city of Ulaanbaatar, the horse is still the main mode of transportation. Horse races are a favourite pastime, and are integral to the *Naadam* festival, Mongolia's national game that is celebrated every year on July 11, which is National Day. Mongolians are fiercely proud of their millennia-old nomadic ways, best personified by the deification of Chinggis Khan, the thirteenth-century leader whose warriors on horseback conquered much of Asia and Eastern Europe and established the biggest Eurasian land empire in human history. Today, it is known as one of the last countries of nomads on earth, and it is believed that Mongolia is the crucible of the unique nomadic culture that shaped Mongolian identity.

Despite the fact that mining and tourism form a major part of the Mongolian economy, a third of the population still depends entirely on nomadic style of animal husbandry for its livelihood. Roughly 30 per cent of the population are now nomadic or semi-nomadic. The Mongols practise Buddhism but initially were adherents of shamanism. Over centuries, the nomadic Mongol culture has been influenced by the cultures of Tibet, China, Central Asia and Russia. Even today, many Mongolian families migrate seasonally three or four times a year with their herds to customarily assigned pastures. Traditional Mongolian society is known for its strict adherence to proper behaviour. Like every other nomadic culture, Mongolian culture too is well-known for its hospitality which is evident from the fact that upon guests' arrival, traditional food is served that includes dairy products in summer and meat during winter. According to tradition, even during his absence, a Mongolian will prefer to leave his *ger* (felt tent) unlocked in order to allow any passer-by to rest and enjoy the food left at home.[3]

In the twentieth century, these traditional practices were disturbed when Mongolia became closely aligned with the former Soviet Union. The Soviet destruction of the Buddhist *sangha* (clergy) and nobility, elimination of archaic customs and the establishment of universal education impacted on Mongolian society. As the world's second Socialist state after the Soviet Union in the years following 1921, industrialisation and farming were strongly encouraged to diversify and modernise the economy, and Western science, technology and culture, filtered through the Russian language, became increasingly significant in Mongolian society. Since the democratic revolution of 1990, there has been a call to revive traditional culture and Mongolian identity despite the fact that privatisation and globalisation have been followed as matters of national policy.

Such arguments about nomadism or traditionalism juxtaposed to modernism featured prominently in the debates about Mongolian identity. It would be pertinent to analyse how historical and political circumstances, as well as strategies and orientations of various groups and individuals, have led to multiple interpretations on this subject. One of such interpretations is by B. Batbayar, popularly known as Baabar, a historian and one of the well-known leaders of the democratic movement in Mongolia: "national language and national culture are indispensable elements for any ethnic group to not only survive but also discover a collective national identity and establish its statehood."[4] He emphasises his point by arguing that all other things such as territory, statehood, sovereignty and independence are of secondary importance.[5] The state-led revival of religious practices based on Buddhist rituals and ceremonies began to take place in order to build a "national brand of public culture" that could make its worthy contribution to identity formation as well.

Western writings focus on urban debates centred round Mongolian identity. According to Marsh, there is a generation-wise variation in ideas and this is indicated by young peoples' role in forging contemporary identities through music. This trend is quite distinct from the preceding Socialist-era trend which was centred round romantic "traditional" ballads about the countryside, nature and rural livelihoods.[6] This distinction is indeed important. Caroline Upton considers mining as another key issue that has recently been given wider attention. Having minerals in abundance, especially gold and copper, Mongolia has become a focus of interest for foreign mining companies. The exploitation of mineral wealth offers the prospect of the country's transformation as well as individual prosperity. The questions that are raised are about its impact on Mongolian national identity due to the strong presence of foreign companies, the place of nomadic pastoralism as a livelihood strategy and as the main ingredient of cultural identity, its relations with land, and what it means to be Mongolian in the twenty-first century.[7] These issues, as Uradyn Bulag describes, take on a particular complexion in Mongolia, a country recently described as "a thriving mixture of nomadism and urbanism" and wherein the nature of modernity is particularly contested.[8] Nevertheless, the first and foremost name, which became the symbol of modern Mongolian identity, is Chinggis Khan.[9]

Chinggis Khan as a Symbol of Modern Mongolian Identity

It was during the struggle for democratic reforms in 1989-1990 that the Mongolian identity issues came to the forefront. The young Mongolian Democrats aspired among other things, for "the revival of traditional Mongolian culture, reintroduction of the old Mongolian script, rehabilitation of Genghis [Chinggis] Khan and encouragement to Buddhism."[10] In this dramatic turn of events, Chinggis Khan, the father of the Mongolian people, was pulled from the rubbish heap of history by the young Mongols not only to criticise their Communist elders but also to identify him as the symbol of new nationalist identity.[11] In 1991, in an effort towards redefining national identity and restoring tribal and family identities, the then Mongolian President P. Ochirbat issued a decree by which people were allowed to choose their own name. Surprisingly, over 60 per cent of the people opted for the name of the clan of Chinggis, the Mongol *ovogton*, Borjigid.[12]

This clan identification points to "the strong identification the Mongols continue to have to a common ancestor of the Borjigid royal lineage."[13] In yet another decree issued in 2010, the current President of Mongolia declared that *The Secret History of the Mongols* (*Monggol-un Niguca Tobciyan*), which is the earliest surviving literary monument of the Mongolian people probably written in AD 1240, should be preserved by all Mongolian families in a sacred place.[14] This is the more so because not only does it recount the genealogy of earlier Mongol khans and the life and times of Chinggis Khan but also provides a unique and authoritative account of the nomadic way of life, patterns of thought and belief of the thirteenth-century Mongols.

Considered to be one of the greatest statesmen in the medieval history of the world, Chinggis Khan, born as Temujin, united all Mongol tribes in AD 1206 in the valley of Tuul, Orkhon and Onon (known as Mongol people of three rivers) and conducted a series of conquests, bringing the tribes of the great Steppe under his leadership. He also gave the Mongols their own script based on the Uighur script and first Constitution *Ikh Yassa*, and the most important, a confederative tribal unit. The year AD 1206 marked the opening of a new era in the history of Mongols in particular and the history of nomadism in general.[15] In fact, the Chinggisid era has a role to play in the socialisation process: "Chinggis Khan's image set free from the 'adhesion' of power and benefit and becomes a special symbol of Mongolian's psychological 'focus,' such as ancestor adoration, hero adoration, god adoration and so on; it is also a special symbol by which Mongolians 'unite' their blood identity, national identity and cultural identity together."[16]

Chinggis Khan is not only a symbol of national unity and independence but is also considered to be the trendsetter in initiatives like postal services, diplomatic immunity and global contacts. As Sh. Bira, the renowned Mongolian historian, writes:

The world was interconnected by the communication network of the [Mongolian] Ortege system of horse relay stations, which was the most efficient means of world communication at the time. Along the roads of the Ortege, peoples, ideas, information and commerce between different countries flowed freely. Relations between East and West had, thus, never been so close and productive as it was during the period of the Mongol rule.[17]

Chinggis Khan has been described by Sabloff as the "democratic leader" of his times.[18] The 800th anniversary of Mongolian statehood (*Yeke Mongol Ulus*) founded by Chinggis Khan was celebrated in 2006 with fanfare and various events marked the occasion. During these celebrations, the capital city Ulaanbaatar witnessed a significant change in the structure of the southern face of the State palace, which houses both the Parliament and the Government. It has been reconstructed to erect the "Chinggis Khan Memorial Complex" by displacing the former mausoleum of Sukhbaatar and Choibalsan, the leaders of the 1921 People's revolution. Chinggis Khan became the symbol of modern Mongolian identity. Most of the Mongolians, irrespective of their profession, tend to agree with Baabar when he writes:

For Mongols who traditionally revered their ancestors, Chinggis Khan was a god. If Napoleon and Alexander of Macedon are national heroes and the pride of the French and Greeks, Chinggis Khan is something more than that for the Mongols: their lodestar, spiritual force, and the object of not only national but of personal pride.[19]

The Chinggisid regime is also associated with Buddhism because "Chinggis Khan was recognised by the Mongolian Buddhists as the reincarnation of the Bodhisattva Vajrapani."[20] This becomes evident particularly after the expansion of the Chinggisid regime when Chinggis Khan began to be worshipped as the universal ruler with the mandate of Buddhist tradition. Bareja-Starzynska and Havnevik remind their readers of the pan-Mongolist vision of Chinggis Khan that has become ingrained in the memory of the observes that "Chinggis Khan reminds the Mongols of their glorious past … the cult [now] is actively used to strengthen the Mongolian national identity and is … explicitly used by those who maintain a pan-Mongolist vision."[21] This idea has been reiterated by Wallace while giving an eyewitness account of the *Naadam* festivities, in which the glorious imperial history and tradition of Mongolia are celebrated. He emphasises the slogan during *Naadam* by the standard-bearers when they dismount from their horses: "Hurrah! Hurrah! Hurrah! Our Lord Chinggis Khan, Vajrapani."[22] According to him, every three years, the new President of Mongolia worships and makes offerings to Vajrapani on behalf of the Mongol state at *Otgontenger* Mountain, which is believed to be an earthly home to Vajrapani and his mountainous emanation. In addition to *Chakravartin*, Chinggis Khan is also said to bear the titles of *Devaditya* and *Arya* as mentioned in some of the colophons of *Kanjur* volumes.[23]

Buddhist Factor in Mongolian Identity

Buddhism also symbolises modern Mongolian identity. The revival of Buddhism in Mongolia after 1990 is an unprecedented development. The 1930s were a period of repression and during that time nearly all Buddhist monasteries and temples were destroyed and a large number of monks were killed. In a joint publication, the fact of repression has been emphasised and the main accusation is against the Stalinist era purges carried out between 1937 and 1939 under the leadership of Kh. Choibalsan, who was popularly known as Little Stalin. Under his instructions, nearly 12,000 Buddhist monks were killed in Mongolia.[24] Buddhism in Mongolia saw its worst times under Soviet vassalage. It is sad because the deep philosophical strength that Buddhism imbibed was forgotten. In the pre-1921 period, Mongolia used to be the second stronghold of Buddhism after Tibet, with more than 100,000 monks taking care of Buddhist tradition in the country. But that tradition was forcibly erased from memory during the early twentieth century when Mongolia became a Soviet vassal and got its independent statehood in 1924. Religion as an embodiment of national culture was hardly recognised by the Socialist regimes of this period.

Mongolia was the classic case of such a situation. Seven decades of communist rule (1924-1990) had impacted on Mongolian society to the extent that the leadership of the ruling Mongolian People's Revolutionary Party (MPRP) was blamed for eroding the traditional national culture. But, at the same time, Soviet support in terms of technical know-how and expertise as well as aid effectively gave Mongolia a new international look due to the industrialisation programme initiated by the Communist government. But tradition in Mongolia faced the challenge of survival as its modernisation according to the Socialist line was completely at odds with contemporary ideas of modernity—a dichotomy that has been pointed out by scholars who have traced the impact of the two types of modernity since the onset of the democratisation process in Mongolia in the late 1980s.[25]

Tibetan form of Buddhism was said to have arrived in Mongolia as early as the third century BC with silk traders travelling from India but later it developed spiritual links with Buddhism in Tibet as both followed the similar lineage.[26] Further, in the thirteenth century, Buddhism received the patronage of the Mongol ruler Khubilai Khan who patronised this religion by placing a Tibetan Buddhist monk the Phags-Pa Lama Lodoijalsan as the "State Preceptor" (*kuo shih*).[27] Significantly, from the Phags-Pa Lama he adopted the concept of dual authority—the sacred and the secular.[28] Though the dual authority principle ended with the downfall of the Yuan dynasty, it became the ideal that was preserved in both Mongol and Tibetan traditions.

There was an exchange of scholars and monks between the Mongols and the Tibetans, and the Mongol ruler Altan Khan conferred the title of Dalai (meaning "ocean of wisdom") to the Tibetan lama Sonam Gyatso in 1577. With this began the lineage of the Dalai Lamas. It has been revealed that the Tibetan schools of Buddhism passionately continued their missionary work among the Mongols.[29] For many centuries, Buddhism became one of the most important decisive factors of Mongolian nomadic identity, and Buddhist monasteries turned into the cultural centres of society. Several traditions and customs of the Mongols were enriched by Buddhist meanings, and by the seventeenth century the Mongol-speaking Buddhist nomads were quite different from the Muslim nomads in general, both in terms of religion and language. In fact, Buddhism gave the final shape to the nomadic Mongol entity.

The quest for Mongolian identity has not been limited to individuals, and has included the Mongolian state, which has been able to revive Buddhist tradition and symbolism. It is widely believed that Buddhism is a moral support in times of social instability. Since 1992, freedom of religion has been granted by the new Mongol Constitution. The separation of religious and secular authority was a constitutional provision. The

Constitution deals with the emblems of national identity and these national emblems, which consist of the State Emblem, the Banner, the Flag, and the Seal, are described in terms that refer both to the traditional religion as well as Buddhism.[30] It is thus obvious that Buddhism is recognised as being of prime importance in the Constitution of Mongolia so far as sociocultural and religious life of the Mongols is concerned. Today hundreds of monasteries and temples have been restored throughout the country. Several thousand monks are registered now, and there are ongoing teaching activities mostly carried out by the Mongolian and Tibetan teachers trained in India, Nepal and elsewhere.[31] More specifically, over 3,000 monks are now registered and teaching. They are mostly Tibetan teachers from the Tibetan exile community in India.[32] Besides, rebuilding of monasteries and construction of new ones can be seen in the cities and in the countryside. In this direction international Buddhist institutions have helped immensely, particularly in disbursing the necessary financial support to revive Buddhist traditions. On the other hand, there are instances of Mongolian people donating money for the restoration of old monasteries, temples, and stupas, like Darhan temple, apart from building such new establishments throughout the country.[33]

Nevertheless, there is also a fear among Mongolian Buddhists that Buddhism may be discarded amidst Mongolians' exposure to a growing display of alternative world views, values and lifestyles.[34] Yet, it is the Mongolian variant of Buddhism and Chinggis Khan's memory that have a greater role in the reconstruction of Mongolian cultural and religious identity in the twenty-first century. During the time of Chinggisid rule, there were developments that characterised the regime which was not just a world empire in name only. According to Bira, "the precepts of Tengrism were based on the worship of Tengri (Heavenly God), which was a fundamental precept of Shamanism, the old folk religion of Mongolian and Turkic nomadic peoples." He argues that Tengri religion had a holistic vision like globalisation today.[35]

Nomadic versus Modern Identity

Commenting on what will happen to the nomadic identity of the Mongols in the twenty-first century, Mongolian and Indian authors point out divided opinions: nationalist writings of M. Zenee and those of the poet O. Dashbalbar, both of whom strongly backed the catchy phrase, "Let Mongols remain as Mongols." They laid stress on the purity of Mongolian nomadic heritage.[36] In contrast to such opinions, the publicist B. Baabar and others have argued that in the twentieth century, westernism inducted through Russian influence has taught Mongols to be competitive to the extent that they can abandon their identification with nomadism.[37]

The Mongolian identity issue can also be studied from the standpoint of a geopolitical debate. Batbayar believes that Mongolia's dilemma of making a choice between Central Asia and Northeast Asia as a regional unit indicates the struggle between the nomadic and modernised identification of the Mongols.[38] The Mongolian ruling elite subscribes to this view. In 2001, during his interview with the *Far Eastern Economic Review*, Nambariin Enkhbayar, the then Mongolian Prime Minister who later became President, laid stress on adopting the path of modernisation. He stated that, "It is not my desire to destroy the original Mongolian identity but in order to survive we have to stop being nomads."[39] Enkhbayar's vision points to taking the country on the road of modern development in the twenty-first century by way of building cities along a 2,400-km east-west highway, called the "Millennium Project," and urbanising up to 90 per cent of Mongolia's population over the next 30 years.[40]

However, there is also no denying the fact that Mongolia's nomadic heritage has had a lingering effect and influenced the Mongols to preserve their traditional culture. Different educational, cultural and political organisations assert strong traditionalist agendas and project traditional values and culture as guidelines for the nomadic pastoralists.[41] Some scholars however have doubts about the practice of nomadism because it is not economic in a modern market. The alternative view suggests that Chinggis Khan's vision was actually well received among Western circles."[42] The issue has attracted attention from many sides. There is an overriding view that Chinggis Khan and nomadism are synonymous with a Mongol legacy and need to be preserved as integral to a modern Mongol identity.

Despite its rebirth in 1990, Mongolia has been facing serious challenges. The only hope for both traditional nomads and modernised city dwellers is survival—and that can happen if better living conditions are made available for the younger generations. The contradictions of urban life have created an urge to preserve the old cultural heritage by reviving not only Buddhist monasteries but also the ancient Uighur script. In the opinion of some Mongolian scholars, it is imperative to find a proper combination of modernity and tradition in Mongolian society."[43] The distinctiveness of Mongolian tradition, customs and cultural heritage needs to be acknowledged. It is also important to understand the realities of the modern world and adjust to changing circumstances.

In conclusion, it may be pointed out that 800 years ago, Chinggis Khan succeeded in building the largest empire in Eurasian history. In memory and reverence to Chinggis Khan's role, the indigenous nomadic culture of the Mongols has come into the spotlight. It is the diversity of nomadic cultures that need to be analysed.[44] The idea is to revive past trends, not segregate them from contemporary ones. The strength and vitality and resilience of Mongolian character have a deeper impact on the market system, and one needs to comprehend the market values in order to make social relationships in a globalised world sustainable.[45] Since market values can transform social relations among the Mongol people, "both traditionalism as a form of national identity and democracy as a new morality need to be researched upon extensively as legitimising discourses for emergent social relationships in Mongolia."[46] In this regard, Buddhism too has been playing a significant role as "it has always been the link among Mongolian nationalities."[47] So, the Mongolians must adopt a balance between tradition and modernity as a rationale for development.

Notes

1. Ministry of External Relations of Mongolia, *Mongolian Foreign Policy Blue Book* (Ulaanbaatar: Policy Planning and Coordination Department, 2000), p.7.
2. Sharad K. Soni, "Promoting Traditional Culture in Contemporary Mongolia," *The IAMS Bulletin*, 2007 and 2008, no. 2 (40) and no.1 (41), p. 106.
3. "Discover Mongolia: Culture and Custom," July 8, 2011, http://sansaratour.blogspot.in/2011/07/culture-and-customs.html

4. See Ts Batbayar and Sharad K. Soni, *Modern Mongolia: A Concise History* (New Delhi: Pentagon, 2007), p. 135 and note 2, p. 143.
5. Batbayar and Soni, *Modern Mongolia.*
6. For more details, see Caroline Upton, "Introduction: Focus on Mongolia," *Central Asian Survey* 29, no. 3, 2010, p. 247.
7. Upton, "Introduction: Focus on Mongolia," p. 244.
8. Uradyn Bulag, "Mongolian modernity and hybridity," *MINPAKU Anthropology Newsletter* 19, nos. 1-3 (2004), cited in Upton, "Introduction: Focus on Mongolia," p. 244.
9. For more details, see Paula L. W. Sabloff, "Genghis Khan and Modern Mongolian Identity: The Democracy Connection," *The Mongolian Journal of International Affairs*, nos. 8-9 (2002), pp. 38-56.
10. Cited in Sharad K. Soni, *Mongolia-Russia Relations: Kiakhta to Vladivostok* (Delhi: Shipra, 2002), p. 223.
11 Alicia Campi, "Mongolia's Position in the World on its 800th Anniversary," *Mongolica* 19, no. 40 (2006), p. 237.
12 Cited in Campi, "Mongolia's Position in the World," p. 239. Further, in his work on the history of Mongolian nationalism, Lkhamsuren Munkh-Erdene points out that the primary basis for Mongol statehood was the Borjigid lineage (Mongol *ovogton*), which preserved the Mongol ulus as a historical community. One can find this in native *Mongol Chronicles* in which "Chinggis Khan and his descendants are glorified as having divine origin and the Mongol people (Blue People) as being the heart of an Empire made up of other inferior peoples," see Lkhamsuren Munkh-Erdene, "Inquiry to Mongolian Nationalism through Terms and Concepts: From Late Nineteenth Century to Mid-1920s," Unpublished Paper, Sapporo, Japan, 2004, p. 2, cited in Campi, "Mongolia's Position in the World," p. 233.
13. Campi, "Mongolia's Position in the World," p. 239.
14. "The Secret History of the Mongols to be Honoured by All Mongolian Families," *Nomadic*, nos. 66-67, 2010, p. 2. The exact date of composition of *The Secret History of the Mongols* is still a matter of debate among historians around the world.
15. Sharad K. Soni, *Mongolia-China Relations: Modern and Contemporary Times* (New Delhi: Pentagon, 2006), pp. 4-5.
16. Bao Shengli, "Chinggis Khan Legends and the Political Culture of the Ancient Mongolia," in B. Enkhtuvshin, *Nomadic Civilizations in Cross Cutural Dialogue* (Ulaanbaatar: IISNC, 2011), p. 133.
17. Sh. Bira, "Mongolian Tengrism and Modern Globalism," *Some Problems of the History of Mongolian Statehood*, Ulaanbaatar, 2006, p. 137.
18. See Sabloff, "Genghis Khan and Modern Mongolian Identity," p. 39.
19. Baabar, *History of Mongolia* (Ulaanbaatar: Nepko, 2006), p. 13.
20 Agata Bareja-Starzynska and Hanna Havnevik, "A Preliminary Study of Buddhism in Present-Day Mongolia," in Ole Brunn and Li Narangoa (eds.), *Mongols from*

Country to City: Boundaries, Pastoralism and City Life in the Mongol Lands (Copenhagen: NIAS, 2006), p. 225.

21. Bareja-Starzynska and Havnevik, "A Preliminary Study of Buddhism," p. 225
22. Vesna Wallace, "Surviving Modernity in Mongolia," p. 97. http://sarr.emory.edu/MAS/MAS_Chap7_Wallace.pdf
23. Raghu Vira, "Imprints on Mongolia," in Chaman Lal (ed.), *India Cradle of Culture* (New Delhi: Oxford, 1978), p. 183.
24. D. Dashpurev and S. K. Soni, *Reign of Terror in Mongolia, 1920-1990* (New Delhi: South Asian Publishers, 1992), p. 42.
25. Contemporary modernity is dominantly characterised by materialism, individualism, and capitalism, see Wallace, "Surviving Modernity in Mongolia," p. 90.
26. "Buddhism in Mongolia—Threat & Revival," at http://www.4ui.com/eart/173eart2.htm
27. For more on Khubilai's religious policy and his relationship with Phags-Pa Lama, see Sh. Bira, "Qubilai Qa'an and Phags-Pa Bla-ma," in Reuven Amitai-Preiss and David O. Morgan (eds.), *The Mongol Empire and its Legacy* (Leiden: Brill, 1999), pp. 240-49.
28. While Khubilai himself retained the task of ruling the secular sphere, the position of ruler of the sacred sphere was given to the Phags-Pa Lama. See Larry Williams Moses, *The Political Role of Mongol Buddhism* (Bloomington: Indiana University, 1977), p. 78.
29. Bareja-Starzynska and Havnevik, "A Preliminary Study of Buddhism," p. 215.
30. Sharad K. Soni, "Exploring Mongol-Tibetan Relations: The Contribution of Buddhism," *Mongolian & Tibetan Quarterly* 22, no. 2, 2013, p. 59.
31. For more details see Batbayar and Soni, *Modern Mongolia*, p. 139.
32. See "Introduction to Mongolia," http://www.jetsundhampa.com/pages/mongolia.html
33. Batbayar and Soni, *Modern Mongolia,* p. 140.
34. Wallace, "Surviving Modernity in Mongolia," p. 96.
35. For more on Mongolian Tengrism, also see Sh. Bira,"Mongolian Tengrism and Tengrisation," (in Mongolian), *The IAMS Bulletin,* 2006 and 2007, no. 2(38) and no. 1 (39):5-67.
36. In the eyes of the nationalists it is the nomadic heritage that defines Mongolia, and, therefore, must be protected from external threats or internal corruption. See Batbayar and Soni, *Modern Mongolia,* p. 142 and note 8, p. 145.
37. They warn that the desire of Mongols to stay as nomads can turn them into "living museum exhibits." For example, they cite current attempts to associate everything with the lineage of Chinggis Khan, especially in re-educating the people in the old Mongolian script, keeping nomadic lifestyle intact and continuing the tradition of entertainment, i.e., *Naadam*, the national sports festival. See Batbayar and Soni, *Modern Mongolia,* p. 142.
38. Ts. Batbayar, "Mongolia's New Identity and Security Dilemma," *The Mongolian Journal of International Affairs*, nos. 8-9 (2002):5.

39. See Enkhbayar's interview in David Murphy, "No Room for Nomads," *Far Eastern Economic Review* 164, no. 21, May 31, 2001, pp. 30-32.
40. Murphy, "No Room for Nomads."
41. Daniel M. Rosenberg, "Across the Border: Mongolian Ethnic and National Identity," *Reviews in Anthropology* 27, no. 2, 1998, p. 171.
42. Campi, "Mongolia's Position in the World," p. 240.
43. Otgonbayar, "Crisis of Cultural Identity in Mongolian Nomadic Civilization," *http://ignca.nic.in/ls_03011.htm*
44. Jacques Legrand, "Some Roots of Cultural Diversity: Nomadic Pastoralism, Migration and other Alternatives," *Nomadic*, no. 84 (2011):7.
45. Rosenberg, "Across the Border," pp. 170-71.
46. Rosenberg, "Across the Border," p. 171.
47 Udo B. Barkmann, "The Revival of Lamaism in Mongolia," *Central Asian Survey* 16, no. 1, 1997, p. 78.

7. The Central Asia Factor in India-Afghanistan Relations

Anwesha Ghosh

Afghanistan can be seen as a "hyphen" connecting India and Central Asia. According to common consensus, no study of Indo-Afghan relations is complete without a cursory look at the century old common cultural and economic heritage of the people of India, Afghanistan and Central Asia. From the security point of view, Afghanistan is critical to the entire South and Central Asian region. In the last four decades, Afghanistan has witnessed diverse projects of nation building and socio-political transformation. The Soviet attempt to transform Afghanistan into a Communist buffer resulted in massive loss of lives and displacement of approximately six million Afghans across the world but mainly in its neighbourhood. Subsequently, when Pakistan attempted to push backward theocracy in the country, the world faced several fateful consequences including 9/11. Apart from disabling half of the population, this period also marked an acute phase of food insecurity and severe reduction of social services.

Today's Afghanistan is bereft of nostalgia for India. Today, shared histories seldom stir the feeling of closeness and bonding between the two countries. The growing security concerns in both countries tend to offer a realistic paradigm for discussing security issues that are not country-specific but hold true for India's northwest and the entire South Asian region. The US-led war in Afghanistan following the 9/11 attacks brought the world community together, pledging support for assistance for reconstruction of war-ravaged Afghanistan. India in the changed environment also adopted a remarkably proactive Afghan policy which led to its investment of over $2 billion for Afghanistan's reconstruction and development. Several attacks on the Indian Mission in Afghanistan were seen as a reaction to India's growing influence in the country, and challenged the fundamental priorities of India's Afghanistan policy. The question remains—what are the factors that are propelling India towards this unusually proactive policy in Afghanistan? The attempt in this paper is to understand how far Afghanistan's position as a gateway to Central Asian Republics has shaped India's foreign policy in this region. What sort of economic and geostrategic interest does India have in this region? This paper would try to understand how the Central Asia factor could shape India-Afghanistan relations in the post 2014 scenario that is destined to mark the withdrawal of international troops from Afghanistan.

India, Afghanistan and Central Asia: From a Post-Cold War Perspective

The strong historical linkages between India, Afghanistan and Central Asia undoubtedly have played a significant role in shaping the course of relationships between these countries, yet the foreign policy postures followed by India towards them were dissimilar. Policymakers and analysts in India had maintained that Central Asia is important because of old cultural and civilisational linkages; strategic location; energy resources and trade and economic opportunities. The country has had a rich tradition of Central Asian Studies. However, traditionally, most of the academic work on the region concentrated either on historical and cultural linkages or part of the broader Soviet Studies. It is in the last two decades that new research based on geopolitics and geo-economics has emerged. Despite intentions and rhetoric, India demonstrated a low profile during the initial phase of the so-called new Great Game in the 1990s in which Russia, China, the United States and the European Union are defined as the main players. The shock of Soviet disintegration and changes in post-Cold War world politics influenced India's policy towards CARs.

After the disintegration of the Soviet Union, Central Asia was defined as the pivot of geopolitics and the playground of the new Great Game. Other important players are Turkey, Iran and Pakistan.[1] India, despite her cultural and civilisational ties with Central Asia, remained confused and indecisive with regard to this region for quite some time.[2] In the post-disintegration period, economic relationship with the region had declined considerably, yet Indian policymakers were comfortable in dealing with Central Asian authoritarian leaders as they had provided stability and were committed to fighting religious terrorism.[3] Several developments that were taking place in her neighbourhood as well as in global politics compelled India to spell out its priorities in Central Asia. These priorities have been reflected in India's efforts to develop diplomatic relations, economic cooperation, trade and investment, and energy cooperation with Central Asian countries in the recent past.

Barring the brief Taliban tenure in Afghanistan, India has managed to maintain close relations with different political dispensations in Kabul. The chaos that resulted in Afghanistan following the Soviet occupation and their ultimate withdrawal in 1989 had far-reaching implications for global politics as well as Indian foreign policy. India managed to maintain close ties with the communist regime that followed after the overthrow of Zahir Shah in 1973. Contrary to popular belief, India was less than pleased with the Soviet intervention and occupation of Afghanistan.[4] However, after failing to engage Pakistan with the prospect of a regional solution to the Soviet intervention and faced with substantial American military and economic assistance to Pakistan ($3.1 billion for six years), India avoided any public censure of the Soviet occupation.[5] India chose to work instead with the successive Soviet puppet regimes in Afghanistan because it cared little for the Islamist ideological orientation shared by the bulk of the Afghan Mujahideen groups that Pakistan was supporting on behalf of the United States (US).[6] India was also loath to cede its military superiority over Pakistan and relied on the Soviets to provide advanced weaponry at bargain-basement prices.[7] During the course of the Afghan war, India's support for the Tajik military commander Ahmed Shah Massoud and the Northern Alliance became a predictable move considering his hostilities towards the Pakistan-backed Mujahideen group. India's ability to maintain good relations with Afghanistan drew to a close with the Pakistan-aided and abetted Taliban victory in 1996.

At that time, the non-Pashtun groups opposing the Taliban regime formed the Northern Alliance and controlled areas in the north of Afghanistan, bordering the Central Asian States of Tajikistan and Uzbekistan. In her efforts to maintain her influence in Afghanistan and counter Pakistan's support to the Taliban regime, India maintained links with the Northern Alliance and contributed in strengthening its defence by providing high-altitude warfare equipment worth $10 million through its Research and Analysis Wing (RAW), and Indian defence advisers provided technical advice to the Northern Alliance.[8] Moreover, India had established a hospital in Farkhor on the Afghan-Tajik border and Indian doctors provided medical assistance to the Alliance. It is also believed that India supported anti-Taliban attacks from Tajikistan and Uzbekistan.[9] Throughout the Taliban period, Indian efforts were directed towards forging a closer relationship with countries like Iran, Russia and the Central Asian States which had an anti-Taliban approach. Ever since the fall of the Taliban in 2001, India has pursued a proactive Afghanistan policy and a broad-based interaction has taken place between the two states. This was also a time when Indian capabilities—political, economic, and military—had increased markedly and India had become increasingly ambitious in defining its foreign policy agenda.[10]

India-Afghanistan Relations after the Fall of the Taliban

In the post 9/11 period, India has played an active role and has been part of every international conference and international initiative to advance the Bonn Process and reconstruction efforts. India's assistance activities and development partnership with Afghanistan has covered almost all possible areas, especially humanitarian assistance, major infrastructural projects, small and community based development projects, and education and capacity building initiatives.[11] India turned out to be the sixth largest donor and the largest OECD donor to Afghanistan. India has been able to restore full diplomatic relations and has provided approximately US$ 2 billion in aid for Afghanistan's Reconstruction and Development so far. It entered into partnership with the Afghan Government in a wide range of sectors such as hydroelectricity, road construction, agriculture, industry and telecommunication, information and broad-casting, etc. Today India is among the top four countries actively participating in the reconstruction process.[12]The Strategic Partnership Agreement (SPA) signed in 2011, was seen not only as a significant step in taking the relationship between the two countries forward but also as a much needed demonstration of India's risk-taking ability and a maturing of India's foreign policy.[13] It sent a strong message to Afghans, the region and the international community. By being the first to sign such an agreement, India demonstrated its independence and commitment to rebuilding Afghanistan.[14] Coming ahead of the US-Afghan strategic partnership deal, which is embroiled in differences and conditionalities,[15] the India-Afghan agreement was a demonstration of India's willingness to help a neighbour in need. Given that the agreement was based on requests and conditions set by the Afghans through a series of consultative meetings and deliberations, there were few hiccups in finalising the deal.

Drivers to the Indian Role

The attacks on the Indian mission in Afghanistan were not only seen as a reaction to India's growing influence in the country but also as a challenge to the fundamentals of India's Afghanistan Policy. While some analysts interpreted it as India's zero-sum game for others it was a confirmation of India's growing influence in the region. The question that crops up at this juncture is—*Which are the factors that are propelling India towards this unusually proactive policy in Afghanistan?*

According to experts, by rebuilding Afghanistan, India not only hopes to achieve greater regional stability but also aspires to counter Pakistan's influence in Kabul, while countering terrorism and extremist movements. It is important for India to ensure that Pakistan does not get a foothold in Afghanistan and so, historically, India has attempted to prevent Pakistan from dominating Afghanistan.[16] Pakistan, on the other hand, has viewed Afghanistan as a good means of counterbalancing India's preponderance in South Asia. Ahmed Rashid has argued that the road to Kabul is partly through Kashmir.

Afghanistan is viewed as a gateway to the Central Asian region and India is conscious that it is a potential route for accessing Central Asian Energy. Central Asia is crucial for India not only because of its oil and gas reserves that India wishes to tap for its energy security, but also because other major powers such as the US, Russia and China have started competing for influence in the region.[17] Regional actors view Afghanistan as a potential source of instability even as their geopolitical rivalry remains a major cause of Afghanistan's troubles. The region can become a natural, historically formed buffer zone as well as form the hub of Islamic extremism. Being placed in the middle of the Eurasian Continent, it is also one of the most convenient routes of transit. It is rich in minerals, especially hydrocarbons. As a consumer market, it still remains to be exploited. All these factors lead to increasing interest in Central Asian Republics (CARs) by various countries.

The Central Asia Factor

The pace of relations accelerated post-1998 as a part of a more proactive stance followed by India in its policies in general. By that time, the pace of economic reforms in the country had accelerated and the parameters of India's policy had broadened. [18] India was forced to increase its military profile in Central Asia after the diplomatic humiliation it had to endure in 1999 when an Indian Airlines flight from Kathmandu was hijacked by Pakistan-backed terrorists to Kandahar in southern Afghanistan. India had to negotiate a deal with the Taliban that involved the release of the aircraft in exchange for three hardened terrorists held by India. India then decided to set up its first military base abroad in Farkhor in Tajikistan, close to the Afghan border, which was used to provide assistance to the Northern Alliance fighters and later to provide assistance to the post-Taliban government in Kabul.

As the geopolitical importance of Central Asia has increased in recent years, all the major powers have been keen to expand their influence in the region. India is no exception. It shares many of the interests of other major powers such as the US, Russia and China vis-à-vis Central Asia, including access to Central Asian energy resources, controlling the spread of radical Islam, ensuring political stability, and strengthening regional economies. But, unlike China and Russia, its interests converge with that of the US in Central Asia, and some have even suggested that it is in US interests to have a greater Indian presence in Central Asia to counter growing Chinese or Russian involvement.[19]

While India's "Look North-West" policy has never been as clearly articulated as the "Look East" policy, there have been attempts to promote policies in a multi-dimensional manner.[20] With no direct transportation access plus difficult market conditions, the region did not become attractive to Indian private companies. Many in India believed that Russia will continue to have a decisive role in Central Asia because of its advantage of history and geography, and that would be favourable for India to some extent. Now, China has increased its involvement in the region and created a huge profile for itself through trade, energy deals, military agreements and the Shanghai Cooperation Organisation (SCO). India is watching carefully. The failure of the Afghanistan project poses common security challenges but any positive outcome will open tremendous economic opportunities to both India and Central Asia. In addition, the developments in Afghanistan, particularly in the background of difficult India-Pakistan relations, have added a new perspective to India-Central Asia relations. These two factors have increased the strategic significance of the region considerably and may be fuelling the announcement of India's twelve-point "Connect Central Asia Policy" (CCAP) to strengthen its political, security, economic and cultural relations with the region.

Connect Central Asia Policy: India's Strategic Vision vis-à-vis Central Asia

Due to its strategic and political rationale it has been difficult for India to ignore its "strategic rear" (CAS). Indian policymakers refer to Central Asia as their "extended strategic neighbourhood" as the national security concerns of Central Asia and India are closely interlinked. These concerns involve the containment of cross-border terrorism, Islamic extremism, drug trafficking, strategic alliance, energy cooperation and bilateral trade. Announced by former Minister of State for External Affairs Shri. E. Ahamed at India-Central Asia Dialogue in June 2012, the new Connect Central Asia Policy (CCAP) is a solid step that seeks to strengthen political, economic, security and cultural connections with the region.[21] The policy includes strengthening security cooperation, close consultation on Afghanistan, stepping up multilateral engagement, reviving the North-South trade corridor, setting up Central Asia e-network with its hub in India and the establishment of a new Central Asian University.[22] A substantial improvement in air connectivity between the regions ensures, and encourages, people-to-people contact. Two of the most crucial reasons that pushed the announcement of a defined policy perhaps are: (a) the post-2014 Scenario in Afghanistan and (b) China's growing profile. It is known that the failure of the Afghanistan project poses a common security challenge, but any positive outcome will open tremendous economic opportunities to both India and Central Asia. In Central Asia, India may be expected to play a relatively bigger role in the backdrop of increasing Chinese dominance. Therefore a major challenge for Indian and Chinese policymakers in Central Asia would be to manage their relationship in such a way that there is limited competition and expanding cooperation.

Building on its past linkages and goodwill, India has already developed strong political and developmental relations, including a Strategic Partnership Agreement and an agreement on uranium trade with Kazakhstan. India is developing stronger trade ties with the Central Asian states in a bid to link up with the emerging east-west economic corridor to secure its strategic and economic objectives.[23] The then Indian Minister for External Affairs Shri Pranab Mukherjee, identified the nurturing of a web of cooperative energy security networks in Central Asia as a primary goal of Indian foreign policy.[24] India's strategic vision is guided by the following concerns:

- India does not want unjustified strategic influence of outside powers in the regional context.
- India aims to gain from the economic ties with CAS and is a potential consumer of their energy resources.
- Rise or spread of Islamic extremism is not acceptable to India.
- Countering Pakistan's influence in the region.

Quite naturally, India welcomed the decisions of the member states of the SCO to expand the observer's role, and stated its intention to more actively participate in SCO activities. Building on its past linkages and goodwill, India has developed strong political and developmental relations with CAS, including "strategic partnership" and an agreement on uranium trade with Kazakhstan. In the midst of serious competition, India is slowly entering the energy scene. Concrete results have emerged lately in the form of an agreement on 25% stake in Satpayev block in Kazakhstan. It has also agreed to supply 2,100 tonnes of uranium to India's nuclear plant by 2014. The TAPI Pipeline project is on the agenda.[25] Central Asia also provides good investment opportunities for Indian business as shown by London-based Indian steel tycoon, Laxmi Mittal, who owns a steel plant with a capacity of 6 million tons in Kazakhstan, employing more than 40,000 people.[26] Some positive developments have happened in respect of TAPI as well as India-Pakistan Trade. In January 2012, India and Pakistan agreed on the principle of "Uniform Transit Fee" (50 cents per million metric Btu as transit fee to PAK, AFG). The current trade with Central Asia is small and unlikely to expend remarkably in the near future. However, the importance of regional trade needs to be evaluated in the context of India's rapidly increasing continental trade. It is expected that by 2015, India's trade with Europe, CIS plus Iran, Afghanistan and Pakistan would be about $500 billion annually. Even if over 20% of this trade were conducted through road, about $100 billion of trade from India would be passing through Central Asia and Afghanistan.[27] With the possibility of this trade passing through the region, most infrastructural projects planned by multilateral organisations in Central and South Asia will be economically viable. The US wants India to be its partner in laying the groundwork for the long-term vision of a New Silk Road that connects markets, businesses and consumers from the Caspian Sea to the Ganges and beyond.[28] India is positive about this strategy of the US administration. This appeared to be a good blueprint for Afghanistan, but unfortunately has been mixed with regional geopolitics and exit strategies from Afghanistan.

India at the moment is not specifically connected to Central Asia through any significant regional organisation. In the absence of any other organisation that can establish linkages between Central and South Asia, the role of SCO is likely to be more important. As the 2014 deadline for the withdrawal of international troops is drawing close, a greater role played by SCO in the post-2014 scenario is a strong possibility. In the light of these developments, India would be interested in joining the organisation.

India's other major initiative in the region, along with Russia and

Iran, was building of a new trade corridor, the International North-South Transport Corridor (INSTC) in the 1990s. Subsequently, other countries have joined the project. The main transport project undertaken in this initiative by India is the development of a new port complex at Chabahar on the Iranian coast, from where a road goes to Afghanistan. It is closer to India than the existing port at Bandar Abbas. India is also planning to construct a 900-km railway line that will connect the Chabahar port with Hajigak region of Afghanistan, where a consortium of seven Indian companies led by the Steel Authority of India has won a $10.3 bn deal to mine three iron ore blocks. India has also completed the construction a 218-km road link from Zaranj on the Iran-Afghan border to Delaram, from where all major cities in Afghanistan and further north Central Asian republics are connected. Despite ambitions, the INSTC has not really taken off in the last decade. It is likely that the Indian government will give a big push to this trade corridor in the coming years.

Since 2001, the proactive foreign policy posture that India has adopted indicates that it is broadening its concentric circles and is not just focusing on South and SouthEast Asia but also Central Asia and Afghanistan. India's priority in the region is based on certain key issues, challenges and advantages. India is a growing power aspiring for global acceptance. In South Asia, India is facing numerous challenges which hinder its expansion of relations with Central Asia. Extremism, Islamic fundamentalism and terrorism, instability in Afghanistan, the uncertain nature of India-Pakistan relations, a deteriorating US-Pakistan relationship, China's increased engagement in the region and problems in Xinjiang region are some of the issues of concern. The growing energy demand compels India to access energy rich Central Asia. These priorities are reflected in India's efforts to develop diplomatic relations, economic cooperation, trade and investment, and energy cooperation with Central Asian countries. In order to fulfil India's interests in Central Asia, connectivity remained a major obstacle. India does not have direct borders with any of the Central Asian states, and has to depend on Pakistan, China or Iran for access to Central Asia.[29]

The year 2012 marks the twentieth year of India-Central Asia relations in the post-Soviet period. There were indications that India was finally moving towards establishing its presence in Central Asia. This became evident from high-level cooperation in the field of defence, intelligence sharing, training and assistance, education and ITEC programmes. Many Central Asian students are given scholarships by Government of India for higher education in Indian universities.[30] In Afghanistan, Indian engineers had completed a transmission line to carry Uzbek electricity into the country and possibly beyond. With a broad understanding that a peaceful and stable Afghanistan is crucial for regional stability, India is also playing an active role in Afghan reconstruction with a commitment worth $2 bn. In a way, India's engagement in Afghanistan has boosted its policy towards Central Asia. India is now attempting to build military ties with Kyrgyzstan, agreeing to train UN Peacekeeping troops and establishing a joint high-altitude military research centre in Bishkek. Former Indian Defence Minister, A. K. Antony visited Bishkek in July 2011 and announced the initiatives.[31] These initiatives can be seen as indications that India wishes to have a greater role in Afghanistan after the allied forces leave, and it wishes to build stronger ties with the Central Asian states.

Pakistan Factor in India's Post-2014 Central Asia Vision

The last ten years of US military intervention in Afghanistan have provided vital space for India to extend its political and economic influence in Afghanistan. The large US/NATO military presence in the region so far has allowed India to extend its influence—without committing any significant military forces itself—much to Pakistan's discomfort. As relations between the US and Pakistan have hit an all-time low, it is often believed that the US would back a continued consolidation of Indian influence. However, it is important to note that the imminent US exit from Afghanistan in 2014 has further enhanced doubts centring round Afghanistan's future. One of the possible scenarios is the quick revival of the Taliban, something both India and CAS would be uncomfortable with. Even if that is not the case, one can be certain that radical forces will continue to whip up jihadist ideologies in Af-Pak in a bigger way. Though India officially projects that it does not contemplate scaling down its presence in Afghanistan, the thrust of Indian projects in the recent past have witnessed a shift from infrastructure creation to humanitarian assistance and service delivery. This shift can be interpreted as a decision taken based on the ground realities in the country. In its extended neighbourhood India might want to balance its interests with the big powers, butwhether India has the resources and influence to be able to do that remains to be seen. Pakistan's role has always been crucial for the region, and will continue to be.

Pakistan's position on the subject of India's role in Afghanistan is a complex one.To interpret it simply as "reflexively anti-India," may have its own limitations. Pakistan is poised to broaden its economic and trade relations with India. In recent years, one fundamental principle which has deeply informed Pakistan's Foreign Policy thinking and approaches on Afghanistan has been: "A Peaceful and Stable Afghanistan is critical to Pakistan's own long-term core interests of growth, prosperity, security and stability."[32] Decades of war and instability in Afghanistan had a huge impact not only from Pakistan's security point of view, in a way Pakistan's macro-economic stability and growth have also been devastated, and future prosperity threatened. From that perspective, an "anti-India" card works well to excite the sentiments in that country. Recently, Pakistan and Afghanistan have decided in principle to include Tajikistan in the Afghanistan-Pakistan Trade Transit Agreement (APTTA). India has to synchronise these developments and the emerging Eurasian Customs Union space within its evolving new Central Asia Policy.

India's huge investments in Afghanistan, its growing energy requirement, requirement of balancing Pakistan and Chinese influence and agenda of a stable Afghanistan compel it to continue (and enhance) its presence in the region. Some strategic thinkers in India are of the opinion that Central Asia can actually provide the much needed "strategic depth" India is looking for.[33] However, considering the geographical distance, this does not seem to be a practicable idea in military terms. A more nuanced look at the region suggests that soft power and non-military engagement have become a part of the quest for strategic depth, and that offers some opportunity to India's "Look North-West" policy towards Central Asia. The situation perhaps would have been different if the five Central Asian countries were united—the fact that these five countries have disagreed over several regional issues adds to the problem of finding solutions to the region's problems.

Conclusion

The geographical distance from Afghanistan and Central Asia has not left India in a disadvantageous position. There are certain problems and complexities of "closeness," which India has been able to avoid by maintaining positive and friendly relations with Afghanistan and Central Asia. Over the past decade India's capabilities have increased to a considerable extent. The Indian strategic community tends to believe that Afghanistan is a test case for India as an ascendant regional and global power. India's strategic capacity to deal with instability in its own backyard will, in the ultimate analysis, determine India's rise as a global power of major import. In other words, an Indian failure in Afghanistan is not really an option. India's posture towards Afghanistan has given its policy towards Central Asia a much required boost over the past ten years. The Connect Central Asia Policy (CCAP) can be seen as a concrete step in that direction. Russia, US and Chinese interests in the region need to be taken into account; subverting their influence should not be in the Central-Asia-India equation. The concept of linking Central and South Asian economies (New Silk Road Strategy, as an example) makes some sense, but due to difficulties in its relations with Pakistan, India will also continue to work with Iran to fulfil its objectives. Despite a plethora of regional organisations in Central and South Asia, there is no single organisation where both the regions meet together. In the absence of such an organisation, the Shanghai Cooperation Organisation (SCO) is likely to play a critical role in the post-2014 phase. It can therefore be said the Afghanistan's uncertainty will push India towards asking for Afghan membership in that organisation. For India, the priority in the region should not be to seek the role of a regional hegemon but to adopt policies that forge partnerships within the current power structure in the region. The Central Asia factor might turn out to be one of the most important factors determining the success or failure of India's Afghanistan project.

Notes

1. K. B. Usha, "India's Foreign Policy Priorities in Central Asia," *Foreign Policy Research Centre Journal,* New Delhi, 2012.
2. K. B. Usha, "India's Foreign Policy Priorities ..."
3. Gulshan Sachdeva, "India's Objectives in Central Asia," International Conference, The US, China and the Future of Central Asia, at NYU Centre on US-China Relations, February 6-8, 2011. http://uschinacenter.as.nyu.edu/docs/IO/23889/Sachdeva_Abs.pdf (accessed on October 10, 2012)
4. G. S. Bhargava, *South Asian Security After Afghanistan* (Lexington: Lexington Books, 1983).
5. S. Ganguly and N. Howenstein, "India-Pakistan Rivalry in Afghanistan," *Journal of International Affairs*, vol. 63, no. 1, Fall 2009.
6. Steve Coll, *Ghost Wars: The Secret History of CIA, Afghanistan and Bin Laden from the Soviet Invasion To September 10, 2001* (Penguin Press, New York, 2004).
7. Nihal Singh, "Why India goes to Moscow for Arms," *Asian Survey Journal*, 24, no. 7, July 1984, pp. 707-20.
8. Ramesh Trivedi, *India's Relation with her Neighbours* (New Delhi: Isha Books, 2008).
9. Rahul Bedi, "India Joins anti-Taliban Coalition," *Jane's Intelligence Weekly*, March 15, 2001.
10. Harsh V. Pant, "India in Afghanistan: A Test Case for a Rising Power," *Contemporary South Asia,* 18: 2, 2010, 133-53.
11. Anwesha Ghosh, *Afghanistan from Enduring Freedom to Enduring Chaos? Implications for India* (New Delhi: KW Publishers, 2012), p. 45.
12. Mondira Dutta, "Empowering Grassroots through Capacity Building Measures: Indian Initiatives in Afghanistan" in Arpita Basu Roy and Binoda K. Mishra (eds.), *Reconstructing Afghanistan, Prospects and Limitations* (Shipra Publishers, 2011), pp.156-69.
13. Anwesha Ghosh, *Afghanistan From Enduring Freedom ...*
14. Coming ahead of the Partnership agreements with the US, UK, EU, France and others, India is the first to lead, rather than being part of an orchestra, thereby avoiding implications associated with such perceptions. Author's discussions with senior diplomats in New Delhi and Kabul, October 2011.
15. Shanthie Mariet D'Souza, "The Emerging Fault Lines of the US-Afghan Strategic Partnership," ISAS Brief no. 210 (August 10, 2011), http://www.isas.nus.edu.sg/Attachments/PublisherAttachment/ISAS_Brief_210_-_Email_-_The_Emerging_Faultlines_15082011115335.pdf. Accessed on October 20, 2011. "US seeks India-Afghan strategic partnership-document like deal," *The Indian Express*, New Delhi, October 13, 2011.
16. Harsh V. Pant, "India in Afghanistan: A Rising Power or A Hesitant Power," *Centre for International Peace and Security Studies Working Paper,* 2011.

17. Harsh V. Pant, "India in Afghanistan …
18. Harsh V. Pant, "India in Afghanistan …"
19. Stephen Blank, *US Interests in Central Asia and the Challenges to Them* (Carlisle, PA: Strategic Studies Institute, US Army War College, 2007), pp. 31-32.
20. Anita Sengupta, "India and Central Asia, Multidimensional Perspective," *Foreign Policy Research Centre Journal,* New Delhi, 2012.
21. "India's Connect Central Asia Policy," Keynote address by MOS Shri. E. Ahamed at India-Central Asia Dialogue, June 12, 2012. Source: Ministry of External Affairs India website http://meaindia.nic.in/mystart.php?id=530119616 (accessed on October 12, 2012).
22. "India's Connect Central Asia Policy," footnote 21.
23. Asma Shakir Khwaja, "The Geostrategic Dimension of India and Central Asia Bilateral Relations: An Analysis," *Foreign Policy Research Centre Journal,* New Delhi, 2012.
24. For further details, see Vidya Nadkarni, Central Asia and South Asia: India and Pakistan, Department of Political Science, University of San Diego, cited by Asma Shakir Khwaja, "The Geostrategic Dimension of India and Central Asia Bilateral Relations: An Analysis," *Foreign Policy Research Centre Journal,* New Delhi, 2012.
25. "India-Kazakistan Agree to Expedite Satpayev Block," December 6, 2012, Source: www.gulfoilandgas.com, http://www.gulfoilandgas.com/webpro1/MAIN/Mainnews.asp?id=13307 (accessed on August 28, 2012).
26. Cristopher Leake and Will Stewart, "Tony Blair, the billionaire donor Laxmi Mittal ... and a major deal in Kazakhstan," *Mail Online News,* October 30, 2011. http://www.dailymail.co.uk/news/article-2055223/Tony-Blair-billionaire-donor-Lakshmi-Mittal--major-deal-Kazakhstan.html
27. Gulshan Sachdeva, "India's Objectives in Central Asia." Abstract of the presentation on the International Conference, "The US, China and the Future of Central Asia" at NYU Centre on US-China Relations, February 6-8, 2011. http://uschinacenter.as.nyu.edu/docs/IO/23889/Sachdeva_Abs.pdf (accessed on October 10, 2012).
28. "India and US must work together for New Silk Road," *The Economic Times*, June 12, 2012. http://articles.economictimes.indiatimes.com/2012-06-13/news/32215426_1_india-us-strategic-dialogue-regional-architecture-south-and-central-asia
29. K. B. Usha, "India's Foreign Policy Priorities in Central Asia," *Foreign Policy Research Centre Journal,* New Delhi, 2012.
30. Information shared by Central Asian students studying at Ravenshaw University in Cuttack during an interview with the author in July 2011 at Cuttack, Orissa.
31. Anita Sengupta, "India and Central Asia …"
32. Simbal Khan, "Afghanistan: Post 2014 Strategy and the Regional Framework," *Foreign Policy Research Centre Journal,* New Delhi, 2012.
33. Shalini Sharan, "Central Asia: India's Real Strategic Depth?" February 27, 2012.

8. Nation-building or National Revival in Turkmenistan: From Dependence to Independence

Lopamudra Bandyopadhyay

The gradual transition of Turkmenistan from that of dependence to independence and socialism to market economy has been in effect since 1991. Turkmen national identity was the result of an amalgamation of unstable conditions that befell the newly independent state immediately after the dissolution of the erstwhile Soviet Union. Following the declaration of independence, the process of nation-building was initiated by President Saparmurat Niyazov—better known as Turkmenbashi—to eradicate the identity vacuum and create a new homogeneous Turkmen national identity.[1] It may be pointed out that President Niyazov used the term "national revival" as an alternative to nation-building. This was in sharp contrast to nation-building as primarily seen in the Central Asian region.[2]

Since its inception, the Soviet Union was the primary architect of Turkmen nation-building. Following the establishment of Turkmenistan SSR, the Turkmen nation met Stalin's four criteria of nationhood: unity of language, territory, economy and historical culture.[3] However, Turkmen nation-building was not consolidated in the Soviet era. On the other hand, Moscow promoted Russian language and culture in Turkmenistan instead of genuine Turkmen values and prohibited nationalist studies and movements. Following the declaration of independence, Turkmenistan has focused on a coherent system of nation-building, which has two main objectives: the unity of the tribes and gradual sociocultural de-Russification. The novelty of the Turkmen process of nation-building as compared to the other Central Asian countries lies in the fact that even at present Turkmenistan is gradually moving towards its dream of an elevated Turkmen nation.

Evolution of Turkmen Identity in the Pre-Soviet Period

Turkmenistan is surrounded by Uzbekistan and Kazakhstan in the north, Iran in the south, Afghanistan in the east, and the Caspian Sea in the west. The advent of the Turkmen tribes in the lands known as Turkmenistan date back to as far as the ninth century.[4] Coming from Mongolia and southern Siberia, they were an informal confederacy of nomadic tribes organised along lines of patriarchic descent and tracing their ancestry to the mythical Turkish warrior, Oghuz Khan. In the beginning of the eleventh century, one of the Turkmen leaders, Seljuk, established a dynasty in Merv. The Seljuks extended their domain and a Seljuk empire was formed through military campaigns to the south and west. However, in the late twelfth century, the Seljuk Empire began to crumble. Mongol invasion of Turkmen lands in 1221 was followed by a destruction of Merv and massacre of many of the inhabitants, while driving the survivors westwards. Nonetheless, they could not maintain strong political control over Turkmenistan after the death of Genghis Khan in 1227. Eventually, they retreated by the end of the fourteenth century. Following the departure of the Mongols, Turkmenistan was a battlefield for continuous conflicts among the Turkmen tribes themselves as well as receiving attacks from Persia, and from the khanates of Khiva and Bukhara established in present-day Uzbekistan.[5] It was during this period of constant turmoil that the Turkmen formed large tribal and kinship groups which have remained an important foundation of contemporary Turkmen society.[6]

In absence of a state to regulate social life, customs and traditions were attributed vital importance unparalleled among other Turkic republics of Central Asia.[7] In order to be respected as a "real" Turkmen, one had to live in conformity with the customs and traditions. *Adat,* the all comprehensive customary law, was interpreted and enforced by the elders, known as *yashlys* and *aksakals*, who gave judgement on ways of living—from marriage and family relations to conduct of war. Further, the Turkmen people were followers of Sufism and were guided by relationships between the individual, the soul and God. The doctrines of Sufi saints were followed by groups descending from their lineage.[8] Turkmen customs and traditions not only regulated social life but also defined hierarchies within the tribes. The principal source for differentiating the levels of hierarchies was descent. There were Turkmen of the pure-blood who were distinct from *yarimcha,* the mixed-blooded, and *kul*, the descendants of non-Turkmen captives.[9]

It should also be noted that Turkmen tribes were generally organised as a flexible confederation. The major Turkmen tribes used to be the Tekke in central Turkmenistan, Ersary in south-eastern Turkmenistan, Yomud in the west, Göklen in the south-west, Salyr in the east and Saryk in the south. They were independent entities and never acted together, but they fought against, allied with, and each other.[10] Most of the time conflicts were due to disputes over territory. In the nineteenth century, the neighbouring states began to establish their control over the Turkmen tribes. By the time the Russian empire expanded its domain through military conquests in Central Asia in the second half of the century, many Turkmen tribes had already become subject to different powers, such as Persia, Khivan and Bukharan khanates.[11] After defeating the khanates of Bukhara and Khiva and annexing their territories, the Russian imperial army encountered the Tekke Turkmen in Goktepe. At the end of a two-year struggle, which cost the Turkmen thousands of casualties, the Russians captured Goktepe in 1881. Following the Goktepe defeat, the Turkmen resistance was broken. By 1885, all of the major Turkmen tribes had submitted to Russian rule and Turkmenistan was annexed to Transcaspia, a subdivision of Russian Turkestan.[12]

Russian imperial rule had important effects on the Turkmen confederation, both in economic and political terms. Although it did not bring tangible benefits to the local people, the construction of the Transcaspian Railway was an important development in economic terms as it opened the region to the outside world and facilitated trade to a great extent. In political terms, the foremost influence of the Russian rule was the introduction of new conceptions of identity based on ethnicity, language and territory. Definition of identity, apart from genealogy but linked to land and ethnicity, was a completely new understanding for the Turkmen, and would constitute the foundations of both Turkmen SSR as well as independent Turkmenistan.[13]

Evolution of the Turkmen State during the Soviet Era

The effect of war and revolutions following the outbreak of World War I was catastrophic. After the February Revolution of 1917, different political forces competed for support in the region, while the Turkmen themselves were divided between traditionalists and reformist intelligentsia.[14] Following the October revolution, Turkmen resistance was part of the *Basmachi* uprising of Central Asia. Finally, in 1920, the Red Army drove the resistance forces into the Kara-Kum Desert and secured most of the Turkmen territories. *Basmachi* forces, nevertheless, continued to fight in the area of Krasnovodsk and the Kara-Kum Desert until 1936.[15]

The Soviet leaders believed that creating territorial republics based on nationalities would undermine pan-Islamic and pan-Turkic sentiments, which were thought to contain seeds of a possible total rebellion in Central Asia, while satisfying nationalist aspirations. Accordingly, Central Asian lands were divided along national lines according to Stalin's four criteria of nationhood, defined as unity of economy, culture, territory and language. An autonomous Turkmen region was created in 1921, and succeeded by Turkmen SSR in 1924 within the borders that have remained as the country's boundaries today.[16] Receiving its own flag, national emblem, anthem and constitution, Turkmen SSR had all attributes of a nation-state except sovereignty.

Nation-Building Policy of Saparmurat Niyazov

Saparmurat Niyazov, elected as the first Turkmen president in 1990 and as president for life in 1999, ruled Turkmenistan for a decade through an authoritarian regime.[17] He was given the name of "Turkmenbashi" (the head of Turkmens) following independence. The legislative bodies, the *Mejlis* (Parliament) and *Halk Maslahaty* (People's Council), remained mere rubber-stamp bodies during his tenure. The ministers did not have real power and were frequently humiliated and sometimes forced to resign by the President. Military/civil bureaucrats were also unable to limit Turkmenbashi's charismatic authority. Turkmenbashi's most significant policy, "10 Years Stability," was declared in December 1992. This policy aimed to preserve political stability and socio-economic development, avoiding opposition and political crisis. As a result, Turkmenbashi's Democratic Party of Turkmenistan (formerly the Communist Party of Turkmenistan) became the only political party in Turkmenistan.[18]

Following the declaration of independence, the Turkmen State initiated a nation-building policy in order to seal the ideological vacuum, maintain the source of legitimacy for the new nation-state, and adapt to the international system. The nation-building policy primarily focused on the unity of tribes. Tribal identities, especially the five largest—Teke, Yomut, Ersary, Salyr and Saryk, were still influential in social life.[19] The lack of a hierarchical mechanism and leadership within the tribes has been a historical legacy.[20]

Turkmenbashi defined the governmental policy on the unity of tribes as "national revival" by returning to the real history and spiritual sources, rather than "nation-building."[21] According to him, what was happening in Turkmenistan is only the rediscovery of the forgotten national identity. "By forming an independent and totally neutral Turkmen state, by uniting a number of tribes into a whole, we did not create a new nation; what we did was to return its national pivot, which used to be strong and powerful but has been shattered by the blows of the historical fate."[22]

Benedict Anderson's "Imagined Communities"

Benedict Anderson describes a nation as an "imagined community" because "the members of even the smallest nation will never know most of their fellow members, meet them, or even hear of them, yet in the minds of each lives the image of their communion."[23] He emphasises the development of vernacular languages-of-states and print-capitalism as two of the roots of nationalism. Print-capitalism symbolises the "interaction between a system of production and productive relations (capitalism), a technology of communications (print), and the fatality of human linguistic diversity."[24] According to Anderson, narratives and symbols, such as the tombs of "unknown soldiers," are also crucial elements in national imagination. Similarly, he points to museums and history writing as significant means for the determination of national identity. The selective interpretation of history, on the one hand, emphasises historical heroic martyrdom, wars and genocide, in order to maintain national solidarity, while, on the other, it consciously omits some events, which undermine national integrity.[25]

Anderson also explains the historical trajectories of nationalism in three groups concerning their chronological order: creole, popular linguistic and official nationalism. "Popular linguistic-nationalism" in Europe depends on the development of vernacular languages-of-states and popular nationalist movements. The features of "official nationalism" in dynastic and aristocratic empires (e.g., Tsarist Russia) are official rewriting of history, state-organised propaganda, and state-controlled education. The success of popular linguistic-nationalism in Western and official nationalism in Eastern Europe has encouraged the political elite in non-Western countries, especially in the newly independent states, to use nation-building policies. The nationalism in these newly independent states is a mix of popular linguistic and official nationalism. Therefore, in the process of nation-building in the new states: "one sees both genuine, popular nationalist enthusiasm and a systematic, even Machiavellian, instilling of nationalist ideology through the mass media, the educational system, administrative regulations, and so forth."[26] It is through Anderson's paradigm that the development of vernacular language, media, history writing, propaganda and education in Turkmenistan can be analysed.

Domestic Tools for Nation-Building in Turkmenistan

The Development of Turkmen as the Primary Language of Turkmenistan

The development of Turkmen as the primary language is the main pillar of Turkmen nation-building. After the declaration of independence, a constitutional change made Turkmen the official language, reversing the linguistic deterioration of the Soviet period.[27] In October 1999, the state radio ceased its Russian language news broadcast.[28] In July 2000, Turkmenbashi declared that all officials must speak Turkmen. He also fired Boris Shikhmuradov, his foreign minister since 1993, criticising his knowledge of Turkmen. At present, it is popular to replace Russian names with Turkmen alternatives. The administrative terms, such as *oblast* (province), *rayon* (district or small city), and *kolhoz* (farmer union) have been replaced with *welayat*, *etrap* and *dayhan birles¸igi*. Official slogans such as *garas¸syzlyk* (independence), *bitaraplyk* (neutrality), *agzybirlik* (solidarity), *galkynys¸* (development) and the names of political institutions, e.g., "Halk Maslahaty" and the "Mejlis," are all selected from original Turkmen rather than Russian.[29]

The Role of the Media

Television, radio and newspapers are important means of governmental nation-building policy in Turkmenistan. They focus on the propaganda of nationalism and on praising the President. Turkmenbashi is accepted as the main symbol of nation-building representing national solidarity. When speaking about the President, the TV and radio commentators used epithets, such as compassionate, merciful and esteemed. Similarly, almost every other day, large photos of Turkmenbashi graced the first page of all newspapers.[30] In addition to media propaganda, hundreds of places and institutions had been named or renamed "Turkmenbashi" all around Turkmenistan. Turkmenbashi's posters and sculptures decorated the main buildings of Ashgabat. His picture also appeared on the national currency, *manat*.

Historical figures have also been used as the symbols of nation-building. Magtymguly (1733–1797), for instance, became one of the significant symbols. He was not only a pious poet, but also a wise social leader. Many of his creations have found importance as official slogans in Turkmenistan. The most widespread official motto, "*Halk, Watan, Tu¨rkmenbas¸y*" ("People, Motherland, Turkmenbashi"), can still be seen in many places in Turkmenistan. Turkmen government also creates narratives to promote the imagination of national identity. The main narrative is *baki bitaraply k* (permanent neutrality), the main pillar of Turkmen foreign policy, which provides an example of interplay between identity and foreign policy in Turkmenistan. The permanent neutrality of Turkmenistan was accepted by the UN in 1995. Given the neutrality status, Turkmenistan is committed to peace-loving principles, refusing to maintain or produce weapons of mass destruction, to participate in military pacts and to start or to take sides in military conflicts.[31]

Rewriting History

One of the pillars of Turkmen nation-building is the writing of history, which focuses on the transmission of national history in schools and by the media. Official Soviet history emphasised the civilising and progressive mission of the dominating Russia, and tried to suppress Turkmen nationalism.[32] After 1991, Turkmen history writing has focused on three issues: changing the Soviet paradigm, emphasising unique Turkmen national history rather than shared Turkic history and maintaining national solidarity by uniting the history of tribes and regions. It emphasises historical events like the Goktepe War as a part of common national history, while omitting the clashes between tribes. The golden age of Turkmen history writing was the era of the Seljuk Empire (1040–1194). A large museum was built in Ashgabat to exhibit the remains of the Seljuk Empire as well as the history of independent Turkmenistan. As a part of its history policy, many places, including the streets and institutes in Ashgabat, have been named or renamed after historical figures, such as Magtymguly, Azady (the father of Magtymguly, 1700–1760), and Gorogly (a legendary hero). Commemorative holidays are one of the main ways to celebrate national identities.[33] Turkmenistan officially accepted many memorial days honouring national history.[34]

Another important project of history writing is Turkmenbashi's book titled *Ruhnama* (the soul book), which will include historical, cultural and other aspects of the "Turkmen soul." *Ruhnama* was also the name of Turkmenbashi's policy of cultural and spiritual revival. This policy sometimes resulted in autocratic manipulation of historical facts. In September 2000, Turkmenbashi ordered the destruction of 25,000 new history textbooks, arguing that their authors had committed treason against the country's past by ignoring "the Turkmen origin and character" of Turkmenistan, overstating the role of other nations in its national history and writing that Turkmens originated not in what is modern Turkmenistan but in the Altai mountains. He criticised the author: "You hardly mention the Turkmen people in your book. … You apparently did not listen to what I said in my speeches."[35]

Education and Propaganda

The Turkmen government since the time of Turkmenbashi focused on the propaganda and indoctrination of national idealism and self-sacrifice to prevent egotistic tendencies. Turkmenbashi emphasised the significance of the spread of national feeling as follows: "The country will flourish when each person in it, young or old, strongly develops the feeling of patriotism."[36] Turkmenbashi attempted to set up a direct relationship with citizens in order to ignite national consciousness by using such methods as a direct mail system and visits to urban and rural areas. Another source of contact between the President and citizens was dialogue meetings.

The "sacred oath" (*kasem*) was recited each day in schools and frequently in public events, aimed to consolidate the loyalty of citizens to the Turkmen nation and its President:

> Glorious Turkmenistan, my motherland, I would sacrifice my life for you!
> For the slightest evil against you, let my hand be lost!
> For the slightest slander about you, let my tongue be lost!
> At the moment of my betrayal, to my motherland, Turkmenistan,
> To my President, let my life be annihilated![37]

This oath reflects three governmental principles. First, the Turkmen motherland, for which citizens could sacrifice their own life, and its President are glorified. Second, collectivism is desired more than individualism. Finally, the concepts of obedience and betrayal are understood in a monolithic and rigid manner. Education is crucial both to indoctrinate national imagination and feelings and to maintain social control. There was a course called "The Policy of Turkmenbashi" taught in schools and universities, which aimed to propagate official policies of national revival. Turkmenbashi stressed the importance of patriotic and moral education.

The Personality Cult of the Leader

When Turkmenistan became independent following the collapse of the Soviet Union, Niyazov abandoned his Communist roots and rebranded himself Turkmenbashi. In the ensuing years of his rule, from 1991 to his death in 2006, Niyazov created a personality cult and instilled a highly repressive regime. He banned opera, ballet and the circus, gold teeth, long hair or beards for men and playing recorded music. He also ruled with a heavy hand, crushing all opposition and controlling all branches of government and the media. In 1999, the Parliament in Turkmenistan voted to allow Turkmenbashi to serve as president for life, thereby eliminating any accountability he may have had to his own people. As a result, upon his death the "Father of All Turkmens" left behind a grim legacy: a crumbling infrastructure, egregious human rights abuses, and a poor quality of life (including rumours of starvation outside the capital) despite the country's vast natural gas reserves.[38]

Cultural Interplay

Three different reasons have been cited for cultural issues having a significant influence on the construction of Turkmen identity. First, Turkmenistan is geographically located at the crossroads of Russian, Islamic and Turkish cultures. Second, it has faced a cultural vacuum and instability since the end of the Russian dominance, which allows the penetration of several cultures. Finally, globalisation has encouraged intercultural relations and interaction mainly because of permeation of cultures across state borders. For these reasons, although the Turkmen state has minimised the role of society in the nation-building process, it cannot disregard Russian, Islamic, Turkish and Western cultures. In this perspective, the interaction between the state and these cultures needs to be analysed in order to understand the essence of Turkmen identity.

Islamic Identity

Turkmens have always tried to preserve Islamist customs during the Soviet era despite state pressure. With Independence, Islamism has reinvented itself in Turkmen society with traditional Islamic customs, such as respect for religious holidays and family values. The increasing number of mosques in Turkmenistan during the pre-Niyazov and the Niyazov period, from four in 1979,[39] 30 in 1990 and 56 to 223 (nine in Ashgabat) in 1999,[40] shows the phenomenal popularity of Islamic practices. Foreign aid has played a crucial role. The United Arab Emirates, for instance, sponsored two mosques in Ashgabat. Turkey's Foundation of Religious Affairs (TDV) also donated a large mosque, *Ertogrul Gazi Metjidi*, in Ashgabat.[41] This mosque also has a cultural centre where TDV distributes free religious books. This is significant since there is a scarcity of books on Islam in Turkmenistan.

Because of the dearth of Islamist scholars, Uzbek *madrasas* and *mullahs* have been the main source for Turkmen education since the pre-

Soviet period. To satisfy the need for religious scholars and officials, TDV opened a theological college in Ashgabat, in 1996, in addition to an Islamic high school. This college, where the mediums of education are Turkmen, Turkish and Arabic, is the main Islamic educational institution in Turkmenistan. Its students were offered official positions before graduation because of the immediate need for religious officials. Additionally, some Turkmen students are educated in theological colleges and high schools in Turkey. Iran has tried to spread its culture in Turkmenistan by founding an educational institution in Ashgabat. Although Turkmenistan is a secular state, it officially accepts Islamic holidays, i.e., *Ramazan* and *Kurban Bairam*, and directly controls and regulates religious affairs through the Council of Religious Affairs. There is neither an Islamist political party nor Islamist organisational networks as the opposition.

Islamist revivalism is sought after for improving Turkmenistan's good Muslim image. This image also became a source of legitimacy for rulers showing their respect for national identity. The Turkmenbashi, for instance, went to *hajj* (pilgrimage to Mecca) with the entire cabinet of ministers in 1992.[42] The large mosque in Goktepe, which is called *Haji Saparmyrat Turkmenbasy,* was built as a memorial to this *hajj*. This mosque honours the Goktepe Wars and their location, Turkmenbashi's respect for Islam and Turkmen nationalism.

Russian Influence

Russian culture, which impacted on Turkmen culture and identity, has still survived. Those who are currently middle-aged, especially the political elite, were educated in the Soviet period and were strongly influenced by Russian culture. Although Turkmen is developing as the vernacular language, Russian language is still used in state bureaucracy, universities, courts and even daily life. Most members of the Russian minority and *Russophones*, who are ethnically Armenian, Azeri, or Turkmen, are unfamiliar with the Turkmen language. These members of the Russian minority have faced isolation since Independence. The main sources of Russian cultural influence are the Turkmen schools which use Russian as the medium of language. Another significant means of Russian cultural influence in Turkmenistan is the TV channel, ORT, which belongs to the Russian Federation and also broadcasts the Turkmen TV programmes. The Turkmen government imposed restrictions on this channel for financial and ethical reasons. In this restrictive environment, Turkmens have sought access to private satellite links. ORT and other Russian channels, as well as Turkish channels, are watched in Turkmenistan via satellite. Russian channels, however, have a greater advantage in this competition than the Turkish ones.

The Turkmen government still publishes a Russian newspaper, *Neutralniy Turkmenistan.* Additionally, the weekly official news reports, the *Turkmenistan News Weekly*, are published in Russian, English and Turkmen. Islamist and Turkic cultural links are stronger in Turkmen society because of historical connections.

Turkish Influence

There are strong ethnic links between the Turks and Turkmens, both of whom belong to the Oghuz group of Turkic nations. Historically, the Seljuk Empire is the common ancestor of Turks and Turkmens. Moreover, the Turkmen language has the closest resemblance to Turkish. The transformation from Cyrillic to Latin alphabet further indicates the linguistic affinity though Turkmen Latin is different from the Turkish variety. Turkey supports Turkmen education, donating school textbooks and providing scholarships for Turkmen students to study in Turkish universities.[43] The Turkish government has opened a language centre and a high school in Ashgabat. Thousands of Turkish businessmen, workers and educators live in Turkmenistan, especially in Ashgabat. A Turkish weekly newspaper, *Zaman*, published in Turkmenistan has a decent nationwide circulation.

Western Impact

The impact of Western culture on Turkmen nation-building was intensified by globalisation and the international system. The main tool of Western cultural influence in Turkmenistan is the English language. Since Niyazov's rule, the English language has been introduced into business, universities as well as the bureaucracy. The American Council for International Education has been coordinating educational exchange programmes for students, teachers and scholars since 1992.[44] The Peace Corps, an American NGO, which is officially supported by the US government, has also implemented a number of educational projects, including summer camps, since 1993.[45] Similarly, German and French education and cultural centres are functioning in Ashgabat, which provide language courses, library services and student exchange programmes.

The Turkmen government supports Western influence in order to assist it in adapting to international systems. Turkmenbashi stressed: "The alphabet transformation, from Cyrillic to Latin will make it easy to learn English, in the same way that Cyrillic made learning Russian easy, and learning English will result in the adaptation to world civilisation."[46] On the other hand, the Turkmen government rejected Western influence based on democratic ideas and political culture.

Nation-building under Gurbanguly Berdymukhamedov

Berdymukhamedov assumed presidency in December 2006, prompting many to hope that he would give the country a new international image by lifting restrictions on the freedom of its citizens and easing access for foreign investors. In his inauguration speech, he vowed to continue the work of his predecessor, while calling for change and suggesting the possibility of increased openness. He also promised to encourage entrepreneurship and allow private ownership, reform the educational system, offer access to the Internet, improve health care, and restore pensions. He moved to dismantle the Niyazov cult of personality by removing hundreds of the omnipresent photographs of Turkmenbashi and by removing Turkmenbashi's image from all banknotes, except the 500 manat note.[47] He restored pension for the elderly and established a new oversight commission for law enforcement agencies. He signed a decree making a fundamental change—increasing compulsory education from nine to ten years.[48] He lifted the previous ban on opera and the circus, and also suggested restoring the names of the months.[49]

But these reforms proved to be measures that were two steps forward, one step back. Authoritarianism returned to Turkmenistan with a new face—Berdymukhamedov. Turkmenbashi's photographs were replaced by ones of Berdymukhamedov. He adopted a similar honorific title—*Arkadag,* the Turkmen term for "protector." Internet in the public domain was curtailed with expensive fees and the presence of armed guards at the doorstep. More disconcerting was the lack of change in the spheres of political and press freedoms. The only legally registered political party has been the government-sponsored Democratic Party of Turkmenistan (formerly the Communist Party of the Turkmen Soviet Republic). Independent media outlets remain stifled as the government maintained near-total control over the media. Despite the cosmetic changes, as time passed, Berdymukhamedov appeared to be following closely in the footsteps of Niyazov, creating his own dictatorial regime rather than choosing to open up his isolated country. Gurbanguly Berdymukhamedov secured a second five-year term in February 2012, winning more than 97% of the vote. In the election, Berdymukhamedov faced several other candidates from his own party, all of whom expressed their support for him. The Organisation for Security and Cooperation in Europe (OSCE) declined to send a mission to monitor the poll, saying there was little point, given the limited freedoms and lack of political competition in the country.[50]

Interestingly, after a decade of tutoring students based on the former president's "book of the soul," there is a new change—this autumn Turkmenistan is said to remove the *Ruhnama* from its school curriculum. A news website run by Turkmen exiles in Vienna reported recently that a new academic programme drafted by Turkmenistan's Education Ministry for the country's secondary schools did not include Saparmurat Niyazov's *Ruhnama*, which was once required reading not only for students, but for government employees, too. According to the *Chronicles of Turkmenistan*, subjects like economics will replace classes dedicated to the book, which became part of the curriculum in 2002.[51]

Russia's RIA Novosti news agency confirmed the report and, citing an unnamed ministry official, stated on August 1, 2013 that "prospective university students will still have to study the Ruhnama for their entry exams." Niyazov had instructed the youth to read the spiritual guide three times a day in order to secure a place in heaven. Two years after Niyazov's death, the *Ruhnama* was removed from the university curricula and was taught only one hour per week in secondary schools.[52]

Conclusion

Historically the power of nationalism has often been related to the emergence of individuality—it is indeed a necessity, because people have been since time immemorial socialised with the extreme need of defining themselves: as a clan, tribe or ethnic group. In case of Central Asian states, they have defined geographical borders, dominant ethnic identities and societies that tend to be more homogeneous with respect to the theory of nationalism.

Two divergent forms of psychological behaviour have emerged in Central Asia that distinguishes the colonial and post-colonial setups in this region. Post-colonial attitude is reflected in a conscious effort by Central Asian leaders to order their economies and politics, but in accordance to Russia's CIS policy. This phenomenon has its reflection in the cases of Kyrgyzstan and Tajikistan. Kazakhstan, Uzbekistan and Turkmenistan are more independent-minded and are confident in steering their own course of politics. A post-colonial attitude in which Russia is identified as big brother and the latter tries to preserve its leadership position in the post-Soviet area is a known fact. However ethnic conflicts in Chechnya and economic crisis in 1993 had destructive effect on Russia's foreign affairs, especially towards the Union states. Emergence of weak governments, lack of budget/exhausted budget, distribution of ethnic conflicts because of land and water, drug trafficking, growing gap between different layers of society, labour migration and low quality of education were results of critical social problems that arose after 1991 in Central Asia.

In conclusion, it may be stated that despite inherent weaknesses of Central Asian states, each country has evolved since 1991 in its own unique way. Nation-building had always been an important factor since ancient times. However, it was given immense importance in the post independence period. The uniqueness of Turkmenistan's mode of nation-building lies in the fact that the state is still in the process of evolution, and despite an authoritarian government being at the helm of administration, the Turkmen population has been able to inculcate within itself the uniqueness of its culture, history, language and other such civilisational attributes. It may be worthwhile to state that the distinctiveness of Turkmenistan's nation-building programme lies in the fact that not only is there an active participation by the state, but also of the people who have played a dynamic role in the preservation of their civilisational heritage.

Notes

1. Ahmet T. Kuru, "Between the State and Cultural Zones: Nation-building in Turkmenistan," *Central Asian Survey,* vol. 21, issue 1, 2002, UK, pp. 71-90, accessed at http://grad.sdsu.edu/~akuru/docs/Kuru_CAS.pdf, on May 15, 2013.
2. See, for nation-building in other Central Asian republics, Azamat Sarsembayev, "Imagined Communities: Kazak Nationalism and Kazakification in the 1990s," *Central Asian Survey*, vol. 18, no. 3, 1999, pp. 319-46; Shahram Akbarzadeh, "Nation-Building in Uzbekistan," *Central Asian Survey*, vol. 15, no. 1, 1996, pp. 23-32; Pal Kolsto, "Nation-Building in the Former USSR," *Journal of Democracy*, vol. 7, no. 1, 1996, pp. 118-32.
3. Kuru, "Between the State and Cultural Zones ..."
4. Adrienne Lynn Edgar, *Tribal Nation: The Making of Soviet Turkmenistan* (Princeton: Princeton University Press, 2004), pp. 22-23.
5. Edgar, *Tribal Nation ..., p.* 20.
6. "History of Turkmenistan," *Embassy of Turkmenistan,* Washington, DC, at http://turkmenistanembassy.org/history-of-turkmenistan/ accessed on June 25, 2013.
7. See Alexandre Bennigsen and S. Enders Wimbush, *Muslims of the Soviet Empire: A Guide* (London: C. Hurst and Company, 1985), pp. 94-106.
8. Kuru, *Between the State and Cultural Zones ...*
9. Edgar, *Tribal Nation,* p. 271.
10 Edgar, p. 20.
11 Annette Bohr, "Turkmen" in Graham Smith (ed.), *The Nationalities Question in the Soviet Union* (London: Longman, 1990), p. 228.
12. "History of Turkmenistan."
13. Edgar, p. 31.
14. Edgar, p. 2. Also see Ronald Grigor Suny, "State Building and Nation-making: The Soviet Experience" in *The Revenge of the Past: Nationalism, Revolution, and the Collapse of the Soviet Union* (Stanford: Stanford Press, 1993), pp. 84-126.
15. Olivier Roy, *The New Central Asia: Geopolitics and the Birth of Nations* (New York, London: New York University Press, 2000), pp. 86-89.
16. Aleksandr Bushev, "A Kind of Prosperity," *Bulletin of the Atomic Scientists*, Chicago, vol. 50, no. 1, 1994, pp. 44-47.
17. John Anderson, "Authoritarian Political Development in Central Asia: the Case of Turkmenistan," *Central Asian Survey,* vol. 14, no. 4, 1995, pp. 509-27.

18. Following the declaration of independence, two opposition parties were constituted: *Agzybirlik* (Solidarity) and the *Democratic Party*. These parties have been suppressed and are now banned. The *Peasant Party* was planned as a non-opposition party. Although it was registered, this party became inactive.
19. Some of the other tribes are; Ogurcaly, C¸owdur, Go¨klen¯, Nohurly, Mu¨rceli, Alili, Sakar, Yemreli, Garadas¸ly, Hydyr ili, Ata, Hoca and Sih. Marat Durdyy´ew and S¸ohrat Kadyrow, Du¨nyedeki Tu¨rkmenler.
20 See, Mehmet Saray, *The Turkmens in the Age of Imperialism: A Study of the Turkmen People and Their Incorporation into the Russian Empire* TTK, Ankara, 1989. Also, Paul Georg Geiss, "Turkmen tribalism," *Central Asian Survey,* UK, vol. 18, no. 3, 1999, pp. 347-57.
21. Kuru, *Between the State and Cultural Zones.....*
22. Kuru, *Between the State and Cultural Zones....*
23. Benedict Anderson, *Imagined Communities: Reflections on the Origin and Spread of Nationalism* (London: Verso, 1998), p. 6.
24. Benedict Anderson, p. 43.
25. Benedict Anderson, pp. 9, 199-206.
26. Benedict Anderson, pp. 113–14.
27. David Nissman, "Turkmenistan: Just like Old Times," in Ian Bremmer and Ray Taras (eds.), *New States, New Politics: Building the Post-Soviet Nations* (Cambridge: Cambridge University Press, 1997), pp. 644-45.
28. "1999 Country Report on Human Rights Practices Released by the Bureau of Democracy," *Human Rights, and Labor, US Department of State*, February 25, 2000, at http://www.state.gov, on March 3, 2013.
29. Ibid.
30. Most of the well-known newspapers, such as Turkmenistan, *Neutralniy Turkmenistan* (Russian), Galkynys, and Adalat were sponsored by Turkmenbashi.
31. Permanent neutrality of Turkmenistan was accepted by the UN with the unanimous support of 185 countries on December 12, 1995. Turkmenistan is committed not to start military conflict or war except in self-defence; to refrain from political, diplomatic, or other moves that might lead to armed conflict or to take sides in a conflict; not to participate in military pacts; not to maintain, produce, or transfer nuclear, chemical, biological and other weapons of mass destruction; and to refrain from leasing its territory for the deployment of foreign military bases.
32. See John Glenn, *The Soviet Legacy in Central Asia* (New York: St Martin's Press, 1999), pp. 86-88.
33. Fred Halliday, "Nationalism," in John Baylis and Steve Smith (eds.), *The Globalization of World Politics*, (New York: Oxford University Press, 1998), p. 368.
34. Some of these days are: Anniversary of Turkmenistan Independence, The Renaissance and Unity Day, Holiday of the State Flag and the Birthday of the

President, and Day of Turkmenistan Neutrality. There are also many special days that are not official holidays, such as the Election Day of the First President of Turkmenistan, the Turkmen Horses Holiday, the Magtymguly Poetry Day, and the Turkmen Carpets Holiday.

35. Paul Goble, "Turkmenistan: Analysis from Washington. Rewriting the Future," *RFE/RL Newsline*, October 2, 2000.
36. Goble, "Turkmenistan."
37. Kuru, *Between the State and Cultural Zones ...*
38. Kuru, *Between the State ...*
39. Bennigsen and Wimbush, p. 101.
40. *BISNIS Country Reports and NIS Market Contacts*, "Country Commercial Guides FY 1999: Turkmenistan," at http://www.state.gov/www/about state/business/com guides/1999/europe/turkmen99 10.html on June 2013.
41. Kuru "Between the State and Cultural Zones: Nation-building in Turkmenistan," *Central Asian Survey*, vol. 21, issue 1, 2002, pp. 71-90.
42. Michael Ochs, "Turkmenistan: The Quest for Stability and Control," in Karen Dawisha and Bruce Parrott (eds.), *Conflict, Cleavage and Change in Central Asia and the Caucasus* (Cambridge: Cambridge University Press, 1997), p. 338.
43. Ochs, "Turkmenistan ..."
44. Kuru "Between the State and Cultural Zones: Nation-building in Turkmenistan," *Central Asian Survey*, vol. 21, issue 1, 2002, pp. 71-90.
45. Kuru "Between the State and Cultural Zones: Nation-building in Turkmenistan," *Central Asian Survey*, vol. 21, issue 1, 2002, pp. 71-90.
46. Kuru "Between the State and Cultural Zones: Nation-building in Turkmenistan," *Central Asian Survey*, vol. 21, issue 1, 2002, pp. 71-90.
47. "Ex-Turkmen Leader's Statue Moved," *BBC News,* May 3, 2008, at http://news.bbc.co.uk/2/hi/asia-pacific/7382512.stm, on July 15, 2013.
48. "A Crack in the Isolation of Turkmenistan: Internet Cafes," *USA Today,* February 16, 2007, at http://usatoday30.usatoday.com/news/world/2007-02-16-turkmenistan_x.htm, on July 26, 2013.
49. "Turkmen Go Back to Old Calendar," *BBC News,* April 24, 2008, at http://news.bbc.co.uk/2/hi/asia-pacific/7365346.stm, on June 15, 2013.
50. "Turkmenistan Profile," *BBC News,* July 3, 2013, at http://www.bbc.co.uk/news/world-asia-16095366, accessed on July 16, 2013.
51. Murat Sadykov, "Turkmenistan: Schools to Scrap Late President's Holy Book," *Eurasianet.org,* August 2, 2013, at http://www.eurasianet.org/node/67336, on August 3, 2013.
52. Sadykov, "Turkmenistan ..."

9. Post-Soviet Media in Central Asia: With Special Focus on Coverage of Presidential Elections of Kyrgyzstan

Mohamad Reyaz

After Communism was discredited in Central Asia, there was a lot of euphoria about democratic experiments in the Central Asian Republics (CARs). Globalisation and liberalisation increasingly were viewed upon as essential remedies of the economic ills. However, each of these countries charted its own trajectory and had varying levels of transition in the past two decades. While most of the Central Asian ruling elites tried to control it, the liberal leaders in Kyrgyzstan insisted upon a larger role for civil society. This paper attempts to analyse the state of the media in the region based on available literature. In the second part of this essay, the inference drawn on the basis of analysis of the coverage of the 2011 Presidential elections in the country is brought to test.

Background

The local print trade, mostly in Arabic, became popular during the Tsarist period. In 1870, the official journal *Turkistan Wilayatining Gazeti* (TWG) began its circulation. TWG[1] was one of the first Turkic language periodicals in the Russian Empire and progressive reformers, namely, the *jadids*, became the real powers of the print. Newspapers for them became the source of enlightenment and symbol of progress. With the Bolshevik Revolution, by the summer of 1918, all print matter, including those in the vernacular languages, was nationalised. *Ishtirakiyun* (Communists) became the official organ of Turkomnats, and judging by its Arabian title, Adeeb Khalid argues, it retained a "Muslim flavour"—at least in the initial period when the *jadids* won some goodwill.[2]

During seventy years of the Soviet regime, the Russian as well as the native press had worked as a "mighty propaganda machine," and Soviet media played the role of "collective propagandist, agitator and organiser."[3] Gorbachev, however, revamped Soviet policies to take direct challenges from the West after assuming office as General Secretary in March 1985, especially since the April Plenum.[4] In the sphere of public information and knowledge, *glasnost* promised freedom of the spoken and the printed word in real socialist and pluralist terms.

According to most accounts, the indigenous intellectuals from the Central Asian republics were lagging far behind their counterparts in other parts of the Soviet Union in taking advantage of the changing political situation. Several rights groups and civil society members had, by 1990, nonetheless started their own newspapers and journals which were local in character, for example, *Mustagil Haftalik, Erlc Tumaris,* and *Munsobatin* in Uzbekistan, *Jam-iJam, Charogi Ruz*and *Adolat* in Tajikistan. These—as well as several government-run newspapers—now started expressing their opinions about the aspirations of the people and were critical of the establishment. This development, according to Haghayeghi, played a critical role in the adoption of national language laws in respective countries.[5]

The Media of Central Asia after Independence

It is generally believed that 1991 marked the end of "relative freedom" that the indigenous press had enjoyed during *glasnost*. The reason for this curtailment of rights of the press was because the authoritarian state was apprehensive of the widening role of civil society and the media was critical about the activities of corrupt politicians. Consequently, despite the effects of *glasnost* and the euphoria of independence, the little progress that was achieved was fast disappearing. The bureaucracy and party organs that developed during the seven decades of Soviet rule continued to dominate politics, with one single transformation—the Communist leaders converting themselves to "nationalist" ideologues who tried very hard for political stability—often at the expense of personal and political freedom. Severe restrictions were imposed both on the so-called independent media as well as the state controlled organisations in the formative years of post-Soviet administration.

Table I. **Freedom Indices of Central Asian Countries***

Country	Freedom Status	Political Rights	Civil Liberties
Kazakhstan	Not Free	6	5
Kyrgyzstan	Partly Free	5	5
Tajikistan	Not Free	6	5
Turkmenistan	Not Free	7	7
Uzbekistan	Not Free	7	7

* Source: *Freedom in the World 2012*, annual survey of political rights and civil liberties by the Freedom House. 1 reflects the "most free" and 7 the "least free" rating.

While the state media was subsidised in all these countries, independent media was allowed very little scope. In Tajikistan, Uzbekistan and Turkmenistan, the opposition press were closed by the end of 1992. Those that did survive, as in Kazakhstan and Kyrgyzstan, succumbed to economic pressure as circulation of papers had decreased sharply. Registration and circulation of newspapers were restricted. For example, of "an estimated 453 officially registered newspapers published on a regular basis until 1989, only 78 (old and new) survived the post-independence financial crisis in Kazakhstan. Similarly, in Kyrgyzstan, of the 114 newspapers published in 1990, only two could survive by 1994."[6]

The current state of media in all five CARs is somewhat ambiguous—both in paper as well as in practice. Table 1, shows the level of "freedom" in CARs as per Freedom House reports. Kyrgyzstan, for long, liked to project itself as an "island of democracy." The country still respects pluralism, like Kazakhstan. Uzbekistan and Turkmenistan, on the other hand, adopted an authoritarian stance. While their respective constitutions guarantee press freedom, in practice the public domain is highly regulated, and ambiguous constitutional amendments negate any positive effect. The situation is further complicated by a prejudiced judiciary.[7] The media of Central Asia had three broad categories, according to senior Uzbek journalist, Alisher Juraev: Kazakhstan and Kyrgyzstan being "authoritarian democratic," Tajikistan displaying a "post-conflict' syndrome" and the attitude in Turkmenistan and Uzbekistan as that of "total control."[8]

Table 2. **Media Sustainability Index (MSI): Overall Average Scores***

	Country	**MSI Score**
UNSUSTAINABLE ANTI-FREE PRESS (0-1)	Turkmenistan	0.30
	Uzbekistan	0.64
SUSTAINABLE MIXED SYSTEM (1-2)	Tajikistan	1.65
	Kazakhstan	1.68
	Russia	1.75
	Ukraine	1.81
	Georgia	1.88
	Kyrgyzstan	1.89
	Azerbaijan	1.89
NEAR SUSTANBILITY (2-3)	Armenia	2.01
	Kosovo	2.34
SUSTAINABLE PRESS (3-4)	None of the countries from South-east Europe, Caucasus, and Eurasia considered for the survey has sustainable press.	

* Source: The 2012 Media Sustainability Index (MSI) prepared by IREX with funding from USAID on the "development of sustainable independent media in Europe and Eurasia." (Average scores of free speech, professional journalism, plurality of news, sources, business management and supporting institutions.)

Media Sustainability Index (MSI), as displayed in Table 2, shows the following trends:

- Not a single country in the region has "sustainable press."
- Uzbekistan and Turkmenistan have "unsustainable anti-free press," while other three CARs—as also Russia—fall under "sustainable mixed system."
- It is interesting to note that several countries, including Kyrgyzstan has a relatively better average score than Russia.

In post-Soviet CARs journalists were expected to be loyal to their respective governments. Their goal was "not a vibrant press, but one that was uncritical of regimes."[9] To curtail pluralist voices, media houses were subjected to various restrictions—from registration to tax laws, anti-defamation, contempt, libel and secrecy laws to hostile situations. Those who are brave can try to be critical, but in a "diplomatic way, not in a sharp or hard way."[10] Besides, journalists also have to cope with financial pressure as remuneration for reporters is very low, and often many of them end up doing "hidden advertisements" or public relations (PR). Investigative articles have rarely been published. An editorial in the Media Insight Central Asia in 2002 made an opening statement: "Investigative reporting in the true sense of the word is a rarity in Central Asian countries."[11] Reporters are often asked to "tone down" sharp details from their articles by their editors.[12] The main problem for media organisations is that financially they are not able to sustain themselves, and ruling oligarchs exploit their precarious economic condition to their advantage. Media companies are thus reduced to "philanthropic" investments of mega companies.[13] The ruling elites increasingly use the media for their respective political agendas and to improve their image. Speaking of questionable ownership links of "independent" media organisations in Kazakhstan, Barbara Junisbai writes:

> In the last decade or so, financial and industrial groups with close ties to the President (owned by political elites and akin to oligarchs) have purchased or gained control over much of the country's print and electronic media ... For the most part the media avoid subjects that could get them in trouble with government officials ...[14]

It is not just political rivals who are using media for political gains, but even ruling elites use it to their advantage—taking a cue from the Soviet system—for "reinforcing authoritarianism through media control." This is common in countries like Uzbekistan and Turkmenistan. Practically there is not a single legal independent media house in Turkmenistan.[15]

Studies in the West are emphatic about seven "paralysing problems" about Tajik media, which, to a large degree, holds true for the entire region. These are: no independent news distribution, poor financial market conditions, high taxes, unprofessional journalism, unwilling to produces stories based on facts, censorship and self-censorship.[16] They cite "fear of authority" and "forced patriotism" imposed on journalists as the main reason behind self-censorship. However, it is not just the authoritarian politics, but also social norms and culture, family/clan traditions that often hold them back as journalists are discouraged from questioning traditions or even to be critical to them.[17]

Compared to other Central Asian states, media freedom is prominent in Kyrgyzstan. *AkiPress* and *Maiya Stolista* (My Capital), with generous US funding, brought before public glare the corruption inside Presidential circles. These papers played the role of "opposition" media during the Tulip Revolution in 2005."[18] Many question the veracity and inspiration of the 2005 "Tulip Revolution" and its April 2010 replication, and believe it to be "sponsored." While some argue that the "colour revolution" was an "indigenous" movement fuelled by unemployment, corruption, inflation and anger against the authoritarian regime, an equally large number of scholars are insistent about a "foreign hand." In 2010, when Roza Otunbayeva became interim President, the panel for the Media Sustainability Index (MSI) of International Research and Exchanges (IREX) had observed that the "legal framework was liberalised," that guaranteed freedom of speech and freedom of media.[19] But during the Osh ethnic riots between the Uzbeks and the Kyrgyz in June 2010, regulations had mounted and self-censorship was also frequent. The same report noted: "The vast majority of journalists and media played down the negative and suppressed photos and videos for fear of provoking a new wave of violence and an escalation of the conflict."

After the April Revolution, a considerable boom in Kyrgyz language press is noticeable.[20] It must be noted, though, that the degree of freedom in all CARs is certainly much better than it was in the Soviet period, when citizens had no civil or political rights.[21] Moreover, where traditional media appears to be failing, new media along with the international media appear as "beacons of hope" and "harbingers of change," much to the dislike of the authorities in the region. In "Blogging Down the Dictator ...," Kulikova and Perlmutter recorded how, despite very low internet users (11 out of 100 persons)[22] in Kyrgyzstan, blog reports played a "critical role in meaningfully contributing to the coverage of the Tulip Revolution" on the internet.[23] In April 2010, Roza Otunbayeva, former Kyrgyz Foreign Minister and the "coup" leader, who later became the interim President, used social media (Twitter) to beckon the "revolution." On April 7, 2010 Otunbayeva tweeted: "We want a free Kyrgyzstan! Bakiyev and his cowards are no match against the will of the Kyrgyz people!"[24]

It is true that international media organisations have their own interests and agendas in reporting. But in a media-space where information is often "censored" or suffer from local interests or are not available at all, international broadcasts of BBC, RFE/RL are often considered to be the only sources of "uncensored" character.[25] Many "independent" media organisations have also provided foreign aid and a number of news websites have been started by international organisations that focus either exclusively or extensively on the CARs. *Integrated Regional Information Network (IRIN)* News is part of United Nations Office of Humanitarian Affairs. Its Central Asian coverage includes Pakistan, Iran, Iraq and Afghanistan, besides the CARs. The *Institute of War and Peace Reporting* (IWPR), *EurasiaNet* and *Central Asia Online* (CAO) similarly cover the region and its vicinity. Russia-based *Ferghana.ru* often attracts attention for its "controversial" stance and was banned by the Kyrgyz authorities.[26]

Coverage of the Kyrgyz Presidential Election

The next part of this paper is a content-based analysis of a Kyrgyzstan based news agency *24.kg (www.24.kg)* and comparisons are made with those news reports made by Western agencies or sponsored by them in the context of 2011 Presidential elections. Contents of news updates on *24.kg* are compared and contrasted with samples from *IWPR*, *EurasiaNet* and *CAO*.[27] For the purpose of this study, the contents in English were accessed from the above four websites.[28]

This study focuses on the events stretching over a period of two months—between September 1 and December 1, 2011. The official campaign for the October 30 Presidential election in Kyrgyzstan began from September 25 and gradually peaked as the final date approached. With Almazbek Atambayev assuming responsibilities as President on December 1, 2011, the cycle of events that had begun in April 2010 with the removal of Kurmanbek Bakiyev and Roza Otunbayeva as interim President, completed its full circle. This research concentrated specifically on the events and articles concerning the much publicised Presidential elections in the country. However, articles that may not be directly related to the election, but those that might have had direct or indirect bearing on its outcome, or that might have reflected on the policies of the new government after the election, or those that appeared keeping in mind the next election have been considered here to get a complete image of the Kyrgyz elections in the aftermath of revolutionary upsurges. For example, ethnic tension in South Kyrgyzstan after the June 2010 riots and confidence-building measures among the Uzbek minority are connected to the election outcome. Normal court proceedings related to the ethnic riots have not been considered, exceptions being those articles that have expressed election-related opinions.

Table 3. **Election-related articles in *24.kg***

Dates	**Election**	**Related**	**Total Articles**
1-5 Oct	18	11	79
6-10 Oct	13	11	89
11-15 Oct	18	15	107
16-20 Oct	09	09	114
21-25 Oct	25	06	80
26-31 Oct	119	05	178
1-5 Nov	45	15	87
6-10 Nov	08	07	66
11-15 Nov	13	08	71
16-20 Nov	05	10	75
21-25 Nov	00	09	115
26 Nov-1 Dec	05	23	108
Total Articles	278	129	1,169
Total Articles in the Sample	**407 out of 1,169**		

Figure 1. **Frequency of Articles on Elections and Related Issues in 24.kg**

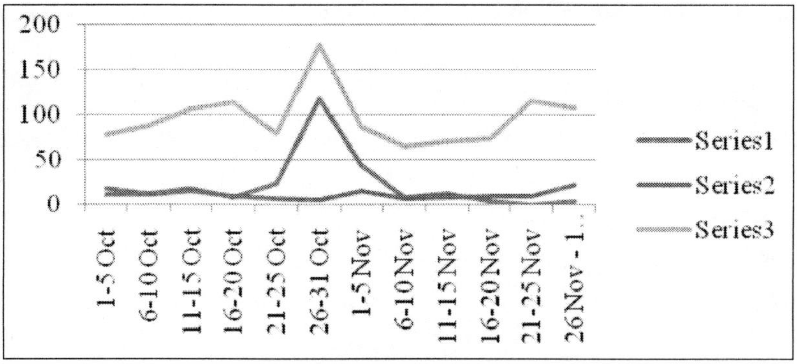

Contents of *24.kg* have been analysed quantitatively as well as qualitatively. This data is then compared with the coverage of the same event in West-sponsored news portals. A total of 470 articles in *24.kg* were considered for this study. From *CAO* 43 articles in the election category have been reviewed, from *EurasiaNet* 11 articles and from *IWPR* 9 articles in this period have been considered.

24.kg

Table 3 and Figure 1 show that of the total 1,169 articles, published on *24.kg* during this period, 407 articles, i.e., 34.8% of the write-ups were on election or related matters. A total of 278 articles were directly related to the election. In the election month of October, a total of 259 articles were published, of which 202 were directly related to elections, while 57 were on related issues.

On October 30, 2011, the agency filed a whopping 67 news updates, all of them concerning elections, from announcing its commencement in the morning till the time it ended. It also filed a number of stories on that day based on allegations and accounts of politicians and activists regarding ballot staff, administrative resources, unfair means adopted by authorities, etc. The following day (i.e., October 31) carried the second highest number of stories related to the election. Of the total 37 updates on the day, 30 were related to the events of elections, continuing the previous day trend of the stories concerning protests against the election result, accusations, counter-allegations and updates by the government on the ground situation. The high numbers of articles on election-related events continued to pour in, in the coming week as unsatisfied supporters of the defeated candidates were not ready to accept the result. In the week following the election, a total of 75 articles appeared. However, the number dwindled as the days passed, and rose slightly on December 1, when Atambayev took oath—3 directly related to the election and appointment of the President, and 6 dealing with other matters. After the global leaders hailed the constitutional process of Presidential elections in Kyrgyzstan, assurances of financial support began pouring in. In the month of October, there were just two news items on some kind of assurances by foreign countries or donor agencies—one about assurance of aid by Russia (on October 17)[29] and the other about UN's assurance to render aid (on October 24).[30] But in the month of November at least 16 items appeared acknowledging congratulatory remarks, from the US President to Chinese authority and other international agencies, or on assurances of aid. There were also cautious remarks about investigating the reasons behind allegations that cropped up after election results were announced.

Articles which were not directly related to election preparations, but were somehow connected to it, fell under seven broad categories, namely, consequences of the April uprising and the "authoritarian" regime of the deposed President Kurmanbek Bakiyev; the June 2010 Osh conflict; the question of Uzbek minorities and the North-South divide; religious extremism and economic statistics and reports especially by international agencies.

Table 4

Index	
Elections **(E)**	Economic Reports **(R)**
April Uprising/Bakiyev**(B)**	Parliament **(P)**
North-South Division/Uzbek Minority **(U)**	Foreign countries/agencies **(F)**
Religious Extremism/Terrorism **(T)**	Generally **(G)**

Coverage of Election in 24.kg									
		Related to the Election							
Dates	**E**	B	U	T	R	P	F	G	**Total Related Articles**
1-5 Oct	18	4	0	5	1	0	0	1	**11**
6-10 Oct	13	1	0	4	1	4	0	1	**11**
11-15 Oct	18	4	2	3	0	1	0	5	**15**
16-20 Oct	09	1	0	2	0	1	1	4	**09**
21-25 Oct	25	0	3	0	0	0	1	2	**06**
26-31 Oct	119	1	1	0	1	0	0	2	**05**
1-5 Nov	45	0	2	0	0	3	10	0	**15**
6-10 Nov	08	1	0	0	0	2	2	2	**07**
11-15 Nov	13	0	0	0	0	5	0	3	**08**
16-20 Nov	05	2	2	0	0	5	0	1	**10**
21-25 Nov	00	1	0	0	0	4	1	3	**09**
26 Nov-1Dec	05	1	1	0	0	7	2	12	**23**
Total Articles	278	16	11	14	03	31	17	36	**129**
Total Articles in the Sample: 278 + 129 = 407									

There were some other stories that did not directly fit in any of the above divisions, but appeared to be consequences of the election, or would have a certain degree of influence on its outcome. For example, on October 12, it ran an interesting "opinion" column correlating the current situation in the country with Sicily or Chicago of the 1930s when "crime was an integral part of the authorities." Titled "Godfather deputy?" the article talked of corruption among political elites.[31]

The fight against corruption in the KRG is confined to detention of university teachers, public employees and officials of middle management for taking bribes. Catching larger fishes is out of the question. Although senior officials are not tired of saying that corruption has reached the highest echelons of power.[32]

Figure 2. **Election coverage in *24.kg***

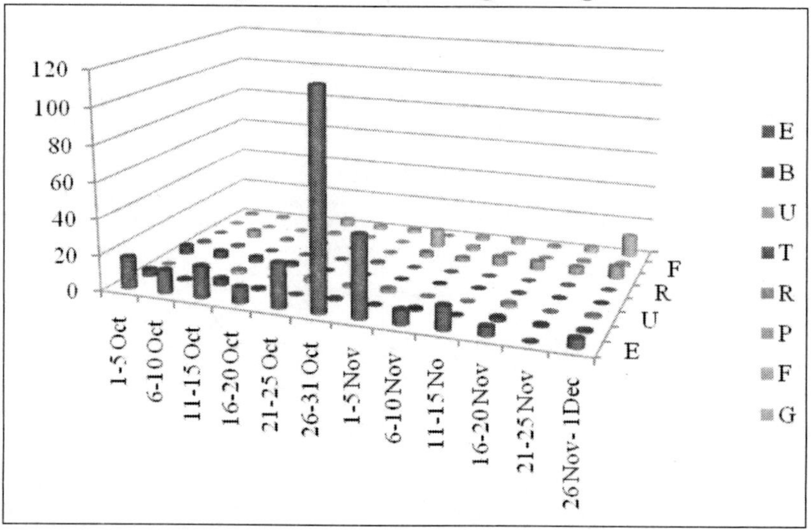

In all, 129 articles under the aforementioned seven related categories were considered for this study. In the election month a number of commentaries appeared that may have helped readers to make an enlightened choice. These articles critically looked at the campaigning race, the televised Presidential debate, election manifestos of respective candidates, corruption among ruling elites, the relevance of parliamentary form of government, etc. An interesting piece on November 1 asked the blunt question straight away: "Voted for what?"[33]

On December 1, in an opinion column, Asel Otorbaeva reflected upon the inaugural Presidential address and noted how, to the surprise of many, Almazbek Atambayev invoked God and "flavoured his inaugural speech with religious attributes."[34] The article further probed and cross-examined his speech, on his assurances for establishing "fair and honest government," and to work in coordination with other branches of the government.

Central Asia Online

CAO published 43 articles during the period October 1 to December 1 on the Presidential elections. Of these 43 write-ups, 21 directly covered the elections, while 22 were on related issues (see Table 6). A total of nine features were published on election or related issues, of which six were on election, North-South divide, and discontent among Uzbek minority. There were two features on the outgoing President for the transitional period Roza Otunbayeva—on November 1 and December 1—and one on investment policies (October 7).

Table 5

In-depth Articles on 24.kg between October 1 and December 1, 2011								
	Related to the Election							
E	B	U	T	R	P	F	G	Total Related Articles
20	2	0	1	0	4	0	12	**19**
Total Articles				**20 + 19 = 39**				

EurasiaNet

During two months under review *EurasiaNet* published 11 featured articles on election or related issues. Six of these were directly related to the election—all of which appeared between October 25 and 31, 2011.

Table 6

Election coverage between October 1 and December 1, 2011										
	Related to the Election									
Organisation	E	B	U	T	R	P	F	G	All Related Articles	**Total Articles**
24.kg	279	16	11	14	03	31	17	36	**128**	**407**
CAO	**18**	01	02	03	05	01	04	09	**25**	**43**
EurasiaNet	**04**	00	03	02	02	00	00	00	**7**	**11**
IWPR	**07**	00	01	00	00	00	00	01	**2**	**09**
Total Articles in the Sample:										**470**

Institute of War and Peace Reporting (IWPR)

IWPR published about nine articles during the period under review that were related to the Presidential elections in Kyrgyzstan. Seven of these were directly connected with the developments leading to the election and its result, while one article on October 24, 2011 voiced the concerns of Uzbek minorities who were "unsure whom to vote for," and according to this article, were looking for a candidate who is "not an avowed Kyrgyz nationalist."[35]

Comparison

24.kg, a private national news agency in Kyrgyzstan, no doubt publishes more articles about events in Kyrgyzstan, covering a wide spectrum of areas—protocol, business, and official news—the *ofitsioz*—compared to international organisations. However, most of the articles were brief news updates, often based on the statements or press conferences by one individual official, politician, activist or "expert." News organisations or news portals sponsored by the West thus play a critical role in filling this information vacuum. Features on *EurasiaNet* and *IWPR* particularly are stories that emphasise popular mood. Comparatively, both "indigenous" *24.kg* and West-sponsored news organisations lagged behind on this criterion. Although everyone agreed that after the transition government of Roza Otunbayeva took charge, media houses enjoyed greater freedom, and this was reflected in the stories that appeared even on *24.kg*. Experts, activists and politicians appeared to be openly criticising the government and its policies. Commentaries and opinion columns on *24.kg* were intensely critical of government policies, and were often interesting to read, although not always well organised. However, *24.kg* hardly encouraged "investigative journalism" during the period under review on election-related issues. The agency relied more on copy or desk editors, whose job is to write beautiful "copies" based on the statements or press releases, and on commentators, and not so much on "reporters."

Furthermore, from the qualitative analysis of articles, it appears that on some issues they followed the State's version and did not appear to critically explore the subject, maintaining a degree of caution and self-restraint. This was quite clear on their coverage of "growing religious extremism," "regional rift" and minority issues. Not a single story—not even columns—appeared to look critically at these subjects. *EurasiaNet* and *IWPR*, on the other hand, appear to be solely concerned about regional rift, minority issues, religious extremism, etc. In fact, all their articles, except those on economic policies, mentioned the lack of trust among minorities and the regional rift. Religious extremism might have been a major issue after June 2010 ethnic conflict, but it was naive of them to say this was the only issue during the elections. One region that found little or no mention in any of the articles, in not only Western-based news sites, but also in *24.kg,* was the northern region of the country. From the coverage it appears as if the voters in the North had no issue or grievances and that they all had decided well in advance whom to vote for. In fact going by the articles that have been published, it appears that the "developed North" was distinctly different from the "underdeveloped South."

In the emergent media-space of Central Asia, "insider" stories of a Kyrgyz news agency and a Western agency complement each other and help in better understanding of concerned subjects and issues. Such expectations have been echoed by various observers: "Western-based Web news sites provide alternative venues for some Central Asian journalists to independently cover such issues," it was said. Furthermore, "even journalists reporting on issues for Western-based media operate under tight constraints, including risk of official retaliation."[36]

Conclusion

In their zeal to guard their newly found independence and to maintain stability, the regional elites of Central Asia are trying to maintain, negotiate and accommodate political and cultural solidarity based on clan, tribe and regional loyalties.Thus what is often termed as post-Communist "reforms from scratch" is nothing more than "minor shift" in relative power of these ruling elites.[37] Soviet legacies still largely influence the attitude of the ruling elites, and affect their decision-making process. This is also evident in the centrally controlled media apparatus. Experts, authorities and most of the people expect the media to play a "constructive" role in development and integration of these newly found nations, and lament crass commercialisation and trivialisation of content in market-oriented media houses. On the coverage of the Presidential election, an OSCE report criticised the media for negligence and bias: "... a lack of independent editorial coverage undermined the quality of information available to voters to make an informed choice. Regrettably, most broadcast media refrained from covering the candidates outside of free and paid campaign spots and did not engage in analysis."[38]

All these countries, however, repeatedly articulate their "commitments" to the ideals of freedom and dissemination of information. There were mixed results too. For example, in Uzbekistan, the film industry considerably opened up to the market economy, while still retaining the "goods" from its Socialist era. The film industry enjoyed "complete creative freedom" unlike the Soviet era when films were made according to Socialist diktat.[39] While it is often pointed out that all CARs today certainly enjoy much more freedom than they supposedly had during Soviet days, there is no denial of the fact that today's media space in Central Asia is worse than most of the post-Soviet republics, with the possible exception of Kyrgyzstan. Globalisation has certainly brought new opportunities and opened up new horizons. Russian media still dominates the region, but Central Asian states have been able to express their pluralist choices with regard to information sources. Turkey, China, the USA and the European Union vie for a share in that media space.

Notes

1. Adeeb Khalid, *The Politics of Muslim Cultural Reform: Jadidism in Central Asia* (Berkeley: University of California Press, 1998).
2. Khalid, p. 291.
3. Lenin, quoted in Brian McNair, *Glasnost, Perestroika and the Soviet Media* (London: Routledge, 1991), p. 20.
4. A Central Committee Plenum held in April 1985 marked a major break with past policies, and initiated "revolutionary restructuring" of society.
5. Mehrdad Haghayeghi, "Media and Politics in Central Asia," *Demokratizatsiya*, www.demokratizatsiya.org/bin/pdf/DEM%2003-2%20Haghayeghi.PDF (accessed on September 14, 2011).
6. Haghayeghi.
7. International Research and Exchanges (IREX), "The Media Sustainability Index

(MSI)," prepared annually with funding from USAID (Washington DC: 2011), p. 267.

8. Alisher Juraev, "The Uzbek Mass Media Model: Analysis, Opinions, Problems," *Central Asia and the Caucasus*, vol. 13, no. 1 (2002), pp. 130-38.
9. Olivia Allison, "Loyalty in the New Authoritarian Model: Journalistic Rights and Duties in Central Asian Media Law," in Eric Freedman and Richard Shafer (eds.), *After the Czars and Commissars: Journalism in Authoritarian Post-Soviet Central Asia* (East Lansing, MI: Michigan State University Press, 2011), p. 144.
10. Umed Babakhanov, a Tajik media owner. Cited in Timothy Kenny and Peter Gross, "Journalism in Central Asia: A Victim of Politics, Economics, and Widespread Self-censorship," *The International Journal of Press/Politics*, no. 13 (October, 2008), pp. 515-25.
11. Aleksandr Khamagayev, "Investigative Reporting in Central Asian Countries," *Media Insight Central Asia,* pp. 30-31. URL: http://www.cimera.org/files/camel/en/30-31e/MICA30-31E-Editorial.pdf (accessed on January 5, 2012).
12. Khamagayev, "Investigative reporting….
13. MSI 2011, p. 256.
14. Barbara Junisbai, "Oligarchs and Ownership: The Role of Financial-Industrial Groups in Controlling Kazakhstan's 'Independent' Media," in Freedman and Shafer (eds.), *Journalism in Authoritarian Post-Soviet Central Asia*, p. 39.
15. Luca Anceschi, "Reinforcing Authoritarianism through Media Control: the Case of post-Soviet Turkmenistan," *Journalism in Authoritarian Post-Soviet Central Asia,* p. 73.
16. Peter Gross and Timothy Kenny, "Journalist Self-Censorship and the Tajik Press in the Context of Central Asia," in Freedman and Shafer (eds.), *Journalism in Authoritarian Post-Soviet Central Asia*, p. 124.
17. Timothy Kenny and Peter Gross, "Journalism in Central Asia: A Victim of Politics, Economics, and Widespread Self-censorship," *The International Journal of Press/ Politics*, no. 13, (October, 2008), pp. 515-25.
18. Charles Buxton, *The Struggles for Civil Society in Central Asia* (Boulder, CO: Kummarian Press, 2011), p. 75.
19. MSI 2011, p. 263.
20. MSI 2012, p. 289.
21. Phool Badan, "State and Democracy in Central Asia," in Ajay Patnaik and Tulsiram (eds.), *Globalisation and Eurasia* (New Delhi: KW Publishers, 2010), pp. 91-102.
22. According to World Bank Data in 2005, Internet penetration per 100 persons in Kyrgyzstan was 10.69. URL: http://data.worldbank.org/indicator/IT.NET.USER.P2 (accessed on September 15, 2011).
23. Svetlana V. Kulikova and David D. Perlmutter, "Blogging Down the Dictator? The Kyrgyz Revolution and Samizdat Web Sites," in Freedman and Shafer (eds.),

Journalism in Authoritarian Post-Soviet Central Asia, p. 283.

24. Roza Otunbayeva's Twitter feed, http://twitter.com/otunbayeva. Also cited in MSI 2011, p. 263.
25. Navbahor Imamova, "International Broadcasting to Uzbekistan: Does It Still Matter?" in Freedman and Shafer (eds.), *Journalism in Authoritarian Post-Soviet Central Asia,* p. 210.
26. March 1, 2012 statement by Lydia Imanalieva, the Permanent Representative of the Kyrgyz Republic to the OSCE. URL: http://www.osce.org/pc/88749 (accessed on March 5, 2012).
27. EurasiaNet is affiliated with the New York-based Open Society Institute's Central Eurasia Project, and covers Turkey, Azerbaijan, Mongolia, Armenia, Georgia and Afghanistan, besides the five CARs. IWPR is a London-based organisation focusing on regions of conflict, including Iraq, Caucasus, Afghanistan and the CARs. Stories related to the region on IWPR and EurasiaNet are available both in Russian and English. CAO is sponsored by the United States Central Command (USCENTCOM) and covers the CARs as well as Afghanistan and Pakistan. CAO too publishes articles in Russian and English as well as in Persian and Urdu.
28. Same contents are put in Russian and English versions on these websites. Here, only English content have been used.
29. "Russia Will Invest $12 Million in the Development of the Southern Regions of Kyrgyzstan until the End of 2011-Valentin Vlasov," *24 kg* (October 17, 2011). URL: http://eng.24.kg/community/2011/10 /17/20966.html (accessed on May 15, 2012).
30. "The UN to Render aid to Kyrgyzstan in the Amount of $186 M," *24 kg* (October 24, 2011). URL: http://eng.24.kg/community/2011/10/24/21087.html (accessed on May 15, 2012).
31. Tolgonai Osmongazieva, "Godfather Deputy?" *24.kg* (October 12, 2011). URL: http://eng.24.kg/vi ewpoints/2011/10/12/20880.html (accessed on May 15, 2012).
32. Osmongazieva, "Godfather Deputy?"….
33. Julia Mazykina, "Post-election Kyrgyzstan: Voted for What?" *24.kg* (November 1, 2011). URL: http://eng.24.k g/politic/2011/11/01/21326.html (accessed on May 15, 2012).
34. Asel Otorbaeva, "What the New President of Kyrgyzstan Has Brought to Us (Reflections on the Inaugural Speech)," *24.kg* (December 1, 2011). URL: http://eng.24.kg/politic/2011/12/01/21 83 1.html (accessed on May 15, 2012).
35. "Uzbeks Unsure Who to Pick in Kyrgyzstan Election," *Institute of War and Peace Reporting* (October 24, 2011). URL: http://iwpr.net/report-news/uzbeks-unsure-who-pick-kyrgyzstan-election (accessed on May 23, 2012).
36. Eric Freedman, "Coverage of the Central Asian Political, Press, and Speech Rights Issues by Independent News Websites," in *Asia Pacific Media Educator*, no. 16

(2005), pp. 71-88. URL: http://ro.uow.edu.au/apme/vol1/iss16/10 (accessed on May 23, 2012).

37. For details see Pauline Jones Luong, *Institutional Change and Political Continuity in Post-Soviet Central Asia* (Cambridge: Cambridge University Press, 2004).
38. OSCE/ODIHR Election Observation Mission Final Report on the "Kyrgyz Republic Presidential Election." Office for Democratic Institutions and Human Rights is a principal institution of the OSCE. URL: http://www .osce.org/odihr / elections/86926 (accessed on April 15, 2012).
39. Rashmi Doriswamy, "Dynamics of Transition: Films from Central Asia," in Suchandana Chatterjee and Anita Sengupta (ed.), *Communities, Institutions and "Transition" in Post-1991 Eurasia* (New Delhi: Shipra Publications for MAKAIAS, 2011), pp. 445-65.

10. Europeanisation at the "Grassroots" Level in Moldova: What Are Effective Ways to Deal with the Transnistrian conflict?

Keiji Sato

Transnistria (*Pridnestrovskaia Moldavskaia Respublica*) is defined as a case of "unrecognised state" or "de facto independent state" of the former Soviet republics, which possesses an independent government, financial system and security force, and whose territory Moldova, its de jure host country, is unable to control. The resolution of the Transnistrian conflict is one of the priority state tasks for the Moldovan government, which images early EU integration as cyanotype. However, since the outbreak of the armed conflict between the Moldovan National Army and the Transnistrian paramilitary forces in June 1992, there has been no effort to resolve the conflict through political dialogue and negotiation tables among key members, despite intermediation by OSCE, Russia, Ukraine, the USA and the EU. It is no exaggeration to say that the conflict is "frozen" in terms of diplomatic methods.

Under such conditions, the "grassroots" approach drawing on the basis of "Europeanism" has lately attracted considerable attention for resolution of the conflict. In contrast to a short-term resolution by way of diplomacy, it is a long-term one to promote and deepen mutual understanding among local inhabitants beyond borders. International societies and organisations, such as OSCE, the UN and the EU, have financially supported the "grassroots" activities of NGOs and other associations in order to lay the groundwork for the penetration of European standards among non-political people in the field of finance, law, education and culture in Transnistria. It is expected that such common groundwork would at last help to preserve public order in society, albeit in any kind of future political changes in the concerned area.

This paper analyses, using the case of Transnistria, by what vision, idea and strategy international organisations and NGOs contribute to cross-border non-political activities for resolution of the Transnistrian conflict. This paper also focuses on the concept of Europeanism as one method of conflict resolution of the former Soviet space.

"Deadlock" of the Transnistrian conflict

The Transnistrian conflict, unlike the other cases of unrecognised states such as Nagorno-Karabakh, South Ossetia and Abkhazia, has shown a lesser tendency of ethnic and religious hostility among the people concerned. In the beginning of the conflict, however, there was the issue of "ethnicity." In March 1989 the conflict originated from an ethnic confrontation between Moldovans, who tried to establish a more powerful political voice and domestic political influence, and non-Moldovans, mainly Russian speakers in Transnistria, who were opposed to the nationalist and radical movement of the Moldovans. As time has passed, however, there have been political struggles between the centre, Chisinau, and the periphery, Transnistria, where there is Russian predominance, and Gagauzia, where there is a Turkish presence. After January 1991, when the Moldovan government suspended payment to the union republic's quota of the USSR budget, regional politicians and entrepreneurs in Transnistria declared the intention of forming a special regional economic zone, and becoming economically and politically independent of Chisinau control. After the collapse of the USSR, the conflict finally turned to a central-peripheral one, involving Transnistrian politicians and entrepreneurs whose aim was the preservation of their own vested interests in that region.

From another aspect, the Transnistrian conflict was expected to be resolved relatively more easily than other complicated ones of the former Soviet states with ethnic and religious overtones. Firstly, this conflict has features different from interstate war such as the Nagorno-Karabakh case. About cases of "frozen conflict," the major difficulty of resolving them lies in dealing with interstate conflicts.[1]

Secondly, unlike the cases of the Caucasus area, Moldova and Transnistria are located more closely, next to the sphere of EU influence. Compared with other secessionist cases, Transnistria is closer to the EU and the process of Europeanisation—defined in terms of norms and values—will therefore take shorter paths.[2]

Thirdly, the resolution of the Gagauz conflict in December 1994, which erupted in the southern part of Moldova, gave Moldovan authority a hope to resolve the Transnistrian conflict by the same manner, to provide "wider autonomy."

Despite such hope, however, the conflict has not been found an exit towards resolution; what is called "deadlock" or "blind alley" in diplomacy. The main reason is the high-level of industrial potentiality and power in Transnistria: Transnistrian authority controls regional heavy industry, which makes it possible to earn foreign currency by trading with neighbouring countries without legal restrictions and to organise a Transnistrian state budget. As a result, the Transnistrian side does not accept any kind of proposal which could compromise the existent vested interests by reconciliation with Moldova and observation of the Moldovan constitution and international laws. The Moldovan government is offering "wider autonomy" to Transnistria, while Transnistrian authorities are demanding an independent subject with independent security and financial systems under a confederative framework with Moldova. The two sides still remain as far apart as ever from resolution of the Transnistrian conflict.

Europeanism in Moldova

Twenty years since the outbreak of the violent outcome in Moldova, there have been two geopolitical consequences on the Black Sea region. One is the colour revolution—the Orange revolution in Ukraine and the Rose revolution in Georgia in 2005—and the other is the EU integration of Romania and Bulgaria in 2007. As a result of these two influences, the distance between the EU and Transnistria becomes geographically shorter. This shortening of distance has affected a larger EU political influence on Moldova, with the EU having greater opportunity to intervene in the Transnistrian conflict.

Among all actors, Russia, which acts as a "mediator" of the conflict and deploys the Russian army in Transnistria, has been the greatest influence in the resolution of the conflict. The Transnistrian case has shown strong ethnic links as "the Russian diaspora" more than in any other secessionist movement. High-ranking sources in the Russian Foreign Ministry assured that it would agree to unite with Moldova if consolidated pressure on Tiraspol is strengthened.[3]

However, Russia will never renounce the right of patronage because Russian speakers in Transnistria strongly demand its protection, even with the help of armed forces. The Russian military in Transnistria also provides employment and security for separatist force.[4]

For these reasons, Russia did not and will not take up the role of a "fair" intermediary between Chisinau and Tiraspol.

Due to Russian interests, the US and the EU could not intervene and exercise their power for the resolution of the conflict. Mediation by the US and individual European states failed in the 1990s. After this, direct intervention by the West meant an increased risk of antagonising the Transnistrian authorities against them. It was alleged that the West stimulated the collapse of the Soviet Union and social chaos in the former Soviet countries. Many inhabitants in Transnistria, among whom the majority are Russian speakers, have had a negative image towards interference (intermediation) in the conflict by the West. Therefore, the EU is more concerned with cooperation with international organisations and NGOs in the long run and avoids short-term policies like intervention by individual countries such as Germany or the UK. This policy focuses more on grassroots approaches to resolution on the basis of confidence building in border regions. For promoting confidence building between the EU and regional inhabitants in Transnistria and for stabilising regional security, the measure of sharing identity based on Europeanism is one of the most important ideas. Europeanism in this context means the action promoted by the international organisations and NGOs, by which all political actors of conflict integrate into the European institution in various fields step by step.

Even though the West is not directly involved in the activities, the penetration of Europeanism could be a menace to the authority of the unrecognised state if it has the tendency to take a pro-Russia or anti-West position. In fact, the Transnistrian authority, which was led by the former Transnistrian president Igor Smirnov for many years, shows distrust of international organisations and NGOs financed and supported by EU member states. A symbolic case is the "school war" in Transnistria. The six Moldovan schools, in which the medium of instruction is the Latin script, had less than 4,000 students in Transnistria in 2006.

The Transnistrian "constitution" defines three state languages, Russian, Ukrainian and Moldovan, and among them, Moldovan must use the Cyrillic script in continuation of the Soviet period. The Romanian language (Moldovan language with Latin script) that is taught in the six Moldovan schools is partially supported by the OSCE in terms of distribution of teaching material. The Transnistrian authorities tried to close these schools several times. In 2004 July, then Minister for Education, Elena Bomeshko, forcibly closed three among the six schools and stressed that the schools did not comply with local education laws and had neither the licence nor accreditation.[6]

The EU and the Council of Europe expressed alarm at the closure of the schools. The EU requested the Transnistrian authorities to restore the status quo for Moldovan-language schools. Furthermore, the EU began introducing visa restrictions against the individuals responsible for the decisions leading to the closure of the schools.

Finally the Transnistrian authorities had to stop the closure.[8]

Despite such debate and tussle, most of the leading political figures, including local inhabitants, have a strong desire to belong to the wealthy EU countries. The Europeanisation dream continues.

CBM as a case of Europeanism

Compared to less visible post-Soviet states, Transnistria has a good resource base with heavy and light industries. This has both negative and positive effects in terms of resolution of the Transnistrian conflict. The negative effect, as mentioned before, is that Trasnistrian entrepreneurs and politicians try to retain their vested interests and never lose them. High population density and development of industry in major Transnistrian cities produce more human and physical resources, and have a greater possibility of keeping the status of de facto independence than Abkhazia or South Ossetia. The positive one is, on account of this highly developed area, that Transnistria needs to establish economic relations with wealthy EU member states.

The main industry in Transnistria, Ribnita steel plant, depends mainly on trading with EU member states, Ukraine and Russia. The Moldova Steel Works in Ribnita was founded in 1985 and is a modern highly productive steel company with CIS and major international standards. [9]

Transnistrian domestic market and the CIS market are limited, therefore the steel plant needs stable access to the EU market. The Transnistrian state budget can hardly survive without proper trading relations with neighbouring states, including the EU. In this sense, Trasnistrian companies find high profits and interests through the smooth traffic of trading and a common value and legal standard of economic activities, following the EU standard. It is assumed that mastering the common trading norms and business rules brings great profit for Transnistrian entrepreneurs.

One of the materialised aspects of Europeanism, promoted by NGOs and international organisations, is the Confidence Building Measure (CBM). The economic aspect is also important in the CBM. In the case of the Transnistrian conflict, there are two types of confidence building measures—one is by UNDP and the other by working groups monitored by OSCE. UNDP's CBM shows more neutral and non-political colour. It supports the building and repair of schools and infrastructure, opening of business schools in accordance with European standards, and supply of medical facilities. Among these, the scheme of building and repairing schools resulted in conflict with Transnistrian authorities, which is a by-product of "the school war" that cropped up since 1992. In the course of the author's interview with the project manager of UNDP, the Transnistrian authorities showed lack of support for UNDP's CBM, but could not deny it either. Local inhabitants in Transnistria especially benefit from projects to repair water pipelines and functioning clinics, and entrepreneurs from mastering business contracts and rules followed by EU standards. Transnistrian authority cannot always regulate such projects that may increase the standard of living of local inhabitants.

Another CBM monitored by OSCE is based on the cooperation between the Moldovan government and the Transnistrian side. Unlike UNDP's CBM, this OSCE-monitored CBM has wider political features because both political parties are required to collaborate. Working groups of CBM consist of eight categories, (1) economy and trade, (2) agriculture and ecology, (3) railways, transport and infrastructure, (4) law enforcement cooperation, (5) humanitarian aid, (6) health and social issues, (7) education, science and youth and (8) demilitarisation and confidence building in the military sphere. The aim of the working groups is to inculcate European standards and international norms into Moldovan society andTransnistria. The eighth working group is dysfunctional because of opposition from the Transnistrian side. This case shows that Transnistria is quite sensitive to the political aspect. Furthermore, most of the working groups do not work well owing to lack of cooperation from Transnistria. These working groups, five years after their establishment, had yet to bring about remarkable achievement. However, in 2011 after interaction between Igor Smirnov, the former Transnistrian President, and Vlad Filat, the former Moldovan Prime Minster, the working group of railways, transport and infrastructure began to function for reopening telecommunication and railroads. As a result, freight trains partially go from Odessa via Tiraspol to Chisinau.

The full-scale functioning of these working groups is expected to help the establishment of common European standards and promote mutual understanding of regional inhabitants beyond borders. In the course of this author's interview with members of the Moldova OSCE mission, it was evident that the players concerned are not at ease with physical and mental borders between Moldova and Transnistria, and wish to keep all channels of dialogue among them open at any cost, because these might make way for future reconciliation among political actors and local inhabitants. The present situation of working groups of OSCE's CBM shows that such participants have a greater possibility of reaching a compromise in the economic and trading field than in the security and cultural field. Relationships in the border region in neutral and profitable fields may be extended further to other fields. This will generate a positive effect on the future relationships among local people in border regions, not only of Moldova and Transnistria but also of the greater EU and the post-Soviet space.

Border Control by EUBAM

Besides two CBMs, there is a remarkable measure concerning border control for the resolution of the Transnistrian conflict. The border regions between Moldova and Transnistria are not completely closed; for instance, university students from Transnistria still have the ability to study in Chisinau. That is a clear contrast to the Abkhazian-Georgian, South Ossetian-Georgian and Nagorno-Karabakh-Azerbaijan borders, which are completely closed from both sides. In a wider sense, Moldova, unlike Georgia and Azerbaijan, still manages to maintain territorial integrity, and has inflow and outflow of people and goods beyond the border.

European Union Border Assistance Mission to Moldova and to Ukraine (EUBAM) indirectly assists in solidifying Moldovan territorial integrity. Until the time when the former Ukrainian president, Yushchenko, agreed border control with Moldova, the Moldovan border control authorities did loosen control in the border of Moldova along Ukraine, which was de facto controlled by Transnistria. By conducting the EUBAM border control system in 2006, which is financed by EU member states, Moldovan and Ukrainian joint customs function along the Transnistrian-Ukrainian border. Following the EUBAM system, the Moldovan government gave rights to trading in the EU zone to Transnistrian entrepreneurs with official documents of registration as companies, with such registrations headquartered in Moldova. Without the registration, companies based in Transnistria cannot officially trade with companies in the EU. The number of the registrations is increasing rapidly every year.[10]

This author's interview with an expert reveals the doubt about actual economic and legal control over Transnistria by the Moldovan government. Several companies just register and do not pay any tax to the Moldovan government. Also, some of them are not functional.

The EUBAM system cannot be managed by Moldova itself and depends greatly on the Ukrainian government. EUBAM was organised by the strong leadership of Victor Yushchenko, when he was the Ukrainian president after the Orange revolution. There was doubt that Victor Yanukovich might abolish the EUBAM system for supporting the Russian stance against the unrecognised states. However, till now, the Ukrainian government officially does not recognise the independence of Abkhazia and South Ossetia, and on the same lines, Yanukovich does not recognise the independence of Transnistria. It is more important for Ukraine to control Crimea than to show "loyalty" towards Russia. In any case, the Ukrainian government takes a careful attitude in abolishing EUBAM which might strengthen the de facto independent status of Transnistria. Also, we should notice that the current Moldovan "national integration" depends largely on Ukrainian policy and is quite fragile.

National territorial integration is one of the indispensable factors for an independent state. While the Moldovan government appreciates border control by EUBAM, which Moldova could not conduct by itself, Transnistrian authority opposed it as a sort of "economic sanction to Transnistrian general public." EUBAM also functions as a working group, which instructs local inhabitants of the importance of border control and the observation of international laws. It promotes the Europeanisation of Transnistria.

NGO

UNDP, OSCE, USAID and EU member states jointly endorse the confidence-building measures, aimed at increasing confidence among people living on both sides of the Nistru River. According to the actual results of 2012, 116 project proposals based on the programme have been submitted by non-governmental organisations and 12 proposals from both sides were selected.[11]

The project proposals are also evaluated by the Government of the Republic of Moldova. The programme has five core areas: business development, civil society, renovation of social infrastructure through local development, health care and environment. To conduct the programme, active involvement and participation of local authorities are required just as is required the involvement of civil society, business communities and other stakeholders from both sides of the Nistru River,

Chisinau and Tiraspol. The budget of the CBM is valued at 13.1 million euros for 2012-2015; 12 million euros were allotted by the European Union, whereas another 1.1 million euros were assigned by UNDP.[12]

Among the best examples of non-political activities by NGOs that are supported by UNDP and EU member states, is the *WE.Bridge* project in Chisinau. The project aims at building bridges in order to remove the communication gap between the youth on the left and right banks of the Nistru River. The Institute for Public Policy, a think tank in Chisinau, technically supports this project. The project uses an interactive web platform for creating favourable grounds for interaction and constructive dialogue between the both sides of the Nistru River. The *WE.Bridge* emphasises—"the youth are the main Internet users and the cyber environment has no borders, it is censorship-free, the language audience is broad, and an unlimited number of youth can interact."[13]

Considering the fast pace of IT innovation, the more the younger generation is involved, the more it will help in conflict resolution.

The Information Resource Centre *Common Home* in Tiraspol is also activated toward the same goal with *WE.Bridge*. *Common Home* aims at building a multicultural, tolerant and diverse society in Transnistria through cultural dialogue and civic diplomacy, tolerance and diversity, human and minority rights and active participation of young people on both sides of the Nistru River. Their areas of work include human rights, peace building in Transnistria, free access to information, education for all, European house-building and visit-Transnistria project. *European House* was established for learning more about the work in different EU institutions for Transnistrian local inhabitants. The visit-Transnistria project is quite unique, especially as it is supported by the Transnistrian youth who welcome foreigners and visitors from Chisinau to visit Transnistria. So this project expects that foreigners and people from Chisinau visit to Transnistria and remove the biased view about "Europe's Northern Korea." The *Come Home* project attaches greater importance to interactive relationships. The main tools for "enlightenment" of Europeanism are: information campaigns through training, round tables and debates, experience of actual immersion in European Union environment in the field of economic strategy, media and culture, social issues, and legislation. There are many non-political organisations with similar aims, and therefore the Transnistrian authorities can hardly regulate them.

Individual EU member states with own state funds assist in development of civil sector in Transnistria, which is expected to be the long-term support of small NGOs and initiative groups. In the case of the Czech Republic, the activities of the 2010 project were: small sub grants for NGOs and initiative groups, seminars, English courses for NGO representatives, study trip to the Czech Republic for selected NGO members and two-month long internship for two representatives of Transnistrian civil sector.[14]

Conclusion

The environment of the Transnistrian conflict has been changing every moment. The Transnistrian conflict as well as Abkhazian and South Ossetian conflicts emerged due to confrontation between titular nations of republics and non-titular nations due to decrees about official languages of the republics. After that first step, however, each case was directed to different ways. The case of Transnistria was viewed in terms of a political struggle—looking at whether a highly industrialised zone could be separated from Moldova and could survive as an independent entity at the beginning of 1991. As this paper has discussed, the substance of the Transnistrian conflict became a central-periphery conflict over the economic and political interests. The Transnistrian authorities that have vested interests as a "de facto independent state" are satisfied with the status quo that Chisinau cannot interfere in Transnistrian politics. Under such conditions, Transinistria will hardly accept becoming a part of Moldova without guarantee of "large autonomy" in the framework of a confederation.

Another difficulty for the resolution of the Transnistrian conflict is that Transnistria and Moldova are located on the "border" of sphere of interests between Russia and the EU. That is to say, the area is in a fault line of Russian and Western civilisations. The outbreak of "school war" in Transnistria is an exclusive example that the Moldovan government and Transnistrian authority were still in a state of confrontation along border lines of "East" and "West," and between Russia and Europe.

At the same time, the fact is that the mental and physical border between West and East in the European continent is shifting, and moving to the East year by year. Moldova is not yet an EU member state, but has already been an EU neighbouring state since 2007. The EU has great concern in resolving the Transnistrian conflict in order to secure the EU. Natalia German, the Deputy Ministry of Foreign Affairs and European Integration in Moldova, believes that the expansion of the EU visa regime toward Moldovan citizens may provide a great impact in resolving the Transnistrian conflict, because it would be attractive to Transnistrian inhabitants to obtain Moldovan citizenship as "EU citizens," and finally push forward the national unification among people. The composition of visa regime with UNDP's CBM, OSCE's CBM and EUBAM may only be a promising method for resolving the Transnistrian conflict.

Notes

1. INFOTAG, November 20, 2006.
2. BASA-PRESS, July 19, 2004.
3. INFOTAG, August 12, 2004.
4. REPORTER .MD, August 30, 2005.
5. http://www.undp.md/presscentre/2012/CBM_13December/index.shtml (access: 2013. 06. 10).
6. http://www.allmoldova.com/en/moldova-news/1249052731.html (access: 2013. 06. 10).
7. http://www.webridge.md/en (access: 2013. 06. 10).
8. http://www.mzv.cz/jnp/en/foreign_relations/human_rights/transition_promotion_program/target_countries/moldavia_1/strengthening_of_civil_society_v.html (access: 2013. 06. 10).
9. JSC Moldova Steel Works, *http://www.aommz.com/pls/webus/webus.main.show* (accessed on October 6, 2013).
10. EUBAM annual report 2009, *http://www.eubam.org/files/EUBAM%20AR%202009%20EN.pdf* (accessed on October 6, 2013); *Summary EUBAM Activity Report*, December 1, 2009–May 31, 2010.
11. http://www.undp.md/presscentre/2012/CBM_13December/index.shtml (accessed on October 6, 2013).
12. http://www.allmoldova.com/en/moldova-news/1249052731.html (accessed on October 6, 2013).

13. http://www.webridge.md/en (accessed on October 6, 2013).
14. http://www.mzv.cz/jnp/en/foreign_relations/human_rights/transition_promotion_program/target_countries/moldavia_1/strengthening_of_civil_society_v.html (accessed on October 6, 2013).

References

Bridge over the Dniestr: Confidence-Building Measures in Moldova, International Peace Institute, 2011 March, http://www.operationspaix.net/DATA/DOCUMENT/4266~v~Bridge_Over_the_Dniestr__Confidence-Building_Measures_in_Moldova.pdf (accessed on October 6, 2013).

Viacheslav Chirikba, "Geopolitical Aspects of the Abkhazian Statehood: Some Results and Perspectives," *Iran & the Caucasus*, vol. 8, no. 2, 2004.

Bruno Coppieters, "The Georgian-Abkhaz Conflict," in *Europeanization and Conflict Resolution: Case Studies from the European Periphery*, edited by Bruno Coppieters, Michael Emerson, Michel Huysseune, Tamara Kovziridze, Gergana Noutcheva, Nathalie Tocci and Marius Vahl (Gent: Academia Press, 2004).

Countdown to War in Georgia: Russia's Foreign Policy and Media Coverage of the Conflict in South Ossetia and Abkhazia(Minneapolis: East View Press, 2008).

Mark Duffield, "NGO Relief in War Zones: Towards an Analysis of the New Aid Paradigm," *Third World Quarterly*, vol. 18, no. 3, 1997.

EUBAM annual report 2009, http://www.eubam.org/files/EUBAM%20AR%20 2009%20EN.pdf (accessed on October 6, 2013).

EUBAM annual report 2010, http://www.eubam.org/files/MR_2011_ENG_FINAL_EUBAM.pdf (accessed on October 6, 2013).

EUBAM annual report 2011, http://www.eubam.org/files/20120530124428564363 annual_report_2011_eng.pdf (access: 2013. 06. 10).

EUBAM annual report 2012, http://www.eubam.org/files/Report_2012_ENGL.pdf (accessed on October 6, 2013).

Maria Raquel Freire, *Conflict and Security in the Former Soviet Union: The Role of the OSCE* (Burlington: Ashgate, 2003).

Dmitry Furman and Carl Johan Asenius, "The Case of Nagorno-Karabakh (Azerbaijan)," in *Peacekeeping and the Role of Russia in Eurasia*, edited by Lena Jonson and Clive Archer (Boulder: Westview Press, 1996).

Nicole J. Jackson, *Russian Foreign Policy and the CIS: Theories, Debates and Actions* (London and New York: Routledge, 2003).

JSC Moldova Steel Works, http://www.aommz.com/pls/webus/webus.main.show (accessed on October 6, 2013).

Charles King, "The Benefits of Ethnic War: Understanding Eurasia's Unrecognized States," *World Politics*, vol. 53, Cambridge University Press, July 2001.

Pal Kolsto and Andrei Edemsky with Natalya Kalashnikova, "The Dniester Conflict:

Between Irredentism and Separatism," *Europe-Asia Studies*, vol. 45, no. 6, 1993.

Florian Kucher, *The Role of the European Union in Moldova's Transnistria Conflict* (Stuttgart: Ibidem-Verlag, 2008).

Dov Lynch, "Separatist States and Post-Soviet Conflicts," *International Affairs*, vol. 78, no. 4, 2000.

OSCE Guide on Non-military Confidence-Building Measures (CBMs), http://www.osce.org/cpc/91082 (accessed on October 6, 2013).

Summary EUBAM Activity Report, December 1, 2009–May 31, 2010.

UNDP Moldova, Support to Confidence Building Measures, http://www.undp.md/projects/Transnistria.shtml (accessed on October 6, 2013).

11. Comparing Post-communism "Big" and "Small": The Inaugural Elections in Russia and Macedonia

Dmitry Seltser

The Argument

This paper aims to compare the inaugural elections in Macedonia and Russia. At one point in time, both countries were Socialist states. Macedonia used to be part of former Yugoslavia while Russia was the main state belonging to the former Soviet Union. There is, however, a difference in the scale and degrees of comparison between the two countries. The population of Macedonia is slightly above 2 million people. The population of contemporary Russia is currently above 143 million. The Macedonian territory comprises roughly 25 thousand square kilometres while Russia is gigantic—nearly 18 million square kilometres. Russia was the most developed among the Soviet Socialist Republics. Macedonia was the least developed republic in former Yugoslavia. The Soviet Union as a body was formed literally around Russia, while the Yugoslavian Federation was formed around Serbia, with Macedonia being a small part of its periphery.

This is the broad reason why this paper is entitled "Comparing Post-communism Big and Small." The title, of course, is just wordplay: it is understood that there is no such thing as large post-communism and small post-communism formally. Rather, the aim here is to show how the democratic political process developed and evolved in both the biggest and smallest Socialist countries.

What tasks and/or problems do "inaugural elections" decide and solve?
Democratic transition theory considers "inaugural elections" as the crucial starting point.[1] It is the first cycle of free elections taking place after a people have rejected authoritarianism. In this process of democratic transition, "inaugural elections" are meant to do several things: first, create a new system of political institutions; second, form a party system; third, legitimise the new political regimes; and fourth, limit and hinder the possibilities for any return to non-democratic forms of government. In other words, "inaugural elections" are the first and most essential stage for democratic transition.

What kind of transition results ought to be seen in real terms?

- "Inaugural elections" need to reflect an understanding among elite groups. That is, we should get a sense of political agreement and consensus between governing elites and the opposition groups.
- "Inaugural elections" ought to be on the fast track. That is, they should be held immediately after the fall of the authoritarian regime.
- "Inaugural elections" should be all-encompassing. That is, power must be democratically chosen from all levels of the society.
- "Inaugural elections" ought to take place under the conditions of a functioning multiparty system. These last two aspects are absolutely complementary to each other.
- "Inaugural elections" ought to be the way and means for democratising an all-encompassing socio-political system. In other words, the elections themselves are not only a mechanism for the realisation of technical problems, but are in fact an instrument for the real-term democratisation of society as a whole.
- The people must have trust in the outcome of the "inaugural elections."
- Finally, "inaugural elections" must change the attitude of political elites. In any case, this is the experience of most of the countries that have undergone transition—after losing the people's faith, the elites end up losing the inaugural elections.

What are the election trends and results of the "inaugural elections" in Russia and Macedonia?

The Russian Case

1. Pact/Consensus

It is difficult to find direct evidence of "pacts"/agreement/consensus in Russia. The elite and opposition groups never reached a consensus until now. The various branches of power began to confront one another. This confrontation led in part to the storming of the Russian White House in 1993 and the dissolution of the entire system of representative government. In fact, this was a massive inter-elite collision. In light of this, it is important to emphasise that in August 1991 the President of Russia and the Supreme Soviet were steadfast partners in the fight against the leadership of the Communist Party of the USSR.

2. Speed

Boris Yelstin did not fast-track the "inaugural elections" and decided upon them only when he was certain that the state was secure to the greatest extent possible. Until then it was highly likely that he was ready to postpone it, if not outright cancel the presidential elections in 1996. If that had taken place, then the "inaugural elections" in Russia would have formally been illegitimate. That is, the "inaugural elections" in Russia would have in large measure been a deferred project. How is this so? Analysts of the party "Democratic Russia" had themselves predicted large-scale defeats of Yeltsin supporters (for example, they predicted only 10-12 victories across in all gubernatorial elections). It was this very prognosis which served as the basis to realise the plan that would come to be known as the "executive vertical." The establishment of the Congress of People's Deputies of the Russian Federation on November 1, 1991 created a moratorium on all elections across the board until December 1, 1992. There is one small caveat to add here, however: I should note that in Russia at the time it was highly unlikely that there were any civil service cadres not, in one way or another, connected to the Communist Party of the USSR.

3. *The Levels of Hierarchy Where Elections Took Place.*

With the onset of transition, President Yeltsin ended up not conducting elections of any kind: there were no presidential elections (one needs to recall that Yeltsin himself was appointed President by the RSFSR on June 12, 1991); there were no parliamentary elections (the All-Union RSFSR was appointed in the spring of 1990); there were no gubernatorial elections (they were all initially appointed); there were no regional legislative elections (they were appointed in 1990 and still carried Soviet nomenclatures); there were no elections for the heads of administrations of cities and regions (governors appointed them); and finally there were no elections for local municipalities (the subregional *soviets* were appointed in 1990). Even after the storming of the Russian White House, authorities did not conduct elections across the board, even though it is likely that it would have been popularly supported and easy to enact. In the end, only the Federal Duma (December 1993) and regional legislatures (Spring 1994) were elected. Few today seem to remember these facts, but it is important to point out that from 1993 to 1995-96 local self-administration (i.e., the city and regional administrative heads) in "democratic" Russia was represented only by appointees!

4. *Party System*

There was a sharp dichotomy in the party system of Russia—drawn along "communist-democratic" lines. There was no multiparty system that developed—only diametrically opposite poles emerged as choices: "Democrats" on the one side and "Communists" on the other.

5. *The Democratisation of the Socio-political Set-up*

The possibility to democratise the socio-political set-up was ultimately blocked by the refusal to conduct quick "inaugural elections," establishing the practice of naming appointees, and creating the "power vertical" in 1991. The "power vertical" was NOT an intellectual product of the Vladimir Putin team, but rather was the norm of governmental foundations under Yeltsin.

6. *Societal Trust in Power*

Yeltsin during *perestroika* was the idol of tens of millions of Soviet people. The people believed in two "miracles"—Yeltsin and the elections. But Yeltsin did not conduct elections, and as a consequence the people once again lost faith and trust in the power of government. However, this general phenomenon still survives today, only with a different degree of poignancy.

7. *Elite Transition*

The current Russian experience about elite attitude will be examined based on the evidence across seven regions of the former Soviet Union and present-day Russian Federation. More detailed analyses can be found published with various authors in monographs and co-authored articles.[2] In this article the logic and results of elite transition across the seven regions of Russia (Ryazan, Samara, Ulyanovsk, Tambov, Mordovia, Udmurtia, and Chuvashia) are being compared to the Macedonian case. To be more specific, the local level was specifically examined in Macedonia. The issue was that the former Soviet Union/Russian Federation has three administrative hierarchies—federal, regional, and subregional—whereas in Macedonia there are only two levels: national and local.

Thus, in 1991 the new authorities underwent a "democratic" transition. The procedure they developed, born from the President's inner circle, was quite simple: the President would appoint governors while these, in turn, would appoint the heads of subregional administrations.

Table 1. **Recruiting the heads of city and county administration (1991-1992)**

Heads	RYAZAN	SAMARA	TAMBOV	ULYANOVSK	MORDOVIA	UDMURTIA	CHUVASHIA	IN SUM	%
1st secretary	4	10	4	7	2	4	1	32	16.2
2nd secretary		1		1				2	1.0

Chair, Dep. Chair Soviet	1	1	1	1		1	3	8	4.1
Chair, Dep. Chair Exec. Soviet	22	21	15	10	15	13	14	110	55.8
Directorate	2	2	6	3	5	10	6	34	17.3
Others			4	1	3	1	2	11	5.6
Total	29	35	30	23	25	29	26	197	100

In more than half of the cases (52%), the heads of administration were recruited from the chairs of the city and county executive committees. The directorate and first secretaries lagged significantly behind, with only 17.3% and 16.2% respectively. The deputy chairs of the executive committees, the chairs and deputy chairs of the *soviets* added to the impressive success of Soviet *apparatchiks* (5.1% and 4.6% respectively). In total, it worked out that 118 people came to leadership positions in the subregions (59.9%) directly from the Soviet nomenclature apparatus. Most importantly, there were no striking inter-regional differences in terms of percentage, barring a few exceptions. In Ryazan Oblast the chairs of the executive committees of the Soviets achieved an extraordinary 75.9%. In Samara Oblast the divergent result came from the first secretaries with 28.6%. In Udmurtia, the agricultural directors were greatly represented with 34.5%.

This collision acted as a direct hit on the authority of the first secretaries acting as the new chairs of local *soviets* and figuratively felt like someone was playing a cruel joke on them (in Tambov Oblast and the Republic of Chuvashia, for example). This "contra-elite" worked against the first secretaries/new *soviet* chairs, blocking all their attempts to penetrate the elite local power structure. Recruiting for the new elite thus came mostly from an old reservoir of power—the old guard Soviet party nomenclature with its preservation of an unadulterated pre-*perestroika* rhetoric. In opposition to this development a democratic movement did emerge but in reality the aforementioned contra-elites had, by 1991, formed the foundation of regional power.

In regions where the first secretaries performed less creditably in 1990, an immediate replacement was made in favour of the chairs/

mayors of the city and county executive committees. Thus by 1991, the new federal authorities had a disclaimer connected with their performance. This was evident in President Yeltsin's decree of July 20, 1991—"About the dismantling of the party" (*O departizatsii*). In the Republic of Mordovia, for example, the local *apparatchiks* reacted sharply to the decree and started looking for new engagements. In the Republic of Bashkortastan only 34 city and county secretaries remained, in Tambov Oblast only 13 remained. In most cases the replacements would lead to a demotion—being replaced as second secretaries with no future prospects. These arrangements worked at the most for a few weeks. These people were devoid of decision-making in the real sense and were wholly unsuited as heads of the local administration. The only option was the First Secretaries who became a source of regional support for the federal centre, but was not, in any way, better.

The changes are connected with different circumstances. Perhaps the major change was the shifting of the bosses of various regions. This change was the main mechanism for establishing appointees belonging to Yeltsin's power structure. It is appropriate to consider them as "agents of influence" for the federal centre across the regions.

Table 2. **"Agents of Influence" for the federal centre in the regions**

Region	**Name of regional leader**	**Mini-political bio**	**Subregional politics**
Ryazan	L. P. Bashmakov (appointed)	Industrial director, Chair of Oblast Exec. Committee (1988–1990)	The domination of the chair and his recent subordinates
Samara	K. A. Titov (appointed)	Deputy director of "Informatika," Chair of city *soviet* (1990)	Support the exec. committee chair and his recent subordinates
Tambov	V. D. Babenko (appointed)	Chief doctor of Oblast Hospital (1977–1991), People's Deputy of RSFSR (1990)	Support the exec. Committee chair and agricultural directors

Ulyanovsk	V. V. Malafeev (appointed, 10/24/1991-11/2/1991) Y. F. Goryachev (appointed)	Director of *Kontaktor*, First secretary of oblast committee of CPSU (1990), chair of oblast *soviet* (1990)	Support the executive committee chair and agricultural directors
Mordovia	V. D. Guslyannikov (elected President of Mordovia, 12/22/1991)	Senior scholar of NPO, People's Deputy (1990)	Support the exec. Committee chair and agricultural directors
Udmurtia	V. K. Tubilov N. E. Mironov	Chair of Supreme Soviet (1990) Chair SM (1989)	Support the exec. Committee chair and agricultural directors
Chuvashia	Presidential elections in 1991 did not achieve results E. A. Kybarev N. A. Zaitsev	Chair of Supreme Soviet (1991) Chair of SM (1989)	Support the exec. Committee chair and agricultural directors

"Partycrat" Y. F. Goryachev (Ulyanovsk Oblast), industrialist L. P. Bashmakov (Ryazan Oblast), academic V. D. Guslyannikov (Republic of Mordovia), Dr. V. D. Babenko (Tambov Oblast), duma deputies V. K. Tubilov, N. E. Mironov (Republic of Udmurtia) and E. A. Kubarev, N. A. Zaitsev (Republic of Chuvashia) all acted according to one logic: the chief support was for the chairs of the local executive committees as they were the least politically dangerous. If, for any reason, the chairs were considered ineffective, the choice would fall on the industrialists. Only in those cases in which both the chairs and the industrialists were not available did they seek out "loyal" first secretaries of the new authority, capable actors of the democratic movement, or people who had fallen out of favour of the *nomenklatura* during the Soviet era. Indeed this process of appointing First Secretaries was done only with great reluctance. The one exception to this process was K. A. Titov in Samara.

It was because of all this that the First Secretaries only managed to maintain their positions in 15% of the cases. Simultaneously a small part of their number (less than 10%) did not fall from the nomenclature but simply exited into the oblast structures as the new heads of local administration needed experienced and young administrators. These first secretaries of the provinces who ended up in the oblast centre were considered not dangerous and therefore acceptable. For example, First Secretary of the Kotovsk city committee of the Communist Party of the Soviet Union, O. I. Betin, became the First Deputy Head of the Tambov Oblast administration in 1999. Nowadays, Betin is now Governor of Tambov Oblast. In this way, nearly a quarter of the leaders of the subregions were able to preserve a primary spot for themselves in the local organs of power.

The Macedonian Case

As politologists, we can ideally speak about the case-to-case democratic trends in the aftermath of Socialist order in the Communist bloc. The first step to democracy in Macedonia was quite different and unexpected.

1. *Pacts/Consensus/Agreement*

In Macedonia, in strong contrast to Russia, the elite pact/consensus was an objective reality. Here the stark division of society into proponents and opponents of socialism are not seen. My field research in the Macedonian republic based on in-depth interviews with Communist Party cadres was conducted during April and May 2012. All interviewees—whether it was the former Secretary of the Central Committee Union of Communists of Macedonia or the Heads of Party Committees from cities all over the republic had one common perception—there was "another socialism" in Yugoslavia. This socialism was different from Soviet socialism. Both the elite groups and society in general in Macedonia wanted a democratic transition. Consequently, there was no room for lack of consensus or to reject the political arrangements. Civil war or social tension was to be avoided. The leaders of the Macedonian Communist party wanted to hold power in new Macedonia but wanted to achieve that status through elections. The opposition too was extremely hopeful about regaining power through elections. This mutual interest became the motivating factor for the two sides to come to an arrangement or a pact.

2. *Pace/Speed*

Elections took place in Macedonia in 1990 even before there was an official declaration of independence from Yugoslavia. These elections decided the most critical political problems and whoever won the elections would be the de facto power.

3. *On the Levels of Hierarchy Where Elections Took Place*

In Macedonia elections were held simultaneously at the level of the government as well as at the level of society. The first multiparty parliamentary elections in Macedonia took place on November 11 (this was the first round) and December 23 (this was the second round) in 1990. The democratic nature of the elections would have had a general consensus and would have been unchallenged were it not for the country's presidential elections. On January 27, 1991 Kiro Gligorov was appointed as the First President of the Republic of Macedonia not through popular elections but through the session of the General Assembly of the Republic. In this discrepancy, we see the defect in the "inaugural elections" of the Macedonian case.

But this is not the only thing to talk about. The election to the post of Heads of the local assemblies was also not open to all. They were elected through an electoral college—formed from the Deputies of the local assemblies. In an interview to the newspaper *Focus,* President Gligorov explained the logic behind this decision: the authorities of Macedonia at that time were afraid of separatist leanings cropping up in various parts of the country. They knew about political forces, both inside and outside the country, which had plans of new autonomous ethnic enclaves. Ultimately, this line of strategic thinking could be seen as leading to the demise of the said enclaves and the formation of new neighbouring states now "adjacent" to Macedonia instead of being part of the Republic. For this reason, they devised a strategy that would make Heads of local assemblies loyal to the centre.

4. *Party System*

The Macedonian case had a lot of public attention especially as it indicated trends of a multiparty system. This phenomenon was noticeable in 1990 just as it is today. It is possible that the level of societal attention was higher here in Macedonia than in the rest of the Communist bloc. This is just a hypothesis, of course, but it certainly deserves greater attention and empirical research. Moreover, it was acknowledged by society in general, and specifically by the leadership of the Union of Communists of Macedonia, that elections needed to take place on a fair, honest and multiparty basis.

Here it is necessary to elaborate on the logic of the working of a multiparty system in Macedonia: it needs to be pointed out that, in contrast to Russia, there were no Communist Parties in the strict sense of the term and, in the broader sense, there was no strong ideological representation within society. There is an important difference between Macedonia and Russia: the former did not have the pronounced conflict between "Communists" and "democrats" compared to the latter in 1990.

In Macedonia the law on elections of June 17, 1990 created a very simple registration system for political parties. In essence, the registration procedure was very simple. The Ministry of Internal Affairs confirmed the decision about official registration of a party. The Communist Union of Macedonia added the words "Party of Democratic Transformation" and became the Communist Union of Macedonia—Party of Democratic Transformation (CUM-PDT). Petar Goshev, the earlier Secretary of the CUM and a member of the Presidium of the Communist Union of Yugoslavia, was appointed head of the party. The party ultimately won 31 out of 120 seats in the first parliamentary elections in 1990, which made it the second largest party in the Parliament.

Similar to the CUM-PDT was the Reformist Union of Yugoslavia (RUY) which was created on October 16, 1990. The head of the party—Stoyan Andov—was a former Yugoslav Ambassador to Iraq from 1991 to 1996 and was the Chair of the Assembly of the Macedonian Republic from 2000 to 2002. The Socialist Party of Macedonia (SPM) was founded in July 1990 and Lyubisav Ivanov was appointed its head. What this signifies is that most of the influential political parties in Macedonia were founded on the basis of the original Macedonian Communist party. Eighteen political parties and unions took part in the first parliamentary elections with 11,550 candidates, signifying an intense level of party activism within Macedonia.

The democratisation of the socio-political system—it was a democratic and politicised system.

5. *Societal Trust in Power*

Societal trust in Macedonian take-over of power was high from the very beginning.

6. *Elite Transformation*

The elections for the heads of local municipalities were not universal and direct. An electoral college of sorts voted for them, consisting of members of municipal assemblies that were originally elected to those positions on a multiparty basis. Just as with the parliamentary elections, these elections at the local level progressed in two tours—on November 11 and December 23, 1990. For the posts of deputies of municipal assemblies there were in general 1,510 places with 5,546 candidates competing for the openings (nearly four candidates for every single deputy post).

Table 3. **Indices for Electoral Lists for the Posts of Local Municipality Deputies, 1990**

№	Electoral List	No. of Candidates	No. of Deputy Posts
1.	SKM-PDP	1,320	512
2.	SPM	1,203	174
3.	SRSM	942	312
4.	VMRO–DPMNE	530	210
5.	MAAK	460	34
6.	PDPM	356	226
7.	SDPM	246	10
8.	Democratic League	166	2
9.	Yugoslavian Position in the SRM	121	5
10.	MDPSM (Young Democratic Progressives of Macedonia)	64	8
11.	PPETSRM	44	7
12.	Democratic Union—Farmers' Party of Macedonia	34	8
13.	Independent candidates	15	4
14.	DSTM	19	0

15.	NDP	13	7
16.	DKhPM	8	0
17.	RPM	4	0
18.	NPM	1	0
19.	SPOB (Pensioners' Union of the Local Bitola)	1	0
	TOTAL	5,546	1,510

The deputies of the local municipalities were sworn in on January 30, 1991. In turn sessions were organised to conduct the elections for heads of local municipalities. The deputies elected these heads from their own representatives in the General Assembly. The overall democratisation of this event became evident as these elections proceeded in consultation with the political parties represented in the General Assembly.

And so, what were the electoral realities? In the final tally there were representatives from six political parties filling the chairs of local municipality chiefs (in all there were 29 positions).

Table 4. **The Correlation between Parties in the Deputy Assembly and Heads of Local Municipalities (HLM)**

№	Electoral List	# of Deputies	# of HLM
1.	SKM–PDP	512	17
2.	SPM	174	1
3.	SRSM	312	4
4.	VMRO–DPMNE	210	4
6.	PDPM	226	3

A decisive victory was achieved by the SKM-PDP party (a total of 17 seats). All of the remaining political parties were able to occupy a mere 12 seats. How was it possible for the secretaries of the local municipality committees of the SKM to achieve such a decisive victory? Were they able to hold on to power continually in 1991? This analysis answers some of the key questions regarding these issues. For instance, how did their political and economic careers fare moving on into the future?

Out of the 31 seats for the heads of local municipalities, there were six former committee secretaries of the Communist Party. In three instances these Heads also became Deputies of the General Assembly. What happened to the remaining Heads? Three among them turned into professional activists with the recently created Social Democratic Union of Macedonia and subsequent Deputies of the Republic of Macedonia Assembly. Seven became Directors of state-run industrial enterprises. Nine people returned to work according to their expertise and among them were university professors, schoolteachers, engineers, economists, lawyers, and medical doctors. Thus, 10 people in one way or the other continued their political career (either as heads of local municipalities, deputies of the parliament, or party activists); seven former party secretaries, utilising the terminology of some of the first Russian research on transition, “exchanged power for property.” The rest simply returned to their civilian lives and to their respective spheres of influence. The logic of the Velvet Revolution and the traditionally peaceful and stable conditions across local communities created for them comfortable opportunities to reintegrate into the life of post-socialist Macedonia. That is, 10 of the most influential party officers at the local level perfectly transitioned into the politico-administrative context of the new Macedonia; seven became the owners of powerful industries in Macedonia as a result of privatisation; the remaining number became specialists with decent incomes. In other words, the local communities were not averse to the former party leaders. The majority of these people came for party work “from their professions”—this often meant they were coming from the now defunct Communist Party of Yugoslavia. At the time of elections, they were replaced for the post of heads of local municipalities in 1991 by the same group of lawyers (8), economists (7), engineers (6), pedagogues (5) journalists, sportsmen, technologists, veterinary surgeons and doctors. Moreover, the former secretaries of the committees of the SKM once again became the leaders of local administration (not as secretaries of the party organs but as the heads of local municipalities).

To sum up, firstly, it is apparent that (a) local elections in Macedonia created in the municipality assemblies a situation of domination for the

SKM/SKM-PDP; (b) a marked reinvigoration of activists at the party level took place, particularly visible at the level of Macedonia's local municipalities; (c) it is obvious that former party actors re-entered transitional phase politics in independent Macedonia.

Conclusion

What are the similarities and differences in the Russian and Macedonian cases of "inaugural elections?"

There are similarities in the fact that there were fundamental limitations in both Russian and Macedonian cases. In Russia those limitations were large, while in Macedonia they were less significant but still present. In both countries authorities were not consistent in the manner in which democratic elections were established and conducted. In fact, it is more accurate to say that Russian authorities more consistently lacked the desire to conduct such elections. Such elections were held only after the events of 1993. The Russian "inaugural elections" can be arguably categorised as deferred. In Macedonia, meanwhile, only the country's Parliament was elected through classical democratic mechanisms.

What hindered democratic processes in Russia and Macedonia? In Russia there were two main reasons: first, the fear of the Yeltsin team about losing power. His analytical team predicted that the group of August 1991 events would not have been victorious if there were direct Presidential, parliamentary or gubernatorial elections. Second, there was hardly any effective governance in the regions and there was no governor upon whom the Yeltsin team could rely.

One must not forget that Macedonia is part of the Balkan peninsula. A very strong nationalist factor is in play here. The country's new authorities were not, therefore afraid of a so-called Communist renaissance. They were more afraid of Albanian separatism and the further division of what was an already small state.

The biggest difference resides in the fact that democratisation in Macedonia took place with much less political conflict and was faster, more consistent and more purposeful. The country did not divide along "red" and "white" lines. Political parties played and continue to play a major role in national politics. Successive parliamentary elections always produced new party leaders in Macedonia. Consequently, there was and is always a revitalisation of the political elite in Macedonia.

In Russia, throughout the 1990s there were conflicts and societal divisions. "Inaugural elections" were therefore delayed and when they did take place, analysts were motivated to call them democratic. This is especially so when one discusses the Presidential elections of 1996.

Reference

Samuel P. Huntington, *The Third Wave. Democratization in the Late Twentieth Century* (Norman, Oklahoma and London: University of Oklahoma Press, 1991).

G. O'Donnell and P. C. Schmitter, *Transition from Authoritarian Rule: Tentative Conclusions about Uncertain Democracies* (Baltimore and London: Johns Hopkins University Press, 1986).

A. Stepan and J. J. Linz, *Problems of Democratic Transition and Consolidation. Southern Europe, South America and Post-Communist Europe* (Baltimore and London: Johns Hopkins University Press, 1996).

Adam Przeworski, *Democracy and the Market: Political and Economic Reforms in Eastern Europe and Latin America* (Cambridge: Cambridge University Press, 1991).

Dmitry Seltser, *Vzlioty I padeniia nomenklatury* (The Flights and Falls of the Nomenclature). Tambov, 2006.

Dmitry Seltser, and M. Crosston, "Mutating Power: Tracking the Changes in Authority of the Sub-Regional Communist Party Nomenclature During Late-Stage Soviet and Post-Soviet Socialism (1985-2005)," *Bulletin of Tambov State Technical University*, no. 2B, vol. 11 (2005), pp. 578-89.

12. The Boundaries of EU Norms: Examining EU's External and Internal Power Using Aboriginal Subsistence Whaling as Case Study [1]

Minori Takahashi

Introduction

The fact that the European Union (EU) is gaining influence as an agent that formulates norms has been pointed out on a number of occasions.[2] In such debates, as indicated by Ian Manners and other researchers, the spotlight is on "normative power" as an aspect of EU's influence on other regions. The "EU as a normative power" does not only connote a passive meaning in which the EU is only creating standards and models for action, but also possesses a dynamic role: EU's orientation or normative influence on other regions and EU's creation, maintenance and management of global markets through the exercise of that influence. Since, as a normative power, the EU projects its influence on the global arena, it is often called "an externally-oriented power." The EU's external power, of course, does not arise spontaneously. It is institutionalised based on the premise of a consensus between 27 countries (28 countries from July 2013 onwards) and then projected outside the EU area. In that sense it may be said that the consensus between the 27 member states is an internally-oriented power that supports the Union's externally-oriented power. In other words, EU norms are shaped through the interaction of such internally and externally oriented powers.

The EU, which today comprises 27 state political actors, has created space for conflicting interests and a competition of opposing ideas. However, when a certain premise is transformed into a norm through a consensus of 27 different countries, the universality of that norm becomes relatively pronounced in comparison to a norm put forward by a single actor (as in the case of the US or Japan). As a result, the EU is, to a certain degree, able to functionally expand its influence through the development of the so-called "European standards." Of course, there is criticism of this claim, which questions the methodology behind it and states that there are issues that cannot be explained solely from the viewpoint of norms.

Nonetheless, the attempt to analyse EU's influence from the standpoint of normative power is an effective argument for understanding the EU's realities, and this view is supported by many scholars. In explaining this normative power of the European Union, there is no example as appropriate as its handling of the whaling issue since 2008.

This paper focuses on the nature of EU's influence on areas outside of it and aims to shed light on a new aspect of that influence (that has not been visible so far). In doing so, the paper takes up Denmark and its autonomous region Greenland as a case study—Denmark being a member state which, although an agent that participates in the creation of the internal power, is also influenced by EU's projection of norms and standards on external areas and is also an object on which EU's external power is applied.

The Significance of this Study

Why is there a need to address EU as a normative power at all? Here I wish to draw attention to two points. The first is the significance of this approach in terms of the study of international politics, since it offers a valuable perspective for understanding contemporary global order. While, as a reaction to the demands of the post-Cold War era, the re-examination of the power structure in the global order was becoming widespread, a perspective rooted in the emphasis of the power shaped by military and economic might was, with a few exceptions, widely advocated. The argument for the creation of G2 in the post-Cold War era is a typical example of that trend. If we consider what has happened in Iraq and Afghanistan, it is clear that the perspective represented by the G2 argument has not been functional. It has, therefore, been pointed out that the view which emphasises only "material power," such as military and economic, is insufficient, and that attention should also be given to the "ideational power" which tends to be underestimated. One instance of such dissent was Manner's "normative power," the argument which took the EU as its main example.[3] The concept of the EU as a normative power, was the result of an attempt to rethink the power of thought and norms that took place within the process of the examination of the post-Cold War set-up, as well as an attempt to assess the role of the EU as an agent that creates, maintains and manages the global order by using its normative power.

The problem with this approach to the study of international politics was that, not only were there discrepancies in the strength of the individual norms, the influence stemming from them, and in their implementation from one policy area to another, but also that the research and analyses of to whom the EU normative power was really being applied and what impact it had were also lacking. One of the goals of this paper, is, while bearing in mind the above problems in past research, to bring attention to a new aspect of EU's qualitative influence.

The second reason for examining EU norms is that such an endeavour may present a contribution to the research on the EU in that it brings to light the essence of EU's norms. Past research has tended to equate and use as synonyms "the EU influence" on outside areas and its "external power." However, as will be shown in this paper, when it comes to the boundaries between "the inside" and "the outside," norms that have been projected to the outside world also have a boomerang effect and tend to reorient policymaking within the EU camp. This phenomenon cannot be well explained by the frame of reference employed in past research that is premised on the distinction between "the inside" and "the outside." The present paper strives to make visible this oft neglected fact.

The EU Environment Ministers Council

The argument begins with the Ministerial Council meeting on whale protection that took place in Luxembourg on June 5, 2008.[4] There the EU reached a consensus on the protection of whales for the first time in its history as a union. The whale protection norm in this case carried a more radical meaning, something akin to an anti-whaling stance. To the common value of whale protection, however, a clause stating that "the EU is not opposed to aboriginal peoples' whaling for their subsistence" was added. That is, the EU is not opposed to any whaling process, and, at least at that point, in June 2008, the EU made clear that it would tolerate whaling by indigenous people for subsistence purposes (Figure1).

Figure 1. **Aboriginal Subsistence Whaling**[5]

COUNTRY **Region** ***Ethnic group***	**Subject**	**Type of Whale**	**Numbers alive (presumed)**	**Quota (per year)**[6]	**Catch (per year)**
USA Alaska *Inupiat, Yupik*	Indigenous peoples	Bowhead	11,800 (2004)	51	38 (landed)
USA Washington *Makah*	Indigenous peoples	Gray	20,110 (2007)	4	0
RUSSIA Chukotka Autonomous Okrug *Chukchi, Yupik*	Indigenous peoples	Gray	20,110 (2007)	120 (140 Max.)	127 (landed)
		Bowhead	11,800 (2004)	5	2 (landed)
DENMARK **Greenland** ***Kalaallit***	**Indigenous peoples**	**Fin**	**4,700 (2007)**	**19**	**11 (landed)**
		Minke (West Greenland)	**10,800 (2005)**	**200**	**148 (landed)**
		Minke (East Greenland)	**Unknown**	**12**	**1 (landed)**
		Bowhead	**6,300 (2008)**	**2**	**0**
SAINT VINCENT & GRENADINES *Bequia Islander*	Non-Indigenous peoples	Humpback	10,750 (1992)	4	1 (landed)

The Environment Ministers Council is one of the EU's administrative bodies consisting of government bureaucrats—an institution for decision-making in which each member state is represented. Decisions made at its meetings have legal binding power for the member states. Decisions on whaling which are under the jurisdiction of the council are made through the system of qualified majority voting in which each of the 27 states are allotted a certain number of votes based on the size of their population. A minimum number of votes needed to prevent the adoption of a decision (blocking minority) is also set, so a bill or a motion can be blocked if the opposing side has a minimum of 91 votes.

For that matter, on many occasions voting on whaling has not been a conflict-ridden issue on which the opinions were sharply split. This is because in the legal system called *acquis communautaire*, which EU states are obliged to follow, there is a clause prohibiting the killing and transportation of whales.[7] This is clearly laid out as an EU directive (Council Directive 92/43/EEC of May 21, 1992). That is, if a state aspires to join and become a member of the EU, it is obliged to follow the directive that prohibits the killing and transportation of whales in EU waters. For that reason, although there might be sentimental issues surrounding it, in purely institutional terms, whaling does not instigate confrontation. At the same time, in the Copenhagen criteria which spell out the conditions for joining the Union, the EU has established provisions which uphold the right to self-determination by ethnic groups. The statement that the EU will not oppose subsistence whaling by indigenous peoples that was added to the 2008 decision on the protection of whales is based on those provisions.

Struggle within the International Whaling Commission

What, then, can we gain from examining the EU decision on whale protection by taking Denmark's autonomous region of Greenland as a case study? The material for our analysis comes from the meeting of the International Whaling Commission (IWC) that was held immediately after the EU formulated its standards regarding whaling protection in June 2008. At the 60th Annual Meeting of the IWC in June 2008 Denmark/Greenland requested that a new catch quota of 10 humpback whales be approved under the framework of subsistence whaling by indigenous people.[8] In its request that it be given a new quota, Greenland referred to the scientific research by the Greenland Institute of Natural Resources and the IWC's Scientific Committee that indicated that the number of humpback whales had increased as a consequence of a whaling moratorium introduced in 1986.[9] This request was an attempt to make up for the shrinking numbers in the whale quota approved to Greenland. Also behind the request was the preference of the indigenous Inuit people in Greenland for humpback whales.[10] Furthermore, another reason for such a request was that there was a gap in numbers between the quota approved by the IWC Scientific Committee and the actual quota given. This issue had been brought up in the report submitted by Greenland's home-rule government to the IWC in 2007.[11] That is, the IWC Scientific Committee had approved a catch of 670 tons, but in reality only 540 tons had been lifted to the shore. It is this gap that Greenland was seeking to close by submitting a request for a new quota (Figure 2).

Figure 2. **2007 Report**[12]

Types of Whale	**Tons of meat per whale**	**Yearly quotas (2003-2007)**	**Meat available per year**
Humpback	8 tons	0 head	0 ton
Finback	10 tons	19 heads	190 tons
Minke	2 tons	175 heads	350 tons
Total			540 tons

However, all the EU member states attending the IWC meeting (except Denmark), which respect the right to self-determination and allow for subsistence whaling by indigenous peoples, formed a single block[13] opposing Denmark/Greenland's request for a new whaling quota, thereby acting in unison with the anti-whaling countries belonging to the so-called "Buenos Aires group," which consists of South and Central American states and Australia. For the request for the change in the whaling quota to be approved, the majority of votes was needed, but since, out of the total of 65 votes, only 29 (including the vote by Denmark) were in favour, while 36 were against (including 19 EU member states other than Denmark), Greenland's request for the new quota was turned down.

Figure 3. **Votes on Greenland humpback quota at the IWC 2008 meeting**[14]

	Yes	**No**	**Abstention**
EU	1	19	0
Other	28	17	2
Total	29	36	2

Denmark/Greenland repeated the request in 2009, as well as at the annual meeting in 2010. In 2009 they proposed the reduction of the already approved catch quota for minke whales from 200 to 178 in order to have the 10 humpback whale quota approved.[15] The basic idea behind this was to adjust for the fall in the number of minke whales observed in nature and to make up for that loss with humpback whales. However, Denmark/Greenland did not manage to reach an agreement with the rest of the EU on this, so the voting outcome was the same as in 2008. In 2010, in addition to the proposed reduction of 22 minke whales, Denmark/Greenland offered to settle for 9 instead of 10 humpback whales and, on top of that, promised that it would catch no more than a combined total of 25 (previously approved) finback whales and humpback whales.[16] That year, Denmark joined hands with the United States which has the same native people living in it, and after some negotiations behind the scenes, finally had Greenland's request approved. This, it can be said, was truly the product of a compromise.

Figure 4. **The result of negotiation**[17]

Type of Whale	**Quota (per year)**[1]8
Fin	19→16
Mink (West Greenland)	200→178
Minke (East Greenland)	12
Bowhead	2
Humpback	9 (new)

However, the fierce debate about Greenland's whaling quotas was reignited at the IWC meeting in 2012. At this, the 64th Annual Meeting, quotas for subsistence whaling were approved for indigenous peoples in the US, Russia and Saint Vincent[19] but not for Greenlanders.[20] At the end, the existence of Greenland's whaling quota itself came to be questioned.

Figure 5. **Votes on Greenland quota at the IWC 2012 meeting**[21]

	Yes	No	Abstention
EU	1	17	0
Other	24	17	3
Total	25	34	3

Reasons Why Greenland's Requests Have Been Viewed Negatively

There are three main reasons why Greenland's requests for a new whaling quota and its whaling quotas as such have been perceived negatively. The first one is that the definition of aboriginal subsistence whaling itself is vague. Aboriginal subsistence whaling has been defined in Attachment 13 of the International Convention for the Regulation of Whaling (ICRW), but in it expressions that leave room for different interpretations, such as "exclusively for local consumption" or "to satisfy aboriginal subsistence needs," have been used. It is worth noting that anti-whaling and whale protection advocates interpret "local consumption" as a hand-to-hand internal exchange, whereas in Greenland whale meat is distributed widely and sold in supermarkets. Because of that, the proponents of anti-whaling and whale protection charge that whale consumption in Greenland is not local at all.[22]

The second reason, which is similar to the first, is that the aboriginal subsistence whaling was envisioned as a non-commercial activity, so that each time a request for a new whaling quota in that category is put forward the debate comes down to whether this would constitute commercial whaling or not.[23] This stifles the debate, leads to various irrelevant conclusions on whaling and thereby contributes to the creation of an environment in which constructive arguments cannot arise.

The third reason is that, since the fierce debate on the introduction of a moratorium on commercial whaling in the IWC in 1986, Greenland has had a history of making claims regarding the legitimacy of its whaling and has been making frequent requests regarding new catch quotas.[24] As evidenced by the events following its request in 2008, it may be said that Greenland's course of action in which it made repeated demands despite a rejection has led to a lot of questioning about whaling and whale protection.

It is under such circumstances that Denmark/Greenland has continued negotiations regarding its requests for new whaling quotas. But, since in Greenland whales that do not belong to the 13 large species regulated and controlled by the IWC are also hunted, concerns have been voiced that the IWC decisions regarding Greenland's requests may also affect whaling that falls outside of the IWC's regulatory scope. Also, an opinion has been voiced that, if so, Greenland should withdraw from the IWC and completely dedicate itself to the North Atlantic Marine Mammal Commission (NAMMCO), an institution for managing ocean resources of which it is already a member.

Denmark's Dilemma since 2008

Against such a background, Denmark has continued to support Greenland's whaling campaign. That is why Ole Samsing, head of the Denmark/Greenland delegation who is in charge of relations with the EU and the IWC in the Danish Ministry of Foreign Affairs, has criticised EU's actions as "cultural imperialism" and "hypocrisy."[25] His statements seem to contain a feeling that Denmark is becoming increasingly isolated within the EU due to the whaling issue.[26]

Regarding this, attention should be paid to the situation *before* and *after* 2008 when the EU toughened its stance on whaling. Up until 2007 Denmark skilfully balanced and performed its role as a member state of the EU and the mainland of the Danish Realm. Denmark's stance, sometimes negatively portrayed as "the double role," was protected by "Declaration 25" of the Maastricht Treaty. "Declaration 25" demands that member states that possess territory outside of the EU area develop their national strategies and policies in mutual agreement with the territories.[27] So, until 2007, Denmark, acting as the "mainland of the Danish Realm," continued its support for whaling in accordance with the declaration and in mutual agreement with its overseas territory, Greenland (which falls outside of the EU).

The reason why Denmark was able to clarify its position in such a way was that, until 2007, the EU did not have a common policy with which to appear on the global stage. The EU had, indeed clearly expressed a policy stance on whaling through its *acquis communautaire* directives and the Copenhagen criteria, but that stance referred only to the prohibition of the killing and transportation of whales within its own territorial waters. In fact, in a 2008 document issued by the EU it is clearly stated that: "The European Union has not yet been able to use its political weight within the IWC because of the lack of a coordinated and agreed EU position."[28] That is, no guidelines were given as to how EU member states should behave at a real venue of international negotiations that was the IWC.

In contrast to that, since 2008 the EU has been participating in international negotiations with a common position shared by its 27 member states in which whale protection is a common norm. For example, Stavros Dimas, an EU environmental committee member has given the following statement: "With this decision, the European Union can now take a strong role at the International Whaling Commission and use its political, moral and economic weight to ensure a more effective protection of whales worldwide."[29] Thus, it may be said that the EU switched its policy stance from prohibiting the killing and transportation of whales in its own waters to the protection of whales worldwide. In other words, because in its policies regarding whaling the priority in thinking had been placed on "the inside," it had been difficult for the EU to achieve interaction and synergy regarding "the outside," but ever since it defined its common position on whaling through the consensus at the meeting of the Environment Ministers Council in June 2008, the EU's influence on the outside has strengthened, and it has become able to promote whale protection as the common voice of its 27 member states.

This also means that the boundary between the inside and the outside has become ambiguous. That is, one of the factors that made it possible for Denmark to respect Greenland's whaling initiative while simultaneously carrying out its duties as an EU member state was that, due to systemic reasons, the EU's influence on the outside was insufficient. However, when in 2008, following the adoption of the common norm regarding whaling, the EU's internal power began to be transformed into an external power, Denmark found itself forced to simultaneously carry out its duties as a member state in EU foreign relations and its responsibilities as "the mainland Denmark" (the ultimate decision-maker) in possession of a territory outside the EU area.

If we were to name the elements on the EU side that contribute to generating Denmark's dilemma that, I believe, would be EU's low-key influence and its high ability to set agendas that can be effectively implemented. What I refer to as the EU's "low-key influence" is the fact that the EU has not directly made statements about what whaling should be like in Greenland. Since in principle it does not oppose aboriginal subsistence whaling, the EU has not directly imposed its standards on Greenland. The important point to remember is that the EU, while institutionalising whale protection on the one hand, also respects whaling by indigenous people, on the other. That this respect comes with strings attached is, I think, visible in the fact that Greenland's request for a quota of 10 humpback whales has been voted down at IWC annual meetings since 2008.

When this, in a sense, low-key influence is paired with the ability to effectively set agendas, the EU's power to influence is further strengthened. Here the EU's agenda-setting ability is understood as the thinking that emerges through debates on how the EU can meaningfully present its norms in foreign relations and the ability of the EU to determine and efficiently present what the problems are in the global dimension and what issues need to be solved in a way that does not blatantly irritate the other (in this case, Greenland, which is an agent outside the EU area). The whale protection norm of 2008 was not simply scattered in all directions, but rather, the IWC was clearly defined as the main battlefield where this norm was then implemented by fully utilising legitimacy stemming from collective action in order to make the IWC a more stringent controller of natural resources. That is what created the situation in which Denmark has to simultaneously fulfil its duties as an EU member state in EU's foreign relations, and its responsibilities as the mainland Denmark that possesses a territory outside the EU zone.

Conclusion

This paper has attempted to shed light on the following two points: (1) to whom and with what impact is the EU normative power really applied, and (2) what is the essence of EU norms. Put succinctly, the tentative answer is: EU norms should not be viewed solely in the context of EU's foreign influence, as something that is projected onto areas outside the EU, since their nature is such that when they are projected to the "outside" they can also manifest themselves by affecting EU member states. That is, since in a lot of past research too much attention was given to the external orientation of EU norms, the realities of the member states which, as a consequence of the implementation of the norms, are also affected, have not been fully understood. Or, at least, it can be said that past research, insofar as it was following the old paradigm of EU norms as something projected on the outside areas, was not able to identify cases of EU member states such as Denmark.

The instability related to the attempts to exercise influence by formulating a common position shared by all the member states was exemplified by the failure of the EU to achieve a unified stance toward the protection of Bluefin tuna at the meeting of the Washington Treaty signatories held in Doha in March 2010. That showed just how difficult it is to come up with a compromise based on the consensus of as many as 27 countries. EU's normative power can be seen at work in a variety of situations, from addressing environmental issues to the promotion of the abolition of the death penalty, and is exercised based on the premise that it presents one side of the coin, the other side of which is instability. There is a need to theoretically account for this two-sidedness of the EU's qualitative influence. Although the work is still in progress, this paper is a small contribution towards that goal.

Notes

1. I would like to thank Ilja Musulin (University of Tokyo) for his constructive comments and warm encouragement in completing this paper. This paper was supported by JSPS, Grant-in-Aid for JSPS Fellows.

2. For example, Ian Manners, "Normative Power Europe: The International Role of the EU," Paper presented at the European Union between International and World Society, European Community Studies Association, Biennial Conference, Madison, Wisconsin, May 2001.
3. Ian Manners, "Normative Power Europe: A Contradiction in Terms?" *Journal of Common Market Studies,* 40, no. 2 (2002): 235-58.
4. EU Observer. *EU Accused of "Cultural Imperialism" on Whaling*. Brussels: EU Observer, 2008. European Union. *Strong EU Support for the Protection of Whales (IP/08/896)*. Brussels: European Union, 2008.
5. Related material offered by Hisashi Hamaguchi (Professor, Sonoda Women's College, Japan), IFERI Joint Seminar, Tsukuba: Inter Faculty Education & Research Initiative (IFERI), University of Tsukuba, January 25, 2010.
6. Five-year block quota expediently calculated in one year.
7. The Council of the EC. *Habitats Directive: Council Directive 92/43/EEC of 21 May 1992 on the Conservation of Natural Habitats and of Wild Fauna and Flora.* Brussels: The Council of the European Communities.
8. The International Whaling Commission. *IWC/60/23 rev (Agenda item 5.3.2) IWC-Scientific Committee Report (Final, 1-13 June 2008, pp. 28-29)*. Cambridge: The International Whaling Commission, 2008.
9. Grønlands Naturinstitut. *Pressemeddelelse. Biologisk rådgivning til IWC; grønlands satsning på hvalforskning giver resultater.* Nuuk: Grønlands Naturinstitut/ Pinngortitaleriffik, 2008.
10. Interview with Ole Samsing, Copenhagen: Ministry of Foreign Affairs of Denmark/ Udenrigsministeriet. August 25, 2009.
11. Greenland Home Rule Government Ministry of Fisheries, Hunting and Agriculture. *White Paper on Hunting of Large Whales in Greenland.* Nuuk: Greenland Home Rule Government, 2007.
12. The International Whaling Commission. *IWC/59/ASW/8rev (Agenda items: ASW 4, 6.4 & 6.5; INF 4; WKM&AWI 3 & 4)*. Cambridge: The International Whaling Commission, 2007.
13. The notion that the EU itself presents a single block is somewhat inaccurate. According to Ole Samsing from Danish Ministry of Foreign Affairs, the strongest opposition to whaling within the EU has been coming mainly from the following four countries: France, the UK, Germany and Luxembourg. These four countries have tended to secure the minimum necessary number of 91 votes for blocking proposals under the qualified majority voting system on their own (with France, the UK and Germany possessing 29 votes each, and Luxembourg having 4 votes).
14. Poll results offered by Ole Samsing, Copenhagen: Ministry of Foreign Affairs of Denmark/Udenrigsministeriet. September 4, 2009.
15. The International Whaling Commission. *IWC/61/11Rev (Agenda item 5.3.2),*

Proposed Schedule Amendment (Greenland Catch Limits). Cambridge: The International Whaling Commission, 2009.

16. The International Whaling Commission. *IWC/62/26 (Agenda Item 3). IWS Quotas Submitted by Denmark and the USA*. Cambridge: The International Whaling Commission, 2010.
17. The International Whaling Commission. *Aboriginal Subsistence Whaling; Strike/ Catch Limits*. http://iwc.int/aboriginal (accessed June 16, 2013). Cambridge: The International Whaling Commission.
18. Five-year block quota expediently calculated in one year.
19. The International Whaling Commission. *IWC/64/Status. Vote2: IWC/64/10 (Aboriginal subsistence whaling catch limits)*. Cambridge: The International Whaling Commission, 2012.
20. The International Whaling Commission. *IWC/64/Press Release Day 4*. Cambridge: The International Whaling Commission, 2012.
21. The International Whaling Commission. *IWC/64/Status. Vote3: IWC/64/12 (Greenland Aboriginal Subsistence Whaling Catch Limits)*. Cambridge: The International Whaling Commission, 2012.
22. For example, World Society for the Protection of Animals. *Exploding myths: An Expose of the Commercial Elements of Greenlandic Aboriginal Subsistence Whaling*. London: World Society for the Protection of Animals, 2008.
23. M. M. R. Freeman, "Is Money the Root of the Problem?" in R. L. Friedheim (ed.), *Toward a Sustainable Whaling Regime* (Seattle and London: University of Washington Press, 2001).
24. Iwasaki Masami, "Whaling in Greenland and its Current Issues" (in Japanese). *Hokkai-GakuenDaigakuJinbunRonsyuu*, 2010, no. 46:1-39.
25. Interview with Ole Samsing, Copenhagen: Ministry of Foreign Affairs of Denmark/ Udenrigsministeriet. December 13, 2010.
26. Grønlandsposten. *Uenighed om hvalfangst truer med at splitte IWC*. Nuuk: Grønlandsposten, June 2008. Politiken. *EU fejer danske hvalkrav til side*. Nuuk: Politiken, June 2008.
27. Det Europæiske Fællesskab. *Maastricht-traktaten. Erklæring (nr. 25), om varetagelse af interesserne for de i artikel 299 (tidl. artikel 227), stk. 3 og stk. 6, a) og b), i traktaten om oprettelse af Det Europæiske Fællesskab om handlede oversøiske lande og territorier. Erklæring knyttet til Maastricht-traktatens slutakt*. Brussels: Det Europæiske Fællesskab, 1992.
28. European Union. *Strong EU Support for the Protection of Whales (IP/08/896)*. Brussels: European Union, 2008.
29. European Union. *Strong EU Support for the Protection of Whales (IP/08/896)*. Brussels: European Union, 2008.

13. Eurasian Economic Union: Opportunities and Challenges

R. G. Gidadhubli

On November 18, 2011, the former President of Russia Dmitri Medvedev, Kazakh President Nursultan Nazarbayev and Belarus President Alexander Lukashenko signed an agreement, setting a target of establishing the Eurasian Economic Union (EEU) by 2015.[1] After taking over the presidency of Russia in May 2012, Vladimir Putin reiterated his policy for the establishment of EEU. This supranational body has the potentiality to assume great geopolitical and geo-economic significance in regional and global affairs. Hence an effort has been made in this paper to examine both the opportunities and challenges for the setting up of the EEU.

At the outset it is relevant to understand the basis for setting up of the EEU. As opined by some analysts, the EEU has been a brainchild of Vladimir Putin himself which he initiated at the end of his second term as President of Russia in 2007. In fact, the President of Kazakhstan should also be given due credit for this concept as he did make a similar suggestion way back in 1994 in his address at Moscow University. Hence it is creditable that not only has this idea been mooted but efforts have also been made by taking several measures and working out a roadmap for setting up this body.

Firstly, all these three states Russia, Kazakhstan and Belarus have already entered into an agreement for Customs Union. During the last two decades several efforts have been made for promoting political and economic cooperation among the former Soviet States even as the outcome of these efforts is not uniform. According to official sources, the Customs Union of Russia, Belarus and Kazakhstan has been fairly satisfactory since it has brought some economic unity among these three states. In fact this positive outcome seems to have encouraged the leaders to form the EEU.

Secondly, it is important to note that since January 1, 2012 the organisation known as Eurasian Economic Space has started operating which may significantly facilitate the formation of the EEU. The seriousness of the leaders in pursuing their vision is evident from the fact that with effect from January 1, 2012 one of the most important institutions of the Eurasian Economic Community, namely, the Court of the Eurasian Economic Community, started working, the legal basis for which was established in 2000. This Court has its headquarters in Minsk, the capital city of Belarus, which shall adjudicate economic disputes between the member states of the Eurasian Economic Community. The Eurasian Economic Commission has been established with this economic objective in mind. Russia's seriousness for creating EEU is evident from the fact that in December 2011, the Russian Industry and Trade Minister Viktor Khristenko took over the charge of the responsibility of the head of European Economic Commission to integrate the three states within a common economic space. This is a supranational body to manage economic integration of the three former Soviet states. The Eurasian Economic Commission will be headed by the Vice Presidents of the three countries. Hence, apart from Khristenko of Russia, the Vice Presidents of Belarus and Kazakhstan will look after the affairs of this Commission.

Thirdly, apart from these measures, Vladimir Putin seems to be particularly influenced by the European Commission set up by the major West European states. In October 2011, when he was still the Prime Minister, he brought this matter to the attention of the leaders of these countries. He specifically pointed to the success of integration achieved by the West European states and benefits of such a Union. Hence there is a strong reason to believe that the concept of EEU might emulate several features of this International organisation of West Europe in working out details of its own institution.

Fourthly, the concept of EEU was showcased by Putin in his article entitled, *A New Integration Project for Eurasia: The Future Starts Today,* that was published in *Izvestia* in October 2011. In this, he reiterated his vision of Eurasia and to accelerate the process of formation of the EEU.[2] Vladimir Putin, therefore, succeeded in eliciting the support for reviving his original idea of setting up EEU as a viable case for economic development of Russia, Kazakhstan and Belarus.

There are several objective factors for promoting this concept of EEU. Firstly, there is geographical contiguity between Russia, Kazakhstan and Belarus, which may give some advantage in promoting cooperation among the three states. Secondly, being part of the former Soviet Union there were certain commonalities in economic institutions, structures and relations. Moreover, even after the Soviet breakup as opined by some analysts, these three states have sustained a fair degree of cordiality in relations among themselves to a great extent, even as some differences persist.[3] Hence it is worth considering the opportunities for the member states with the creation of EEU.

Benefits for Member States

All the three member states will have certain opportunities and benefits with the establishment of the EEU. Firstly, both Russia and Kazakhstan, being major energy rich countries, the share of EEU, so far as global oil and natural gas resources are concerned, will be quite significant—i.e., about 10-12 per cent of oil and over 35-38 per cent of natural gas. Hence from geo-economic and geopolitical perspectives, Russia and Kazakhstan will have a better bargaining power both with the West as also with the East. Being a major supplier of oil and gas to West European countries, on the western front, Russia might not face problems and hurdles in maintaining flow of energy through Belarus. According to N. Kuzmin, the Kazakh political scientist and foreign policy expert, "the proclamation of the Eurasian Union is a campaign with a very powerful symbolic resource."[4]

Secondly, the levels of productivity in Russia, Belarus and Kazakhstan are more or less the same. Hence if efficient coordination mechanisms at the level of the branches of finance and economy are put in place, the EEU might be able to achieve sustained economic growth. It is creditable that the first step has already been taken by the three states by signing an agreement comparable to the Maastricht Treaty in January 2012 which sets maximum levels for debt-to-GDP, inflation, and budget deficit.

Thirdly, the creation of the EEC will contribute to the economic development of the three countries in terms of modernisation and industrialisation, cut down transaction costs and promote international division of labour. The three states have entered into Customs Union which helps the free flow of capital and labour so that basic differences could be resolved. This will facilitate achieving the objective of full macro- and micro-economic integration as the key goal for the EEU. In fact, the impact of signing Customs Union, and other measures initiated by the three countries, has been evident from the fact that trade between the three countries has been increasing since the last couple of years. For instance, in 2011 the trade turnover between Belarus, Russia and Kazakhstan exceeded $110 billion—40 per cent more than in 2010. It may be noted that as per some reports while Kazakhstan and Belarus benefited from favourable gas tariffs, the Russian market was filled with cheaper goods from Belarus and Kazakhstan.[5]

Fourthly, the treaty between the three states on the creation of the Eurasian Economic Commission (EEC) was signed in Moscow on November 18, 2012 and ratified by the State Duma on November 22, 2012. The open-ended list of EEC activity includes such macro-economic issues as customs, tariff and non-tariff regulation, establishment of trade regimes with respect to third countries, industrial and agricultural subsidies, state and municipal procurement, currency policy and labour migration. It is claimed by some analysts and policymakers, and debated by others, that the EEC decisions will be binding; disputes will be referred to the court of the Supreme Eurasian Economic Council, which consists of the heads of state and governments of the partner countries. It is argued that the treaty benefits all three countries because, for the first time in 20 years, a new economic—not political—entity has emerged in the former Soviet space, and it is an entity that preserves the national identities of all the parties.[6]

Fifthly, in the opinion of some analysts, Russian entrepreneurs will stand to gain from the formation of the EEC because it has allowed them to register their enterprises in Kazakhstan, for example, where the taxes are lower, as is the level of corruption. Already, during the last couple of years, the first several hundred enterprises have been re-registered in

Kazakhstan.[7] Over time, the EEC will enable Russian businesses to hire more and better workers as and when the visa regime is abolished.

Reactions of the West

The United States and West European states seem to have mixed reactions with regard to the emergence of EEU. They have reason to be cautious about EEU since they have geopolitical and geo-economic interest in the region—Ukraine, Caucasian region and in Central Asia, particularly their energy resources. But at the same time US policymakers have legitimate concern about security scenario after its withdrawal from Afghanistan since Tajikistan, Kyrgyzstan could face serious threat from radical groups, the drug mafia, etc. Hence, the emergence of the EEU is considered to be an effective mechanism that can counter such challenges and is therefore in the West's interest too. The West also realises that Eurasian integration can promote stability and prosperity in the region which would help promoting trade and economic ties. Observers feel that the West should have no objection to the establishment of EEU, but membership of EEU should be voluntary, non-exclusive and designed for the benefit of all member states. According to Jeffery Mankoff, Russia's proposal of economic integration could strengthen some weak economies of Central Asia, particularly Tajikistan or Kyrgyzstan.[8] His apprehension, however, is that it might also bring negative consequences because of overdependence of these countries on Russia, which might lead to a compromise for the countries concerned in terms of economic development and foreign policy. Therefore, by 2015, Washington will have both the military and diplomatic resources available to renew its attention to the Eurasian region. In addition, by that time the American policymakers might revive the objective of setting up ballistic missile defence sites ready for deployment in Central Europe.

Some western analysts have expressed the concern that, by forming the EEU, Vladimir Putin actually intends to revive the Soviet Union. But this is rather far-fetched, imaginative and highly unrealistic considering the political differences that have emerged among the Commonwealth of Independent States during the last two decades. But there is a different perspective, too. The Western commentator Neil Buckley opined in 2011 that Vladimir Putin, the then Russian Prime Minister, was pursuing a different goal—that of building a "quasi-European Union" out of former Soviet States. There is a possibility that the EEU might be keen to expand, and then there is the strong possibility that some more countries of the former USSR, particularly Kyrgyzstan and Tajikistan, might join the EEU. Positive indications to that effect became evident in an official report of July 12, 2012.[9] Valentina Matviyenko, the Chairperson of Russian Federation Council, after her meeting with Armenian President, Serzh Sargysyan, stated that Armenia might join the Customs Union and the Eurasian Economic Union. Hence theargument that Putin intends to revive the former Soviet Union in a different form. The Russian political scientist, Dmitry Orlov, has even speculated that the Eurasian Economic Union, which embraces both Europe and Asia, could be expanded to include many neighbouring countries including Bulgaria, Finland, Mongolia, China, etc. But this is an extremely speculative argument. At any rate, as per some reports, Putin has frankly stated that in establishing EEU, he would like to take the best examples from the former Soviet Union and the European Union. In this paper I would argue that Putin has legitimate ambitions to bring about higher economic integration that will enable all members of the EEU to prioritise higher growth rates.

The China Factor

EEU's stakes are growing with the involvement of Asian countries especially China. During the last two decades, China has already emerged as a major partner of both Russia and Kazakhstan in terms of bilateral trade, investment, joint ventures, etc. Political relations are also close and cordial. At the same time, there are some genuine concerns for both Russia and Kazakhstan so far as China is concerned. For instance, China is posing serious competition to the Russian economy, especially in the eastern regions of Russia. With the declining population growth of Russia, which has resulted in a shortage of labour force, there has been a huge influx of Chinese migrants, numbering over several million, into Russia's Far Eastern regions, East Siberia and so on. Similarly, in the case of Kazakhstan, at present as many as 50 per cent of Kazakhstan's companies cooperate to varying degrees with Chinese partners. As analysts have observed, China's hold on Kazakh's energy sector has been increasing both by way of investment for exploration and exploitation and for laying pipelines to supply oil from Central Asia to China.[10]

Hence Russia has genuine concerns in Central Asia and its neighbourhood because Russia has had a historical presence in the region. With growing importance of the energy sector of Central Asia, a new great game is being played by major global players, including Russia and the US. China is also a strong contender in the region by virtue of its growing demand for energy with its high and sustained economic growth during the last few decades. In view of this, Russia has been concerned with the growing role of the West, particularly the US, on the one hand and China on the other. Hence, there is a possibility that besides other issues, the creation of the Eurasian Union could provide an economic shield against Chinese expansion.

India and South Asia

The establishment of the EEU might increase trade and economic ties with the region so far as India and South Asian countries are concerned. In the past, the former Soviet Union was an important trading partner of India. During the last two decades there have been changes concerning economic relations, even though political relations continue to be close and cordial with Russia and with all former republics of the USSR. The quantum of bilateral trade turnover has significantly declined, while imports of military equipments from Russia into India have shown appreciable standards.[11] A new set of economic relations has evolved between India and the rest of the CIS states. There are some improvements in relations with Russia and Kazakhstan in the energy sector. Moreover, India can benefit with the emergence of a large market for establishing joint ventures in certain areas such as information technology, pharmaceuticals, etc., apart from increasing exports of certain traditional goods.

Considering the fact that there is geographical proximity between EEU and South Asian region and that there are no conflicts of geopolitical interests, one could visualise prospects of regional cooperation to the extent that economic ties between the emerging EEU and South Asian states of India, Pakistan, Bangladesh, Sri Lanka, etc., can be improved. Hence, it is in the interest of these South Asian states that the proposed EEU should materialise.

Challenges

Notwithstanding the above discussion, there are several challenges and constraints in the task of setting up of EEU. Firstly, even as efforts have been made by the three CIS states to promote economic relations in the form of the Customs Union and the EEC, there is speculation regarding the performance of these institutions. In the opinion of A. Vlasov, Editor-in-Chief of VK, who analysed the working of the EEC:"the contradictions between the three major players of the Customs Union and the EurAsEC have reached a new qualitative level, where most of the questions would not fit into the agreement circle." Some critics argue that several decisions taken by the government remain on paper and are not implemented. For instance, the Eurasian Economic Community already existed much before recent efforts to showcase it as an institution. Its origins can be traced to March 1996 when the Customs Union, comprising the Commonwealth of Independent States and all the three states, Russia, Belarus and Kazakhstan, was formed. The performance of the EEC today is far less than what was expected of this former organisation.

Secondly, while the concept of the EEU on the lines of the European Union is laudable, the experience of European integration is hardly relevant for the post-Soviet space, where Russia, with its enormous size overshadows other potential partners. Moreover, it is argued that Russia has enormous economic potential and military might and hence would be the "natural leader" of any union. Russia's dominating presence might create a perception problem which could be a challenge for Putin as to how he will overcome this constraint in making the EEU all-encompassing.

Thirdly, while Russia wants to accelerate the path of economic integration, contrary opinions of analysts indicate that the aftermath of the formation of the EEU might have negative results. The concern is whether the economic union will lead to political integration. Having attained political independence after the Soviet break-up, no member would be prepared to lose it. During the last two decades most of the former Soviet Republics have succeeded in establishing their political and economic ties with other major powers in the world. They have evolved their own national identity and national interest which they would like to retain, even as EEU becomes a reality.

Fourthly, as stated above, EEU is a supranational body which would ensure the interest of the member states. In one of the summit meetings in 2011, as reported by the Russian daily, *Kommersant,* one of the issues that caused controversy was the authority of the EEU with third-world countries.[12] According to some analysts, Russia holds the view that the authority is the prerogative of the Eurasian Supreme Economic Council, which consists of the heads of member-countries. But, it appears, Belarus has insisted that all contracts should be agreed at the national level (with preservation of the nation state's right of veto). During the summit, the Belarus president Lukashenko even insisted that member states had the right to veto decisions of the future structure. To sort out such differences will be a challenge for the three states before it is formed in 2015.

Fifthly, all the three states are facing socio-economic problems, including unemployment, poor performance of the private sector, declining tax revenues, protests by workers and so on. The possible impact of the EEU on many of these issues is still uncertain. Soliciting public support from various sections of society for all the three countries will be a challenge for their leadership. Putin has been persistent in giving intensive push for the establishment of the EEU, and he had no hesitation when he campaigned for his third Presidential term. Hence the year 2015 has been considered, by which time major problems are expected to be resolved.

Sixthly, Russia and Kazakhstan are concerned with the security scenario and political developments in Afghanistan once USA and the Western countries withdraw from the region. The ongoing political unrest and protests in the Middle East and the Arab world are quite serious. The establishment of the EEU is essential and, at the same time, a challenging task for ensuring security of the Central Asian States as also of Russia. The interest of Tajikistan and Kyrgyzstan to join the proposed EEU could also be due to speculation about security lapses in the region. Moreover, according to Western experts, Moscow's push for acceleration and deepening of integration processes is associated with the desire to protect Russian interests in the event of upcoming possible changes of political elites in Central Asia.

Seventhly, Ukraine is an important country in the region but its political and economic relations with Russia are not always steady and consistent. The symbolic sequence of Putin's visits after he took over the presidency of Russia for the third term —Belarus–Germany–France–China–the countries of Central Asia—clearly shows the foreign policy priorities of the current Russian leadership. This also indicates that Ukraine was not on the priority list of Putin. In this context, it is important to note the views of V. Tkachuk, the director general of Ukrainian Foundation for Democracy "People First," who has opined, "within the framework of establishment of the Eurasian Union, Russia insists on the entry of Ukraine into the Customs Union. Moscow is closely interested in its resources, infrastructure and human capacity." But in setting up EEU, Russia will face the challenge and uncertainty of Ukraine's participation. Similarly, Roman Rukomeda, a political analyst for the Ukrainian Foundation for Democracy "People First," has been candid in his statement that the final goal apparently is the Eurasian Union, where Moscow will have the last word. In addition, this Union is perceived to become a powerful global player which is interested in partnership with the EU in the west, and with East Asian countries like China and South Asian countries like India. Now Ukraine wants deeper and closer integration with Western Europe instead of the East. It has so far resisted joining the Customs Union despite pressure from Moscow and incentives that offer lowering of tariff for energy.

Eighthly, as reported by *RIA Novosti* on June 15, 2012, Russian Prime Minister Dmitry Medvedev, proposed to introduce a single currency within the Eurasian Economic Union. But this is an over-ambitious proposal and a challenge for Russia. Both Kazakhstan and Belarus might have their own objections on this issue. All the economies are at present passing through a difficult phase. Belarus is in virtual crisis. Hence, it might take several more years for the EEU to introduce its own currency.

Conclusion

It may be pointed out that the realisation of the idea of the Eurasian Union is Putin's master plan to unite the efforts of the former Soviet republics to strengthen Russia's position vis-à-vis geopolitical competition with the US, EU and China. Thus some critics argue that the EEU, which is essentially a Russia-led organisation, partially integrates some of the former Soviet states. Putin tries to use this as a weapon to prop up his declining popularity and even legitimacy. By setting 2015 as the deadline for the formation of the EEU, Moscow has an end in view—to gather US attention in the aftermath of US military withdrawal from Afghanistan and the Middle East. Economic integration within Eurasia has potential benefits not only for the three original member states but also for many regional states. In the opinion of some analysts, regional integration is a reality (not just through the EU but also via NAFTA, ASEAN and Washington's proposed Trans-Pacific Partnership, among others). In that context, the post-Soviet space has nothing exclusive to offer. The most significant advantages of a new Eurasian Union would be the creation of a large single market and the lowering of barriers to the movement of goods and people. Economic integration could lower production costs by letting each member focus on areas in which it has a comparative advantage. EEU has major geopolitical and geo-economic significance and relevance for the West as well as to the East. India and South Asia might also gain certain advantage with the formation of the EEU.

Notes

1. "A Russian Bridge Across Eurasia," *The Hindu*, November 3, 2011.
2. Vladimir Putin, "A New Integration Project for Eurasia: The Future Starts Today," *Izvestia*, October 15, 2011 (in Russian).
3. "Putin's Grandest Dream: Could His Eurasian Union Work?" *EurasiaNet,* May 18, 2012.
4. A. Kuzmin, *RIA Novosti*, June 25, 2012.
5. *Kommersant* (in Russian), July 10, 2012.
6. *RIA Novosti*, November 23, 2012.
7. Sergei Ivanov, "Russia's Commercial Interests in Central Asia," *Kommersant* (in Russian), April 5, 2012.

8. Jeffrey Mankoff, "What a Eurasian Union Means for Washington?" *The National Interest*, April 9, 2012.
9. *Itar-Tass Report*, July 12, 2012.
10. N. Aldabek and K. Gabdullin "Oil and Gas Factor in the Foreign Policy of Kazakhstan" in Ajay Patnaik and Tulsiram (eds.), *Post Soviet States: Two Decades of Transition and Transformation* (New Delhi: KW Publishers, 2012).
11. Hari Vasudevan, *Shadows of Substance: Indo-Russian Trade and Military Technical Cooperation since 1991* (New Delhi: Manohar Publishers, 2010).
12. *Kommersant*, November 25, 2011 (in Russian).

14. Silk Road as an Integrative Concept: The Twenty-first Century Scenario

Sreemati Ganguli

The Eurasian or the post-Soviet space has become an arena where there is a multitude of regional cooperation organisations with different aims, objectives and nature. There are organisations on security cooperation like the Collective Security Treaty Organisation (CSTO) and the GUAM (Georgia-Ukraine-Azerbaijan-Moldova) Organisation for Democracy and Economic Development, organisations for economic cooperation like Eurasian Economic Community (EURASEC) and Economic Cooperation Organisation (ECO). There are also organisations which aim at both security and energy cooperation, like the Shanghai Cooperation Organisation (SCO). These organisations are promoted mostly by post-Soviet states of the CIS—apart from ECO, promoted by Iran and SCO with support from China and Russia.

There are also a number of projects that are being promoted under the name of the Silk Road—the historically famous corridor from East to West. These Silk Road initiatives include a wide array of projects—trade and transport corridors, energy pipelines, educational initiatives and the like. This article attempts to discuss the integrative character of the Silk Road concept, as is manifest through these projects.

Silk Road Initiatives

The first such initiative is TRACECA—the Transport Corridor between Europe, Caucasus and Asia. It was established in Brussels in 1993 by eight countries under the European Commission. This project was funded by TACIS Programme with the purpose of developing trade and transport along the Corridor. In 1998, the Basic Multilateral Agreement (MLA) was signed at the "TRACECA Summit-Restoration of the

Historic Silk Route" in Baku, and the TRACECA Intergovernmental Commission was set up in Tbilisi in 2000. Armenia, Azerbaijan, Bulgaria, Georgia, Kazakhstan, Kyrgyzstan, Moldova, Romania, Turkey, Ukraine, Uzbekistan, and Tajikistan are the member countries. The TACIS TRACECA Programme aims at the development of economic, trade and transport communications among the member states, facilitation of access to the international market by road and railway corridors, air and commercial maritime navigation, and promotion of international transport of passengers, goods and hydrocarbons.[1]

The planned project by the United Nations Economic and Social Commission for Asia and the Pacific (UNESCAP) to build a transcontinental railway network between Asia and Europe is another such project. It includes countries like China, South Korea, Thailand, Vietnam, Laos, Vietnam, Indonesia, Cambodia, Myanmar, India, Bangladesh, Sri Lanka, Nepal, Mongolia, Iran, Turkey, Armenia, Azerbaijan, Kazakhstan, Tajikistan, Uzbekistan and Russia. The initiative was taken in 1992 by the Transport and Tourism Division of UNESCAP, under the Asian Land Transport Infrastructure Development Project. Later the Project was formalised under the Trans-Asian Railway Network Agreement in November 2006. This Project is also termed as the Iron Silk Road Project.[2]

In August 2005, an International Symposium on Regional Economic Cooperation was held in Urumqi on the development of a New Silk Road (formerly known as the New Eurasian Continental Bridge) from Liyanyungang in China to Rotterdam in Netherlands. It was jointly hosted by the UNDP and the China National Coordination Mechanism of the New Eurasia Continental Bridge and the Chinese Ministries of Commerce, Railways and Civil Aviation. The Meeting was attended by Ministers from the five Central Asian Republics and Pakistan, Mayors from the cities along the New Silk Road, private sector representatives from the sixteen countries which would be covered by this route and experts from the World Bank, and the World Trade Organisation.[3]

International Road Transport Union (IRU) initiated a project to interconnect Asia with Europe through land transport under the programme of NELTI (New Eurasian Land Transport Initiative). The project is promoted as an initiative to revitalise the Great Silk Road in the twenty-first century.[4] The Project envisages the development of truck routes along three directions: the northern route from Uzbekistan via Kazakhstan, Russia and Belarus to the European Union; the central route from Central China via Kyrgyzstan, Uzbekistan, Turkmenistan, Azerbaijan and Georgia to the EU; and the southern route from Kyrgyzstan via Uzbekistan, Turkmenistan and Iran to Turkey.

The North-South Transport Corridor is another initiative, jointly promoted by India and Russia. This corridor, connecting Mumbai-Bandar Abbas-Astrakhan-Moscow-St. Petersburg was planned in 2000 by a tripartite agreement among India, Iran and Russia. The significance of this route is that it will provide better connectivity among the regions of Central, West and South Asia. The economic potential of such a corridor has caught the attention of regional countries and now the Corridor has eleven new members— Armenia, Azerbaijan, Belarus, Bulgaria, Kazakhstan, Kyrgyzstan, Tajikistan, Ukraine, Turkey, Oman and Syria, besides the three founder members. The Corridor has been claimed to have the potential of becoming the Silk Road of the new millennium.

CAREC-ADB Initiative is another project that aims to become a transport corridor across Eurasia in order to promote regional cooperation under the identical name of the Silk Road.

The BTC or the Baku (Azerbaijan)-Tbilisi (Georgia)-Ceyhan (Turkey) Pipeline is termed as another initiative to revive the Silk Road. Kazakhstan also joined the project in 2006. It is called by various analysts and observers[5] as the "Silk Road of the 21st Century" for its potential to promote energy transport within the region and beyond. This 1,760-kilometre long pipeline connects the Azeri-Chirag-Guneshli fields of Azerbaijan in the Caspian to the Mediterranean Sea port of Ceyhan. In 2006, Kazakhstan also agreed to join the project. The estimated cost of this pipeline is $3 billion but it is a part of a larger $12 billion upstream project of developing the Shah Deniz gas fields of Azerbaijan and of constructing the Baku-Tbilisi-Erzurum pipeline to carry gas from this field.

In May 2009 in Prague, the EU troika-meaning the Czech Presidency, the European Commission and the General Secretariat of the Council, met the countries of the Southern Corridor (Georgia, Azerbaijan, Turkey and Egypt) in the "Summit Southern Corridor-New Silk Road."[6] The Southern Corridor energy pipelines are Nabucco (Turkey-Austria), the White Stream (Georgia-Romania through the Black Sea), the Interconnector pipeline between Turkey, Greece, and Italy and also the Trans-Caspian energy pipeline projects.

NATO termed its project to provide high-speed and effective satellite channel access to the Internet and to the European Scientific and Educational Networks in the region as the "Virtual Silk Highway." The beneficiary states are Azerbaijan, Armenia, Afghanistan, Georgia, Kazakhstan, Kyrgyzstan, Tajikistan, Turkmenistan, and Uzbekistan.[7]

The series of Silk Road Strategy Acts of the US government also are pointers to the new approaches in the relations between the United States and the post-Soviet states of Eurasia.

In September 2011, Secretary of State, Hillary Rodham Clinton, Afghan Foreign Minister, Zalmay Rassoul, and German Foreign Minister, Guido Westerwelle, co-chaired the New Silk Road Ministerial, hosted by the German Mission in New York City on September 22, 2011. It was a follow-up of what Secretary Clinton outlined a speech in Chennai on July 20 about her vision of a "New Silk Road" linking markets in South and Central Asia, with Afghanistan at the centre. The idea is that "lasting stability and security go hand in hand with economic opportunity" and so, an Afghanistan with better economic partnership with its neighbours, would become the reason for enhanced security and stability for the region covering Central and South Asia as a whole.

Promotion of Regional Cooperation

The concept of a road expresses that of movement from one place to another. It breaks the barrier of a mentality that refuses to look beyond the immediate surroundings, the mentality that fears the adventure to face the new, the unknown—a mentality that is aptly termed in Sanskrit as *Kupamandukata* (the mentality of a frog, satisfied in the closed dwellings of its well). The Silk Road, with all its different and varied routes, offered the region an option to reach out to the outside world. The Road offered an access to the larger market for not only silk but other goods as well. The ideas of different religions, art (the most prominent example being the Gandhara art), architecture and civilisations were also carried along this Road.

The new Silk Road initiatives are developed and promoted in a different global scenario. The context has changed, and there has been a marked change in the connotation of globalisation—increasingly a link between globalisation and Westernisation is being explored. And along with the core values and ideas of globalisation, that are pursued and projected, are regional economic cooperation through interaction in areas of trade and energy, economic reforms, democratisation, protection of human rights, non-proliferation and the like. While the TRACECA Programme (1998 Baku Declaration) highlights the particular role of the region in the architecture of the ongoing process of Eurasian integration, and calls for closer integration of the regional projects with international trade and transport systems and for establishing new cost-effective transport infrastructure for goods and energy to global market, the BTC Project signifies increased mutual interdependence between Europe and South Caucasus in energy sphere, and it is hoped that the process of integration of these states into a broader transatlantic partnership and in NATO[8] may be expedited. The series "Silk Road Strategy Act" (of 1997, 1999 and 2006) of the US government[9] also spells out the tasks of the promotion of democracy, protection of human rights, development of economic cooperation in spheres of transport, communication, education, health, energy and trade as well as market economic principles, and assistance for regional conflict resolution, in the context of the relationship between the US and the countries of South Caucasus and Central Asia.

Notably, there are a number of significant features in this Silk Road promotion drive.

First, the initiatives do promote and support regional cooperation. It is more accurate to say that these are inter-regional or trans-regional cooperation as each of the initiatives breaks the boundary of the region of Central Asia, the Caucasus or in a wider sense, Eurasia. The economic and trade interactions between regions, that were long stalled, can be called the positive signs of globalisation, and this is true to the nature of the original Silk Road, that was the first experiment of globalisation. The essential idea of globalisation entails the exposure to the outer world, breaking the barriers of boundaries and expanding the horizon through interaction in various spheres and different forms. These initiatives are meant to generate flows and networks of activity and interaction across regions and continents. D. Held[10] defined globalisation as "a process (or set of processes) which embodies a transformation in the spatial organisation of social relations and transaction-assessed in terms of their extensity, intensity, velocity and impact-generating transcontinental or inter-regional flows and networks of activity, interaction and exercise of power." He referred to "flows" as movements of physical artefacts, people, information, etc., and to "networks" as regularised or patterned interaction between independent agents, nodes of activity or sites of power.

All these are economic initiatives, promoting economic interaction among regions within a broader perspective to achieve a sort of an economic integration that verily suits the interests of the powers that are involved. The TRACECA initiative demonstrates the magnitude of the EU's interests in developing the region's economic and energy potential and in connecting the region to the European market through a multimodal transport corridor, just as the NATO is keen to extend its economic and technological reach in the region. The BTC Project has been a US initiative to provide the region an alternative route for energy transport to the Western market. But the underlying interest was to deny Russia (and to a certain extent, Iran) a monopoly over the energy transport network from Central Asia to the global market. The North-South Transport Corridor provides India with an alternative route to get connected with the region. India lacks direct connectivity due to its strained relations with Pakistan and the instability in Afghanistan. A unique feature of this corridor is that it is the only initiative that includes Russia and Iran. Stephen Blank has remarked—"This programme is central to Russian and Iranian aspirations in Asia because it counters the EU's East-West Silk Road and US pipeline programmes that exclude those states."[11]

Also, these initiatives do provide the states of Eurasia a wide choice of markets—the European market through TRACECA, the Chinese market through the Iron Silk Road (possibly the market in the Middle East as well) and the South Asian market through the new Silk Road project. These Corridors are expected to ease the trade and transport bottlenecks of each country in the project, so trade and transport become hassle-free and smooth. For these states, this means more economic opportunities that are vital for their economic restructuring.

But the more significant aspect of the Silk Road dynamics needs serious analysis. The region, comprising mostly those states which were once part of the Turkic civilisation, stands to gain the most from this attempt to revive the Silk Road that has taken a variety of forms and routes. These countries are rich in energy reserves, minerals and other natural resources. But they face problems of connectivity to the world market—these are landlocked, and the rail and road transport infrastructures do not possess intercontinental reach. The Silk Road initiatives try to provide these countries with more investments to restructure their economic systems, and better access to the global market through flows and networks of activities and interaction across regions and continents. Here the process of globalisation has a direct and positive impact upon the economies of these countries. These countries have much greater interest in these initiatives, and so are engaged directly in all these Corridor projects, not as silent spectators of a group headed by a major power, but as confident partners who are well aware of their contribution as well as their stakes.

It is important to note that these initiatives do project economic competition between China and the West—of providing the landlocked states with access to global markets through these Corridors. There is also geopolitical competition among them in order to posit themselves in the post-Soviet space as powers to reckon with. It is true that the powers involved in the Silk Road initiatives use these as a geo-economic strategy to become geopolitically relevant in the region, and it is also true that save and except the North-South Transport Corridor, Russia has not been included in any other Silk Road initiative. At the same time, there is tacit competition of marketing of history. And, surely, China has a definite advantage in this arena—the Silk Road had its origins in China and China still represents the most popular cultural image of being a Silk

Road space. But the West does have another advantage—the values that get transmitted through these initiatives, are all that the West stands for, especially economic reforms and democratisation.

Aftab Kazi has put forward a new dimension to the study of regional cooperation in his argument of "geopolinomics."[12] He argued that geopolinomics "is a spatially oriented region-specific analytical model that identifies hitherto ignored historical, economic and cultural links responsible for successful trade during ancient and medieval times that continue to play an equally important role in the concurrent geopolitical environment."[13] In his opinion, "geopolinomics" derives its strength from culture, history and economics, and is more interdisciplinary in nature. Pressing issues in the form of need for energy pipelines, climate change, cross-continental routes of trade, terrorism and space security have all contributed towards a new form of regional interdependence. He preferred this term to geopolitics as geopolitical issues are influenced by external powers. But in the contemporary scenario of Eurasia, external powers have significant involvement—be it transport corridors (TRACECA), energy pipelines (BTC and Southern Corridor Pipelines), education (NATO's Virtual Silk Highway Project) and even promotion of democracy (a number of US Silk Road Strategy Acts have promotion of democracy as an agenda). So regional cooperation does have extra-regional involvement, and geopolitics is there even in cooperation among regional countries—the competition between Uzbekistan and Kazakhstan for regional supremacy—is a case in point

Interestingly, Afghanistan is being focused in a number of initiatives as the bridgehead of inter-regional trade cooperation between South and Central Asia, a welcome change from its stigma of being the centre of insecurity for the last thirty years. Frederick Starr and Andrew Kuchins put forward a Modern Silk Road Strategy[13] involving Afghanistan in 2010. This Strategy focuses on re-establishment of Afghanistan's traditional role as a hub of transport and trade linking Europe and the Middle East with the Indian subcontinent and the whole of South and South-east Asia. To them, the US-led Operation Enduring Freedom opened up Afghanistan's Northern and Eastern borders to long-distance trade for the first time since 1936, and it "is one of the most transformative developments on the Eurasian landmass in the past century." And so, America should carry on with this "transformative transport-based strategy." In the 2014 onwards post-withdrawal phase, the Silk Road initiatives represent an alternative scenario for the US as well as for the regional countries and most importantly for Afghanistan. For the US, the strategic dilemma remains how to engage itself in Afghanistan and in the wider region even after the completion of its military withdrawal from Afghanistan. The promotion of Silk Road initiatives is a better strategy for prolonged engagement with Afghanistan: it has geo-economic advantages that provide greater strategic sense in the long-term scenario.

The security situation in Afghanistan is evolving—there is insecurity in the present situation and there is uncertainty about the future. The main challenge is as much to ensure peace and development, as to handle this task simultaneously. It is not which would be the first task to accomplish. It is about how to balance these twin tasks at the same time, even if not at the same pace. And the successful accomplishment of this complex task in Afghanistan demands involvement of regional and global powers, as the making of the current situation there has had the fair, or rather unfair, share of regional and global power rivalries. There are a number of international and regional initiatives to help the Afghan reconstruction process, such as the Central Asia Regional Economic Cooperation (CAREC) and Regional Economic Cooperation Conference (RECC). The Silk Road initiatives offer possibilities of cooperation in the same direction but in a new way. If properly implemented, Afghanistan is likely to be the centre of activity for trade and transport corridors and the energy pipelines linking South and Central Asia leading to China in the East and Turkey to the West, and then eventually to Europe. Moreover, development in the area of national and regional infrastructure would help economic reconstruction efforts in Afghanistan and, in the long term, political stabilisation. Economic benefits would, hopefully, help ensure the active involvement of regional countries as stakeholders in the process of development there, not as power-brokers in a new geopolitical game.

Interestingly, the New Silk Road Initiative (NSRI) provides a scope for inter-regional cooperation between the regions of Central and South Asia. As Robert Blake, the US Assistant Secretary of State for South and Central Asian Affairs, commented—"that economic integration is the new 'Great Gain' that can animate our regional strategy."[14] For the South Asian region, the Initiatives offer another opportunity, apart from SAARC, to connect and cooperate in areas of trade and transport and energy cooperation. TAPI (Turkmenistan-Afghanistan-Pakistan-India) pipeline might be the first such case of inter-regional energy cooperation, if successfully implemented. Two developments have made Central-South Asia energy cooperation even more meaningful in the present context: the first is the New Silk Road Initiative of the US which emphasises making Afghanistan the transit hub of trade and transport corridors, and also of energy pipelines between Central and South Asia. And the second is the development of the SCO Energy group as it is an imperative for the group to include both India and Pakistan, the two observer states that will make the grouping economically viable as both India and Pakistan are large emerging energy markets. More significant, through this prism of inter-regional energy cooperation, the countries of the regions would at least attempt to see the age-old bilateral security problems, less as inimical neighbours, but more as joint stakeholders in a long-drawn peace process. We can think of today's EU that started as the ECOSOC in the early 1950's against the backdrop of a Europe ravaged by two World Wars. South Asia is also plagued by a plethora of problems—some internal, some bilateral and some regional. There is a logical issue of which follows what—regional stability first, energy cooperation later, or the urge to achieve viable energy cooperation leading to greater sense of mutual trust in establishing regional stability. In this region, where economic insecurity and regional instability are interlinked, this issue demands a long-term solution through a process that may be complex and multidimensional. But, regional and inter-cooperation involving various sectors may offer some hope for this complex but workable peace solution. A region where past memories of partition and present politics of distrust are the main impediments to cooperation and development, the Silk Road initiatives might offer prospects for a better future through inter-regional cooperation. The Silk Road is a metaphor of regional and inter-regional cooperation, and this might help the countries of this region to be more practical and come to terms with each other's historical limitations.

Conclusion

Significantly, these initiatives do promote regional economic cooperation. But it is of a different kind. Here the goal of regional cooperation has a different geostrategic method. The revival of the term Silk Road projects the relevance of the concept of Silk Road, which essentially means the development of cooperation through exchange—exchange of trade, values, cultures and civilisations. In this post-Cold War scenario, the trend is towards balancing of interests. So the economic imperatives of the promotion of trade and transport corridors do coexist with the geo-cultural use of marketing of history. At the same time, all these projects are strategic in nature—these initiatives constitute an essential part of the promoter states' comprehensive policies towards the region that are competitive at times. Still, through all these Initiatives, a bond of regional as well as inter-regional cooperation is being evolved. Such forms of cooperation are inter-connected with the integrative vision of the Silk Road that promotes not only inter-regional but inter-cultural and inter-civilisational integration as well.

The Silk Road concept in the twenty-first century, as in the past, offers a vision of a shared future between states, regions and continents, a vision for better integration through better connectivity.

Notes

1. See *www.traceca-org.org/ docs*, accessed on February 5, 2007.
2. UNESCAP "Iron Silk Road," UN Treaty, Press Release, *http://www.rmtbristol.org,uk/2006,* accessed on July 10, 2010.
3. International Symposium on Regional Economic Cooperation along the New Silk Road, *www.undp.org.cn*, accessed on July 23, 2010.
4. See *http://www.iru-nelti.org*, accessed on July 11, 2010.
5. See "Silk Road of 21st Century Baku-Tbilisi-Ceyhan Pipeline Opened," *www.Today'szaman.com/tz-web,* accessed on April 10, 2007.
6. See *http:// ec.europa.eu/external-relations/energy/s_corridor*, accessed on March 16, 2010.

7. See http://www.nato.int/science/virtual-silk/ 2003, accessed on April 10, 2007.
8. Svante E. Cornell, M. Tsereteli and V. Socor, "Geostrategic Implications of the Baku-Tbilisi-Ceyhan Pipeline" in S. F. Starr and Svante E. Cornell (eds.), *The Baku-Tbilisi-Ceyhan Pipeline: Oil Window to the West*, 2005, www.silkroadstudies.org, accessed on February 2, 2009.
9. http://govtrackus/congress/bill.xpd?bill=s109-2749, accessed on July 5, 2010.
10. D. Held et al., *Global Transformations: Politics, Economics and Culture* (Cambridge: Polity Press, 1999, p. 17.
11. Stephen Blank, "India's Rising Presence in Central Asia" in Ariel Cohen, (ed.), *Eurasia in Balance: The US and the Regional Power Shift,* (England: Ashgate, 2005, p. 191).
12. Aftab Kazi's talk in the international conference, *Energy, Transportation and Economic Links in Eurasia* (New Delhi: IDSA, January 16-17, 2012). *www.idsa.in/EurasiaConference2012_Session5.htm,* accessed on December 5, 2012.
13. Frederick Starr-Andrew Kuchins, "The Key to Success in Afghanistan: A Modern Silk Road Strategy," *www.silkroadstudies.org/new/docs/silkroadpapers/1005Afghan.pdf,* 2010, accessed on October 3, 2011.
14. Stephen Kaufmann, "State's Blake Sees Growing Economic Integration in Central Asia," *iipdigital.usembassy.gov/st/English/article2013*, March 2013, accessed on April 14, 2013.

15. Contextualising Anton Chekhov in the Literary Traditions of His Time

Joyshree Roy

This paper is an attempt to delve into the intellectual preoccupations of the "literary man" in Russian society in the middle and late nineteenth century. Here I would like to position Anton Chekhov at the central point of my discussion. Chekhov's amazing journey from a writer of light-hearted stories to a litterateur of iconic proportions commanding universal appeal with his nuanced short stories (*povesti)* and plays was intercepted specially during his early years, by critical traditions which sought to dominate Russian culture. However Chekhov, by not only initiating *avant garde* stylisations in his writing, but by championing aestheticism in art as well, carved out a unique place for himself in a rather complex literary environment. Critical traditions at that time focused on utilitarian ethics and insisted on creativity for a social purpose. My objective here is to place Anton Chekhov in the context of the debates that were raging in Russian society at a very crucial phase in its history when Westernisation, the spread of education, the struggle for a national identity and at the same time a desire to surmount the obstacles posed by the Autocracy gave rise to certain canons of culture that all were expected to adhere to.

In the early years of the nineteenth century which may perhaps be regarded as the take-off phase of the golden age of Russian literature, attitudes regarding the problematic of the true purpose of literature remained equivocal. Politically this was a time of disquiet, with the Autocracy overpoweringly in control of every aspect of society and extremely wary of the emergence of any new ideology. Whatever tenuous links literature forged with the reader remained confined to the upper strata of society, as till the 1820s, cultural cognisance remained the privilege of an aristocratic and elite set. The character of the educated elite changed somewhat in the 1830s and the intelligentsia now comprised men from both noble and non-noble backgrounds.

This subtle transformation in the composition of literate people in Russia maintained an element of continuity with the spread of education, initially from the top downwards which had the cumulative effect of increasing the volume of the reading public. In fact, its growth was to reach phenomenal proportions in the final decades of the nineteenth century and the early years of the twentieth, though literary tastes were to remain split between the Western educated upper classes and the newly educated rural reader. With the progression of literacy, the writer rapidly established his position as an intellectual guide who helped infuse Russian mentality with a new consciousness. Situated in a society of layered complexities, the literary man in Russia was unmatched in terms of his diverse preoccupations: he was at once a writer, a philosopher, a political thinker and a social activist. On the creative front, too, the display of remarkable genius (especially on the part of literary greats like Pushkin, Dostoevsky, Tolstoy et al.) earned for him a permanent place in world literature.

The idea of harnessing literature and the authorial voice to help an adolescent nation strive towards intellectual maturity and self-sufficiency was the brainchild of Vissarion Belinsky, the father of literary criticism in Russia. In the 1830s, Belinsky emphasised the need to use literature as a tool for providing proper cultural guidance to a society which had the task of eliminating social and economic backwardness at hand. His vision also pointed to literary criticism as an important force to be used in the political struggle against the Autocracy. Petr Chaadaev's *Philosophical Letters* which projected the Kantian concept of society transcending individual aspiration, possibly gave a priori strength to the Belinskian vision of using literature for the purpose of enhancing social cohesion.

On the question of art, Belinsky believed that nature was the permanent model for the artist, who could thus never completely divorce himself from his social surroundings and raise art to a level of pure abstraction. He wrote "... while fully admitting that art must first of all be art, we are nevertheless of the opinion that the idea of pure abstract art, living in its own sphere and having nothing in common with other aspects of life is a dreamy abstraction."[1] In his view, literature should possess the qualities of reality and naturalness which should be the result of the artist's skill by which he transformed ordinary reality into his ideals. Literary criticism likewise was forced to turn away from pure aestheticism and had to take into consideration "the place and time when the poet wrote and the circumstances that paved the way for his poetical career and influenced his poetical activities."[2] Belinsky thus proceeded to reject as inferior the literature in which the normative elements of utilitarianism were absent. However his outstanding intellect prevented him from being simply the theorist of a realistic art which was to serve only a utilitarian function. Belinsky, as pointed out earlier, admitted that art must first be art and only afterwards can it be the spirit and drift of a society in a given age.

With the agenda of creative activity having been specified thus, criticism emerged as a special discipline serving as the moderator of cultural tastes, as abundant literature reached the public through journals. The 1840s saw voluminous literary output as well as the emergence of literary criticism as a regular academic discipline being subject to intellectual discourse.

In fact Russian educated society was able to absorb, within a short span, changes in literary form ranging from poems, odes and epics (Lomonosov, Kantemir, Derzhavin) in the eighteenth century, to the sophisticated novel and drama (Pushkin, Lermontov, Gogol) in the nineteenth. The quest for *narodnost* was spearheaded by Pushkin through his prose works, mutating into the naturalism of Gogol, which with its emphasis on Russian reality brought the struggle for a national literature to its logical conclusion. All this was achieved with the ideology of the Decembrists and Slavophil-Westerniser controversy in the backdrop.

Belinsky's views on literature and literary criticism were echoed by the Russian intellectuals of the 1860s, namely, Chernyshevsky, Dobrolibov and Pisarev, who set the literary standards of their age. However an element of inflexibility characterised their ideas about art and society as they lacked the insight and sensitivity of Belinsky. All of the above subscribed to a body of doctrine known as Russian Populism.

In the context of Czarist repression, the populists decided in the 1870s to give practical manifestation to their ideals of constructive programme through their "Going to the People" and "People's Will" movement. On the intellectual front they attempted to use literature as a means of eluding the censor and emphasised that literary works should resort to overt moralising.

The doctrine of utility turned out to be the underlying principle of all Chernyshevsky's theorisation, be it on philosophy, art or aesthetics. This leading intellectual stalwart of the 1860s held that "art is the reproduction of reality" and that the essential purpose of art is to "explain life" and to pronounce judgement on the phenomena depicted and thereby place art "... among the moral activities of man."[3] In writings such as *The Anthropological Principle in Philosophy* and *The Character of Human Knowledge,* Chernyshevsky was to concern himself totally with the utilitarian aspects of aesthetics and was to proceed well beyond Belinsky's theorisation on art and nationalism. He rejected almost totally almost any aspirations to pure beauty in art in the absence of material motivations.

Chernyshevsky, perhaps more than Belinsky, had an even more complex situation to reckon with, considering that he was witness to a series of failed attempts at agrarian reform by the Autocracy, resulting in peasant discontent as well as rejuvenated intellectual unrest in the context of reversion to repression of thought after a brief period of concessions to liberalism.

N. A. Dobroliubov and Dmitri Pisarev, two of Chernyshevsky's disciples, were at one with the spirit of the 1860s so far as literary criticism was concerned. To Dobroliubov, the methodological orientation of the critic should ideally be an objective analysis of a piece of creative writing as a sociological document. He asserted that the critics' sole task was to adjudicate on the extent to which a literary work adhered to reality. Pisarev, a strong believer in nihilism, highlighted the need for social goals and an automatic negation of the motive of pleasure. Any striving for aestheticism was considered to be a waste of human effort by Pisarev who felt that music and the arts in general had very little role to play in the enhancement of the "intellectual and moral standards of humanity."[4]

It would be worthwhile here to contextualise Anton Chekhov amidst the polemical engagements of writers and thinkers who dictated artistic thinking and literary tastes. This was done through their monitoring of material published mostly in the journals of the time. In fact, journals comprised the principal literary fare made available to the Russian reader in both towns and provinces as books were rather difficult to come by. The journals in their turn were categorised into "thick" ones that were ideologically motivated and contained serious literature meant for the discerning and sophisticated reader. *Notes of the Fatherland* was an overtly populist journal while *Russian Thought* was reputed to be liberal in outlook. *Northern Herald*, *Russian Wealth*, *Messenger of Europe* and *Russian Notices* were some of the leading newspapers and thick journals of the period. On the other end of the scale was the "thin" magazine to which the newly educated low-brow public was partial. These magazines were expected to entertain through the written word and convey at a very superficial level an idea of popular science, history and current events. *The Cornfield* can be cited as a classic example of a thin magazine. By the time Chekhov was in the fray, trying to establish his reputation as a writer, readership had increased considerably in Russia, though literary tastes remained somewhat divided. The circulation of "thick" magazines remained essentially limited to the readers from the intelligentsia who confined himself to *belles lettres* and maintained an exclusiveness from the rest of the low brow public.

Meanwhile critical traditions in the Chekhovian era witnessed a general decline epitomised by a very narrow interpretation of Belinskian approaches. Literature now even more than before was used as a didactic tool with the innate objective of fomenting dissent. The populist interpretation bolstered up by Gleb Uspensky and Mikhailovsky prompted the latter to dismiss the value of Chekhov's story *The Steppe* as being devoid of worthwhile causes even though Mikhailovsky did recognise the writer's undoubted talent. Skabichevsky of the *Northern Herald* also prophesied ultimate doom for Chekhov's literary career, a stand which he modified later in the face of Chekhov's obvious success. Chekov's relation with Vukol Lavrov started on a note of bitterness (though this was to be mended later) as the publisher of *Russian Thought* described him as an unprincipled writer.

Chekhov was quite conscious of this downward trend in criticism as well as the decline in the standard of thick magazines and commented … "The idea that talented people must work only for large magazines is narrow-minded. It did have a certain justification when real personalities like Belinsky and Herzen were at the head of publications and they, in addition to remuneration used to influence, guide and teach … But now … petty groups and yokels are in charge of publications … ."[5] Chekhov had scant respect for contemporary critics such as Tatischev, Mikhnevich and Burenin (who were no major names but nevertheless important at that time).

It is in the context of this matrix of populist criticism, that we find socially conscious writers such as Gleb Uspensky and Nikolai Zlatovratsky writing their stories in the 1870s and even in the early 1880s with the peasant utopia uppermost in their consciousness. Uspensky wrote his story *The Incurable* in 1875, confirming that the true force in Russian life was represented by peasant existence. Zlatovratsky nurtured no pretensions of artistic objectivity in stories like *Peasant Jurors, The Foundations*, etc. All populist writers were ultimately to equate Russia's fate to her villages and its inhabitants. It was this sense of commitment to rural Russia, to faith in simplistic solutions, that begins to change in the 1880s—with Anton Chekhov serving as a catalyst to this kind of change.

However, Chekhov had to go through the litmus test of censorious appraisal, often by critics of mediocre standing, before he could achieve any kind of literary reputation. Notwithstanding the near abysmal state of literary criticism, Chekhov interestingly enough was a man actually made by the critic. He was spotted by Nikolai Leykin, editor of the humour magazine *Fragments*, adopted by Alexei Suvorin, owner of the conservative journal *New Times* and befriended by Lavrov of *Russian Thought*, all of which contributed to his meteoric rise as a writer. That the marked imprint of Belinskian ideals of converting criticism into an important cultural conduit in Russian society was still at play can be sensed here.

Chekhov stood out from the rest of his contemporaries where the question of art was concerned. With his remarkably wide-ranging literary output he marked a watershed in the literary evolution of Russia in more ways than one. He was in one sense a link between the didactic approach and the later modernist schools of Symbolism and Futurism which were to break out of all creative stereotypes. In his enumeration of what he felt were the duties of the author, Chekhov believed that subjectivity on the author's part tended to undermine the quality of creativity. It was therefore the artist's duty to depict things as they existed and to restrain from passing any judgement on issues he really did not understand. Formulating questions correctly was all that was required of a writer—answers to these questions would automatically follow from among the readers who would judge problems in their particular way. His individualistic temperament rejected regimentation of any kind. Freedom of the artist had an overriding importance in his particular world view. Chekhov's maturity and talent were revealed in thematically diverse and stylistically nuanced stories such as *The Steppe* (kaleidoscope of impressions of the countryside), *Lights* (theme of pessimism), *The Party* (scathing view of intellectuals), *A Dreary Story* (ideals and values discerned in the everyday existence of individuals), *The Duel* (superfluous man), *Ward No. 6* and *The Black Monk* (two intense stories about the human psyche) and women-centric stories like *Ariadne, Ionich, The Darling, Lady with the Dog*, etc. The fact that he published not only in "thick journals" after he attained success, but also in "thin journals" like the *Niva* is a pointer to the ease with which he straddled the two worlds of serious and popular literature.

While acquiring a stature that was perhaps comparable to Tolstoy and Dostoevsky, Chekhov became the initiator of a new genre in the sphere of Russian literature. The short story on which his fame primarily rested was taken up by other writers of his time and by some of those following him—the two most important being Alexander Kuprin and Ivan Bunin. Chekhov himself felt at one with the writers of the "end of nineteenth century" among whom he included "Tikhonov, Korolenko, Scheglov, Baranstevich and Bezhetsky."[6] All of them taken together could represent a "guild" of creative artists who would observe society and formulate the correct questions. The men of the eighties, as he called them, were a varied lot—most of them were to lapse into oblivion as authors, but formed an important literary circle in Chekhov's time, influencing to a certain extent the trend of literary creations of the period. The impact of the likes of Uspensky, i.e., populist writings, was tending to get somewhat dispersed.

Vladimir Korolenko's works fitted in quite well with the fading out of politicised literature with conspicuous tendentious leanings towards the end of the nineteenth century. His stories like *In Bad Company, The Strange One*, *Escapee from Sakhalin, Going the Same Way, The Blind Musician* were marked by a versatility of thematic preoccupations surpassed only by Chekhov himself. In fact Maxim Gorky remarked that reading Korolenko's stories in 1889 evoked a "new impression that did not accord with the one received from the literature of the populists ... it is clear that Korolenko's stories in no way set out to coerce either the mind or the senses."[7] The *Narodniks* too discarded them as being socially unimportant.

Alexander Kuprin's affinity to Chekhov, in terms of plot formation and compact narratives, was remarked upon by contemporaries and friends. Ivan Bunin wrote of Kuprin's stories *Solitude, Sacred Love* and *Night Lodgings* that they were written in a manner imitative of Maupassant and Chekhov. By imbibing the Chekhovian structural pattern, of commentary but no comment, Kuprin was contributing to the formation of a new kind of literary craftsmanship, different in content and form from the writings of the previous era. Chekhov's place in the history of Russian literature as an innovator of thematic and stylistic formats was therefore all the more assured through the works of his followers like Alexander Kuprin, who more often than not relegated ideology to the background for the sake of purity of their art. The short story had carved out a permanent niche for itself and the plotlessness of style and thematic unconventionality were to serve as a platform for greater innovations in the craft of writing in the next phase of literary development in Russia represented by the Symbolist and Futurist movements.

While didacticism in literature was anathema to him, Chekhov was not indifferent to the imperfections of the social milieu and the need for social rejuvenation. From the man who wrote stories with zero endings or no endings at all, we have a book *The Island of Sakhalin* where he studied the living conditions of the prisoners in the penal colony of Sakhalin. Here Chekhov described the degraded lifestyle of the convicts in the colony, the poor utilisation of the natural resources available on the island and the ruthless attitude of the authorities at Sakhalin towards the indigenous population. Active participation in famine relief work and census operations in Serpukhov districts contradicts any impression of the writer's apathy to Russia's diverse problems that are so underplayed in his literary creations. Chekhov represented the real thinking man in Russia, committed to aestheticism in art, a trendsetter through the absolutely brilliant exposition of his craft and yet an important intellectual force sensitive to the needs of society through his practical endeavours for societal change.

Notes

1. V. G. Belinsky, "A View on Russian Literature," *Selected Philosophical Works* (Moscow, 1948), p. 424. Also Belinsky, "Vzgliad na Rysskyu Litaraturi 1847 Goda. Statia pervaia." *Polnoe Sobranie Sochinenii,* Moskva, 1955, 1956, vol. 10, p. 304.
2. V. G. Belinsky, "A View on Russian Literature," *Selected Philosophical Works*, Moscow, 1948, p. 426. Also Belinsky, "Vzgliad na Rysskyu Litaraturu 1847 Goda. Statia pervaia," *Polnoe Sobranie Sochinenii,* Moskva, 1955, 1956 vol. 10, pp. 305, 306.
3. N. G. Chernyshevsky, "The Aesthetic Relation of Art to Reality," *Selected Philosophical Essays*, Moscow, 1953, pp. 374-75.
4. Quoted in Andrzej Walicki, *A History of Russian Thought from the Enlightenment to Marxism*, tr H. A. Rusiecka (Oxford: Clarendon Press, p. 214).
5. A. P. Chekhov, *Polnoe Sobranie Sochinenii I Pisem (v tritsati tomakh), Pisma v dvenatsati tomakh.* Moskva, 1975, vol. 2, (*Pisma*), pp. 117-78. (Letter to Y. P. Polonsky from Moscow, January 18, 1888.)
6. A. P. Chekhov, *Polnoe Sobranie Sochinenii I Pisem (v tritsati tomakh), Pisma v dvenatsati tomakh.* Moskva, 1976, vol. 3, (*Pisma*), p. 174. (Letter to Tikhonov from Moscow, March 7, 1889.)
7. V. G. Korolenko, *Selected Stories* (Moscow: Progress Publishers, 1978), p. 7. Maxim Gorky, *Reminiscences of V. G. Korolenko,* tr. Suzanne Rozenburg.

16. Representing the Caucasus in Russian Literature: Creative Writings "Then" and "Now"

Ranjana Saxena

Introduction

The last two decades and a half of the twentieth century had been one of the most disturbing periods in the history of contemporary civilisation. Perhaps this holds truer for the Eastern and Central parts of Europe as many horrifying memories of ethnic, nationalist hostilities that erupted after the disintegration of the erstwhile Soviet Union and fall of the socialist regimes in the East Central parts of Europe are still vividly etched on sensitive minds. As Meredith Tax, writer and feminist political activist, while arguing for the reasons of these kind of changes in the world, says, in the "past ten years, nationalist, communalist and religious fundamentalist social movements have surfaced all over the world, moving into the power vacuum created as local elites have been overwhelmed by the new global financial ruling class. The emerging struggle is not between East and West, as Samuel Huntington would have it, but within both; it is a struggle between the forces of globalisation and the atavistic social movements that have sprung up to oppose it"[1] The massacre of the minority communities and the great divide between "them" and "us" on religious lines in those parts of Europe, as well as the former Soviet union, perhaps, could be termed as shattering of the vision of the "multicultural dream."

We know that the "great shift" from socialist command economies to "free markets" took place in the larger context of the processes of globalisation, these processes created a world where "the material sphere of human life has increasingly become integrated and homogenised at a level of humankind. Though, the ethical-cultural and the spiritual sphere remain divided and the traditional, religious and national lines of demarcation have got even more accentuated. Such is the fundamental contradiction of our times."[2] It is this fundamental contradiction that has also given rise to divisions on lines of ethnic identity.

As Tony Wood remarks that "in the decade and a half since the end of the cold war, the map of Eastern Europe has considerably been redrawn. More than a dozen countries have appeared as a result of the break-up of the Soviet Union and the Yugoslav wars of succession, an arc of newly sovereign states stretching from Estonia to Azerbaijan."[3]

The formation of new states has been an outcome of the people's demand for reassertion of their own identity, often suppressed in the past as part of bigger and powerful nations' quest for geopolitical expansion. It is here that history comes in conflict with the demands of "social memory."

The Caucasus has been one such region that has seen much clash of nationalities and identities. Throughout the last couple of centuries, the shared history (past and present) of Russia, the former Soviet Union and now the Russian Federation with the region of the Caucasus, has been one of strife and conflict. These disputes have taken very ugly dimensions in the last twenty years, resulting in new warfare in different regions and/or countries of the Caucasus, as well as the entire region's relationship with the Russian Federation. The present crisis has its roots in the past historical background of annexation and/or surrender in context with the Russian expansion. The reasons for the continued hostilities are many. As the critic remarks, "more interesting than its geographical features and material resources are the peoples of the Caucasus. In no other region of its size in the world are there so many different races and languages. Macedonia contains seven or eight nationalities, but in comparison with the Caucasus, with its fifty or sixty, it is but a poorly-stocked ethnographical museum. Since the earliest times, this country has been famous as a meeting-place of many races and many tongues."[4] This rich and diverse multi-ethnic, multicultural region had also been rife with tensions from time to time. Never having been a homogenous region, there was conflict amongst nationalities arising out of multi-confessional and multi-ethnic contradictions. The highlanders, fiercely valuing their freedom, had resolutely resisted the advances of intruders. The advances from the Russian state were also resisted. The tradition was carried forward during Soviet Russia also, though for exigencies related to Soviet Union's quest for assimilation of these people into Russia. Some of the areas under major conflict are:

- Abkhazia—the Abkhaz ethnic minority, falling under Georgia, declared independence in 1992. In the ensuing war Georgia, supported by Russia, lost the war. This soon was followed by ethnic cleansing and mass exodus of Georgians from Abkhazia.
- South Ossetia was an autonomous district of Georgia during the times of the Soviet Union. Now exists as an independent unrecognised South Ossetian Republic.
- Nagorno-Karabakh is yet another independent republic located in the South Caucasus that borders with Azerbaijan and Armenia. In the centre of Azerbaijan, this region is populated by two-thirds by Armenians.

The region occupying most of the national and international newsprint and the bane of the Russian Federation is Chechnya which is located in the North Caucasus. During World War I Chechens were deported en masse out of their homeland for their alleged collaboration with the Germans. One of the expressed views is that the "Chechens remained impervious to the numerous attempts to Sovietise them. Their clan-system was quite strong and governed the main social aspects of life. The Communist Party had little influence, given that religious leaders and elders retained their social positions. The traditional and the Soviet systems were superimposed one onto the other, and most of Moscow's decisions gave rise to resistance and revolts. Thus, Chechens met the Soviet authorities with strong opposition when they imposed brutal collectivisation tactics. Several uprisings occurred in the Republic during the 1930s. Likewise, the war aggravated this very complex situation. A part of the Chechen population was openly hostile towards Soviet rule. Some tried to make contact with the Germans, as Ukrainians or Russians had done. A few of the insurgent group leaders viewed Germany's advance as an opportunity to gain autonomy or even independence. However, the Germans refused to accede to their demands, and Chechens consequently cut off all discussions."[5]

After the fall of the Soviet Union the region comprises the three countries of the South Caucasus, namely, Armenia, Azerbaijan, and Georgia. The Russian part consists of Adygea, Karachay-Cherkessia, Kabardino-Balkaria, North Ossetia, Ingushetia, Chechnya, and Dagestan. Presently Russia is embroiled in an armed conflict with Chechnya. During *perestroika* the Chechens had come up with the demand to secede from the Russian Federation, which was not acceptable and a series of wars followed since 1991 between the Russians and Chechnya.

History of the Region and the Russian Factor

There have been a lot of legends about Caucasus. One of the tales about the creation of the world says that Caucasus is protected by three giant-kings—Elbrus, Kazbek and the sacred mountain Ararat—the cradle of human race post-deluge. ... Strabon, the Greek historian, geographer and traveller, had also referred to Caucasus. According to one of the Greek myths Prometheus* was tied to one of the mountains in this region.[7]

The region that is called Caucasia is a land mass between the Black Sea and the Caspian Sea, which has a chain of mountains passing through it. The Northern Caucasus, or Ciscaucasia, merges into the steppes of the Don and the Volga. Southwards is Transcaucasia, having many smaller ranges of mountains. The Caucasus serves as a sharp dividing line between the two continents—Europe from Asia. Despite the barrier this region has been the meeting point and the intersection for the peoples of North, South, East and West. As an encyclopaedic entry informs,

> The two continents overlap, as it were, and we find Christian races of Indo-European stock south of the mountains, and Moslem Turanians in the northern steppes; sedentary and civilised peoples in Asia, barbarian nomads in Europe. But geographically the character of the two regions is quite distinct; the Northern Caucasus is a continuation of the great plains of Russia, while the fertile valleys of western Transcaucasia and the arid deserts of the eastern provinces are redolent of the Asiatic East.[8]

This region has been fought over by the Russians, Persians and the Ottoman Empire. The Russians maintained supremacy in the area after Astrakhan was captured by the armies of Ivan IV in the mid-sixteenth century. The history of the advancement of the Russian Empire towards the Caucasus dates back to the earlier period of the Russian State. At the end of the tenth century the Russian Prince Svyatoslav, having won over the khazars,* reached the mountain region of the Caucasus. The chronicles also mention about marriage alliances* between the Russian princes and the Caucasian princesses.[9] Then in the mid sixteenth century Ivan IV took the north-western region of Karbada under a protectorate and vassalised the tribes of the Kuban river basin. Russia's interest in this revived in the late eighteenth century. This resulted in the uprising of Sheikh Mansur during 1785-1791. According to A. Iyazkova, the Russian czars were spellbound by the beauty of the region and its people. The Caucasus had always attracted the Russians. Chronicles also point towards marriage alliances between the Russian princes and the Caucasian princesses. The beauty of the mountains and the Caucasian women apart, later, it was the policy of imperial Russia during the reign of Peter I to acquire access to the seas, both the Caspian and the Black Sea. The first campaign by Peter I was undertaken in 1722, which laid the foundation of a protracted future conflict between the people of Caucasus and the successive Russian rulers.

One of the most contested issues regarding the Russo-Caucasian war is the issue of its chronology.

> Some historians of Caucasus have the tendency to expand the chronological boundaries of the war and suggest its beginning to the times of Peter I, Catherine I, i.e., to the XVIII century. On the other hand Russian historians tend to reduce the time limits. ... The year 1817 is the commonly accepted date of this war in Russian historiography. ... Though the beginning of the conflict situation between Russia and North Caucasus legitimately can be dated to the year 1764. The year saw the completion of the construction the Mozdok fort that was to be the precursor to the conquest of Caucasus.[10]

The Caucasus had been significant for the Russian state as this region was part of the trade route that connected Europe with Central Asia. Thomas de Waal makes an interesting observation that

> The economic and demographic importance of the area between the Black and the Caspian Seas is small. By no calculation could Georgia, Armenia or Azerbaijan be called strong states; …. Yet by an accident of geography, which has situated them between Russia and the Middle East, Europe and Central Asia, these countries are fated to be the meeting place and a crossroads for the 'great powers.'[11]

This region has been home to various people and nations and seen co-existence of various "languages and dialects, of Islam, Christianity, Buddhism, Judaism and traditional belief patterns. Thus the Caucasian mountainous civilisation and the common Northern Caucasian type of culture got formulated."[12] The alpine Caucasus, that in the past has been a mythical place, being situated at the crossroads of the civilisation drama, came to acquire great importance for many others from time to time. Finally, Russia was able to bring this region under its control by the end of the nineteenth century.

As is known,

> In the course of 180 years, starting from the eighteenth century up to the '80s of the nineteenth century, every 10 years Russia had fought a war. Directly or indirectly these wars were connected with its expansion and widening of its sphere of influence. The only exception was Napoleon's intrusion when Russia had to defend its national territory. There is one more highlight of these wars. As compared to other western territorial conquests that lasted two-three years, the victory over the Turkic and the Caucasian ethno-sphere in the South lasted almost two centuries.[13]

The Caucasus Factor in Russian Literature

Russia's political engagement with the Caucasian region has produced a large body of creative writings of the Russian classicist poets, the romanticists of the beginning from the nineteenth century forming a literary Caucasus of their own kind. Even the end of the twentieth century saw creative responses to this relationship from the past. It is interesting to note that the great writers from the nineteenth to the twentieth century had been captivated by the story of the Russian–Caucasian encounters! Pushkin, Lermontov, Tolstoy and Makanin—all four writers in their own way have told and retold the story of the *Prisoner of the Caucasus*. The Caucasus became the region of captivity not only for Prometheus, the Greek mythical character, but also for many Russians, banished to this region by the orders of the rulers and/or self-will in the XIX century. As the critic remarks, the "Caucasus, for the progressive minded Russian from the beginning of the nineteenth century has been a symbol of free-will, freedom, though, roughly from the same period onwards Caucasus for the Russians becomes the antipode of these concepts—a place of exile, punishment arm postings." Though it should be added that for the "Russians it was a kind of an opportunity to get away from the conditions of repression."[14]

The beginning of the twentieth century saw the powerful representation having anti-czarist political undertones of this crisis-ridden relationship between the captive and the captors in *Hadji Murat*—the masterpiece by Leo Tolstoy. As is known, in his younger days, Tolstoy was posted in the region of Caucasus and he considered the Russian invasion as unjust. Later, in 1902 he again reiterates his earlier views on the issue and writes,

> What happened was what always happens when a state possessing great military strength enters into relations with primitive, small peoples living their independent lives. Either on the pretext of self-defence, even though any attacks are always provoked by the offences of the strong neighbour, or on the pretext of bringing civilisation to a wild people, even though this wild people lives incomparably better and more peacefully than its civilisers ... the servants of large military states commit all sorts of villainy against small nations, insisting that it is impossible to deal with them in any other way.[15]

While the paper would attempt to analyse the above-mentioned works or the "Caucasian text" in detail, it would deal with the images created by the Russian writers over the years. While tracing a trajectory of the image of this region in Russian literature, the paper would eventually look into the new dimensions of the indigenous "image of the region" as projected in the writings of the people from the region itself. There is a long list of writers, ethnically connected to Caucasus, presenting the view from the other side: German Sadulaev, A. Mahmedov, G. Markosyan-Kasper, I. Oganov, F. Iskander, etc. One such work to be taken up for analysis is *I am a Chechen* by German Sadulaev. The work presents a new image of the region and the people.

Coming to the question of the image of the Caucasus in the Russian social consciousness, it would be appropriate to say that the interest of the Russian people in this region got activated as a result of the aggravation of the expansionist policy of the Russian state in the region. This process brought the Russian people into close proximity with Caucasus. In fact, Caucasus also served as a place of exile for many Russian intellectuals, and the area began to be called the "Southern Siberia."[16] L. Gatagova observes that the "image of the Caucasus gets imprinted in the Russian social consciousness under the powerful aura of the creative and literary perceptions about the region."[17] Eventually, the beginning of the nineteenth century witnessed an upsurge of the Caucasian theme in Russian literature. This has been partly attributed to the rise of Russian romanticism and partly to the presence of strong censorship conditions in the czarist Russia which transformed Russian literature into a platform for discussing political, social and cultural issues.[18]

Coming to the question of depiction of the Caucasus in Russian literature, it may be said that Caucasus had been mentioned in the works of the Russian poets of the eighteenth century. The classicist poetry of Lomonosov, Kheraskov, Derzhavin, etc., made mention of this region. In an ode written in 1747 on the occasion of the coronation of Elizaveta Petrovna, Lomonosov refers to Caucasus as part of the Russian empire and in his description, "Russia extends its legs over the steppes, reckoning the prosperity around her, resting with her elbow on the Caucasus." A couple of years later in 1779, M. Khraskov wrote the poem *Rossiada*, which was dedicated to the victory of the Russians over Kazan. He describes Caucasus as a place that is very miserable, cold and unexciting. Caucasus is covered with ice, cold and bereft of any sunlight and it can consume you. Derzhavin, though a supporter of Russia's expansion in the Caucasus, in his poem, "On the return of Count Zubov from Persia" written in 1797, tries to give a balanced view of Caucasus:

> Oh, young leader! You who on campaigns
> Passed through the Caucasus with an army
> Saw the horrors, the beauty of nature:
> How, flowing from terrible mountain ridges
> Angry rivers roared into the darkness of abysses;
> How from their foreheads, snows thundering
> Fell down, after lying idle for whole centuries;

The Russian poets from the period of classicism wrote these odes either to applaud the ruler or the generals of the imperial army on their successful exploits of the Caucasus region. Hence, while describing the Caucasus, they pay attention only to the geographical character of this region. For Lomonosov, for example, the Caucasus is just a region to be put under command of the Russian State. According to Harsha Ram, Lomonosov describes Russia "as a human colossus straddling her own territory and surveying the horizontal expanse that she commands."[19] In the poetry of the classicist poets, references are made to Caucasus in the context of the supremacy and dominance of Imperial Russia. Russia of this period was consistently forging ahead with its policy of expansion in the South. It was Derzhavin who attempted to move away from this paradigm of the literary Caucasus projected by the poets in the period of Classicism in the ode, *On the Return of Prince Zubov from Persia.* Derzhavin expands the framework of the representation of the region as he gives a realistic picture of Caucasus, stressing its beauty also.

In the opinion of L. Gatagova, "The image of Caucasus, in the works of the classicist poets, has not been differentiated or fragmented as a geographical, political or ethnic entity. Caucasus has been represented as an enigma; a mountainous terrain, where behind every step and each cliff bend hid a threat."[20]

According to V. V. Chikhichin, “the region of Caucasus, in the classicist imagination, is only a potent mountainous column, the Southern support of Russia.”[21] While distinguishing between various images of Caucasus emerging at different points of time, the critic divides Russian literature into three stages according to the formation, development and consolidation of the geo-cultural image of the North Caucasus that still dominates the social consciousness. The first stage that begins from the end of the eighteenth century up to the 1820s, is marked by an absence of a geo-cultural representation. This is essentially the period of Lomonosov, Kheraskov, Derzhavin and others. The second stage, that begins around the 1820s and lasts for about two decades, is most remarkable as far as shaping of a geo-cultural image of the region of Caucasus in Russian literature is concerned. The distinctive character of this period is that most Russian writers of this period actively engaged with the region, and their poetical, literary interventions are rooted in their personal experience of the Caucasus. The great Russian poets and writers of this period, the Russian romanticists like Pushkin, Griboedov, Lermontov, Bestuzhev-Marlinsky, Polezhaev, had all visited the Caucasus. This was the time when Russian society was inundated with first-hand accounts in the form of travelogues about this region. Elaborating upon the second stage in the representation of the region, distinguishable by its attraction for Caucasus, it is pertinent to recall that “aggressive tsarist penetration into the Caucasus in the early decades of the nineteenth century coincided with the rise of Russian romanticism.”[22]

The third stage, i.e., the second half of the nineteenth century is marked by a decline in the writing about Caucasus. Though, Tolstoy wrote some significant works about this region during this period.

One of the famous Russian romanticist poets is Bestuzhev-Marlinski who had participated in the 1825 Decembrist uprising against the Czar, and on his own request served in exile in Caucasus. His stay there produced a large body of writing readership like *Ammalat Bek* (1831), *Mulla Noor* (1835), etc. Especially significant are his travelogues containing vivid ethnographic details and account of the Caucasian region. “Apart from describing the local customs and traditions, the dress-code and outfits, Marlinski also made notes of the local folklore and legends."[23]

Pushkin's and Lermontov's oeuvre is replete with poetry and/or poetical references to the region of Caucasus. Pushkin's famous works on the theme of Caucasus include "A Prisoner in the Caucasus" (1822), *A journey to Arzrum* (1836), in which the poet records his impressions of the places that he sees on the way. He acquaints himself with the customs and traditions of the local people. The Cherkessian and the Ossetian people attract his attention by the fact that they are the most poor amongst the clans that inhabit the Caucasus. Pushkin also pays attention to the "quiet and daring" women of this region, their customs of funeral, etc. His other works are *Kavkaz*, *Monastry on Kazbek*, *The Terek flows through the mountains*, etc.

Lermontov's relationship with the region of Caucasus could well be understood by the poet's own admission in the poetry *Aul Bastundzhi*, where Lermontov calls himself the "son of Kavkaz." Kavkaz stroked the poet's love for freedom and free will. The theme of Kavkaz occupies a significant place in his writings. These works include *Izmail Bei*, *Mytsri*, *A Hero of Our Times*, *The Prisoner in the Caucasus* and others. In the poem, *Farewell, unwashed Russia* (1841), the poet explicitly condemns "the unwashed Russia, the country of slaves." The poet is also critical of the lack of freedom in his country.

> Farewell, farewell, unwashed Russia,
> The land of slaves, the land of lords,
> And you, blue uniforms of gendarmes,
> And you, obedient to them folks.
> Perhaps behind Caucasian mountains
> I'll hide myself from your pashas,
> From their eyes that are all-seeing,
> From their ever hearing ears.

In the literary imagination of the Russian poets of romanticism, the region of Caucasus, where most of them found themselves in exile, is a place of comfort and freedom, away from the prying eyes of the authorities. As is known, after the Decembrists' revolt, the czar had told A. Pushkin that he himself would like to be the first reader of his poetry. As already mentioned, many writers were exiled to the Caucasus and many went there for the love of the exotic. It is also a historically corroborated fact that the Russians would be captured by the Caucasians for exchange of their "own captives" or for ransom.

The Russo-Caucasian interaction had produced a vast body of literature having a recurrent theme of the *Prisoner in the Caucasus*. The first work with this title was written by Pushkin in 1822, the second by Lermontov in 1828, the third by Tolstoy in 1872 and the fourth, with modification in the title and the plot, was written by Makanin in 1994, just before the First Chechen War in 1995. The first three stories have the Russian as the prisoner in the Caucasus, while the last has a Chechen as the prisoner of the Russian soldiers.

The romanticist hero of Pushkin's lyrical epic, "Prisoner in the Caucasus," rejects the life of the "civilised high society" and comes to the Caucasus in search of freedom. But here he is taken a prisoner by the highlanders. The Russian prisoner gets used to this life in a natural setting. He is observant of the traditions, customs and norms of the life of the highlanders and is appreciative of their simplicity and hospitality. In the end he is led to freedom by the Circassia girl who had fallen in love with him.

Lermontov's *Prisoner in the Caucasus* is close in its plot to Pushkin's story except that it has more characters and a tragic end. The Russian prisoner is mesmerised by the beauty of the Caucasus, its mountains, the clear river and nature around him, but he pines for his homeland. The Circassian girl in Lermontov's story is more resolute in achieving her love. But her love could not save him. In the end both are killed while trying to escape.

The tragedy of both the captives seems to lie, as articulated by Harsha Ram, in the "double-edged effects of Russia's coercive state apparatus, which stifles the creative artist in the metropolis just as it subjugates the colonised people of the Southern periphery."[24] Tolstoy's *Prisoner in the Caucasus* (1872) follows the plot line of the celebrated work by Pushkin on the same theme; here, not one, but two Russian soldiers are taken captive by the highlanders for ransom. Far removed from the romantic description, Tolstoy gives a realistic interpretation of this already repeated story of the Russian captive and the highlander captors. The two officers, while in captivity with the highlanders, are only bothered about their escape back to the line; even if they venture out in the mountains, it is to acquaint them with the map of the terrain. They are not enchanted by the beauty of the mountains, the Circassian girls, etc. Tolstoy resolutely moves away from the romantic interpretation being convinced that the people did not "swoon over the mountains, nor have love affairs with savages while in captivity, nor conduct war, even die in combat in the ways previously depicted.[25] Tolstoy's *Hadji Murat* (1904) added yet another significant chapter in the Russian-Caucasus literary discourse, Tolstoy's story is dedicated to Hadji Murat, a Chechen separatist rebel and a former associate of Shamil, in the nineteenth-century "holy war against the Russians." He had opposed Shamil and crosses over to the Russians. But, unfortunately, he becomes a pawn in the hands of both the rulers—Shamil and Nikolai I. The story about the life and death of *Hadji Murat* begins with a very symbolic episode of an unsuccessful attempt by the narrator to pluck the wild flower during his stay in the Caucasus:

> I climbed down into the ditch, … , I set to work to pluck the flower. But this proved a very difficult task. Not only did the stalk prick on every side—even through the handkerchief I wrapped round my hand—but it was so tough that I had to struggle with it for nearly five minutes, breaking the fibres one by one; and when I had at last plucked it, the stalk was all frayed and the flower itself no longer seemed so fresh and beautiful. Moreover, owing to a coarseness and stiffness, it did not seem in place among the delicate blossoms of my nosegay. I threw it away feeling sorry to have vainly destroyed a flower that looked beautiful in its proper place.[26]

Tolstoy's story highlights the fact that though the dialogue between the Russians and the Caucasians is of confrontation in nature, yet it is a dialogue. Secondly, Tolstoy emphasises the moral superiority of the Caucasian rebel

Hadji Murat over his conqueror—the Czar. Thus, he moves away from the official paradigm of the "bad vicious Caucasian." Thirdly, in Tolstoy's opinion, not every flower is meant to be a part of one large bouquet. They should be left to bloom where they are! Like flowers, people also have roots in their soil which cannot and should not be uprooted.

As a matter of fact such views were expressed even then at the height of the escalated tension between the Russians and the Caucasus in the mid-nineteenth century. A satirical novel titled *Escapades in the Caucasus*[27] published in 1844, made a lot of noise in Petersburg. The book was written by E. P. Lachinova, wife of a general posted in the Caucasus, and published under the pseudonym of Khmap-Dobanova. Views contrary to the Imperial vision about the Caucasus war were expressed in this novel. The novel was withdrawn, but it became a cult of its times. The last work in the sequel, i.e., Makanin's *Prisoner of the Caucasus* (1994), inverts the Pushkinian plot whereby the captive turns out to be a young Chechen boy in the hands of the Russian soldiers whom they would barter for safe passage in the valley of the Caucasus. But the core question that Makanin seems to be raising in the story is articulated by the conversation between the Russian colonel and the Chechen Alibek—a local dealer. The Russian tries to convince the Chechen that since he is in the territory of the Russian fort, hence he should understand his position of a captive. On the other hand, the Chechen alludes to the broader territorial conditions and tells the Russian that it is he, who actually is the Captive in the region of the Caucasus. The conversation of the Russian colonel expresses the views of the Russians who think that Caucasus has been conquered by them.

As far as the depiction of the highlanders in these stories is concerned, one may put the first three stories in the same category as all three, Pushkin, Lermontov and Tolstoy, project an image of the noble captor, who finally leads the Russian captive to freedom. V. Makanin's the *Prisoner of the Caucasus*, written at the end of the twentieth century, brings in a new understanding that nobody is a conqueror; everyone is a victim in this conflict. Makanin's story presents us with a different paradigm. Makanin's story, set in present-day Russia, "dramatises two exchanges—a financial deal and a military clash—between the Russians and the highlanders.

In both cases, the captive/captor relationship prevailing in the romantic tradition is questioned and inverted."[28] Rubakhin, the main protagonist of the story is captivated by the beauty of the mountains and the beauty of the Chechen boy, whom he, nevertheless, kills. The writer also drives home the point that both Russia and Chechnya are "stuck up" in this situation.

Narratives about Caucasus by the Native: A "Revolt of Social Memory"

This brings us to the memoir-novel by German Sadulaev, *I am a Chechen*, written in 2006. This is a book that tells the history and the story of one of the regions of the Caucasus in the words of the native. The book is based on his own memories, as well as on the collective memories of the entire people of the region.

Sadulaev's take on Chechnya is woven with the legends of the people and the land, images of the exotic regional landscapes, fragmented memories and pain inflicted as a result of the genocide that took place from time to time in this region. Sadulaev beautifully combines the past, his childhood memories of his beautiful country with the present war-torn Chechnya. In this context he says,

> Later I visited Chechnya many times. Today I travel home regularly. And I see a newly built Grozny. I see a Shali which has become twice as big and more beautiful—or so people say. They say everything has been restored. But that's a lie. You cannot restore anything. Once destroyed, it is destroyed forever, just as a dead person cannot be brought back to life. They have merely built a new city....

With these words, German Sadulaev expresses his anguish at the loss of his native land in Chechnya.

Sadulaev's memories seem to retain the pain of all the injuries inflicted on the people from this region over the centuries. The pain when the Russians began their conquest of the Caucasus; the pain when the Russian army under General Ermolov attempted to crush the rebellion of the early nineteenth century; the emotional trauma and the anguish of the people when they were deported out of their homeland during Stalin's regime. And finally the destruction and mass-killing of the people in the two wars between Russia and Chechnya between 1995 and 2000.

> Each night the heavy shells fly howling over the houses in the direction of the mountains and explode with a boom somewhere far away. ... That would indeed be a famous victory. When the mountains die. When they are razed to the earth, and this proud range stands no longer. *Gordost*–pride and *gory*–mountains: they share the same root. There'll be no more pride of the mountains, just the docility of the plains. Or the emptiness of the steppe.

No more mountains, only the Great Steppe, without end and without border."[29] This has the obvious allusion to the intrusion from the North, the steppes, the Russians that time and again made attempts to tread upon the pride of the Caucasian natives.

Sadulaev heavily draws upon his memories from the past and says, "And memories like explosions. Once my memory was a strawberry field. Now it is a minefield."[30] While arguing about the difficult relationship with Russia due to historical reasons, the narrator tries to delineate the basic features of the Chechen people. The writer says "My name is Sadulaev, German Umaralievich. I am a Chechen. I do not know how to feel fear. The part of our brains responsible for fear has atrophied completely."[31] The narrator recalls all the instances of being discriminated against in his own country for belonging to the region of Caucasus: "No matter how hard I tried to leave ... I just couldn't hide from the war. ... The war came to me through the searches at airports and stations, through the detentions 'while we verify your identity,' through blunt refusals to register me, and awkward and sheepish refusals to offer me jobs after reading my application forms."[32]

The narrator is able to drive home the point that his native land had been wronged many decades ago. What followed was a process of forced assimilation which did not take place as the Russians never completely trusted the people of Caucasus. The social consciousness of the people of the Caucasus also holds the pain of the trampling of their pride close to their chests.

This brings us to an important issue of social memory and how events remain preserved and etched in the minds of people and there is no way one can erase them. Histories can be erased and/or rewritten, but memories, individual or collective social memories, do not die. They become part of the oral tradition and are passed down from generation to generation. In the case of the Chechen people, this holds true. "Memory plays a central role, not only in its oral traditions—notably the epic songs, *illi*—but also in the customary duty to remember seven generations of ancestors. History is no dispassionate record of events; it is the basis of Chechen identity itself."[33]

Conclusion

In conclusion, I would like to say that the image of the region of Caucasus emerged as powerful narrative in Russian literature starting from the mid-eighteenth century onwards. This image has been linked with the development of the Russian thought process. Taking shape under the idea of absolutist czarism it moves on towards a geo-cultural image of the region of Caucasus. This image has also been dealt with critically by writers from within Russia. Tolstoy, the giant of Russian literature, having critically questioned the czarist Russian state, treated the subject of the image of the Caucasus in the background of the complex Russo-Caucasian relationship, and forwarded a very radical understanding. In this context most important is the fact that "Caucasus appears not just as a literary, metaphysical image, but also as a conceptual space through which the Russian society and the Russian social thought positioned itself vis-à-vis the czarist Russia."[34] The image of the Caucasus and the Russo-Chechnya conflict that has been so masterly created by Sadulaev, without a linear narrative with memories coming in cyclic manner, makes a compelling case in favour of Chechnya. The book by Sadulaev proves that "pasts that cannot be incorporated are privatised and partcularised, consigned to the margins of the national and denied a full public voice,"[35] still have a life and lies deep down in the depths of social memory. They may spring up at any opportune time. The book by Sadulaev proves just that.

Notes

1. M. Tax, "World Culture War," *The Nation*, May 17, 1999 http://www.meredithtax.org/global-feminist-movement/world-culture-war (accessed on April 20, 2012).
2. G. Abdusalom, "Dialog kultur: vozmozhnosti I predely (Dialogue of Cultures: significance and prospects), http://www.lych.ru/online/index.php/0ainmenu-65/34--s52008/140--- (accessed on July 27, 2013).
3. T. Wood, "The Case for Chechnya," Editorial, *New Left Review*, November 30-December 2004, p. 5.

   * Khazars—a Turkish language speaking people, habituating in the Eastern Europe in the fourth century AD after the invasion of the Huns and moving in the territory of western-Caspian steppes.

   * Reference is being made to the marriage between Prince I. Mstislavovich and the Georgian Princesses in 1154.
4. Luigi Villari, *Fire and Sword in the Caucasus* http://armenianhouse.org/villari/caucasus/caucasus-history.html
5. A. Campana, "The Massive Deportation of the Chechen People: How and why Chechens were Deported," http://www.massviolence.org—ISSN 1961-9898.

   * Prometheus is the name of a figure in Greek mythology, one of the Titans. His name means "forethought." He brought fire to the earth from heaven. Thus, he evoked the enmity of Zeus. To punish this offence he was chained to a rock of the Caucasus (the eastern extremity of the world according to the notions of the earlier Greeks), where his liver, which was renewed every night, was torn by a vulture or an eagle.
7. A. Iyazkova, "Kavkaz I Rossia. Iz istorii rossisko-gruzinskikh otnashenii," *Vestnik Evropi*. 2004, no.11.
   magazines.russ.ru/vestnik/2004/11/iaz11.html (accessed on August 1, 2012).
8. Iazykova.
9. Iyazkova.
10. V. Gutakov, "Russki put' k yugi.", *Vestnik Evropii*. 2007, no. 21 http://magazines.ruus.ru/vestnik.ru/2007/21 «Вестник Европы» 2007, no. 21.
11. Thomas de Waal, "Reinventing the Caucasus," *World Policy Journal*. vol. 19, no. 1. (Spring, 2002). http://www.jstor.org/stable/40209790 (accessed on July 20, 2012).
12. M. Yu. Chotchaeva, "Historical cultural myth" about the Caucasus and separate updatings of a theme of "The Caucasian Captive" in the modern Russian and North Caucasian literature," http://cyberleninka.ru/article/n/istoricheskiy-kulturnyy-mif-o-kavkaze-i-otdelnye-modifikatsii-temy-kavkazskogo-plennika-v-sovremennoy-russkoy-i-severo-kavkazskoy (accessed on August 18,2013).
13. Gutakov.
14. Chotchaeva.
15. T. Wood, "The Case for Chechnya."

16. V. Shaduri, "Dekabristskaia Literatura i Gruzinskaia Obshchesvennost" (Decembrist Literature in Georgian selfhood), Tbilisi, *Zaria Vostoka*, 1958. p. 22.
17. See L. Gatagova, *Obraz Kavkaza v Russkom Obshchesvennom soznanii (XVII–XIX).* In the monograph "Obrazy regionov v obshestvennom soznanii I kulture Rossii (XVII-XIX) Tula, Grif I K, 2011.
18. See S. Layton, *Russian Literature and Empire* (Cambridge University Press, 1994), pp. 33-34.
19. H. Ram, *The Imperial Sublime. A Russian Poetics of Empire*, (Madison: The University of Wisconsin Press. 2003), p. 76.
20. See L. Gatagova.
21. V. V. Chikhichin, Geokulturnii obraz severnova Kavkaza.
22. S. Layton, p. 1.
23. L. Gagatova.
24. H. Ram.
25. Eikhenbaum quoted in Susan Layton.
26. Leo Tolstoy, Murat Hadji, Trans. Louise and Aylmer Maude. A PENN STATE ELECTRONIC CLASSICS SERIES PUBLICATION. 2001, pp. 3-4.
27. *Bolshaya Biograficheckaya Entsiklopedia* http://dic.academic.ru/dic.nsf/enc_biography/69146/Лачинова
28. H. Ram.
29. G. Sadulaev, *I am a Chechen*, (London: Vintage books, 2011), pp. 28-29.
30. Sadulaev, p. 95.
31. Sadulaev, p. 83.
32. Sadulaev, p. 82.
33. See T. Wood, "The Case for Chechnya," Editorial, *New Left Review*, November 30-December 2004, p. 9.
34. Kh. G. Tkhagapsoev, "Pushkinski faktor v dialoge russkikh I kafkazskikh kultur," *Vestnik rossiskikh akademii Nauk.* 2009, vol. 79, no. 7, p. 618.
35. A. M. Alonso, "The Politics of Space, Time and Substance: State Formation, Nationalism and Ethnicity," *Annual Review of Anthropology*, 23, 1994, p. 389.

17. Socialist Realism Architecture and Soviet Cinema: The All-Union Agricultural Exhibition (VSKhV) in *The Radiant Path*

Akiko Honda

As Beatriz Colomina mentioned in her book, *Privacy and Publicity: Modern Architecture as Mass Media* (1996), the centre of architectural work saw a worldwide shift during the first half of the twentieth century. The construction site was no longer the focus as the mass media—newspapers, magazines, and movies—played an increasingly important role. This was especially true for Soviet mass media and socialist realism architecture, the central aim of which was not construction but the promotion of the concept of an ideal community, which would be achieved through architectural images. Among various mediums of art, the cinema was no doubt the most influential one for the general public during pre-war days. People visited the theatre many times to watch the same movie, memorised the songs, and imitated the main character's manner. It was an effective method for implanting images of the brilliant future capital consisting of enormous monumental buildings into people's minds. Most of them could not visit Moscow because an internal passport control system restricted free travel and migration, particularly to the capital. In short, they could know of the capital only through the movies.

From this viewpoint, the All-Union Agricultural Exhibition (VSKhV) held in Moscow was one of the most stimulating shows of Soviet architecture and cinema. The pavilion buildings at the exhibition were considered the best of socialist realism in architecture. In particular, art integration (*Gesamtkunstwerk*) was the primary task for these pavilion architects. They were required to integrate all kinds of art through architecture for the realisation of architecture parlante ("speaking architecture"), which narrated idealised village life in a kolkhoz. Of course, it was a difficult task for architects to incorporate not a chronological but a spatial kind of art.

The question arises: Can architectural spaces speak more fluently in movies than in real space? Based on the hypothesis that this is indeed the case, I would like to analyse Grigori Aleksandrov's film *The Radiant Path* (1940)—particularly the last scene, which was devoted to the VSKhV. The space created by Aleksandrov can be regarded as a model of socialist realism architecture with the integration of many types of art and the full convergence to Joseph Stalin as the leader.

Pavilion as a Model for the Palace of Soviets

The All-Union Agricultural Exhibition opened on August 1, 1939, in Ostankino, north-east of Moscow. At first, the exhibition was planned to open for the 20th anniversary of the Revolution, and was devoted to the success of agricultural collectivisation and mechanisation. However, the construction of the exhibition missed the deadline twice, and the last delay changed its overall character, with the place becoming the centre of a Stalinist cult.

On the pretext of the second delay, the Communist Party intervened in the planning of the exhibition. As a result, Mikhail Chernov, the head of the Exhibition Committee and the People's Commissar of Agriculture, was arrested along with the general planner, Vyacheslav Oltarzhevsky.[1] The opening was postponed for another year, and during this period (1938-39), the entire design was changed dramatically. One of the biggest changes was made to the Pavilion of Mechanisation (Figure 1), which was the official centrepiece of the exhibition. Its tower-shaped pavilion, designed by Oltarzhevsky, was demolished and a huge new arcade-like building was constructed right behind the Mechanisation Square. Instead of housing the Mechanisation Pavilion, the centre of the square was occupied by a 25-metre statue of Stalin. Consequently, the new Mechanisation Pavilion became a frame for the Stalin statue (Figure 2). Also, Oltarzhevsky's main entrance (Figure 3) was replaced by a huge arch with four pillars, decorated with many reliefs (Figure 4).

Figure 1. **The Design of Mechanisation Pavilion by Oltarzhevsky (1937).**
Arkhitektura SSSR, no. 2 (1937): 5.

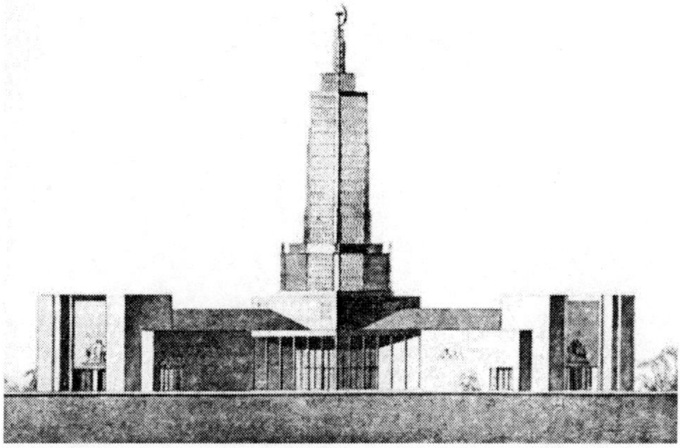

Figure 2. **Stalin's statue and new Mechanisation Pavilion (1939)**
Stroitel'stvoMoskvy, no. 16 (1940): frontispiece.

Figure 3. **Maquette of the Main Entrance by Oltarzhevsky**
Arkhitektura SSSR, no. 2 (1937): 6.

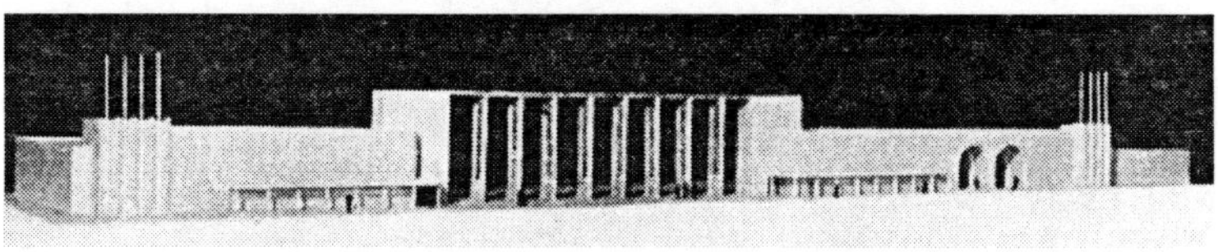

Figure 4. **The new Main Entrance**
Arkhitektura SSSR, no. 9 (1939): 4.

In the exhibition, all pavilions were required to integrate various types of art, similar to other monumental buildings of that time. This meant that various kinds of art should have a mutual relationship by following a common theme. From this viewpoint, existing pavilions were criticised for lacking expression.[2] In response to such criticism, signboard-like wooden pavilions were replaced by stone eclectic neoclassical pavilions made of marble or granite, with ornate reliefs, statues, frescos, and paintings (Figure 5). Eventually, the total number of statues increased to about 1,600, and the total area of majolica and fresco was expanded to 2,000 square metres.[3] These exhibits had a fixed purpose. They were devoted to the goal of socialist realism architecture,[4] namely, erecting the Palace of the Soviets[5] (Figure 6).

Figure 5. **Belorussia Pavilion under construction (1937) and its new design (1939)**
Arkhitektura SSSR, no. 9 (1939): 23.

Figure 6. **Palace of the Soviets**
Arkhitektura SSSR, no. 6 (1937): 26.

Figure 7. **Diorama of** *Georgian SSR*
*Vystavochnyeansambli SSSR 1920-1930-e gody.Mate*rialyidokumenty, Moscow: Galart, 2006, p 267.

Figure 8. **Inside of Moscow, Ryazan and Tura Oblast Pavilion**
Vystavochnyeansambli SSSR, p. 287.

Among these exhibits, one highly praised attempt at art integration was the diorama. For instance, Aleksandr Labas' *12 Soviet Republics* (Figure 7) combined sculptures, reliefs, and paintings to describe each of the nation's characteristics. In addition, the diorama was also required to be capable of stimulating all five human senses.[6] Such an aspiration for the creation of total reality led artists to create a panoramic simulacrum of an ideal kolkhoz life, not only with statues and painted images but also with real people wearing folk costumes in the pavilions, or through the entire exhibition. For example, one of the pictures in the Pavilion of Moscow, Ryazan and Tula Oblast (Figure 8), clearly shows such integration. In this picture, there are two girls wearing typical village costumes. In a slightly unnatural pose, instead of facing the exhibits behind them, they are looking outward as if imitating the Lenin statue or the people in the painting. This is a standard pose of socialist realism figures, which expresses the people's eager expectation of a brilliant future coming soon. Looking at this common pose, the girls in the photo can relate with the Lenin statue and the people in the picture, thus overcoming the difference of each medium. In other words, these figures, though conveyed through different mediums, share the same story, that is, the realisation of the ideal society of the near future.

According to Igor Riazantsev, a historian of the Soviet exhibitions, showpieces in exhibitions from the 1920s to the early 1930s were either "actually existing things or products of exhibition art." However, in the VSKhV, "described reality"[7] was the main theme, and the boundary between real things and imitations became blurred. "The obsession with the authenticity of the object and the rationale for its collection in science,"[8] an ideal of World Fairs in the late nineteenth century, has already disappeared. This is the novelty of socialist realist exhibitions. A Russian historian of Soviet architecture, Irina Belintseva, described the VSKhV as a daydream that integrated "imitations and real things," saying it was "completely unconnected with a real kolkhoz."[9]

Furthermore, in the panorama, a frame that ordinarily divided spectators from artefacts was removed and visitors became part of the exhibition. However, in the exhibition scene of the film *The Radiant Path*, Aleksandrov removed the frame literally, to bring in not only his heroine but also spectators into the social realists' dreamland.

The Space of Stalin

The main character in *The Radiant Path*, Tania Morozova[10] (Lyubov Orlova), worked as a housemaid in the countryside. She was initially an illiterate, unsophisticated girl but with a talent for rationally organising work (which was suggested at the beginning of the film in the scene where a meal is prepared). But an encounter with an engineer who would become her future partner, Aleksei Lebedzev, and a forewoman, Maria Pronina, leads her to go to a school and thereafter to become a factory girl. She began to work in a spinning mill and then a textile factory. She showed her ability to organise things efficiently and established the new record for the number of looms operating simultaneously. Finally, she received the Order of Lenin as an outstanding Stakhanovite worker.

After the conferment ceremony in the palace of the Kremlin, Tania, who has received the Order from Mikhail Kalinin, comes out to an anteroom. Being unable to suppress her joy, she begins to sing and dance. Soon, past images of her as a housemaid and a factory girl appear one after another in a mirror on the wall, and they begin to sing together with the present-day Tania (Figures 9 and 10). Then, Tania's past image at a New Year's party appears in the mirror. Present-day Tania asks the image to show her what will happen in the future. The past image opens the mirror frame like a door and invites her into the mirror world (Figure 11). As soon as Tania enters the mirror, they drive off in a flying car toward the future.

While the car is flying over Moscow and the snow-capped mountains,[11] the mirror frame surrounds the screen as if to emphasise the fictional nature of the scene. However, when the car arrives over the entrance of the exhibition (Figure 12) and begins circling around Vera Mukhina's *Worker and Kolkhoz Woman* statue, the mirror frame disappears (Figure 13).

Aleksandrov often used frames around a screen in his works to visually depict that what we are watching is a pure fabrication. The most extreme example of Aleksandrov's frame play is the last scene in his *Jolly Fellows* (1934). In the last sequence, the camera is continually pulled backward from the stage of the Bolshoi Theatre to its entrance, and the screen becomes surrounded by one frame after another. The first is by the frame of the stage, next by a box seat, then by the lobby's door and finally by the frame of the theatre's entrance (Figure 14). It suggests that the whole story we have watched is not reality, but a fabrication.

In contrast, however, the mirror frame disappears before the ending in *The Radiant Path.* Instead of the frame, the entrance arch of the exhibition surrounds the screen, with the titles "Welcome to the VSKhV!" (Figure 15). At the same time, the car driven by Tania lands. From a simplistic viewpoint, the disappearance of the mirror frame could be regarded as a return to reality. In actuality, the space of the exhibition described by Aleksandrov is as fictional as the mirror world.

Figure 9. **Singing Tania with her past images as a housemaid**

Figure 10. **Singing Tania with her past images as a factory girl**

Figure 11. **The past image invites Tania into the mirror world**

Figure 12. **Tania's arrival at the VSKhV**

Figure 13. **Disappearance of the mirror frame**

Figure 14. **Last scene of** ***Jolly Fellows***

Figure 15. **"Welcome to the VSKhV!"**

For example, Aleksandrov began a space montage from this scene. Nonetheless, we saw the car enter the main entrance, and in the next shot, it appears at the opposite side of the site (Figure 16), in the Mechanisation Pavilion (Figure 17). The car cuts through the arcade-shaped pavilion and goes out to the Mechanisation Square (Figure 18). By montaging shots of the real places, the director created a new non-existent space.[12] This editing makes an especially striking contrast between the dark tunnel-like Mechanisation Pavilion and the bright Mechanisation Square, where the Stalin statue stands. In other words, it is not just space conversion but also semantic inversion, or inversion of a hierarchy of meaning: The Mechanisation Pavilion, which was officially expected to be the centre of the VSKhV, is used as the tunnel for emphasising the Stalin statue as the centrepiece of the exhibition.

After the montage, the car driven by Tania arrives at the front of the Georgian Pavilion and she gets into it. This choice of the pavilion can also be considered as a suggestion to Stalin; however, the pavilion's name is not referred to in the movie. From this point, the background changes to a studio set. In the pavilion, many people are waiting for Tania, who has become a member of the Supreme Soviet in this future world. In this scene, without a doubt, warping of space is the most remarkable point. Despite watching Tania enter the pavilion, we see the sky and the Soviet Palace behind the people (Figure 19). Nonetheless, the palace is located on the west side of the Kremlin where the Cathedral of Christ the Saviour once stood (about 10 km apart from the site of VSKhV), and it looks as if it stands behind the Pavilion. Also, the shortened perspective—similar to a baroque theatre—and the stream of painted people leading from the Palace to real actors at the front of the rostrum, creates an illusion of space continuity.

Figure 16. **Map of VSkhV (1939)**
Arkhitektura SSSR, no. 9 (1939).

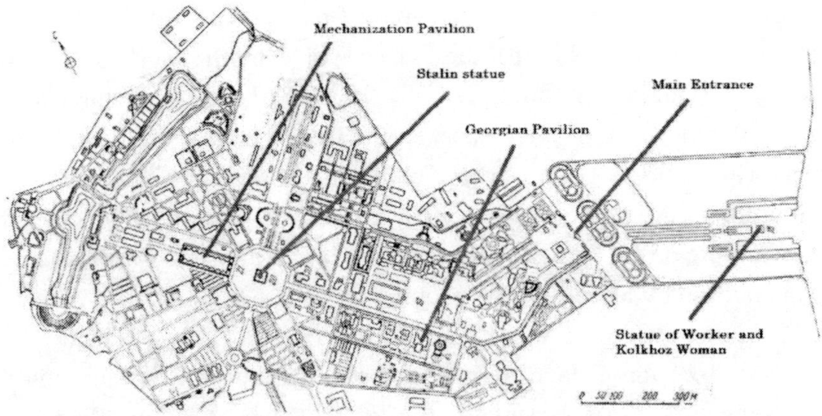

Figure 17. **The car going through the Mechanisation Pavilion**

Figure 18. **The Mechanisation Square and Stalin statue**

Figure 19. **Inside the Georgian Pavilion**

It is worth mentioning that Aleksandrov omitted the statue of Vladimir Lenin, which would be placed on the top of the Soviet Palace, and instead put a Stalin statue right behind Tania. Having this huge Lenin statue (over 100 metres high), the Palace would be the world's highest building (420 metres) at that time. This addition of the Lenin statue also changed the meaning of the Palace. At the first two competitions, it was designed as a complex of a workers' club and a conference hall. But after the addition of the statue, its function as a public institution was replaced by a symbolic one. The main hall changed to the pedestal for the statue and the building was called "the Monument of Lenin."[13]

The perspective of the Lenin statue was the big problem for construction of the Palace. It was colossal so that pedestrians could not see the full statue except for the leader's feet. Vladimir Paperny mentioned this invisible Lenin statue in his book, *Architecture in the Age of Stalin: Culture Two,* as a paradigm of Culture Two or Stalinist culture. According to him, it seems obviously defective; still, it is not a fault under Culture Two. He insists that the world of Culture Two was hierarchical and the top of the building was not merely the highest tier, it belonged to the ideal world.[14] Consequently, it was natural for the statue of Lenin to be invisible to ordinary people on the ground.

However, in the case of the Georgian Pavilion scene, it might be easy to solve the statue's perspective problem. If the director wanted to show an overall picture of the Palace that includes the Lenin statue, it would be enough to draw the Palace smaller and farther apart from the pavilion. Nonetheless, Aleksandrov did not choose such a solution. Was he trying to keep the statue in the invisible, ideal world as the architects of the Palace did? Perhaps not, but this manipulation demonstrates Aleksandrov's intention to emphasise Stalin as a central figure in this space, omitting the Lenin statue, which might threaten Stalin's highest position (in both the literal and symbolic sense) on the screen. This can be observed more clearly in the space order of the Georgian Pavilion.

In the long shots, we see lines of a cornice of a colonnade angling sharply into the depth. These lines are defined by accelerated one-point perspectives meeting at the Stalin statue (Figure 19). Placing a figure of the highest importance at a vanishing point like this was one of the common techniques of socialist realist paintings, as well as realist paintings in former centuries. For example, in *Metro!* by Stalin's painter Alexander Gerasimov (Figure 20), balcony lines are seen merging at the statue of Lenin. These lines, the strongest elements in the picture, guide our eyes to the statue as the initial point of the space. Thus, the perspective system functions not only as a method of describing space, but also as a way of constructing a semantic order. In this painting, Stalin and party executives are looking in the same direction as the Lenin statue, like his faithful successors. As a result, (the statue of) Lenin appears to approve of their project—the Construction of Metro—by being the origin of this space that implies him as the founder of the Party.

It is obvious that Aleksandrov attempted to attract the audience's gaze to the statue of Stalin as the focus of this space by using the perspective. That is to say, on the one hand, the Stalin statue exists inside the space as does Tania and others: on the other hand, it works as the central pillar, constructing the entire order of this space.

Figure 19. **One-point perspective crossing at the Stalin statue**

Figure 20. *Metro!* **by A. M. Gerasimov (1949)**

Ensemble of Tania's Images

In this scene, another strange phenomenon occurs: there are three Tanias. The first Tania is in a painting on the wall (Figure 21), which describes her at the time she was establishing the record in the factory. Introducing

Tania, a chairman on the rostrum points to the painted figure first, after which the real Tania (the second Tania) takes the rostrum for a speech (Figure 22). After her speech, the camera recedes from the rostrum, and the third Tania comes on screen. The third Tania is a carved statue that represents Tania at the time she received the Order of Lenin (Figure 23). From this long shot, we see that the real Tania and her other two images stand opposite each other, constructing a triangle.

In principle, an image depicted as a picture or carved in marble often occupies a higher position than real people in socialist realist paintings. For example, *The Oath of Pioneers* (Figure 24) shows this sort of hierarchy between real people and images. Here, children just joining the pioneer group are described in the right half of the drawing and the statue of a pioneer boy occupies a higher position among them. In the same way, the picture of Friedrich Engels, the teacher of socialism, occupies a higher position than the female instructors and teachers. It means that these images have been physically and also symbolically placed on a higher level than living people, showing them an ideal model.

Figure 21. **Tania in a painting as a factory worker**

Figure 22. **The real Tania as a representative**

However, in this scene the living Tania stands at equal height to both her painted and carved images. Conceivably, in the future, Tania would reach the summit of her career for a worker in the USSR. This means she would have attained the highest rank, which is usually reserved only for images.

Figure 23. **Tania's statue**

Figure 24. *The Oath of Pioneers* **by Ia.Avershina (1965)**

In other musical comedy movies, we see a similar transfiguration of socialist heroes in an image. For instance, in Ivan Pyryev's *They Met in Moscow* (1941), the heroine Grashia knows her future partner Musaib, as an udarnik (strike worker) through his portrait displayed in the VSKhV (Figure 25). She later meets him and falls in love. The next year, Musaib gets to know from Grashia's portrait displayed at the same place that she had also become an udarnik, despite the fact that she does not come to the exhibition. We can see the same pattern in *The Radiant Path*, too. After establishing the new record in the textile factory, Tania disappeared for the celebration with her colleagues, leaving Lebedzev alone. He missed her, looking at her portrait as an outstanding worker displayed at the entrance of the factory (Figure 26). These episodes show penetration of official ideology like the socialist competition or the Stakhanovite movement into private romance (as many studies have mentioned, accomplishment of social tasks promotes fulfilment of their romance in these musical comedies). At the same time, they also remind us of the mythic origin of the picture described by Pliny the Elder in *The Natural History (Naturalis Historia)* as a representation of an absent lover gone to the front.

Figure 25. **Musaib's portrait and Grasha looking at it with her friends**

Figure 26. **Lebedzev looking at Tania's portrait**

But there is a difference that cannot be overlooked between these episodes and the scene of the Georgian Pavilion. In Pyryev's movie, the portraits represent an absent Grashia or Musaib. In the factory scene of *The Radiant Path,* Tania's portrait represents her absence, too. In contrast, however, there is no real absence as the original Tania is also present in the Georgian Pavilion (instead of her being absent, curiously enough, in this scene, it is Lebedzev who is absent and is late for her speech). In other words, the images were not intended to serve as a representation of an absent Tania.

Then what could such images represent? It is nothing but a reflection in the mirror, which is the reason Tania and her images stand facing each other. The space of the Georgian Pavilion can be considered as a sort of extension of the Kremlin's mirror room, just as Tania has been in the mirror world.

As is generally known, mirror motifs appeared repeatedly in *The Radiant Path*. But it is worth mentioning that the mirrors are often connected to Tania's self-realisation in her work. For instance, a mirror appears impressively when she moves to a new house that was given to her as a prize for the new record and, as mentioned above, when she got the Order of Lenin in the Kremlin. The scene titled "The Beehive," especially, clearly shows the relationship between her social self-image and the mirrors: In this scene, Tania throws a flowerpot at her mirror and breaks it after knowing her record was beaten by another worker.[15] The destruction of the mirror suggests that her ideal social self-image is broken.

Accordingly, the correspondence between the original Tania and her reflections in the Georgian Pavilion demonstrates that Tania catches up with her ideal self-image completely and identifies herself with it. In other words, she is at the apogee of narcissism, or Jacques Lacan's mirror stage. According to Lacan's psychoanalytic theory, in mirror stage, infants start to recognise themselves in a mirror as an object from outside; it is easy to identify oneself with it despite it not being themselves but an image. In consequence, Tania's entire self-realisation—which seems possible only in a fairy tale—implies psychological regression.[16]

Furthermore, the correspondence between the three Tanias makes a strong ensemble. Here the diachronic narrative or Tania's Bildungsroman is expressed synchronically as a trinity of delightful Tanias: her past image in the painting, her present image as the statue and her future image as her living self. Through this ensemble, the integration of various kinds of art is completed.

Of course, such a relationship with the painted or carved images also has an effect on Tania's own body. As Oksana Burgakova says, *The Radiant Path* is a process in which the heroine is learning the official gestures,[17] her body fixed on the rostrum, and her gestures strictly restricted during the speech. Comparing with the scene of her earlier speech at the factory (Figure 26), inconsequential movements such as the act of pushing up a strand of hair are eliminated in this scene. As a result, her body has come closer to her static images. Evgeny Dobrenko forthrightly stated that she transfigured to the "speaking statue."[18] And at the end of the film, Tania and Lebedzev are duplicated and replaced by

Mukhina's statue, *Worker and Collective Farm Girl,* standing in front of the entrance arch.

However, petrification is not limited to Tania's body. At the same time, the camera also stops moving. Her speech scene consists of the repetition of a long shot and a close shot, but in both, the camera's viewpoint does not move. Why should the camera stop here, too? This is apparently because of the space order based on the perspective system. If the camera moved on the floor, the optical illusion of the space and the symbolic order constructed by the Stalin statue would soon collapse. Accordingly, in these shots not only the heroine's but also the camera's movement had to be excluded. To put it another way, at the zenith of the story and the art integration, the screen denies the identity as a motion picture and turns to a tableau vivant.

Figure 26. **Tania making a speech at the textile factory**

Conclusion

Bulgakowa pointed out that in the 1930s, Russian directors begun to shoot in a studio more frequently than in a real place, and Moscow was often replaced by a backdrop or sets in their works.[19] The scene staged at the VSKhV in *The Radiant Path* shows this shift clearly. That is, it begins with the montage of shots of real sites in the exhibition and then moves to the pavilion set. Nevertheless, we should not consider the architectural space built by Aleksandrov in comparison with the real exhibition space. As mentioned before, the whole space of the VSKhV was a kind of daydreaming world where the boundary between real things and their ideal models was mixed up. Therefore, the pavilion space at the climax of the film should be regarded as a dream within the dream, or a more perfect dream. In this virtual space, the true theme of the VSKhV—the symbolic order centring on Stalin—was visualised more clearly than in the real exhibition space. In other words, just as Tania demonstrated an ideal model of the New Soviet Woman, this imaginary architectural construction showed the final goal of socialist realist architecture.

On the other hand, this scene demonstrates the impossibility of realising such "speaking architecture." As we have seen, the ideal space constructed by the classical perspective system was very frail; if the viewpoint moved from a link to the character's movement, it would soon be revealed that the space was just an optical illusion. Consequently, in this sense, socialist realism's ideal construction was similar to the Potemkin villages.

Notes

1. After Chernov was shot dead, Oltarzhevsky was exiled to Vorkuta until 1943. After World War II, he was assigned to the Hotel Ukraina project, one of Stalin's Skyscraper Projects in Moscow. As a result, he got the Stalin Prize with other Stalin Skyscraper architects in 1948.
2. I. Belintseva, "Natsional'nayatema v arkhitekturepavil'onov VSXV 1939 g. v Moskve" (The National Theme in Pavilion Designs of the 1939 VSKhV in Moscow; summary in Russian), in *Problemyistoriisovetskoiarkhitektury: kontseptsii, konkursy, vystavki,* edited by T. N. Kotrovskaya. Moscow: TSNIIP gradostroitel'stvo, 1983, p. 83.
3. "Na stroitel'stve VSXV" (VSKhV under Construction; summary in Russian), *Stroitel"stvoMoskvy,* no. 11 (1939): 31.
4. *ArkhitekturaDvortsaSovetov: materialyplenumapravleniyaSoyuzaSovetskikhArkhitektrov1-4iyulya 1939 g* (Architecture of The Palace of the Soviets: Materials of Executive Plenum of the Soviet Architects' Union; summary in Russian), Moscow: Izdatel'stvo Akademiiarkhitektury SSSR, 1989, p. 59, V. Vasilenko, "Narodnyi ornament v arkhitekture" (National Ornaments of Architecture; summary in Russian), *Arkhitektura SSSR*, no. 6 (1939): 44.
5. There is no doubt that the Palace of the Soviets was the biggest project throughout the history of the USSR. A design competition was held four times from 1931 to 1933, and leading world architects like Le Corbusier or Walter Gropius joined

it. In the end, however, an unknown Russian architect, Boris Iofan won the first prize. After the addition of a Lenin statue on the top of Iofan's palace by order of Stalin, the plan was finally completed. But after the beginning of the construction, its enormous scale gave rise to many problems: overload of the Lenin stature, soft ground of the site and a lack of sufficient high-rise experts. When the German invasion started, materials for the Palace were diverted to a munitions' industry and construction stopped. After the war, Stalin told Iofan to make a new plan for the Palace several times, but they were never realised and its foundation pit was converted into an open-air pool. In 2000, the Cathedral of Christ the Saviour, which was demolished for construction of the Palace, was rebuilt at the same place. "The Design and Construction of the Palace of the Soviets of the USSR in Moscow," in *Naum Gabo and the Competition for the Palace of Soviets Moscow 1931–1933* (Berlin: Berlinsche Galerie, 1993), pp. 192-95.

6. G. Rublev, "Ob ekspozitsiivystavki (About Display in the Exhibition; summary in Russian)," *Iskusstvo*, no. 2 (1940): 104.
7. I. Ryazantsev, *Iskusstvosovetskogovystavochnogoansamblya 1917-1970* (Art Ensembles of Soviet Exhibitions in 1917-1970; summary in Russian), Moscow: Sovetskiikhudozhnik, 1976, p. 114.
8. Paul Greenhalgh, *Ephemeral vistas: the expositions universelles, great exhibitions and world's fairs, 1851-1939* (Manchester: Manchester University Press, 1988), p. 88.
9. I. V. Belintseva, *Ansambl' vsesoyuznoisel'skokhozyaistvennoivystavki v konteksteistoriisovetskoiarkhitektury 1930-kh gg* (Ensembles of the All-Union Agricultural Exhibition in the Context of Soviet Architectural History in the 1930s; summary in Russian), Moscow: Vsesoyuznyinauchno-issledovatel'skiiinstitutiskus stvoznaniya MK SSSR, 1989, p. 23.
10. Tania is modelled after a real woman named EvdokiiaVinogradova (1914-1962), a legendary weaver who set a new USSR record and then a world record for the number of looms used at the same time. She got the Order of Lenin in 1935 and was elected as a representative of the Supreme Soviet. Aleksandrov and Orlova interviewed her to study how to dramatise her life.
11. Akira Hasegawa assumes that these mountains are the Pamir Mountains or the Caucasus Mountains, which represented Stalin at that time. In *The Radiant Path* we can find such suggestions of Party leaders in many places. Akira Hasegawa, Grigori Aleksandrovkantoku Akaruimichi no jikukan (Chronotopos of *The Radiant Path* directed by Grigori Aleksandrov; summary in Japanese), *Akitadaigakukyouikubunkagakubukenkyukiyou*, 2004(15): 31.
12. For example, Lev Kuleshov did the experiment called "creative geography" in one of his first montage works. He montaged a film shooting a woman on the Petrovka Street and another film shooting a man on the Moscow River embankment. As

a result, a couple seems to occupy the same space. He connected not only shots in Moscow, but also a shot of the White House in Washington, DC and created new hybrid geography. Oksana Bulgakowa, "Spatial Figures in Soviet Cinema of the 1930s," in *The Landscape of Stalinism: The Art and Ideology of Soviet Space,* editied by Evgeny Dobrenko and Eric Naiman. (Seattle: University of Washington Press, 2003), pp. 52-55.

13. N. Atarov, *Dvorets Sovetov* (The Palace of the Soviets; summary in Russian) (Moscow: Rabochii, 1940), p. 43.
14. Vladimir Paperny, *Architecture in the Age of Stalin: Culture Two* (Cambridge: Cambridge University Press, 2002), pp. 88–90.
15. R. Salis, *"Nam uzhe ne do smekha": Muzykal'nyekinokomedii Grigoriya Aleksandrova* ("We Don't Feel Like Laughing Anymore": Musical Comedy Films Directed by Grigory Alexandrov; summary in Russian) (Moscow: Novoeliteraturnoeobozrenie, 2012), p. 250.
16. For example, Dobrenko points out an infantile characteristic in socialist realism heroes. E. Dobrenko, "Sotsrealizmimirdetstva" (Socialist Realism and Children's World; summary in Russian), in *Sotsrealisticheskiikanon*, edited by Xans Gunter and E. Dobrenko(St. Petersburg: Akademicheskiiproekt, 2000), pp. 31–40.
17. O. Bulgakowa, *Fabrikazhestov* (Factory of Gestures; summary in Russian), Moscow: Novoeliteraturnoeobozrenie, 2005, pp. 208–25.
18. E. Dobrenko, "Iazykprostranstva, szhatogo do tochki, iliestetikasotsial'noiklaustr ofobii" (The Languages of the Space Condensed to points, or Esthetics of Social Claustrophobia; summary in Russian), *Iskusstvokino*, no. 9 (1996): 127.
19. Bulgakowa, "Spatial Figures in Soviet Cinema of the 1930s," p. 65.

18. Presentation and Representation: Subjectivity through History in *The Sky of My Childhood*

Rashmi Doraiswamy

Post-1991 there has been what P. L. Dash calls a "triple transition" in the post-Soviet space. The economic transition envisaged the transition from socialist to market economy, as well as the dovetailing into processes of globalisation; the political transition saw the independent states establishing their structures and institutions for governance; the ideological sphere saw desovietisation and derussification. The supranational Soviet identity had to be discarded in favour of a national identity that now looked inwards rather than outwards. A repertoire of symbols and icons had to be put together to stand in for an identity that was being deconstructed and reconstructed. These were as Brubaker has called them "nationalising" regimes. Their post-Soviet political adjustments made them quite distinct from the internationalist and nationalist orientations of the previous regime. In many of the successor states, the leaders of the previous state set-up merely donned new cloaks and became presidents of the independent states.

> "The existing political institutions the new states inherited were hollow, giving incumbent leaders space to dictate the terms of the post-independence constitutional settlements, and to amass enormous political power and considerable personal wealth. Importantly, the Party bosses, now reinvented as national presidents, also knew from running the increasingly dysfunctional Soviet command economy, how to furnish existing patronage networks with rents derived from oil, natural gas and mineral sales. To reinforce their hegemony, a new ideological template was formulated to replace the discredited creed of Marxism-Leninism and to overlay serious internal, regional, ethnic and clan cleavages."[1]

The nationalism of the nationalising states was not without its internal contradictions. There is an inward gaze that tries to encompass and deal with these contradictions. The new nationalism in Kazakhstan, for instance, had two different impulses as Bhavna Dave points out:

> Two distinct forms of "nationalisms," both promoted by the nationalising ideology and practice of the regime, can be identified in Kazakhstan. The first one is the expedient or instrumental nationalism of the political elites, officials and technocrats, powered by Kazakhstan's economic success and its prominence as a major oil exporter. These rich, upwardly mobile strata, which include members of the former nomenklatura and the "New Kazakhs" (many of these are the offspring of the old nomenklatura), are well plugged into the global consumer structure ...
>
> The second is the quotidian (*bytovoi*) assertion of Kazakhness, including ethnic entitlements, on the street, in public sphere and in interpersonal communication… ."[2]

There is an outward gaze as well, in which the newly independent countries position themselves in the region and the international arena. Despite contradictions, Kazakhstan has emerged as the leading nation of the Central Asian region in terms of the smooth transition and rapid development internally, and as an important global player.

Cinema has played a very important role in the nation-building processes. According to Ismail Xavier,

> "… film production—like the industrial fairs and the crystal palaces of the nineteenth century—became one more forum for the exhibition of national values and technical achievements within the international arena. Film itself became an index of modernisation and power, so that different countries saw their efforts to improve their cinema as a privileged strategy of national affirmation and, at times, as a celebration of hegemony."[3]

Cinema in Kazakhstan has been at the forefront of the ideological transition in terms of how the state has tried to portray itself and its nationalising projects. Cinema has been mobilised to represent the state's outward gaze, and to present a window on Kazakhstan; it has participated in the representation of national identity in the contemporary, post-Soviet sense of what it means to be Kazakh. A cinema industry that produced the Kazakh New Wave during the period of perestroika and glasnost, and continued to produce works even after 1991; the state's investment in the film industry in terms of infrastructure and the state-supported annual Eurasia International Film Festival that brings in people to view the films made in Central Asia and sends out information into the world about this young country and its robust film industry; the state ad film industry positioning themselves as leaders in the region, much in the same way that Tashkent was during Soviet times; and the state actually commissioning and supporting the production of films that in many ways participate in the discourses of nation-building and nation-projection—all these factors make Kazakhstan an interesting case to study in terms of ideological transition and its cultural effects.

Cinema is one of the many fields that Kazakhstan is making a mark with in the international arena. The agenda is one of showing the Kazakh nation in a positive light and of providing a visual representation of what constitutes it as a nation. This is distinct from making money in the international market as an industry venture. Internally, within Kazakhstan, the shift from socialist to market economy has resulted in the development of a commercial cinema that is genre-based, a middle cinema and an auteur cinema. According to Bauryzhan Nogerbek, "… from 2000 onwards, the philosophy and style of the 'Kazakh New Wave' leaves the arena, giving up its place to a different cinema, that was looking for a way to reach the mass audience. In the place of director's cinema, there arrives a producer's cinema, and the authorial art-house cinema is pushed into the second place."[4]

Kazakhstan continues in the Leninist and Soviet vein to view cinema as one of the most important art forms for its mass reach as well as its potential for enlightenment. In 2006, in a meeting between President Nazarbayev and President Bush, the recently released Sacha Baron Cohen's *Borat: Cultural Learnings of America for Make Benefit Glorious Nation of Kazakhstan* and the damage the film caused to the image of

Kazakhstan was on the agenda.[5] President Nazarbayev took personal interest in the scripting and making of the film *Nomad* (*Kochevnik*, 2005) which was intended to place the nomads of the steppes in the same register as the cowboys of Hollywood or the samurai of Japanese cinema.[6] The film was hyped as a blockbuster before its release, but proved to be a failure at the box-office. The President also encouraged and supported the making of *Mustafa Chokai*, on a Muslim leader, who propounded the need for an autonomous Turkestan under Soviet rule and propagated the ideology of Pan-Turkism. Cinema has been used as a tool for nation-building purposes by the Kazakh state and a film on the President seems to follow logically from this premise. In fact, the three films form an ideological trilogy, with each reflecting an aspect of the nation-building strategies of the Kazakh state. *Nomad* deifies the steppe and posits the Dzungars as enemies. *Mustafa Chokai* is about a proponent of Pan-Turkic ideology; as such it represents a particular aspect of the state's political ideology. It also posits a figure from the past as a hero, a man who was never a part of the Soviet pantheon for having collaborated with Hitler. *The Sky of My Childhood* is very mildly critical of Soviet times; it underlines the multicultural heritage of Kazakhstan and projects an image of modernity that is intricately bound to tradition.

Kazakh director Rustem Abdrashov's 2008 film *Gift to Stalin* (*Podarak Stalinu*) was well-received abroad as well as in Kazakhstan. His *The Sky of My Childhood* (*Nebo Moego Detstva*, 2011) is the first of a proposed trilogy of films on the President of Kazakhstan, Nursultan Nazarbayev. The film is based on the President's work *No Lefts, No Rights, Epicentre of the World, Centre of Eurasia. The Sky of My Childhood* deals with the birth, childhood and youth of the President and portrays the rites of passage from one stage of life to another. That a director, who has made his mark on the national and international film scene, makes a biopic on a living President of his country, who still holds office, may seem curious to many. It, however, makes immense sense if one considers the importance the cinema-industry has been accorded in the nation-building discourses post 1991 in Kazakhstan. For the director, too, this seems a logical development from his previous film, *Gift to Stalin*, which is based on real events; this is also representation of real events and people.

How then is the nation imaged in cinema? The most direct representation would be through a plot that proclaims its allegorical intent. These can often be rhetoric or heroic tales. Anthony Smith points out that "… there is more to nationalism and national identity than public moralities and virtuous patriots. In the eyes of its devotees, the nation possesses a unique power, pathos, grandeur, qualities which film, perhaps even more than painting or sculpture can convey … . That is why we find an increasing concern for archaeological verisimilitude and distinctive 'ethnic atmosphere' in the portrayal of national drama."[7] He adds that the visual representation of this atmosphere is done through character development, historical reconstruction, pictorial tableaux, accessories, ethnoscapes and the "people." In the case of Kazakhstan, the state has tapped on the nomadic past of its people and the great steppes as part of the iconography of the new nation. No more is nomadism, for instance, to be viewed in a teleological sense of being a precursor to the historically consequent state of sedentariness, but as an essential characteristic that constitutes the nation of Kazakhs. *Nomad* and *The Sky of My Childhood*, on the other hand, use space evocatively as the constitutive part of nationhood: the steppes in the case of *Nomad* and the mountains in *The Sky of My Childhood*. Anthony Smith states that "… 'ethnic atmosphere' is closely linked to the poetic landscapes of distinctive ethnic communities (ethnies), or 'ethnoscapes.' Here the territory mirrors the ethnic community and is historicised by the communal events and processes whose relics and monuments dot its landscape, so that the land comes to belong to a people in the same way as the people belong to a particular land—creating an ancestral 'homeland.'"[8] In *The Sky of My Childhood* it is the mountains and the sky that impart a sense of aloofness, of distance, of loftiness that craft and cradle the special destiny of the special child, but also show the rigours of daily living, the *byt*, the difficult life of the family of three, who seem to be living in isolation, with very few other families close by for support. The wildness of the natural surroundings is brought out in two sequences, when the wolves attack the sheep and the father loses his arm when the barn catches fire; and when the father goes out into the snowy, dark winter night to a distant neighbour's house, to get apples for his sick son who is asking for them in his delirium.

What is being represented is the memoir of the President, the leader of the State. What is also being represented is the nation. The leader becomes the personification of the nation. According to Ismail Xavier, "… 'the nation,' despite its secular roots in modern history, solicits personifications in fictional narratives, and other allegorical strategies as well, thus confirming its affinities with the sense of the sacred."[9] He further points out that "Many national allegories are based on personifications, as when a single character is taken for a nation, like Maria Braun or Aleksander Nevsky, or when the very idea of a nation is condensed in familial tropes, like Mother Russia or Mother India."[10] In *The Sky of My Childhood* the narrative, though biographical, is being told in the fictional and not documentary mode. While the "real" narrative about the leader of the state unfolds, there is a simultaneous transcendent signification about the nation. Oksana Sarkisova states that "Despite the declared break with the past, characteristic of transitional societies, a closer look at the social and cultural fabric of 'post-Communism' reveals that the simplistic opposition of 'before' and 'after' is subverted by recurrent long-term intellectual frameworks, narrative devices, and visual imagery, employed to make sense of the world 'here' and 'now' as well as 'there' and 'then.'"[11] The "there" and "then" of a socialist past, are being recast into a nationalist present. The film shares an affinity with Aktan Abdykalykov's *Beshkempir* (1998) from Kyrgyzstan. The film deals with the coming of age of an adopted child. Kyrgyz traditions and artefacts are used evocatively, creating a sense of nationhood. The film was foundational in creating a genre, through which the "national in content" could be represented, without the "socialist form." The national now could be linked to the ethnic. The ethnic that evokes the primordial, or at any rate, traditions that have been in existence for generations, is a characteristic feature of these films. *The Sky of My Childhood* partakes of this genre, but in a didactic way. Central to both films is the figure of the grandmother, who nurtures, who is the repository of age-old wisdom, who protects the child and who is very crucial to the child's universe. The parents, in fact, are less central to the child's world. There is a sub-allegorisation, it seems, at work here: the "hoariness" of the nation, its repertoire of ethnic markers, its traditions as invested in the grandmother; the parents are necessary, present, investing in the well-being of the child, but not really crucial in the formation of the child's world view. This loop that the child forms with the grandmother, can be read as the inclination of the young nation to reach out to its past, in order to come of age, taking in its stride the parents and their caring and often disciplining attitudes, a trope for the socialist period, in-between the past and the present.

The Sky of My Childhood is not strictly a "producer's cinema" made for the market; its "producer" is the state itself, and it is about the leader of the state; it is intended for a mass audience, not for the purposes of ringing in box-office receipts, but for an ideological agenda. It is, however, not just a "commercial" film, for it draws on the aesthetic registers of Soviet poetic cinema. As the story of child and teenager Nazarbayev is represented, we are presented with the subjectivity of a future leader that far exceeds the "person" of the growing youth.

The historical events portrayed in the film are the "big" events of the Soviet Union: collectivisation, World War II, the deportation of peoples to Kazakhstan, the events of the 1950s. No re-reading of historical events is offered. Collectivisation is shown as being a cruel imposition; but the conflict is not between the Slavs/Russians and Kazakhs. It is curiously between a Kazakh whose father had previously worked under Abish's father, who now wields power over his son and his property as a functionary of the Soviet state. The events mentioned are shorn of their political intent. Even the deportation of peoples is said to be the decision of some "war commissioner" in Moscow. The multicultural, multinational nature of Kazakhstan's population as a result of these migrations is emphasised. These well-known signposts of history are intertwined with the narrative of the growing child. The child is blessed and ahead of others in studies, sports and the arts; his is an almost conflict-less life.

High up in the mountains there is little of community life. A sage like Aksakal who emerges almost magically from the fog, a Russian family that lives at a distance, a Russian hospital, at also a distance, the exiled family to whom Abish opens his doors until they have a house of their own, a very distant school … .

Joshua First writes in *Kinokultura* that "The film draws extensively on the style and thematic elements of Soviet poetic cinema from the 1960s-70s, with its slow pacing and quiet tone, and its ethnographic focus on folklore, everyday life, kinship, and the landscape. Thus, to dismiss *Sky of My Childhood* as 'authoritarianism in action,' ... however, misses the point. While baby Sultan almost never cries and adolescent Sultan always makes the right decisions, wins the races, performs the best in school, and knows how to dance and recite poetry, the film's nostalgic address overwhelms these attempts at hagiography. The film celebrates Soviet values like multiculturalism, the dignity of manual labour, the discourse of peace (in one scene, Abish and his brother perform the highly symbolic act of re-forging a bayonet into a sickle, which they give to Sultan), respect for authority, and community, while evincing the curious combination of celebrating tradition and lauding Soviet-style modernity that lie at the root of socialist realism."[12]

The *bytovoi*, it is true, is being evoked very consciously and being cast in utopian mode, a happy child growing up surrounded by a family that dotes on him. But this *byt* is very different from the *byt* as represented in the 1960s and 1970s. Then, *byt* was invoked *in contradistinction to* the *klassovost'*, *partiinost'* and *ideiinost'* of socialist realism. While it is true that the slow pace and quiet pacing is reminiscent of the Soviet cinema of those times, the internal logic flowing through the veins of the images, is not an act of rebellion, but invoking a new sense of *natsionalnost'* and *narodnost'*. Instead of class identity, there is a sense of ordinary, humble lives being lived; instead of *partiinost'*, an individual who grows up with a sense of having a great destiny ahead.

There is no re-reading of history, only the creation of subjectivity for the new nationalism and sense of nationhood. The Russian or the Soviet State are hardly critiqued. The only criticism comes in the interference of their way of life (through forced collectivisation), or in taxing the extra trees that the father has grown so lovingly, creating hybrid varieties of apples and fruit. Historical events are viewed through the memories of the protagonist. Madhavan Palat speaks of the dethroning of history as the custodian of truth and the valourisation of memory:

> "It remains for us to ask why there is a 'politics of memory' in the late twentieth century, and why the subject of memory has become so obsessive? If at every stage the experiences of war, genocide, terror, famine, gulag and other horrors are to be inscribed in stone, why is it called the recording of memory rather than of history? ... There is more than a hint … that history has been displaced from its position of authority as the provider of truth; if so, memory, or claims to remembering, replaces it. In the nineteenth century forgotten, suppressed, or non-existent nations claimed to recover their past, their identity, and their glory, through history; today they make comparable claims through the recovery of memory … ."[13]

Height and flight are the two motifs that recur through the film. The opening sequence begins with a plane bearing the name of the country taking off into the skies. This is immediately followed by the grinding of wheat by the grandmother in the traditional grinder's stone that is a pan-Asian image. Most of us would remember our grandmothers with grinding stones of the kind shown in this shot. There is then a regional "signpost" of the child having to learn the names of his forefathers for seven generations. The child is distracted by a small plane that is flying and he runs after it. The run takes him across a mountainscape that is alternated with the plane flying in the sky. There is a gradual opening out of the landscape below and the child surveys the lands as it lies before him. There is a transition in the child's expression: He is gazing into space, but also into time, as we are made aware of his special destiny. The playful child now looks like he knows and self-perceives this special destiny—his as well as that of his land. The music is soaring, uplifting and we hear the voice-over of the narration from the voice of the President (as we see him writing in a plane), talking of planes. He recalls his visits to many countries and states how he first felt the excitement of flying when he stood as a boy atop the hill. He looks out of the window and sees the boy he was, standing on the hill. The child is now the object no longer just of our gaze, but of the memory-gaze of the adult President. The pans and circular movements are now not encompassing the joyous run of the child, but encompassing history, positing the President's forefathers as sedentary and nomadic, highlanders and steppe people at the same time. The birth of the child is also through prayer, ritual and miracle (there is a hint, in the sequence where the mother is underwater in a dream, surrounded by little darting fish, if not of immaculate conception, then at least of otherworldly forces playing a role in the conception). There is the evocation of the pan-multicultural myth of unseasonal rain that heralds the birth. There is also the sub-theme of the exchange of newborns, which again has a long tradition in folk and other traditional narratives. The opening segment ends with the father checking for himself whether the newborn is really a boy.

The opening section of the film thus moves through several registers, all of which insert the film into discourses of nationhood: the plane's flight into the expanses of the sky (rhetorical), the child, grandmother and father (with the flavor of *byt*, with traditional and community values), the child and his land, the relationship with the land, the future, the past, the birth, ritual, mythic, miraculous … . Past (biological, historical and traditional), the present and the future of the country and its rise to unknown heights, are all woven together, to tell the story of the leader, the son of this soil. Nazarbayev is probably the only President who allows himself to be inserted into films. These insertions are in the beginning or end (as in *Nomad* and in *The Sky of My Childhood*), and are very definitive in terms of proclamations about the country and the nation.

Rustem Abdrashov thus skilfully creates a rich tapestry of Kazakh, Central Asian, and Asian images; he draws on the mythic, the *bytovoi* (the everyday) and the rhetorical; he brings together the past, present and future as simultaneous time frames; he creates smooth bridges between tradition and modernity … He presents the subjectivity of the President as well as the subjectivity of the nation. The film provides a narrative of the making of both these subjectivities and their positionings in the region, continent and world.

Notes

1. Michael Denison, "Discipline and Persuade: The Origin and Uses of Central Asia's Leadership Cults," Bhavna Dave (ed.), *Politics of Modern Central Asia*, vol. III, (New York: New York, 2010), p. 243.
2. Bhavna Dave, *Kazakhstan: Ethnicity, Language and Power* (New York: New York, 2007), pp.168-69.
3. Ismail Xavier, "Historical Allegory," in Toby Miller and Robert Stam (eds.), *A Companion to Film Theory* (Oxford: Oxford, 2004), pp. 351-52.
4. Baurzhan Nogerbek, "Natsionalny Kinematograph Kazakhstana," *Kino Entsiklopedia Kazakhstana*, Kazakhfilm Almaty, 2010, p. 20.
5. Rashmi Doraiswamy, "Cinematic Imaginings of the Nation: Spotlight on Kazakhstan" in Anita Sengupta, Suchandana Chatterjee (eds.), *The State in Eurasia: Local and Global Arenas* (New Delhi: Knowledge World, 2013).
6
7. Anthony Smith, "Images of the Nation: Cinema, Art and National Identity," Mette Hjort and Scott Mackenzie (eds.), *Cinema and Nation* (London: Routledge, 2002), p. 50.
8. Anthony Smith, op. cit., p. 55.
9. Ismail Xavier, "Historical Allegory," op. cit., p. 351.
10. Ismail Xavier, op. cit., p. 340.
11. Oksana Sarkisova, "Long Farewells: The Anatomy of the Soviet Past in Contemporary Russian Cinema," in Oksana Sarkisova and Peter Apor (eds.), *Past for the Eyes: East European Representations of Communism in Cinema and Museums after 1989* (Budapest: CEU Press, 2008), p. 143.
12. Rustem Abdrashov, *The Sky of My Childhood* (*Nebo moevo detstva*, 2011), reviewed by Joshua First © 2012, KINOKULTURA, http://www.kinokultura.com/2012/36r-nebodetstvo.shtml
13. Madhavan Palat, "History and Memory, Myth and Tradition" [Special Lecture] in International Seminar, *Eurasia Twenty Years After*, Kolkata: Maulana Abul Kalam Azad Institute of Asian Studies, February 17, 2011.

19. Reinventing Culture: The Tajik Experience of Post-Soviet Years

Nandini Bhattacharya

Culture is a potential factor in redefining identities in the post-Soviet space. For each independent nation of Central Asia, this journey towards a newly contoured identity began experimenting with cultural revival and renovation. In fact, each post-Soviet state began this journey with the introduction of new national flags, symbols and national anthems of their own. In the experiments of the last two decades, the Tajik cultural experience had a distinct character. Being the only Central Asian state with a Persian lineage, Tajikistan has a unique cultural heritage. Her rich culture provides a strong foundation for nation-building despite the reality of mounting economic crises and endless political challenges.

Recovery of the Cultural Face of Post-Soviet Tajikistan

In the ancient past,. Tajikistan, northern Afghanistan, Turkmenistan, and southern Uzbekistan were joined with northeastern Iran in a region historically termed as Khorasan. In fact, this geo-cultural entity goes back to pre-Islamic times. The political upheavals in different phases of history brought into being many artificial boundaries and ruptured the harmony of the space. The contemporary Tajik state cannot identify itself with contemporary Iran for several ideological reasons. But, from the historical perspective, common cultural inheritance is a major determinant for understanding shared identities beyond the Central Asian space. William O. Beeman observed, "Khorasan remains today a somewhat unified cultural region. Residents of the area, whatever modern state they belong to, remain justly proud of the achievements of the poets, writers, and artists of the region, whose works constitute a large part of the canon of Persian cultural heritage."[1] Therefore, Tajiks in the post-Soviet period tend to proudly acknowledge the role of Persian poets like Rumi, Rudaki and Firdausi as literary geniuses in the field of Tajik literature. But there remained an uneasy relation between Iran and Tajikistan in terms of political ideology and religious affiliation. Firstly, Iran embraced Shi'ism in the sixteenth century and drifted away from Sunni Islam which the Tajiks practised. Moreover, the Islamic Revolution in Iran and the Soviet regime in Tajikistan had further drifted the two states in the course of the twentieth century. Even though the Tajiks acknowledge the close cultural connections with Iranian literature and art, there is uneasiness about the religious and political orientation of modern Iran. Iranians are keen on closer cooperation with Tajikistan but face opposition both from the Tajik government and the opposition (who are Sunni Muslim). Despite this, the Tajiks' Persian lineage and Samanid connections (with Ismail Somoni as the iconic figure of modern Tajik state) were a major factor in Tajik state building in the aftermath of Soviet disintegration.

The political journey of Tajikistan began in 1920 as a Soviet autonomous republic and then as a Soviet socialist republic (1924) and culminated with the formation of an independent republic in 1991. The loss of Samarkand and Bukhara that became part of the Uzbek Socialist Republic due to territorial delimitation in 1929, became a part of Tajikistan's tragic memory. The other trans-border geo-cultural linkage that has a deep impression on Tajik national consciousness is the Afghan connection. Afghanistan, the closest neighbour of Tajikstan, has ethno-geographical links with the Tajik people. While the interstate relations suffer from some sort of threat perception and insecurity with cross-border terrorism and drug traffic looming large, the cultural sphere seems much more cohesive, establishing the foundations of a common ethno-linguistic space that lacked harmony with the passage of time.

At the same time, Tajik entity is strongly embedded in the Central Asian psyche that experienced Soviet order. As an inseparable part of a secular socialist experiment for seventy years, Tajikistan still identifies herself first and foremost as a successor state of post-Soviet Central Asia. Although the recent cultural process began as an attempt to recover from the Soviet cultural hypotheses of state-building, it does not denote an outright denial of a Russian influence that was integral to the

Soviet framework. It is not that the Soviet regime had downplayed or suppressed the local cultural expressions. Encouragement for local or regional literary and cultural development was extended in many ways. But the Soviet cultural ethos inevitably and in principle downplayed the nationalist image displayed through indigenous cultural expressions. The Tajik cultural image thus has a civilisational image but has a distinct entity. So, one can rephrase the Soviet proverb "national in form and socialist in content" as "national in form and multicultural in content."

Reinventing Selfhood through Tajik Poets' Imagination

Tajik poets play an active role in the making of her identity and enrich the culture with their profound understanding of their history, situating it in the larger dimension of world history. The journey through the passage of metaphor and rhythm may begin with Bozor Sobir,[2] the renowned poet of Tajikistan whose compositions were greatly acclaimed during the Soviet period. Authors of the post-Soviet generation have high regard for Sobir because of his non-conformist views, referring to his poems *The Stage* and *After Us* in which he condemned Soviet order and its corrupt bureaucracy.

Sobir was committed to his own nation, language and culture. From the very inception of his literary career, he was an advocate of Persian lineage of Tajikistan and in his poems he invoked deep respect for the Persian heritage of Ismail Somoni and the heyday of the Tajiks emanating from a Bukharan legacy. His poem, *The Mother Tongue*, expresses his anger, anguish and despair of the inheritance of loss by the Tajik people in the cruel twists of history, and ultimately revives the confidence of the poet in the sole possession of the mother tongue.

The poem began with a sense of loss, loss of proud heritage, loss of legitimate inheritance … .

> She handed over all her worldly assets,
> She handed over her Balkh and Noble Bukhara,
> She handed over sublime traditions and ways,
> She handed over her throne of Saman.

But towards the end it began to transcend the despair and land up in the realm of an undaunted optimism, thanks to the inseparable inheritance of the mother tongue:

Like a wounded deer,
She repeatedly licked her wounds,
Until she healed them
With the miracle of her tongue.
They climbed a hundred pulpits
So that her language can prosper;
On a hundred gallows appeared her poets
So that the worth of her tongue is upheld.
When we come to determine borders,
Only Tajiki delimits the Tajiks,
As long as she has a tongue she has a homeland,
With her language intact, she remains worthy.[3]

In spite of his strong passion for pre-Soviet past, he was not penalised during the Soviet regime. But, in independent Tajikistan, his political involvement brought him imprisonment, even though for a short period. He then left his party membership and immigrated to the United States. But, this shift in space did not change his commitment to his land and his people. Bozor Sobir recited his own poems that immortalised the notion of *vataan* (motherland) and the glorious memories of the past:

Dubora sozamat vatan, ba khishti joni kheshtan,
Sutun zanam ba saqfi tu, ba ustukhoni kheshtan.[4]

[If I ever live another life
I wish to rebuild my homeland.
Which is in a miserable state.
I want to bring my country into life again … .][5]

A similar craving for the motherland is reflected in other poems too.

Gulrukhsor Safiyeva[6] laments the centuries'-old pain of not being able to protect the motherland:

> …
> Oh Motherland—
> Religion,
> My Golgotha and an Altar!
> My lonely parent,
> My destroyed sanctuary;
> I do not deserve you,
> Living with you,
> Without you!

Unlike Bozor, Gulrukhsor is subtly critical of the denial of the Tajiks' selfhood:

> I am not a refugee—
> I am offended,
> Rushing all over the world,
> Bringing light,
> Burning as candle at the wind,
> The Zoroastrians fire … .[7]

In another poem titled *Home* she laments till the end:

> The past is wrapped up in ashes—
> The future is threatening with tsunami
> I go home…
> And there is no home!—
> O God, what you have done to us?![8]

There are echoes of similar sentiments in the poems of Loiq Sherali, Gulnazar Keldi (author of Tajik national anthem *Surudi Milli*), Fazona Khojandi and so on. One of Gulnazar's poems is dedicated to the classical poets and scientific personalities like Rudaki, Hafiz, Rustam Shohrab, Abu Ali Ibn Sino, etc.

If I see a barbed tongue even for a moment,
and see fluent words choppy,
and see a weak person in the clutches of weakness,
my heart burns for Rudaki,
it burns for life today.[9]

Loik Sherali too belonged to the same genre and was one of the most celebrated Persian literary figures of Tajikistan and Central Asia. He too reiterated similar unhappy sentiments of artificial boundaries among the Persian speaking people:

Maa Keh Khod Parwwardeh e jak maadarum! Tajik o Iraan o Afghaan Cheraa?

Translated as:

We who were brought up by only one mother! Why be dubbed as Tajiks and Iranians and Afghans (today)?[10]

And there are poems of Farzona Khojandi with simple yet unfathomable metaphors that mesmerise human conscience:

There was a boy. He would spread his wares
in our alley. The strength of the hero, Rostam,
roared from his shoulders,
he had the features of a Joseph,
his hair was the torch of Zoroaster,
flaming with ancient times.
The young boy sat on an old stool,
saying goodbye to his rose-scented time.[11]

Therefore, while Bozor Sobir is forthright in registering his protests, Farzaneh or Gulrukhsor are possessed by the inheritance of loss. But while glorifying the years of glory and pride of the past centuries and instilling conscience about shame and dishonour inflicted on the Tajik nation, these poets in practice stirred the feelings of cultural nationalism of Tajikistan vis-à-vis other people with creative pursuits who were responsible for the fractured identity of the Tajiks. Anaita Khudonazar identifies these "other sections" vis-à-vis the Tajik nation in her use of metaphors. For example, Russia was represented as glorious mother at the beginning of the Bolshevik regime but later on had been categorised as the stepmother because it was she, posing as a Soviet entity, who in actuality, separated the Tajiks from the greater union of Persian speaking people of the world, namely, the Iranians and the Afghans. The next group categorised as "the other" is the Uzbek Soviet Republic which thrived over what the Tajiks lost—the inheritance of Samarkand and Bukhara. Bozor Sobir was scathing in his criticism of the Uzbeks.[12]

Olivier Roy is emphatic about the loss of the Tajiks: "The Tajiks having in 1924 lost control of their two historical cultural centres, Samarkand and Bukhara, have difficulty convincing themselves that Tajikistan is a nation-state rather than a collage of autonomous provinces. They feel themselves to be in a minority and under threat. Thus it is no accident that Tajik intellectuals have developed a hardline nationalism, at odds with their actual powerlessness … ."[13]

It was at this phase of cultural regeneration that the Tajik state was caught up by the civil war, and her romantic notion of cultural synergy across borders was torn between the two extremist factions of the Communists who dominated the north and the radical Islamists who dominated the southern part. The civil war brought the region of Badakhshan into the limelight, and the cultural reserves got attention once violence calmed down. Tajik intellectuals and artists articulated their sense of belonging to a cultural heterogeneous entity instead of only emphasising Persian homogeneity of a glorious past.

So an ethno-linguistic delimitation of borders did not only redefine Tajik identity that was considered to be distinct from the Russians, it also situated them within the broader spectrum of Persian-speaking people of the world. Yet, for the independent Tajik state, in spite of all its emotional ties and shared history and culture, amalgamation with the Iranian state was not a serious proposition. The irony of Tajik cultural entity is that it shares nostalgia and sense of loss which are best expressed through a poet's imagination. So, the

Tajik cultural nationalism has no practicable political agenda like a recovery of lost lands. The poetic expressions are introspection about Tajik selfhood through self-confidence and moral strength.

In an article titled, "Tajik Literature: Seventy Years is Longer Than a Millennium," John R. Perry remarked that the evolution of Tajik language and literature during the Soviet and post-Soviet periods took some time. He explained why the Tajiks refrained from becoming full members of the Persian-speaking world, why the connection with the Iranian diaspora and proximity to the Afghan brethren was split. He showed the hope of creating the "independent Tajik poet" whose "mind is enriched with the consciousness of heritage but is free from prejudices of the past and not blinded by hatred and anger that could engulf the nation. This individual may never be as famous as Rudaki, but he is determined at least to be his own master."[14]

Music that Ties up the Past and Present of Tajik Cultural Entity

However, this exclusive emotion about national entity and the ruptures between Uzbek and Tajik identities (despite the fact that they were united by the ethnonym *sart*) has a common factor—that of shared inheritance, especially in the realm of classical music. *Shashmaqam,* the classical music of Central Asia is a combined heritage of Tajik-Uzbek nations. Once again the cradle of this music tradition was mainly Bukhara where all the famous musicians' ensemble took place in the palaces of the great rulers. However, there is a common tendency of connoting this classical musical tradition as "court music" since the Soviet days. Diloram Karomat categorically explains that "in all the countries of the East, traditional professional music, although it is performed in a democratic environment, was nevertheless an 'elite' music, which was heard in the courts of the rulers and by connoisseurs of music and the rich people. Thus in the Bukharan Emirate the best musicians lived in the Court of the Emir."[15]

However, in the early days of Soviet regime, the interest in the *Shashmaqam* did not wane. But, according to Karomat, it was after World War II that the government's attitude towards these song-music traditions narrowed down, as they were not regarded to be in tune with Soviet ideology, but were branded as survivals of feudal culture, generating a mood of parochial nationalist sentiments. However, *Shashmaqam* survived through private initiatives and was performed in private ceremonies like marriage, etc. It was during the last decades of Soviet regime that an attempt to revive this musical tradition started in Uzbekistan with the personal initiative of Karomatli. In the words of his daughter, Dilorom, eager singers and musicians from various parts of Central Asia joined along with some foreign students.[16]

However, this revival of music had been possible mainly after the Central Asian states got independence from Soviet control, and a process of redefinition of this old cultural heritage began with greater enthusiasm. In Tajikistan, after the end of the Civil War, the Aga Khan Music Initiative got a new lease of life. The purpose of committed Tajik musicians and composers is to teach the new generation this unique cultural trait and disseminate information about *Shashmaqam* in their own countries as well as abroad. This musical venture has resulted in a ten-volume series of Central Asian music in collaboration with the Smithsonians. The second volume titled "Invisible Face of the Beloved" is exclusively dedicated to *Shashmaqam* and subtitled as "Classical Music of the Tajiks and Uzbeks."[17]

A renowned expert on Tajik music, Federico Spinetti, analysed the multilayered musical experiments in post-Soviet Tajikistan. Among them, one category of singers showed tendency to revive the pre-Soviet *Shashmaqam* tradition. Among this group are Abduvalid Abdurashidov, head of the *Shashmaqam* ensemble of State Radio and Director of the Academy of Shashmaqam, Dushanbe. In Spinetti's observation—

> "The re-evaluation of tradition which these musicians embody is, I argue, a peculiarly contemporary process related to important issues in current Tajik cultural politics. In addition to an emphasis on nationalism in the wake of independence, these issues also include responses to the concerns of ethnomusicologists for the integrity of native musical practices, to the marketing of traditional music on the world music circuit and to initiatives for the support of artistic activities in Central Asia such as those promoted by the Aga Khan Trust for Culture."[18]

Therefore reinventing and re-allocating a musical tradition does not only pertain to national tradition, but also the packaging in which it will appear more authentic and free from the artificial influence of Soviet training.

But, as seventy years were a long and interactive phase so far as evolution of music is concerned, it is not possible, nor even desirable, to erase the musical memories and experiences of Soviet times. In the revival of *Shashmaqam* many Soviet and Western influences and style of presentations were incorporated. For example, music is played or songs are sung sitting on chairs which are adaptations to the Western style of performance, alien to the traditional milieu.

Anyway, *Shashmaqam* is not the only classical variant of music practised in Tajikistan. There are many more varieties of music, indigenous folk and pop songs of various styles and themes, folk songs with strong regional content and the continued influence of Western music, introduced by Soviet masters. Each of them has their own contribution in the cultural reorientation of the Tajik state in the last two decades.

Falak is one such significant song and music style among mountain Tajiks, with themes like sorrow, loss, exile or loneliness. Literally, *falak* means destiny, fate or firmament.[19] The Music of Central Asia series by the Smithsonians, in its fifth volume, is an ode to the mountain songs of Badakhshan, *Falak* being one of the most prominent musical genres mentioned in it. This volume showcases an optimistic and vibrant singer Soheba Davlatshoeva, who has created the "Badakhshan ensemble" on her own initiative. This organisation caters to some important cultural demands of her native place and has a future vision of establishing a school of music for the upcoming generation. She says rather optimistically: "The kind of music we play and sing has been performed in the Pamir Mountains for a thousand years. My goal is to ensure that future generations of talented musicians will know this music, and perform it with all their soul and heart."[20]

There are, however, plenty of common Tajik songs falling under the category of *Estrada*, or pop songs. They are rather a loose combination of Western music and Tajik lyric and tunes. Spinetti observed that the synthesiser was used on stage for both pop and traditional songs. The performer Gulchehra performed traditional songs along with her sons but used all sorts of Western instruments. "They are inclined to conceive traditional and electrified music as 'old' (*qadima*) and 'contemporary' (*hozira zamon*) music and thus lay emphasis on their being not separate or oppositional spheres, but moments of a coherent, stretched-in time *musiqi-i khalqt* ('popular' or 'people's music')."[21] The line of distinction between folk and pop is also sometimes blurred as there are many popular singers who traverse in both domains and sometimes compose new folk songs of the modern context with contemporary musical instruments. Ma'nisaro Afzalshoh Shodiev is one of the most popular contemporary folk singers in Tajikistan and among the Persian-speaking communities in the world. His songs are about motherland, patriotism, romance and love.

However, it is Ziyodullo Shahidi who is considered to be the musical genius, and recognised as the father of modern Tajik music. Shahidi stands as the icon of harmony between indigenous Tajik music and Western music acquired through the Soviet infrastructure. According to Munira Shahidi, the Director of the Shahidi foundation, and the daughter of late Shahidi, it is his effort that for the first time brought Tajik music and the innate richness of its melodies to the international arena. She remembers her father's contribution in the following words: "Interaction and cross-pollination between traditional Tajik and Russian-European classical music has formed the basis for the creation of a national school of modern Tajik music." In her recollections about her father's musical journey, Munira Shahidi is more candid: "When Central Asian countries adopted the European educational system in the 1920s and 1930s, a common challenge arose: could Central Asian composers master Russian and European styles, while still expressing their own ethno-national musical experience? The response to this challenge was a crucial push towards the formation of a new musical culture, on the cusp of which stood Ziyodullo Shahidi."[22] His inclination towards Western music did not withdraw his commitment towards the songs and melodies of his native land. Since there was no disjuncture in his musical journey from national to the international, there is hardly any relevance of mentioning him as a creator and composer of the Soviet generation that makes him different from the post-Soviet generation. His musical compositions are still alive and highly acknowledged for their depth and range within Tajikistan and abroad. In fact, Shahidi was an institution by himself and has left a very competent legacy within his own family. His house is a museum of music-based collections. It is also a foundation for research in music in Tajikistan. Tolib Shahidi, the son, became an established composer following his father's footsteps, and performs his father's compositions. He has also made his mark with his own symphony that is a combination of both Western and traditional styles.[23]

The contribution of Ziyodullo Shahidi became national news on the occasion of his 90th birth anniversary celebrations in May 2004 in Dushanbe. The First International Festival of Modern Music, held during May 14-19, 2004 and dedicated to the 90th birth anniversary of Ziyodullo Shahidi, coincided with the 80th anniversary of the foundations of the Tajik capital, Dushanbe. This international cultural event was heralded as a great success for the Tajik Republic especially in the aftermath of the Civil War.

Conclusion

A brief and quick overview of Tajik cultural expressions in the post-Soviet phase, whether it is in the literary field or in music and melody, denotes an image of an undaunted spirit, empowered by a rich past cultural heritage. The initiatives for cultural recovery and the accompanying modifications reflect the urge to recover lost entities, even while fighting complexities in the contemporary scenario. Culture carries enormous significance for the Tajik people, instilling a subtle yet distinct sense of self-confidence that has helped them tide over difficult circumstances.

Notes

1. William O. Beeman, "The Struggle for Identity in Post-Soviet Tajikistan," MERIA, *Middle East Review of International Affairs Journal*, vol. 3, no. 4, December 1999.
2. Iraj Bashiri, *Bozor Sobir's Life*, Copyright Bashiri 2000, *www.angelfire.com/mb/Poets/Bozor.html*
3. Translation by Iraj Bashiri, 2000.

4. Bozor Sobir; Dubora Sozamat Vataan, YouTube, www.youtube.com/watch?v=oF9UpKUYiyk
5. Translation by Tajik scholar, Nargis Nurullo Khoja.
6. Gulrukhsor is a poet, write, journalist, playwright, translator. She is author of more than 70 books. Gulrukhsor was the chief editor of many newspapers and magazines; Deputy Chairman of the Union of Journalists; Secretary of the Union of writers of Tajikistan; Chairman of the International Fund of Culture of Tajikistan; Deputy to the Supreme Soviet of the USSR (1989-1991); Member of Union of Writers of the USSR; Member of the Association of Writers of Asia and Africa; Peoples Poet of Tajikistan; Laurie of American Prize of Khamet; (1994); Laurie of Comsomol Prize (1978); Laurie of Tajikistan's Komsomol Prize (1976); www.festivaldepoesiademedellin.org/pub.php/en/.../safieva.html
7. Gulrukhsorsafieva, Golgothaandan Altar (Song on the Wind), www.festivaldepoesiademedellin.org/pub.php/en/.../04_24_04_09.ht
8. Safieva, Golgotha.
9. Gulnazar Keldi, "If I See a Barbed Tongue," translated by Sunil Sharma, *World Literature Today*, vol. 70, no. 3, *Literatures of Central Asia* (Summer, 1996), Board of Regents of the University of Oklahoma, pp. 575-76, URL: http://www.jstor.org/stable/40042073. Accessed: August 20, 2012, 23:56.
10. Loiq Sher-Ali was an expert in classical Persian poetry. The influence of Firdowsi, Khayyam and Molana Jalaleddin-e Balkhi is evident in Sher-Ali's works. He also translated several literary masterpieces into Persian. He was the head of Tajik-Persian Language International Foundation in Central Asia and was called as Shah-Poet of Tajikistan. A chosen collection of his works is published in Iran, 1994. Another collection, "Rakh's Spirit," is published in Iran, 1999, by Mirzo Shakurzoda.
11. Farzaneh Khojandi is a poet who writes in Tajik. Born in 1964 in Khojent province of Tajikistan, Farzaneh Khojandi is widely regarded as the most exciting woman poet writing in Persian (Farsi, Tajik) today and has a huge following in Iran and Afghanistan as well as in Tajikistan, where she is simply regarded as the country's foremost living writer. Her frequently playful and witty poetry draws on the rich tradition of Persian literature in a humorous way. ***http://www.poetrytranslation.org/*** *poets/Farzaneh_Khojandi*
12. Bozor Sobir, "Mother Tongue."
13. Olivier Roy, *The New Central Asia*: *The Creation of Nations* (New York and London: New York University Press, 2007, p. 178.
14. Roy, *The New Central Asia*, p. 573.
15. Dilorom Karomat, "The Fate of the Shashmaqom in Uzbekistan in the 20th century" in Rashmi Doraiswamy (ed.), *Cultural Histories of Central Asia* (Aakar Books, 2009), p. 58.

16. Karomat, "The The Fate of Shashmaqom," p. 70.
17. *Music of Central Asia*, vol. 2, Aga Khan Trust for Culture and Smithsonian Folkways Recordings, 2005.
18. Federico Spinetti, "Open Borders. Tradition and Tajik Popular Music: Questions of Aesthetics, Identity and Political Economy," *Ethnomusicology Forum*, vol. 14, no. 2, *Music and Identity in Central Asia* (November 2005), p. 189, URL: http://www.jstor.org/stable/20184518. Accessed: August 21, 2012, 00:10.
19. Evan Rapport, "Falak: The Voice of Destiny: Traditional, Popular, and Symphonic Music of Tajikistan" by Federico Spinetti (Review Article), *Ethnomusicology*, vol. 51, no. 2 (Spring/Summer, 2007), pp. 358-60. URL: http://www.jstor.org/stable/20174535. Accessed: August 21, 2012, 00:43.
20. Rapport, "Review on Spinetti," p. 18.
21. Spinetti, "Open Borders," p. 191.
22. Ziyodullo Shahidi: Songs and Romances « Shahidi Cultural - Bobojon bobojon.com/shahidifoundation.com/wordpress/?p=2430 June 2011.
23. Tolib Shahidi with Maroon Town Reggae Band, British Embassy in Tajikistan, Shams Band, Radio Tajikistan, Artin Pic Presents, 2011, YouTube.

20 Eurasian Culture/Arts of Central Asia: The Case of Tajikistan

Munira Shahidi

The disintegration of the Soviet Union, the end of the Cold War and the creation of the five independent "*stans*" of Central Asia have opened up prospects for re-envisioning Central Asia within a Eurasian community. The problem, however, lies in the distinctive systems of knowledge of Central Asia and Europe. Although there has been interaction among communities of poets, philosophers, musicians and craftsmen of Central Asia and other countries of Asia and Europe since medieval times, which laid the foundations of academic studies of Tajikistan in the twentieth century, the results of these investigations are not known in the West. That ignorance restricts interest of the global community to the local/national intellectual potential, widening the gap of knowledge about the past and creating a biased view about the future course of developments.

The starting point to bridge that gap is legalisation of the main achievements of Tajik academic school in arts for contemporary development. It is important to know that integration of the local/regional traditional arts of diversity of cultures of Central Asia, has its own periods of development in the twentieth century:

- 1920s-1930s—creating a cultural infrastructure with the inception of intermediate and advanced schools of the study of music and other arts all over Central Asia in partnership with Russian, Iranian, Afghan, Turk and other Eastern European experts in the fields of art and culture.
- 1940s-1950s—organisation of social studies with special branches in artistic traditions in academic and university institutions. International interaction between academic and art institutions for professional development of the study of artistic traditions based on

collaborative projects for the study of manuscripts and lithographs, collected by national academic schools from the entire region.

- 1960s-1980s—deeper links between national institutions of art and other art institutions, defining the common and specific features and dynamics of national art.
- 1990s till now—transitional period in culture and arts and understanding their problems and prospects.

These four periods of formation, re-formulation and transformation of the Bukharan infrastructure to the contemporary independent forms of cultural infrastructure will be discussed and analysed in this paper. Although the common intercultural and cosmopolitan space of the Bukharan Emirate and Russian Turkestan has been divided into national state structures, the idea was to develop the provinces of the Russian Empire that underwent transformation at the time of the October Revolution. Culture and art were the main identifying factors in the vast Soviet space of diverse cultures that stretched between Moscow and Dushanbe. The diverse kinds of relations that developed in this vast space date back to the colonial period and have been gradually merged within the overall knowledge. This had an impact on the creation of new forms of music, theatre, paintings and cinema.

Since the middle of the nineteenth century, there have been local and regional perceptions about European forms of art. These ideas have started to materialise in Samarqand only in the 1920s and 1930s of the twentieth century. The theory of art or poetics, free from religious, linguistic and even political barriers of the time, uniting people of different ethnic groups and nations, however, has been created long ago—during the Samanid period in the tenth century. In practice, its realisation started with the idea of Timur as the symbol of unity between eastern and western parts of the Islamic world in the fourteenth and fifteenth centuries. The encouragement that was given to folk culture in the poetics of *shahroshub* (rebellious citizenship) on the one hand, and the synthesis of religiosity and culture of Islam and Hinduism within the "Indian style of Persian poetry" on the other, expressed diversity of art and craft and community interaction as well as competition in the vast cultural space that stretched from Samarkand to the Mediterranean coast. But that knowledge, despite its dynamic content, was available in a limited way among a section of the highly educated group of people, like Ahmad Danish, Abdurauf Fitrat, Sadryddin Ayni and others, who were the creators of an artistic environment in Central Asia. The October Revolution in Russia was welcomed by most reformers at the turn of the nineteenth and twentieth centuries as a way to engage the masses in the discovery of the world, but that enthusiasm was suppressed by Bolshevik terror and Stalinist repressions which were followed by World War II.

New thoughts percolated with the establishment of academic institutions and universities in Central Asia. The Academy of Sciences of Tajikistan, founded in 1951 as a branch of the Soviet Academy of Sciences, became one of the new national academies that were set up in the region with a focus on socio-economic studies. The First President of Tajik Academy of Sciences was Sadriddin Ayni (1878-1954), an outstanding cultural personality at the turn of the nineteenth-twentieth centuries in Central Asia, a bilingual writer and an academic, who survived the persecution of different regimes—Amir of Bukhara, Stalinist terror and ideological restrictions of the Soviet period. His contribution in the field of literary studies of the last century is outstanding. He studied the syncretic and cosmopolitan character of national identity, encouraged the development of the millennia-old Tajik literary heritage and the new forms of Tajik creativity: national theatre, music, paintings, etc. He was among the initiators of the *jadid* reformist movement in the Bukharan Emirate, arguing in favour of awakening of the mind through the arts. The way to achieve that was cognitive cultural intervention in European classical forms of art: music, theatre, paintings and cinematography. What were the basic ideas of such an intervention? Who were initiators? How were the interpretations of the famous figures of Tajik culture, such as Ibn Sina/Avicenna, Rudaki, Firdawsi, Ahmad Danish accepted by the people? What was the people's response to publication of folk-tales about the "miracles" of Ibn Sina the healer, to selected writings from the heritage past of the classical period, and what were their images in new born theatre and film productions?

The specifics of Tajik Eurasian culture/arts have been formed within the competitive space of classical literary perceptions of the world and the modern European technical interpretation of classical literature. Both these trends were integrated into a newly formed artistic space for indigenous classics, introducing actors of the classical and pre-revolutionary figures of the past as the real stars and heroes of the present. How did that interpretation impact on the formation of national identities among a cosmopolitan population of the region? How was modern Tajik art accepted by the global partners? What could be its role in integrating an emergent Eurasian market in the contemporary period?

It is true that there are new possibilities of getting information from the Internet, which is a new powerful tool for creation of the new intellectual society of the globalising world. But the internet has very few and that too rather narrowed interpretations of Eurasian art. Museum demonstration of artefacts of the ancient Silk Road does remind one of the "glorious past" but is also the reason for indifference to today's reality in the realm of art, sometimes taking it for granted. In a way, the Internet unites people on the one hand but widens the gaps among generations on the other hand—not only between original thinkers and artists and practitioners of consumerism, but also generally, between diversity of categories of society. To restrict the negative usage of knowledge and to empower the nation with positive usage largely depends on the capacity and commitment of the world community to meet the national interests in a globalising world.

My knowledge and experience is based mostly on my own family, scholarly and public activity through building of a new institution for cultural studies in the now independent country of Tajikistan. Formed in 1992 with the aim of restricting destructive tendencies since the dissolution of the Soviet Union, the Ziyodullo Shahidi International Foundation for Culture was strategically oriented to create its own network of researchers in culture and arts, gradually promoting integration of national and regional intellectual potential into the bigger space of Eurasian studies. At the beginning, the aim was to promote Tajik culture, identifying deep links of academic research with the modern arts, both Asian and European. Based on the classical heritage of the region, the literary studies of Tajikistan were oriented towards realisation of its own heritage through interpretations by the non-Tajiks, identifying the inner world dynamic and misinterpretations and biased views. As a consequence, common artistic features, such as literature, music, theatre, painting, etc., were discovered and several misconceptions in Western oriental studies realised. Since 1997, the Foundation has been registered as an independent institution for cultural studies, and has become a member of the Public Council under the President of the Republic of Tajikistan. It developed its own strategy to transform from traditional courses of study of classical heritage into cooperative and informative methods. Paradoxically, the Civil War of 1992-1997 that raised worldwide interest in Tajikistan, which shares its longest borders with Afghanistan and some mountainous lands with China, has created an opening for a number of projects that support peace-building measures. One of these initiatives has a cognitive approach to the problems of peace and war in Central Asia. Due to cooperation with UNDP, the Embassies of Asia, Europe and the USA in Tajikistan, the Swiss office for cooperation and development and the Soros Foundation, the Ziyodullo Shahidi Foundation has been able to widen its national network significantly. The author has had prolonged experience of cultural studies in the field of comparative literature of Central Asia and Europe and the resultant collaboration with academic and university circles in Sweden, France, the UK and Germany, and has gained access as teacher in the premier institutions of art and culture. There has been considerable acquisition of knowledge about new world tendencies in human studies, creating innovative partnerships with a diverse range of scholars and artists. Thus, the following questions that this paper seeks to address are: What is the significance of Eurasian culture/arts for the emerging intellectual market of the globalising world? How and why were they marginalised from the world humanistic studies of the last century? What is the nature of improved contacts and relations between the countries of the former Soviet Union and the "others," especially in the context of Central Asia's independent cultural policies, and how has that contributed to the integration of the vast Eurasian space? What is the role of culture/arts in building Eurasian space in a peaceful and non-violent way? What are the perspectives of integration to the emergent Eurasian space for Central Asian culture/arts?

Some of these issues were addressed in the recently concluded *Eurasia Emerging Markets Forum* in Astana on September 10-11, 2013. The keynote address of the Kazakh President, Nursultan Nazarbayev, pointed to Kazakhstan's 2050 goal of attaining new-age development levels. This author addressed new Tajik institutions in arts. Politicians, experts and leading figures of international institutions and banks were invited to facilitate discussions for the promotion of long-term projects. The aim of the Forum was to create a space of trust between countries of Central Asia and the European Union. Discussing the ways of actualisation of that aim, Michael Emerson, Senior Research Fellow of the Centre for European Policy Studies (CEPS) in Belgium, outlined the problem of negotiations among post-Soviet countries on the one hand and China with other global partners. He said, that "separation of Europe from Soviet Eurasia and China during the twentieth century was the product of historically short-lived iron and bamboo curtains." But these bottlenecks could be overcome by humanitarians and artists: academics, writers, composers, theatre producers and film-makers. That peace-building measure in the countries of Central Asia, including Tajikistan, however, is totally ignored in present-day projects that are intended to improve the image of emerging Eurasian markets. The reformist mind and artistic ideas have been restrained by the political regimes both internally and externally. The deeper levels of creativity have hardly been recognised internationally.

With independence, the Central Asian states got another chance to re-integrate the diverse forms of culture/arts into the vast, fast changing world. But compared to the situation of the 1920s and 1930s, the global situation has changed in a major way. The innovative and scholarly approach to classical art during the Soviet period raised the ability of national art to adapt to a humane environment and European art tradition through national opera, ballet, symphony, theatre, cinema, paintings, etc. Although the present transition period demonstrates their degradation, instead of development, it is important to recognise the achievements of the past century and the coexistence of local and global interests.

The intellectual strength of nations and nationalities in the last century was more significant than artificial borders between the nation states of the region. The theatrical production, film festivals and festivals of arts have widened horizons of understanding among common people and promoted the building of an intercultural space. Cultural policy, while establishing "a progressive, Soviet identity," was exclusive and not inclusive. By ignoring the religious aspect inherent in cultural traditions, the Soviet authorities were actually rejecting the very basic ideas of unity of Islam. What the regime encountered was the artistic interpretation of universal national/global values, and that "hidden" process created risks for Soviet order as a whole. The main concern for the regime was to handle creativity. The aim was to restrict the impact of arts on the people and to keep the cultural aspect as a least priority of development, while politics and economy would take the lead role. These policy-priorities resulted in cultural degradation. In my opinion, the objective reason for the crisis of the 1980s was not only political or economical, but there were ethical and human reasons for the dissolution of the Soviet system. This angle is hardly discussed in the gamut of Eurasian studies.

The reconstruction of the national/regional ethics of relationship depends on how deeply we can understand the problems of Eurasian culture/arts of the Soviet period, and to what extent they can answer the basic challenges of the globalising world, improving the system of knowledge of our contemporary period. But, to understand the situation of the Eurasian space in the Soviet period, one has to be aware of the rivalry and competition among diverse traditions and orientations within the common cultural space.

There were two contradictory tendencies of culture/arts in Central Asia during the Soviet period: official "instructional" institutions and those resisting official policy. There was also another path that tried to combine and harmonise these two contradictory tendencies, thereby building objective, academic foundations for development. The results of academic research, especially during the five-six decades after World War II belonged to such trends—instead of commodity-centric ideas, ideas in poetics and arts of Central Asia tended to be based on Ibn Sina's perception of the world, which is formally conceptualised as "intention-activity-prosperity." But the intention to build own modern national and regional institutions of art has been roughly interrupted due to propagation of radicalisation among the masses, the Stalinist repression of intellectuals, and World War II which disturbed centralised budgets in the field of culture/arts. In Tajikistan, the situation became even worse due to the civil war of 1992-1997. But what are the intentions to build art institutions in the Tajik-world of Central Asia and to what extent are they in demand today?

The intention to build art institutions, oriented to integrate traditional music and dance traditions and diverse ethno-national amateur theatre groups into the European space was seen in the modernisation projects of Central Asian *jadid* reformers in the nineteenth and twentieth centuries. Ahmadi Danish took the initiative of modernising the archaic Bukharan environment by building a new musical theatre. This initiative was inspired by the model of Mariinsky Theatre of St. Petersburg. Academic research of the 1960s-1980s in Tajikistan were dedicated to Danish's heritage and political activity, identifying problems and inner contradictions of power and arts in Bukhara during the nineteenth century. *Rasul Khodi-zoda* initiated the academic approach to Danish's works. This lineage was adopted by the critical edition of *Navodir-ul-vakoe* which was the seminal work of Danish, the poet, politician and diplomat. The critique was published in Cyrillic with a comprehensive introduction and commentaries by A. N. Boldirev. Many sections of that book were translated into Russian and published later as a separate book. A theatre play and a film entitled *A Star at Midnight* were staged by Tajik directors and actors. That genre of academic and artistic writings reflected the change in Bukharan society in the nineteenth century. Through this theatrical composition people became aware that Danish was voicing his protest against tyranny and the feudal system of his times in three different ways: intellectually, politically and artistically. He became a national hero of modernisation of traditional arts of Central Asia. Boldirev's scholarly interpretation was based on the times when Ahmadi Danish visited Mariinsky theatre in St. Petersburg, where he listened to the famous Italian singer, soprano Adelina Pitte, to whom he dedicated a poem. These facts from the angle of cultural policy of the Soviet period had a double social impact—(a) it brought about the synthesis of Tajik-Russian art compositions and (b) it reflected the interest of Tajik musicians to European vocal tradition. This type of academic research was a unique inspiration for national theatre and polyphony music. Thus, both, academic research and artistic activity were united in convincing the society about the humanistic appeal of Eurasian culture/arts.

Central Asian culture/arts also give space to "the other." Muslim culture is a synthesis of diverse cultures, incorporating human studies into an artistic, intercultural vision. This concept of integrating cultures was seen in Europe during the late Middle Ages, and reached its culmination in modern Europe in the eighteenth century in Goethe's composition, *Eastern-Western Divan*. I. S. Braginskii, the renowned Soviet orientalist, interprets Goethe's idea of transforming the rigid antiquated poetical tradition into "the shifting, fluid element of eastern verse." But Goethe's synthesis of European and Persian poetical traditions, according to Braginskii, was not followed universally and in the middle of nineteenth century, the later German poets not only differed from Goethe's style but also openly challenged his poems. Braginskii may not have explained the reason for this. But one may find reasons in the industrial competition which was gaining ground during the middle of the nineteenth century, which transformed into the industrial revolution. The use of armaments and weapons has resulted in the strength and power of nation-states like Germany. The capacity for controlling these weapons lay in the hands of the rich. Consequently, the balance between material and intellectual values was broken and crises of individualism revealed the contradictions of modernity of the European tradition. According to Monique Castillo, a Swedish philosopher, European modernity is responsible for the "lost unity." Although European Union (EU) is a model for most contemporary societies, especially transitional ones like Central Asia, it appears that the union is based on a complex legal system rather than on moral and human values. Morality as a human ideal is the strength of Central Asian arts. Thus, a face-to-face cooperation of artists and researchers in the arts complex of Central Asia and Europe is the challenging factor of our own times.

In the nineteenth and twentieth centuries, Central Asia's opposition against colonisation and Bolshevik regime has been expressed mostly in the concepts of "soft power." There was neither any warfare, nor any serious military confrontation to the military aggression. It is paradoxical that development priorities were based on institutionalisation of knowledge and arts within the models of the colonising powers—Russia and Great Britain. Although the key figure in the reformist movement, Ahmad Danish was inspired by the idea of crucial reform of political and social system of old Bukhara, there was neither social capital for that type of reforms, nor any desire for either internal or external power-sharing by the Bukharan Emirate and Tsarist Russia to invest in such type of reforms. The intellectual revolution was suppressed by the military forces. It also resulted in moral losses for the people of the region.

Empowered with a cultural infrastructure, the Soviet authorities did not fail to adopt a repressive stance towards practitioners of humanities and arts. That is why the veil of fear and caution made it impossible for the marginal elite to bring a full-scale cultural revolution into effect. The policy of divide and rule has impacted on arts and music, where the simplified norm has been chosen either in the form of diverse interpretations of old forms and traditions, or adapting to the ready-made methodology of Western music. Nevertheless, the middle path of interpenetration among indigenous cultural values as a new technique of expression, was becoming more and more acceptable to the people at large.

The emancipation of the academic mind, the freeness of ideas, whether in research or in arts, is reflected in the dialogue of cultures that has transcended the world of Islam, the world of Christianity, the worlds of Hinduism and Buddhism. The study of Chinese, Slavic, non-Slavic and Caucasian (Armenian) images has also given an impression of the cosmopolitan identities of the Central Asian people. Releasing the mind from religious dogmas and cultural isolation of Soviet times, a group of intellectuals became attracted to greater integration and a globalised world. Unfortunately, due to the civil war and large-scale emigration of musicians, actors, vocalists and ballet-dancers, a new vision of Eurasian culture/arts almost totally stopped. To study the past through the lens of the present is still predominant in humanities, and this has created a deterrent in the formulation of "new" art forms. There are a growing number of publications on the challenges of multiethnic and multicultural Central Asian space but most of these are rather politicised, limiting the process of cooperation in the field of arts, as well as in the publication of regional editions. Such is the fate of the journal *Fonus* which focuses on the development of Eurasian arts in the region and seeks to create a bridge between the old and the new in the arts domain through a revitalisation of art institutions created since the last century. The attention goes to the first art institution and the challenges it faced in working towards a unity of diverse ethno-national culture/art forms. One would also like to assess the present situation.

The modern Institute of Art was initiated by Abdurauf Fitrat in 1928 in Samarkand. His book on Uzbek classical music and history (written in the Uzbek language and Arab graphic) was suppressed in 1927. Al Jumaev writes: "Since we have known the first version of that research, we can just suppose, that the reason of persecution might be some reflections of Abdurauf Fitrat in the book" (ignoring the Tajik element in the common heritage category, classification of some Tajik-speaking authors, for example, Najmiddin Kaukabi of Bukhara as "Uzbek scholars in music," etc.). But Jumaev's statement can raise some speculations. First, Fitrat was bilingual like many intellectuals of that time, writing efficiently in Tajik and Uzbek. Second, the political reason of marginalisation of the Tajik-Persian language from the common intercultural space was devised to change the linguistic policy within the "great games" of Russia in Central Asia. Bilingualism had a bizarre form—horizontal bilingualism—whereby Russian language was the dominant language. Finally, Farsi-Tajik as the *lingua franca* of diverse *ethnoi* of Central Asia, as well as Central Asia and India since the time of the Timurids, was out of the games played by superpowers in the Central Asia-South Asia region. Abdurauf Fitrat wanted to create inter-ethnic cognitive balance between urbanised and rural parts of the region, when the cities at that time were mostly inhabited by Tajiks and the countryside was inhabited mostly by Uzbeks.

By 1927-1928, when the Institute's foundations were being planned, the national delimitation of Central Asia was almost complete, and the debates about Soviet linguistic policy were reaching the culmination stage. The disparity about change of the script from Arabic-based Tajiki and Uzbeki-Chaghatay was not given adequate attention. Some reasons were cited to support the change: uneducated masses and necessity of gaining advantage over Western technological education. The intense debates have been argued in the book, published by a group of Tajik researchers, namely, A. Navai, N. Odinaev and P. Olimova. The research material is based on newspapers and magazines of the 1920s and the 1930s, such as *Ovozi Tojik* (Voice of Tajik), *Bedorii Tojik* (Awakening of Tajik), *Tojikistoni Surx* and *Rahbari Donish* (Guide for Knowledge). The research, however comprehensive, has a limited outreach, from the linguistic point of view. One of the most important problems is still missed out in analysis of those debates: what was the view regarding bilingualism and cosmopolitan character of the region, as a whole? Why were most of the bilingual and open-minded Tajiks and Uzbeks repressed—like Abdurauf Fitrat, Mahmudkhodja Behbudi, Gani and Rashid Abdulla, Muqaddaschon Shahidi, Turaqul Zehni and several others? Why were most of the poets, musicians and those who actively built a new artistic space, locally and regionally, persecuted?

My grandfather, Mukadaskhon Shahidi, was a prosperous businessman and a well-known philanthropist in Samarkand in the nineteenth century and the beginning of the twentieth century. His house still stands on one of the small and narrow streets of that ancient city and, due to its typical architecture, is now under protection of UNESCO. At that time, that house was the most visited place by artists of the age: poets and musicians such as Khoja Abdul Aziz, Levicha, Mullogandov and many others. These gatherings were multiethnic and international, but linked by music of Shashmaqam, though initiation to innovate that tradition was already adopted by Khoja Abdul Aziz. The other method of improving traditional melodies, by borrowing European rhythm and declaration of human rights in musical art, was shown by Sadriddin Ayni's interpretation of the French national anthem *Marselieza* in Tajiki. These gatherings were attractive not only for musicians and poets. They were also visited by different types of informers and spies, at the end of nineteenth century, first from the Tsarist army and then from the KGB after the Revolution. When Bolshevik violence started, books written in

Arabic-Persian script were burnt down in huge numbers and the library of Muqaddaskhon Shahidi was one of the first that was eliminated. That was a warning for him to escape. In 1929, when the Soviet Socialist Republic of Tajikistan was established, Shahidi's family and many of his friends and associates moved to Dushanbe, which after a while became Stalinabad, the Tajik capital which was renamed as Dushanbe. Starting his trade here, in the newly built shop, Mukaddaskhon again became the centre of attention of poets and musicians. Among his friends there were Tajiks, Uzbeks, Jews, Russians and people from other nationalities who were extremely enthusiastic in setting up the cultural infrastructure of the new Tajik Soviet Republic. His son, Ziyodullo gained recognition as one of the reputed and talented musicians, playing *tambur*, *du-tar*, *rubab*, with the experience of a school teacher at a new *jadid* school in Jizzak, a countryside of Samarkand. He moved to Dushanbe with his friends who belonged to the roving bands of musicians from all over Central Asia, e.g., Azam Kamolov, Fozil Soliev, Sharifjon Bobokalonov, Nasimjon Pulotov and many others. He was involved in concert performances in the newly built theatres, where they got acquainted with Russian musicians. Some of the stories of those first musical theatres and new music creations are described and analysed in Ziyodullo Shahidi's book, *Musiqi dar haety man*—"Music in my life." The father and son duo created a new circle of artistic gatherings in their own small tent that still exists behind the luxurious building of "Orienbonk" on Rudaki Street amidst the fast-track changes of the city of Dushanbe in the twenty-first century. But that circle of artists was disbanded during the period of Stalinist terror. Mukhadaskhon Shahidi was arrested by NKVD in 1937, and in 1938 he was executed in the Gulag. The events of those years, engraved in the memory of a family, came to be expressed many years later in the famous romantic composition *Zi suzi sina*—The Fire of the Soul—written by Ziyodullo Shahidi towards the end of the 1940s.[5] Altogether about 1,800 persons, most of them in the field of literature and arts, were arrested in a newly built Tajikistan and 4,750 were arrested in Uzbekistan. The Soviet regime was a paradoxical system—on the one hand having created a cultural infrastructure, and destroying the human face of the structure on the other.

Only after World War II was there a radical change when scholarly institutions of Moscow and Leningrad opened their doors for Central Asian students. Professional researchers, musicians, artists and actors, creating their own cross-cultural networks, started to gradually improve the cultural infrastructure. The most important findings of academic research during the Soviet period were the recognition of the role of art in societal development and international affairs. That historically short period of peaceful development of Central Asia, however, is totally ignored by the international academic community of our own times. There are two main reasons for losing the basic, fundamental elements of culture/arts during the second half of the twentieth century, even though independence gave new opportunities for the development of national/regional Eurasian identity. These two reasons are:

- Rivalry and competition in the contemporary world.
- Marginalisation of culture/arts of Central Asia from the contemporary institutional domain that prioritises Eurasian integration.

Contemporary rivalry for selfish economical interests is pretty much obvious in Tajikistan. That policy significantly reduces creativity of society, diminishing youth energy to express the current status about societal problems. Although many governmental and non-governmental institutions all over the world have the aim of promoting arts as a main tool for peaceful development of Eurasian space, there is still no significant interest or investment for promoting the culture/arts of Central Asia. That lack of patronage is seen particularly in the context of the Western world's sole interest in local cultural values. This was the main criticism of Edward Said's *Orientalism.*

The last two decades of independence of the countries of Central Asia has opened prospects of re-integration of Eurasian culture/arts of Tajikistan into the world space of arts. One of the main problems of development, however, lies in the varying "gaps" about the artistic style of thinking, which goes back to the Soviet period. Talking about the poverty of art in the Soviet past, the contemporary Tajik poet Gulnazar has remarked that the reason for backwardness and simplification of artistic imagination at that time was fear and ignorance. But still, there were some inspirational sources of native culture, which was maintained by the significant strides in research and finance. Transition from the planned economy to market economy weakened these two fundamental sources of development of Eurasian culture/arts in the country.

The graduates of the universities of Moscow, Leningrad, Kiev and Tashkent integrated music with theatre and in the 1960s-1980s, linkages pointing to diversity of cultures flourished. Realising a huge potential of Tajik-Persian literature of the classical period for modern literature, music, theatre and paintings, some authors of the new Tajik culture skilfully tried to blend their own with other artistic findings. These innovations have resulted in new and adaptable forms of arts. As a matter of fact, the universal problem of clan rivalries as depicted in Shakespeare's play *Romeo and Juliet*, was uniquely portrayed by Abulqasim Lohuti, the Tajik revolutionary poet of Iranian origin. This was the starting point for the formation of modern Tajik drama. Interpretations and critical observations, however, were restricted and framed by official ideology. Those restrictions are still in place, and as a process of development they are yet to make a progress.

The last decade of the Soviet period is considered to be the dramatic era among the Tajik-speaking people of Central Asia. In art studies, at the turn of the Soviet and post-Soviet periods, the Tajik theatre has been named "Theatre Mecca." Shakespeare, Moliere, Chekhov, Dostoevsky, Khayam, Jami, Abdulqadir Bedil, Rabindranath Tagore, Gani Abdullo, Nur Tabarov—their creations featured constantly in the theatre space at the turn of the century. Over 70 years, the history of art penetrated into the realm of literature, music and paintings. It was also a time of reinvention of tradition. The Tajik producer, Farrukh Kasimov, who was the winner of many international awards, became a celebrity in the new era of Tajik theatre as he stunned the audience with his performance, *Joseph the Beautiful is coming back to Canaan*. The dialogues, decoration, the Sufi dance of "Sama"—all these were innovations that exemplified, according to Barzu Andurasakov, "either dying or a new life of Tajik theatre." The Eurasian art of Central Asia serves as a model and is a real link in the chain as it combines humane and economic traditions, keeping in mind the moral values.

Bibliography

1. Braginsky, I. *Zapadno-Vostochnyi syntez Goethe. Zapadno-Vostochnyi Divan* (Western-Eastern Synthesis of Goethe. Western-Eastern Divan). Moscow: Nauka, 1988.
2. Danish, Ahmadi. *Puteshestvie iz Bukhary v Peterburg. Izbrannoe* (Travel from Bukhara to Petersburg. Selection). Dushanbe: Tajikigosizdat, 1960.
3. Djumaev, Alexander. A*bduraif Fitrat*, http://www.ca-c.org/journal/08-1997/st_22_djumaev.shtml
4. Emerson, Michael. *Emerging Markets Forum*. Astana: Kazakhstan Press, September 10-11, 2013.
5. Liedman, Sven-Eric (ed.). *Monique Castillo. The Dilemmas of Postmodern Individualism. The Postmodernist Critique of the Project of Enlightenment.* Gothenburg, 1997.
6. Khotamov, Namoz. *Ta'richi chalki tojik (az solhoi 60umi asri XIX to soli 1924).* (The history of Tajik people (from 60th of XIX to 1924)). Dushanbe: Donish, 2001.
7. Shahidi, Ziyodullo. *Musiqi dar hayoti man* (Music in my life). Dushanbe: Irfon, 1986.
8. Said, Edward. *Orientalism*. London, 1972.
9. *Zaboni Tojiki dar mabnoi mubochisaho* (The Tajik Language). Dushanbe: Irfon, 2007.

21. India-Tajikistan Relations in the 20th-21st Centuries: The Evolution of Cultural Ties

Umedjon Majidi

Cultural-historical relations between India and Central Asia have deep roots. Since ancient times, these regions have had regular exchanges of culture and trade. Many émigrés, including scientists, poets, artisans and performers have come to India from Middle Asia, bringing in elements of their culture.

Recent archaeological research shows certain typological similarities of culture between south and south-eastern Tajikistan and north-western India during the Paleolithic Period. During the Neolithic Period, similar practices in agriculture gave rise to urban civilisation and state formation in these two regions.

The most significant achievement of Indo-Middle Asian cultural synthesis was the founding of the Kushana Empire. In centres like Bactria as well as North-Western India, the Kushanas made Bactrian their state language, and practised a bilingual linguistic system. The Kushana kings were patrons of all Indian religions—*Shaivism*, *Vaishnavism, Buddhism* and *Jainism*.

India and Tajikistan were united by roads crossing the lands of Kashmir and its surrounding areas. Many scientists, historians, geographers and travellers—including Ibn Batuta, Al-Biruni, Sharafuddin Yazdi, Mirza Haidar Dughlat, Abul Fazl, Jahangir, Nasan Shakh and the Europeans—Francois Bernier, George Foster, Belov and George Trebeck—have written extensively about the Silk Road connecting India and Central Asia through Kashmir. This network connects Punjab-Kashmir-Sogdiana (the territory of Afghanistan and Tajikistan), Andijan, Tashkent, Badakhshan, Bactria, Kandahar (Peshawar) and China through the mountainous regions of the Pamirs, Hindu Kush, Karakoram and the Tien Shan.[1]

The cultural links between the Indian and the Tajik people grew substantially in the tenth century with the Ghaznavid penetration into north-west India especially Punjab[2] and Persian linguistic influence. The bilateral relations between the Tajiks and Indians developed due to historical links as well as interaction between the governments, scientific advancement, cultural and global trends. Such relations deepened during Soviet times when exchanges were established in the spheres of science, politics, economics and culture. The pioneer in the field of promotion of Tajik-Indian relations was the Tajik poet, Mirzo Tursunzade, who visited India just after it attained independence.[3] His well-known works include *Indian Ballad* (1948-49), *I am Free from Asia* (1950-56) and *From the Ganges to the Kremlin* (1970). The Indian freedom movement and the liberation struggles in India and Afghanistan were popular themes of Tursunzade's poems. Mirshakar was another Tajik intellectual who was respectful about Indian nationalists. His novel *English bullet* is about an Indian rebel who sustained bullet wounds inflicted by the British and fled to the Soviet land:

Uslyshal chto u was w strane
Welikhikh mnogo mudretsov jiwet
Chto lyubyat i jaleyut swoy narod
I, mojet byt, oni pomogut mne

Dushoy ko mne, by mojet, snizoydut
I nakonets tu pulyu izwlekut
Proklyatuyu iz tela moego
I bolshe ne proshu ya nichego[4]
I heard in your land

Many wise men live
That love and feel sorry about own people
And may be, they can help me

Purified by soul to concede to me
And finally remove the bullet
From my bloody body
And else asking no more[5]

Literary exchange between Tajikistan and India thrived during the time when the works of the noted Indian philologist, Rahula Sankrityayana, became visible in the public domain. Sankrityayana translated the classic Tajik novels by Sadriddin Aini into Hindi, namely *Odina*, *Dokhunda* (1948). Other popular novels that were translated into Hindi were *Margi Sudkhur* (Death of a Moneylender, 1952), *Yatimon* (The Slaves, 1953) and *Yatim* (Orphan, 1956). In the early twentieth century the *Rubaiyat* of Omar Khayyam was translated by Maithilishram Gupta and Harivansh Rai Bachchan. Today, at the Sadriddin Aini Tajikistan Pedagogical University a cultural centre, "Charogi Zindagi" (Light of Life), organises exhibitions on the life of Khayyam.[6]

In 1977 Dushanbe celebrated the 100th anniversary of the Indian subcontinent poet and philosopher, Muhammad Iqbal. A collection of his poetry is entitled "Voice of East" (Sadoi Mashriq in Tajik). The writings of renowned Indian writers like Rabindranath Tagore, Munshi Premchand, Krishan Chandar, Khwaja Ahmad Abbas, Mulk Raj Anand, Amrita Pritam and others have been translated into Tajik language.

There is acknowledgement about several linguistic commonalities between India and Khurasan. Suniti Chatterji, the linguist has indicated such details in his studies. Many Persian loan words have been borrowed by India—for example—*karsha* in old Persian means coin; *kshatrapa* or *satrap* which is borrowed from old Persian *kshatrapavan*; *dipi, lipi* meaning sign is borrowed from old Persian *dipi*; *napista* means written; *ayatana* (*ayadana* = *ayazana* from the root word *yaz,* equivalent to sanskrit *yaj*) meaning temple; *asavari* (*asabari* or *asvabhara* from Sanskrit meaning horseman; *mudra* (*musra* or *muzra*) derived from the Egyptian meaning of coin; *pramana* derived from *framana* which means decree.

During the period of expansion of Buddhism, links with Parthia and Sassanids were established and these too have been indicated in the loan words borrowed from Prakrit language, which was the language for the spread of Buddhism—*pusta*–book/note (animal leather, where books were written), *pirojaka*–turquoise colour; *mocaka*–a boot, shoe (mocak–a new Persian word *mozah*).[7]

Cultural connections through Buddhist network and Buddhist ideologies are popular in East Asia. Soviet scholars have enthusiastically spoken on the creative pursuits of artists replicated in Buddhist art forms.[8] Buddhist artists of Central Asia and India have a lot in common and the commonalities are visible in the art of Afrasiab, Ajinateppe, Kalai-Kafirnigan and Balalyk-tepe.

Another component of cultural commonality is music. Indian music since the days of the Vedas and at the time of the epics *Mahabharata* and *Ramayana* has been researched into in India, and this work on the ancient Indian musical tradition termed as *Natyashastra* has immense appeal among Central Asian musicologists.[9] Indian music has evolved significantly with the advent of Muslim culture. Cultural synthesis was a significant development and musical notes were made not only in Sanskrit but also in simple Hindi. In the composition of the Persian court poet, Amir Khusrau Dehlavi, (*Śārngadhara paddhati),* we see a lot of musical links between India and Central Asia in general and with the Tajik people in particular. The Hindustani musical tradition and musical instruments like *venu* (flute) and *vinu* (harp) are common to both. Sometimes, musical instruments have migrated from Central Asia to India. One such instrument is the *rubab*. We see a lot in common between the Indian *shehnai* and Central Asian-Tajik *sunray.*[10]

Central Asian music is very similar to the Kashmiri musical tradition *sufiyana qalam* with a specific melody—the *maqam* and a fixed rhythm. This kind of music is accompanied by the use of the *rubab*, *sarang* but is somewhat dissimilar from the group performance in Tajikistan, *Shashmaqam.*[11]

Indian musical genre has survived through the gurukul system—which is very similar to what exists in Tajikistan. The *shishya* (student) lives with the Master (guru) and serves him while the Master teaches his student. This is a tradition of the Master-student tradition that is well known in Central Asia and the knowledge of the Master has passed from generation to generation.

The Sufi tradition of Central Asia is very close to the Sikh saintly tradition. According to legend, the honour of putting the first stone in the Golden Temple in Amritsar was given to Sufi Miyan Mir from Qadiriya Sufi sect. Among other members of the sect were Hoja Moinuddin and

Nizamuddin Auliya (Sheikh of Amir Khusrau Dehlavi). The *qawwali* or religious songs that are sung by a group of people, and also solo singers, are a distinguishable music form.[12]

India became one of the first countries to recognise the independence of Tajikistan in 1991 and diplomatic relations were established on August 28, 1992.[13] An official Indian delegation visited Tajikistan in February 1993 and as a result a six-point Cooperation Agreement was concluded. The fifth point of this agreement addressed questions of cooperation between the Republic of Tajikistan and the Republic of India in the areas of culture, art, science, media, cinema and sports. In December 1995 during the official visit of the President of Tajikistan to India, the Agreement on Science and Technical Cooperation was signed. In October 1998 during the visit of Himachal Som, Director General of Indian Council for Cultural Relations, to Tajikistan, the opening of a Tajik Cultural Centre in India and an Indian cultural centre in Tajikistan were discussed. On March 27, 2002, the Ministry of Culture of the Republic of Tajikistan with the support of the Embassy of India in Tajikistan organised a concert, *Moments with the Poems of Bedil*, at the Sadriddin Aini Opera Ballet Theatre. Tajik artists like Kurbonali Rakhmonov, Somon group and others, attended the concert. In March and April of 2002, the tenth anniversary of the establishment of diplomatic relations between India and Tajikistan was celebrated. Besides classical dance performance, like Bharatnatyam, an exhibition on contemporary graphics, with 81 exhibits of 34 artists was put on show based on the collection of Indian Council for Cultural Relations. Works and creations of artists as Maqbul Fida Hussein, Lakshman Gaud, Gogi Saroj Pal, Shanti Dev, etc., were displayed.[14] Contemporary scholars like Zarina Rahmatullaeva, a Tajik Indologist associated with Tajik National University, published with ICCR support a monograph titled, *Artistic Specialty of Rajendra Yadav's Short Stories,* in 2005.[15] In Tajikistan, there is awareness about the dissemination of writings of Tajik authors in India.[16]

Today, cultural cooperation with foreign countries is promoted by the India-Tajik Friendship Society. The Tajik-Indian Friendship Society has made significant contribution by organising festivals, book exhibits, meetings and lectures, in collaboration with Russian-Tajik (Slavonic)

University. The Department of Linguistics also organises special events. Each year, the Indian Philology Department of Asian and Europe Languages Faculty at Tajik National University organises conferences based on Indian languages and literature. Recent events include a conference dedicated to the 120th year anniversary of the birth of the famous Indian writer, Prem Chand, and the 50th year anniversary of the creation of the Indian Republic. The theme of the conference was, *The Role of Hindi Language in Bringing Together the People of India.* On their part, Tajik specialists regularly participate in international scientific conferences organised in India and scholars like Muzaffar Olimov and Umeda Gaffori, who are associated with the Tajik Academy of Sciences, are regular participants. The Indian cultural centre run by the Embassy of India also makes a sizeable contribution to strengthening cultural relations between the Tajik and Indian people. The centre offers 6-month Hindi language classes, as well as courses in classical Indian dance (Kathak) and instrumental music. Similar short language courses could be organised by the Embassy of Tajikistan in India.

Tajikistan has also been proactive in seeking the attention of the Indian people to the culture and traditions of the Tajik people. In 2006, the Embassy of Tajikistan in India organised a programme on Tajik dance and music in Delhi.[17] In October 2008, the Embassy of Tajikistan and the Indian Council for Cultural Relations organised *Tajik Culture Week* in Bangalore and Delhi that were attended by prominent cultural personalities including the well-known singer Noziya Karomatullo, daughter of late Karomatullo Qurbonov who was studying while living in India during that period.

Screening of Indian films is one form of Tajik-Indian cultural dialogue. The Government of India's scholarship programmes and training programmes have been brought under the rubric of technical and economic cooperation. Tajik diplomats have attended training modules at the Institute of Foreign Service under the Ministry of Foreign Affairs of the Republic of India. Tajik students have shown inclination to attend post-graduate training in India in the fields of economics, political science and business management administered by the Indian Council for Cultural Relations, and there is high demand for Tajik graduates who have been educated in India in the fields of banking, civil service, NGOs and in international organisations. At the same time, Indian students study at the medical and polytechnic universities in Dushanbe, and according to official statistics of the Ministry of Education the scope of study for Indian students in the secondary and higher secondary levels of education in Tajikistan is increasing every year.[18]

It is necessary today for the Government of Tajikistan to look at contemporary educational requirements and to adopt a comprehensive programme especially in connection with diaspora societies within and outside Tajikistan.[19] The Tajikistan Friendship Society can play a significant role in public diplomacy within the structure of the Tajikistan Foreign Ministry. The Society began its activities as a Soviet Society of Culture with focus on promoting information on achievements of the Soviet system.[20] Since the declaration of independence, many countries of the Soviet bloc withdrew their engagement with the Society which brought all normal functioning to an end. However, some countries, after adopting laws on non-governmental organisations (NGOs), renewed the activity within the framework of this law. Some other countries, for example, the Russian Federation, integrated the society within their Ministry of Foreign Affairs as *Rossotrudnichestvo.* This is a model that Tajikistan needs to follow.

In the last two decades the Tajikistan Friendship Society expanded its friendly relations with the Mumbai-based Zoroastrian College. Represented by Meher Master Moos, the College has responded to the Tajik Government's call for opening a Tajik Cultural Centre in Mumbai's suburbs. Suggestions also include opening the Dushanbe branch of the Zoroastrian College. Such initiatives are significant in view of the role of culture in expanding cooperation between Central and South Asia. Dialogues reflecting cultural commonalities between Tajiks and Indians should also be encouraged.

The subject of bilateral cooperation on the basis of historical linkages and contemporary dynamics was studied by Russian orientalists like E. Batalov.[21] Self-perception is an important component of international relations and Tajik scholars Saodat Olimova and Muzaffar Olimov who head the research centre, *Sharq*, have done creditable surveys based on opinion polls that are focused on the perception of Tajik people about regional and global diplomacy. India was rated as a power with enormous potential for cooperation with countries like Tajikistan. India's friendly environment evoked good response in the opinion polls.[22] The memory of Indian films (especially those of film-maker and actor, Raj Kapoor), with a message of peace and brotherhood, is still fresh in Central Asia. The image of India as a friendly nation is also seen in the responses of the Indian diaspora as the flag-bearer of Indian culture overseas. Sanjay Chaturvedi is optimistic about the cross section of Indian residents living in Tajikistan.[23]

India's academic circuit is also optimistic about political and cultural links with Tajikistan. Nivedita Das Kundu is particularly emphatic about such influence on Indian foreign policy.[24] Meena Singh Roy is emphatic about Tajikistan being India's strategic neighbour.[25] According to Sarvajit Chakrabarty, political relations between India and Tajikistan are most cordial.[26] But this has not gone beyond a point because India has only responded to initiatives rather than taking its own initiative.[27] According to Shashi Tharoor, India is a major aid recipient from the West.[28]

Active Indian involvement in Central Asia has been voiced by the Foreign Ministry. E. Ahmad, the former Minister of State for External Affairs expressed the Ministry's interest in multi-level engagement through "Connect Central Asia" policy that became a catchphrase among diplomatic circles ever since the Minister's speech in the First India-Central Asia Dialogue that was held on 12-13 June 2012 in Bishkek.[29] The text of his speech became the essence of India's Connect Central Asia Policy. This policy shall focus on strengthening relations of India with Central Asian nations through different ways—culture, economy, capacity building, and IT development. This has enormous relevance for a region where millennial memories of ties exist. Within the given parameters of this policy, India will initiate the establishment of the IT Centre of Excellence in Dushanbe. It has also planned the opening of an India-Central Asia University in Bishkek. This University is intended to develop a different priority. Unlike the Aga Khan-funded University of Central Asia that has centres all over the region, this new university set-up will focus on studies for Central Asian students for attaining professional and technical education. The recommendations were forwarded by the then Indian Ambassador in Bishkek, Phunchok Stobdan, who is a senior scholar at the Institute of Defence Studies and Analysis in New Delhi. Stobdan also suggested the opening of a Taxila University in Central Asia for the study of ancient Indian and Central Asian cultures.[30]

India's healthcare arrangements in Afghanistan are also raising expectations about India's multifaceted involvement in the frontiers of Central Asia. As far as Tajikistan is concerned, there are certain bottlenecks that have restricted Indian involvement there. The Varzob hydroelectric station stopped getting necessary equipment for a project that has been stopped long ago on the Tajik-Uzbek border, and the completion of the project has taken an unusually longer period. Due to the absence of a direct corridor with Tajikistan, India has limited herself to small projects. The issue is not about a lack of interest in Tajikistan for implementing serious larger projects, but, to deliver equipment necessary for a larger project, India would have no usable corridor for transporting this equipment.[31]

India, owing to its soft power image, has acquired some visibility because of its films, music and food, and has carved a niche in Tajik society. India has also made significant strides at the state level that have proved helpful in initiating programmes like Connect Central Asia. Tajikistan still needs to do a lot to make a real cultural presence in India. A well-conceived state policy with a South Asia programme needs to be carved out. Just like the Indian Cultural Centre that is functioning in the Indian Embassy in Dushanbe, where Hindi language classes are provided for the Tajik youth, a Tajik Cultural Centre can be established in the Tajik Embassy in New Delhi. The potential among the youth may be tapped to establish a working relationship between the two countries.

Students of Persian language and literature with knowledge of the Iranian dialect would be able to provide the right inputs for the proper functioning of an academic-cum-linguistic centre in the Tajik Embassy in Delhi. A government-civil society partnership is essential for promoting a positive image of Tajikistan that would also be helpful in widening the focus of Tajik missions abroad. The *Zaboni Modari* Foundation established in Tajikistan in 2011 can be sufficiently motivated in this direction.

Notes

1. Mushtaq Kaw, "Indo-Tajik Relations: A Historical Perspective," *India-Tajikistan Cooperation—Perspective and Prospects* in K. Santhanam and Ramakant Dwivedi (eds.), *India and Central Asia: Advancing the Common Interest* (New Delhi: Anamaya Publishers, 2007), p. 8.
2. *Encyclopedia of Islam*, vol. II, ed. by B. Lewis et al. (Leiden: Brill, 1983), pp.1050-1055.
3. M. Olimov, "Tajik-Indian relations." (Unpublished) Paper presented in International seminar *Tajikistan Today*, Jawaharlal Nehru University, New Delhi, p. 2.
4. Mirsaid Mirshakar, *Angliyskaya pulya.*
5. Translation by Umedjon Majidi.
6. Habibullo Rajabov, *Ten Years of Cultural Relations of Tajikistan and India, India and Tajikistan Revitalising a Traditional Relationship*. Publication of Maulana Abul Kalam Azad Institute of Asian Studies. New Delhi, 2003, pp.137-42.
7. S. N. Chatterji. *Iranianism: Iranian Culture and its Impact on the Work from Achaemenian Times.* The Asiatic Society, Kolkata, 2008. p. 28. Similar such studies in Laufer B.Sino-Iranica, *Chinese Contributions to the History of Civilization in Ancient Iran, with Special Reference to the History of Cultivated Plants and Products* (1919).
8. B. A. Litvinsky, "Nastennaya jiwopis Kala Kafirnigana" (Mural painting of Kala Kafirnigan) // *Sbornik. Kavkaz I Srednyaya Aziya w drevnosti I srednewekow'e. (Istoriya i kultura)*, Moskva, "Nauka." 1981, p. 126.
9. B. Chaytanya Deva, *Indiyskaya muzyka.* (Indian music) From English t*ranslated by Gorokhovik. E. M..* – M.: Muzyka, 1980. p. 9.
10. B. Chaytanya Deva, *Indiyskaya muzyka*, Indian music, p. 44.
11. B. Chaytanya Deva, *Indiyskaya muzyka*, p. 140.
12. B. Chaytanya Deva B. *Indiyskaya muzyka*, pp. 138-39.
13. Olimov M. "Tajik-Indian relations." (Unpublished) *Paper presented in International seminar "Tajikistan Today,"* Jawaharlal Nehru University, New Delhi. p. 2.
14. Shovkoplyas M. *Kulturnoe sotrudnichestwo Respubliki Tajikistana so stranami Wostoka.* (permanent link - http://history.tj/shovkoplas.php)
15. B. Jayshankar, "Maqsadi mo: bunyodi kuprukhoi dusti" (Our aim is to build bridges), *Jumhuriyat,* 20 Avgusti soli 2005 (from Tajik).
16. H. Rajabov, *In ast Hinduston.* (This is Hindustan) DDMT, Dushanbe, 2007. pp. 220-21 (from Tajik).
17. *Bulletin of the Embassy of Tajikistan in New Delhi*, 2007.
18. *Asia Plus*, September 17, 2010.
19. A. Shamolov, Narodnaya diplomatiya goworit iskrenne (National Diplomat Talks Sincerely). Journal *Dusti*, Obshestvo druzhby I kultury s zarubezhnymi stranami Tajikistana. Dushanbe, no. 1, 2013, p. 7.

20. Interview with Habibullo Rajabov, Chairman of India-Tajikistan Friendship Society in April, 2013 in Dushanbe.
21. E. Y. Batalov, *"O filosofii mejdunarodnykh otnosheny," (On philosophy of International Relations)* Moskva., Nauchno-orbazovatetelny forum po mezhdunarodnym otnosheniyam. 2005, pp. 77-78 (from Russian).
22. Muzaffar Olimov. Saodat Olimova. *Opros sredi naseleniya*. (Public Opinion Poll) Dushanbe, 2010. (from Russian)
23. Sanjay Charurvedi, "Diaspora in India's Geopolitical Visions: Linkages, Categories and Contestations, *Asian Affairs,* vol. 32. no. 3 (Fall, 2005) p. 153.
24. Nivedita Das Kundu, *"India-Tajikistan: An Enduring Relationship,"* Issue Brief. Indian Council of World Affairs, July 30, 2010.
25. Interview with Dr. Meena Singh Roy, IDSA, New Delhi, September 2012.
26. Interview with Sarbajit Chakrabarty, ICWA, New Delhi. September 2012.
27. Among Central Asian diplomatic missions in India, the Kazakh Embassy in India is most active and organizes events in Delhi on a regular basis. Comparatively, the Tajik Embassy has a muted presence. Interview with Dr. Angira Sen Sharma, ICWA, New Delhi, September 2012.
28. Shashi Tharoor, *Pax Indica: India and the World of the XXI century,* Thomson Press India, New Delhi, 2012.
29. India-Central Asia Dialogue is a Track II Initiative and is a dialogue between officials and scholars of India and Central Asia. Its objective is to engage in discussions related to India's foreign policy planning in the region. http://www.mfa.kg/mews-of-mfa-kr/12-13-iunya-2012-goda-v-diplomaticheskoi-akademii-mid-kr-sostoitsya-mejdunarodnaya-nauchno-prakticheskaya-konferenciya-pervii-indi-isko-centralnoaziatskii-dialog_ru.html; Also Jyoti Prasad Das, "India's 'Connect Central Asia' Policy, *Foreign Policy Journal,* October 29, 2012. (http://www.foreignpolicyjournal.com/2012/10/29/indias-connect-central-asia-policy/)
30. Takshila Nalanda University is the oldest Indian educational institution located in Bihar.
31. Conversation with Meena Singh Roy, IDSA, New Delhi, September 2012.

ANNEXURE

(Compiled by Mohamad Reyaz)

Media of Central Asia at a Glance*

Kazakhstan
Print: 937 total including 5 main daily papers and 6 main weeklies. Newspaper circulation statistics: The top two newspapers are *Vremja* (private, Russian language) and *Karavan* (private, Russian language). News agencies: Kazinform (state-owned), Interfax Kazakhstan, KazTAG, and Kazakhstan Today. Television Stations: 3 national channels, more than 100 other terrestrial channels, 14 local cable networks Broadcast ratings: Top four television stations: Khabar TV, Kasakh TV (Kazakhstan 1), KTK (Kazakh Commercial TV) and El-Arna. Radio Stations: 4 national stations, 43 in total.
Kyrgyzstan
Print: 250 including 4 main dailies and 4 other major papers. Newspaper circulation statistics: Top four by circulation: Super Info (circulation 80,000, private, Kyrgyz language), *Vechernij Bishkek* (circulation 50,000, private, Russian language), Pyramid (circulation 40,000, private, Russian language), *Delo* (22,000, private, Russian language). News agencies: *Khabar TV* (state-owned), *AkiPress* (private), and 24.kg (private). Television Stations: 7 main stations, 3 local cable networks. Broadcast ratings: Top two: National TV and Radio Broadcasting Corporation (state-owned, both languages), 5th Channel (private, Russian and Kyrgyz). Radio Stations: 6 main stations, 31 others.

Tajikistan
Print: Print: 268 newspapers, 136 magazines. Newspaper circulation statistics: The top three newspapers by circulation are *Oila*, Asia Plus, and *Charkhi Gardun.* News agencies: Asia Plus, *Avesta, Tojnews*, Pressa.tj (private); *ruzgor.tj* (private) *Khovar* (state-owned); 4 more are registered but inactive. Television Stations: 25. Radio Stations: 19. Broadcast ratings: Dushanbe's top radio stations are Radio*Imrüz*, Radio *Vatan*, Asia Plus, and *Orieno* (Russian-language); in Khujand Tiroz and SM-1.

Turkmenistan
Print: 24 national and local newspapers, 15 magazines. Newspaper circulation statistics: Top two by circulation: *Netralniy Turkmenistan* (Russian language state-owned daily), *Turkmenistan* (Turkmen language state-owned daily). News agencies: *Turkmen Dowlet Habarlar Agenligi* (state-owned). **Television Stations:** 5. Broadcast ratings: Top two: National TV and Radio Broadcasting Corporation (state-owned, both languages), 5th Channel (private, Russian and Kyrgyz). **Radio Stations:** 5. Broadcast ratings: N/A

Uzbekistan
Print: 663 newspapers, 195 magazines, 13 periodical bulletins. Newspaper circulation statistics: Total newspaper readership is estimated at only 50,000; top publications include *Khalq Sozi* (state-run daily), *Narodnye Slovo* (state-run, Russian language daily), *Ozbekistan Ozovi* (published by ruling party). News agencies: Uzbekistan National News Agency (state-owned), *Jahon*, *Turkiston Press*. **Television Stations:** 53. **Radio Stations:** 35. Broadcast ratings: N/A

* Source: The 2012 Media Sustainability Index (MSI) prepared by IREX with funding from USAID on the "development of sustainable independent media" in Europe and Eurasia.